The Enemy Within

SAYEEDA WARSI

The Enemy Within

A Tale of Muslim Britain

ALLEN LANE
an imprint of
PENGUIN BOOKS

ALLEN LANE

UK | USA | Canada | Ireland | Australia
India | New Zealand | South Africa

Allen Lane is part of the Penguin Random House group of companies
whose addresses can be found at global.penguinrandomhouse.com

First published 2017
001

Copyright © Sayeeda Warsi, 2017

The moral right of the author has been asserted

Set in 10.5/14 pt Sabon LT Std
Typeset by Jouve (UK), Milton Keynes
Printed in Great Britain by Clays Ltd, St Ives plc

A CIP catalogue record for this book is available from the British Library

ISBN: 978-0-241-27602-0

To all the victims of terrorism past, present and future: innocent men, women and children who lost their lives as others pursued their violent political goals.

Contents

Introduction: Belonging

'Never apologize for showing feelings. When you do so you apologize for the truth.'

Benjamin Disraeli

It's quite an art to insult someone well, to deliver a phrase that is cutting and effective, the perfectly pitched 'put down' ball, words that leave your adversary winded. Many a mother-in-law has perfected this art. But what's always impressed me more is not the delivery of the insult but the fielding of it.

When I was a child, the two insults that hurt most were 'Paki' and 'specky'. Contact lenses from the tender age of sixteen fixed the latter, but the former took a lot longer. Wandering around the Bradford mela during my youth I came across a young British Pakistani selling T-shirts, one of which simply read 'PAKI'. Not quite sure how my mum would react to such a garment, I resisted the temptation to buy, but it signalled the start of a community owning its identity, insults and all.

Times have changed, 'Paki' is no longer the favoured insult for the likes of me; nor do I much these days mix in those circles where overt racism is worn as a badge of honour. I've been a positive social mobility story, and so my adversaries are no longer intellectually challenged skinheads but respectable, refined individuals where the insult is couched in reason and the words used are sophisticated, almost poetic. Xenophobia as an ideology is a broad church, with adherents ranging from your drunken, street-fighting thug to the chichi academic, commentator and, dare I say, even politician.

An emphasis on difference, an acceptance of that which sets us apart rather than that which makes us the same, can be the start of a positive lifelong learning experience. Acknowledging and accepting difference was the foundation of the multicultural melting pot that is today's Britain, the basis of amazing friendships and loving relationships and the journey in which others change us and we change them. But this same difference can also be the justification for insult.

And for me owning the insult is the most powerful way of neutralizing the words and winning the fight for a diverse and plural society.

We all see difference, we all are different. Our children are now young adults, and often my husband and I will argue a position which makes absolute sense to us but seems alien to them. It's a generation thing, but it's also, as our kids keep reminding us, a Pakistani thing. They keep telling us they are different to us. We agree, and to make the point I recently bought my husband the T-shirt 'It's a Paki thing and you wouldn't understand'. He wears it with great pride.

As a child I knew we were different from our neighbours.

I was six years old when we moved to Falcon Road in Savile Town, Dewsbury. It was the third of what in the end became six different houses we lived in over a period of twenty years in the area. My parents continue to live nearby. Savile Town, which takes its name from the Savile family, has a history stretching back to the 1300s and was part of the famous woollen trade in West Yorkshire. Most of the mills on the banks of the River Calder closed in the 1970s, but the workers the mills had attracted, the migrants from India and Pakistan in the 1950s and '60s, went on to shape the Dewsbury of today.

Childhood in Savile Town during the late 1970s and early '80s involved brass bands, scouts and guides parades, hopscotch and British bulldog games in the street. The Queen's silver jubilee celebrations rubbed alongside a growing Muslim community and the building of what was then the largest mosque in Europe, the Markaz.

Dewsbury has in more recent times lost some of the charm and prosperity of its past. The Victorian houses, the town hall and the now converted mills still stand tall and majestic, the greenery and parks are still beautiful and the market still vibrant, but the general decline is visible in a town centre that is peppered with pawn and pound shops.

The last decade appears to have provided a string of bad-news stories, from the sad saga of the fake kidnap of schoolgirl Shannon Matthews by her mother to the town's tragic association with high-profile suicide bombers Mohammad Sidique Khan and Talha Asmal. But for me Dewsbury is still the place that produced local girl Eileen Fenton, who swam the English Channel, the scientist who invented the first stored-program computer, Tom Kilburn, and the first female speaker of the House of Commons, Betty, now Baroness, Boothroyd. For me this town of my birth, where I made my career as a lawyer and which I adopted in the title I took upon being made a life peer, is what shaped my identity. It is the basis of my success and a place for which I have both great affection and cautious hope.

Savile Town is now almost exclusively made up of a community which is of South Asian descent and Muslim by faith, but as a child I grew up in a Savile Town that was much more diverse. It was a mixed community, a strong white working class and a minority Muslim community, which divided into families originating from the Gujarat district of India and families from the Punjab and Kashmir provinces of Pakistan.

The Goodlads and the Pearsons were our neighbours. Mr Pearson I held in high regard, as he owned the local sweet shop, and the Goodlads had a daughter my age, so provided an extra playmate. Both had immaculate gardens. Orderly, tidy, colourful and calm, whereas ours, however hard my mum tried, always looked like a cheap imitation. They had fairy lights at Christmas, a blow-up swimming pool, fencing which smelled amazing when treated and above all a greenhouse and a caravan, a clean white caravan that whisked them away on holiday usually during the summer, leaving me to contemplate another life that could be, another world, which included the magical place known as Great Yarmouth. I so wanted to go to Great Yarmouth, it seemed far away, exotic, unachievable, and I vowed that one day when I grew up, I would buy a caravan and take my children to Great Yarmouth. To date, I have not done so.

Of all the things the Goodlads had and we did not, it was the greenhouse and caravan I yearned for most. My parents didn't seem remotely interested in investing in either, instead choosing to buy a second-hand glass display cabinet for the posh front room and some property in Pakistan. These were differences I wanted to change, to bridge. I wanted to belong.

We were one of the small number of Pakistani-origin Muslim families. Living there was an active decision taken by my parents, and one that had a profound impact on my upbringing and my identity. It was a decision which would in later life be regularly discussed in the family and one which my mother still cites as one of her many wise decisions. I agree with her. It exposed my siblings and me to a plural and diverse ethnic and religious upbringing, where the world at home was often very different from the world in our local Muslim community, different from the world in the madrasa we attended and certainly different from mainstream Dewsbury. As children, we quickly learned to recognize, rationalize and reconcile difference.

I was born in a small house on Dewsbury Gate Road, the second of what eventually became a family of five girls, though the care and support of a relative in Maidstone, Kent, meant that the family moved within months of my birth. My first two years were spent in Maidstone. I have no memories of Maidstone. Although photographs from the era show a happy childhood, my parents never felt settled there. The Muslim community was small, and everyday practical needs around prayer, support and diet were not easily accessible. My parents would have to order their halal meat in from Gillingham or Chatham as part of a weekly delivery.

A combination of cramped housing, a growing family, my mum was expecting her third child, and a general lack of cultural and religious needs resulted in us returning to West Yorkshire.

And it was upon returning to West Yorkshire that Savile Town became our home. It was an unusual choice, because the majority of the families and the community that my parents were connected to, the Pakistani community, had already started to make other parts of Dewsbury their home.

My parents liked the gentle Gujerati Indians who made up the majority of Savile Town's Muslim community. The difference in background – my parents originating from Pakistan not India – allowed them greater freedom and less community censure. For my mum it opened up a whole new world of Asian cooking and friend-ships that are as strong today as they were then. For my father it provided access to mosques and a very formal and conservative reli-gious community he knew little of as a child.

My parents were bought up as Sunni Muslims, although both have members of the family who are staunchly Shia. They grew up mainly in the Barelwi practice of Sunni Islam, although Sufism also played a big role through the family's association with the followers of the Sufi shrine at Deva Sharif in India. Savile Town and specifically its Gujerati community, however, were mainly linked to Deoband in India, the Tablighi Jamaat movement in Pakistan and India and even-tually the Wahhabi movement in Saudi Arabia.[1]

My parents took to the local Gujerati mosques and madrasas. They liked the formality of the teaching, they liked the way the Qur'an was taught, they liked the emphasis on Arabic pronunciation, something they hadn't been taught growing up in Pakistan, and they saw the additional benefits of the broader religious education being in Urdu, the national language of Pakistan.

The teachings favoured in the local mosques we attended were both conservative and puritanical. Many of the cultural practices which my parents had grown up with were seen as unnecessary at best and forbidden at worst. This didn't seem to worry my parents, who continued marking the Prophet's birthday and holding food and prayer sessions with music and celebrations whilst continuing to send their girls to the local madrasas, where the teachings were at times in direct conflict. They also on occasions took us along to the Shia mosques in Bradford and Leeds during the month of Muharram to mark Ashura. Muharram was a big deal in our home: the mood was sombre and subdued, and the TV became a no-go zone, which caused much angst for us as teenagers, as soaps played an integral part in our lives, and, in these days before catch-up TV, my mum had decided the video recorder was also off limits during the first ten days of the month.

Our parents never taught us that a specific version of the faith was wrong, instead telling us there were many ways to pray and worship, an upbringing opposite to divisive sectarianism, which can be politi-cally exploited and trigger deep hatred. Later, because it didn't form a part of my upbringing, I wrongly assumed sectarianism was an irrelevant distraction and thus failed to respond quickly enough to the growing challenge it posed. More generally, this mistake has contributed to the current failures in policy-making.

But the one identity that was stronger than all others for me as a child was being a girl. It underlay most of the discussions that we had at home and became the basis of most decisions made about my life. It shaped my upbringing, my career, my personality, my drive and indeed the chip on my shoulder.

Each time my parents had another child, it further reinforced this 'female' identity at home. As the tally of daughters increased it signalled, in a male-dominated, conservative society, that once again my parents had failed. As a child I don't recall my father ever expressing disappointment about having 'just girls', and if it hadn't been for an overheard conversation between my mum and her friends, with mum's friends saying that my father 'must be upset', I would never have known there was anything to be 'upset' about.

The birth of Bushra, my youngest sister, was met with almost universal sympathy by visitors. The mood was sombre, more suited to the weeks following a bereavement. Unlike the happy occasions when my aunts and mum's friends would have boys, we never distributed Asian sweets, nor did we have them in the house to welcome visitors with when they came to congratulate my parents on their new arrival. In fact, there were no congratulations, no celebrations and no ladoos, which is probably what attracts me to them even today. The Pink Ladoo campaign launched by Raj Khaira in the UK, Canada and Australia is a very visual celebration of female births and a stark reminder that, four decades on, the war of gender equality is still not won.

In the community where I was born and raised, boys were assets and thus of value, girls were liabilities and thus a burden. Much of this thinking was based on cultural norms in South Asia, which valued a male child for the economic worth they would bring to the family as breadwinners, for their physical worth as protectors and defenders of family honour and property and for their social worth through succession. Boys in South Asia were contributors, girls were responsibilities; boys would add to the family resources, girls would be a drain on them; boys carried honour, girls brought shame.

Our births marked the start of a battle by my parents and us to prove worth and value. Dad's hard labour, Mum's single mindedness in ensuring we bettered ourselves, focusing on education and ensuring that our lives had to be more successful than the generation before us, and our determination to be better than the boys shaped my journey and that of my sisters. The message that we, the girls, were not going to be 'labourers' but professionals was drummed into us on a weekly basis

As a child I thought that the 'boys are better than girls' attitude was something unique in the Asian community. Later experience taught me that the status of women has been an issue in all societies, all of which are at different stages in the journey to genuine equal worth between the sexes. The election of President Trump after a disturbingly sexist campaign signals that some may be in reverse.

Although both my parents come from humble beginnings from a rural part of Punjab in Pakistan, in relative terms my mother's family were comfortable. My mother thinks in middle class. She is one of seven girls and two boys, and despite the boys, my maternal uncles, being spoilt, the girls did not go without. All received a primary and secondary education, and my mum, very much like my grandmother, aspired for better. She embraced the opportunities Britain had to offer for her and her girls. She took up English classes, she learned to drive in the 1970s and she insisted her girls received a university education.

My parents had a very large social circle consisting of family and friends although we were only ever allowed to get to know a few of them well. My own friends were a small group of mainly Pakistani-origin girls whom I went to school with, and then of course there was Sarah, the daughter of our neighbours, the Goodlads. Although Sarah Goodlad and I were the same age and went to the same school, we played much more at home than we played at school.

The Goodlads were a hard, strong working-class family, and I know that our relationship as neighbours was warm and strong. My mum and Mrs Goodlad used to smooth over my many run-ins with Mr Goodlad, mainly connected to leaning against his fence. I know my parents valued this warm relationship and took great pride in nurturing it.

Holidays were mainly a few days at my maternal aunt's house in Kent. While there, we would travel to the beach, mainly the pebbled beaches of Hastings, a quintessentially English seaside town, dressed up in our full Pakistani best. We must have seemed odd, fully dressed on a warm summer's day on the beach, but I certainly never recall being aware of being stared at or not being made to feel welcome – an indication of how most of Britain was indeed tolerant, or at least indifferent.

An alternative to Kent in later years was Blackpool, both in the summer for the candy floss and fairground rides and in the winter for the illuminations.

The other great pastime for us was fruit-picking either in the many apple, plum and pear orchards of Kent or strawberry-picking in Yorkshire. It always seemed the nearest I would get to an adventure, the kind of adventure that I would read about in Enid Blyton books. For my parents it represented a connection with the villages from where they had set out many years earlier, where fruit on trees and crops in fields constituted a way of life. Again, photos from that era show us in the quintessentially English orchards in our home-stitched shalwar kameez, trousers and tunics that my mum would conjure up on her Singer pedal-operated machine that seemed to permanently sit on the coffee table. I never inherited my mum's talent for sewing: failing my CSE needlework miserably at the age of sixteen proved early on that I was going to be an inadequate example of a 'good "Asian" daughter'.

Overall, this feeling of difference always made me feel like we were special. It was only in later life that I understood that many around us didn't see us as a special family but as inferior.

My parents embraced and encouraged us to embrace what they saw as 'good' within Britain, always keen for us to experience what they viewed as moments of great advancement. A family outing to the newly opened Humber Bridge was one such moment. My father decided the newly opened bridge in Hull, which at the time was the longest in the world, was a magnificent piece of engineering, human advancement which his daughters needed to experience. As ever, my mother dressed us up in our best silky shalwar kameez, complete with flowing scarfs, not quite the right attire for a very cold, blustery day as my father marched us along the length of the bridge. The pride they felt at this engineering advancement and the compliments they paid to the great achievements of 'the British' reinforced for us that to aspire to be like 'them', the Brits, was positive.

The big holiday during our childhood, however, was a visit to Pakistan. It was in 1979; I was eight and at middle school. It was my mother's first visit to Pakistan since she arrived in England in 1970.

My parents decided that the girls – at the time there were four of us – should be immersed in Pakistan. What I learned subsequently was that many certainly in our extended paternal family hoped we would settle there. It was based on both a romantic idea that most migrants have of returning to the homeland, with the money to live the life they had always wanted but couldn't afford, and a notion that the real values that they held dear would only be preserved in the next generation by going back.

In the 1970s my father definitely had a wish to eventually settle in Pakistan, to make it his final home. Having come to the UK in 1962, he has spoken to me about how he always intended to return home in 1970, having made enough money to set up a small business and build a home of bricks and render, not loam. In 1962, 1970 seemed a long time away. However, having married in 1968, my eldest sister being born in 1969 and my mother arriving in the UK in 1970, the time for returning shifted. Although there was no longer a date in his mind, I think the desire to return to Pakistan and settle was still there. In many ways that desire increased as he started to have daughters. I'm sure the desire was fuelled as much by others in the Pakistani community in Britain as by relatives in Pakistan who scaremongered about the dire consequences of girls growing up in a western society.

A few incidents of youngsters 'marrying out' during the 1980s, kids from families known to my parents, further heightened my dad's sense of losing control. This was seen as a slippery slope by them, one of which we as girls worryingly could become the victims. My mother, on the other hand, was clear that Pakistan did not provide a future for her girls, that, whatever the challenges were for her and her daughters in the UK, they would be a whole lot worse in Pakistan.

However, she did have a desire to have a home in Pakistan. My parents led a very frugal lifestyle and invested in a home of their own in Pakistan. They continue to maintain a home in Islamabad. It's a property which in the past we girls have tried to persuade them to sell and invest the funds in the UK, but in more recent troubling times we have been less inclined to push them to put all their eggs in basket Britain.

The conversation of where was 'home' was one we grew up with. I know from discussions with friends it was a conversation happening in Asian homes across the country during the 1970s and '80s. What was unusual in our home was that it was a genuine all-family discussion, whereas in many homes the women were excluded. My father became a feminist by default.

Pakistan in the 1970s and '80s was a safe place. Much of the troubles of recent years were yet to manifest. The cities, especially Islamabad, were growing and provided huge opportunity. With money earned in Britain, British Pakistanis could live a very comfortable middle-class life in Pakistan, attend private schools, own nice homes in expensive neighbourhoods and socialize and party in a 'safe environment' in ways that were considered off limits in Britain. So returning 'home' was an attractive proposition, and this was the kind of experiment that many a Pakistani family did during the 1970s, '80s and even '90s. It was an experiment which for almost everybody failed. Once the challenges of everyday bureaucracy, corruption and family feuds kicked in, Britain once more beckoned.

Our own experiment came to a worrying and abrupt end when my mother contracted meningitis. Her illness was both badly diagnosed and badly treated, and we nearly lost her. The fear of her not making it and the possibility that her girls would be left in Pakistan with a village-school education being the best on offer I think gave her the strength to fight back and eventually recover to travel back to the UK, and by the summer of 1980 we were back home in Dewsbury.

Summer also represented another difference for me. My mum has always been a keen gardener. She likes flowers and she likes a nice lawn. We had a heavy, clunky manual lawnmower which she would, after trying to persuade my dad to cut the grass, take over herself to ensure that the lawn was kept neatish. She also had a secret garden, a small, square piece of land that sat between the back of the garage and the boundary wall which she dug up and divided into plots by using old bricks and where she grew coriander, mint and spinach.

The coriander and mint garden was, and still is, a popular feature within Asian households. It provides the essential and almost daily used ingredients for Asian cooking. Indeed my mother-in-law still has an impressive coriander and mint plot. It is something that I have experimented with but always failed at. Unlike many Asian women who have a regular and necessary supply of these important herbs, I still buy them from the Asian shop if I have the time or more regularly and stupidly from the supermarket, where they are still sold in uselessly small packages extortionately priced. My incompetence at growing coriander is another example of me letting down the 'Asian' bit of me.

But where Mum had her secret garden, the Goodlads had a greenhouse, in which they must have grown many things, but the only item I ever recall was tomatoes, because Mrs Goodlad would come round with them during the summer. Although I could see the importance of Mum's secret garden, as I would often be the one, at the most inconvenient times, usually mid comic-reading session, to be sent on the coriander errand, personally I wanted the greenhouse. For me it represented the sophisticated way to grow herbs and veg, and in my childhood it felt more civilized. It was suburban living in the way it should be on our road with its neat semi-detached homes and not the closet 'ethnic village' practices that my mum's back-of-the-garage plot represented.

My upbringing was limited but not limiting. We didn't travel much and, other than to Pakistan, certainly never overseas; we didn't go to the pictures except for the very odd occasion as very small children when we accompanied my parents to Bradford to see Indian Bollywood movies; we didn't go to restaurants, and we didn't have any hobbies, clubs or sports activities. So I was limited in experience yet I always felt there was nothing that was impossible. It never seemed unusual that my mother would want and expect us to one day become lawyers, accountants and members of other coveted professions, and I never felt that I wouldn't get there or deserved not to be there. This can-do attitude and almost blind belief in ourselves my sisters and

I get from our father, who never seems to think anything is unachievable and has never accepted that anyone else is more entitled to success than he is. It's the attitude that took him on a journey from arriving in the UK as a young man in the early 1960s with £2.50 in his pocket to today being the successful owner of two multi-million-pound businesses.

My Pakistani heritage was always a large part of our upbringing. The months spent in Pakistan during 1979 had felt like a new and exciting holiday yet also quite familiar. After the initial trauma of discovering that there were no indoor toilets, that the village schools did not have chairs and tables and that we needed to sit on the floor, that books were not a large part of schooling but personal slate and chalk boards were, and that if you did not eat your meals on time, that was it, there was nothing in between meals to compensate, I very much remember feeling that I was amongst family and people with whom I had a connection: my maternal and paternal grandmothers, my maternal grandfather, my parents' siblings and their children, a huge family who just accepted us as one of them. Nobody felt like an outsider, and after a few weeks the strange surroundings seemed comfortably familiar. It was a place where I felt I both mattered and belonged.

I wasn't aware that this Pakistan visit was a potential experiment that could have become a lifestyle. I enjoyed those months as a great adventure.

Looking back, it now seems surprising that four young girls were allowed out of school for such a long period of time. It affected me academically and has had an impact which even today affects my professional life. I was absent from school at a time when we had just started to learn 'joined-up writing'. It was something that I never learned at the time, and no one subsequently taught me. To this day I still print.

Whether it was the Pakistan visit, the Savile Town upbringing or the all-female family, I was acutely aware of difference from an early age: different from the Asian community in which we lived, because we were all female; different from the Muslim community that surrounded us, because we were of Pakistani not Indian origin; and different from the broader English community in which we lived, because we did not have a greenhouse and a caravan. But I also learned that these differences didn't have to be limiting. Differences could be ignored, different environments could be accommodated in short bursts, differences could be simply kept secret, and differences could be overcome over time through success.

What I did, however, sense both from my parents and my own experience growing up was a desire to try and fit in.

An example was a very childish game that my sisters and I would play in which we would try and convince Sarah Goodlad that we, like her, dressed in a nighty for bed. None of us had nighties or shop-bought pjs as children. My mother had stitched us little cotton trousers and tunics which were effectively our night clothes. Sarah, on the other hand, had a proper nighty. On an evening before we went to bed we would sometimes wave to Sarah from our toilet window which overlooked the two drives and faced their toilet window. On occasions Sarah would ask my elder sister and me if we were ready for bed, and we would say we were not if we were in our Asian night clothes. But to keep the façade of fitting in alive, my sister and I would occasionally raid our mum's wardrobe, find one or two nighties that she possessed, which we never really saw Mum wear but we always saw her pack when she went into hospital to have a baby, pull the nighties over our heads and pop our heads through the window to show that we too had 'English' night clothes. I am sure that I looked odd and I am sure that it didn't fit, but it seemed to work. It made me feel like I fitted in.

In the summertime caravans and greenhouses brought 'differences' to the fore, but winter too brought its own challenges, with a deep desire to fit in during Christmas. Christmas was never celebrated in our homes when we were young, but as children we were hopeful that we would get presents. It must have been during that time when we still believed that Santa Claus existed. One year my elder sister Farkhanda and I had a detailed conversation about why Santa didn't come to our house. I was terribly logical and tried to reason it on the basis that Santa Claus did not come to us because there was no chimney for him to come down. In many Asian homes in the 1970s and 1980s the chimney breasts had been removed to allow the living room to be squared off and provide a bigger seating area. My parents saw alcoves as wasted space. So my sister and I decided to leave the back door unlocked on Christmas Eve. We did it late in the evening after bedtime. The open door was discovered the next day, but no presents had arrived.

I pledged when I grew up that I'd never have the chimney breasts removed, because I needed to create space for Santa. I've done major renovations in our last two family homes, and chimneys have featured in both. In one I insisted on creating a chimney in a new-build where none had existed before and in the second I reopened the old chimneys and restored live fires in a house that is our current family home. Chimneys matter, Santa matters.

As a child I needed to belong, to fit in, to be a part of the world and experiences of my friends and neighbours. I wanted to belong in all the different parts that made up the sum of my world: the Pakistani bit, the Savile Town bit, the English bit, the Asian bit, the western bit, the female bit and the many versions of the Islam bit. As an adult I wanted not just to belong in each one but also for each bit to belong in the others. By my early twenties I'd done with keeping differences neatly compartmentalized; the famous double life that many young Asians lived was tiresome, and I'd managed to grow comfortable in my own skin, flaws and all. We were staying, Britain was home, it's where I belonged, it's where I wanted to matter.

And yet three decades on, it seems interesting how conversations today about identity, belonging and the concerns of some minority communities mirror conversations from my teens. Back then, I would become frustrated with my parents' conversations about maybe one day having to settle 'back' in Pakistan. My father's argument was premised on a rose-tinted, good-life retirement-type dream, set in a northern Pakistan life in the way most Brits dream of southern Spain. My mother, however, based her argument on worry and concern about things becoming so difficult for Pakistanis in the UK that one day we might have to leave.

I was fully reconciled with Britain and my new multicultural, diverse British Asian identity, and it annoyed me that my parents were not.

Unusually, as someone born and raised in Britain, I found it easier to understand my father's position of having a connection and wanting to make a home for his children in a place that in his mind was still his home. Wanting to make another place home I could understand; being forced to make another place home I couldn't comprehend and I would, sometimes rudely, dismiss my mum's position, which I found absurd.

During my twenties I would have heated conversations with my mum, arguing that Britain could never be a place which would be so unwelcoming to a community that a whole group of people would feel they had no choice but to leave and set up home elsewhere. British Pakistanis, I felt, were an intrinsic part of the multicultural nation we had become, a broad set of people from different backgrounds, a multitude of minority races all forming the fabric of modern Britain. I'd convince her that the debate was moving so far in the right direction that her references to Enoch Powell made her sound like she was stuck in a time warp, that Britain had moved on from its heady racist years of the 1960s and '70s that she and Dad had experienced and it was never going to be that kind of an intolerant place again, that there was only one direction of travel, and that literally meant no going back.

Yet, despite arguing so vociferously against my parents in my twenties, I found myself in my privileged, successful thirties dreaming my dad's dream of a nice holiday home in Pakistan and in my forties worrying my mum's worry of things getting tough.

It didn't remotely occur to me that some thirty years after my soapbox speeches to my parents about how there was no turning back my generation would be once again talking of where else could be home. I could never have predicted that in years to come my religious identity would be a basis of non-acceptance and conflict within the UK as great if not greater than my parents' racial identity. Three decades on, these conversations are now happening again amongst people of my generation. A generation born and raised in the UK now regularly talk about their fear of life being made hard and difficult for a specific community simply because of its identity. And it raises the question how a desire to fit in, a pride in Britain, a warmth amongst neighbours and an aspiration to do well and get on, a belief that anything is possible could result in both great success and a deepening alienation. How a community that came to work and go back became a community that worked and settled and is now viewed as neither settled nor belonging.

I want to explore how we got here. The mistakes that were made by the community, society and policy-makers and the reasons behind those mistakes. I will try and unpick myth from reality, headlines from hard facts, and step out of the comfortable world of the converts to the god of diversity and plurality and explain how some people simply do not believe that difference can be accommodated.

Today, Muslims are often painted as not playing by the rules, as having practices and beliefs which are inconsistent, dare I say even incompatible, with being British. They are painted as intrinsically violent, irreconcilably aggressive, and intent on taking over this green and pleasant land.

I will revisit the seminal moments when 'the Muslims' were dramatically brought into the national and international consciousness and explore whether the 'war on terror' set the tone for how we see our Muslims or simply exacerbated a sore that was already festering. When was 'the Muslim problem' born?

I'll try to deconstruct violence in the name of a cause: terrorism. I'll try to explain what makes a violent 'jihadi'. And I will also ask whether the rules we want them, 'the Muslims', to play by are indeed fair or even the rules we ask others to play by.

As a lawyer I have great faith in the rule of law, equality before the law and core principles of fairness consistently and transparently applied. Politicians often quote these as examples of our British values, but having spent nearly a decade working on our policy towards Muslims, I'm not as confident we apply these values as diligently as we assert these values.

It's been brutal being a British Muslim for the last decade or so. Rarely has a Muslim in the public eye escaped either the outright accusation of being an extremist or the nudge-nudge, wink-wink suggestion of being one. The London mayoral election and the campaign against Sadiq Khan, the comments by the *Sun* about Channel Four news presenter Fatima Manji and the hounding of Aaqil Ahmed, the head of BBC faith programmes, are but some examples. Rarely have Muslim organizations, from community groups to youth clubs, faith schools to charitable foundations, been under this level of scrutiny. And rarely has the daily vilification in the media of all things Muslim been so unrelenting and Muslims seen as fair game.

Am I complaining? To pinch Ed Milliband's line, hell no. Now, I'm no fan of sadomasochism, it's not my thing, but I think a bit of pain for the community right now could in the end serve us, 'the Muslims', well. In the past, when I've warned of the changing winds in Britain and urged some of my fellow co-religionists to step up and step out, the response has been abysmal. We've talked a great talk, but I've seen little follow-through. So, however uncomfortable and unfair it is for those of us who face the onslaught on the frontline, I feel we, the Muslims, can make a virtue of this current phase.

Sometimes things need to get really bad for people to be jolted into fixing them. Government policy towards 'Muslims' is often unfair, often unwarranted and often wrong, and this could be the conduit for the change that is needed. It astounds me that even today amongst some community organizations and so-called community and faith leaders the 'business as usual' mentality prevails. The obsession with the minutiae, the irrelevant and the fringe is still a favourite pastime; our commitment to unity is a nice sentiment but vastly outshone by our commitment to doing down every other community organization, activist or Muslim in a position of authority and the passion with which we draw our theological swords on sectarianism is quite breathtaking. We haven't quite worked out that when Islamophobia strikes it doesn't ask whether you are Sunni or Shia, which mosque you go to and which imam you follow. You don't even have to be Muslim to be sworn at, spat at or physically assaulted – ask the poor Sikhs who have been collateral damage for Islamophobes for years.

These internal and external challenges and how this tale of Muslim Britain has developed over the last fifteen years I explore in some detail in the coming chapters. I ask whether our counter-terrorism strategy has been effective or counterproductive. I explore what our Muslim communities would have become had the war on terrorism not happened, what journey they would have been on, whether we would even have identified them as 'Muslim' or simply defined them through their individual origins and race.

Whilst many of us were engaged with racial justice, religion crept up on us as a new dimension: the new race, the point of difference, the characteristic to fear, the focus of the far right, the fair-game group in the media and the acceptable rabble-rousing feature in politics. I will detail this transition.

British Muslims are on a journey. They are coming to terms with a changing world which over the last three decades has placed their religious identity centre stage both domestically and internationally. In fixing 'the Muslim issue', the starting point is knowing and understanding British Muslims in all their glory, failings, difference, diversity and nuance, valuing our intertwined histories, our fractious present and our shared future, and doing so in the spirit of open and inclusive values.

Britain has often found groups within its borders whom it does not trust, whom it feels have a belief, culture, practice or agenda which runs contrary to those of the majority. From Catholics to Jews, miners to trade unionists, Marxists to liberals and even homosexuals, all have at times been viewed, described and treated as 'the enemy within'. The Muslims are the latest in a long line of 'others' to be given that label, from those like my parents who sweated and toiled in the mills of Yorkshire half a century ago to successful, integrated British citizens who now make up the growing Muslim middle class; it was a phrase used to describe me in government.

As the granddaughter of two men who both served in the British Indian Army, I felt it was probably one of the worst insults to be directed at me. It told me that I didn't belong in Britain. This book is my way of fielding the insult, by owning and dismantling the label 'the enemy within'.

PART ONE

How Did We Get Here?

I

Who Are the British Muslims?

'To be yourself in a world that is constantly trying to make
you something else is the greatest accomplishment.'

Ralph Waldo Emerson

The Muslims, or, more politely put, the Muslim communities, are
described and most often referred to as a monolithic block.

Well they – we – are not.

British Muslims come in many forms. Some are black, some
two-thirds are various shades of brown, many are oriental and, yes,
some are even white. They originate from all corners of the world,
including the continent of Africa and the European mainland, with
ancestry which traces back to ancient civilizations in South and Central Asia and Persia; some are simply descendants of your bog-standard
Anglo-Saxon.

Some are old, but most are young: a third are under the age of fifteen. They are male, female and transgender; they are straight, gay
and bisexual. They are monogamous, polygamous, and some, like
the rest of the population, simply sleep around.

Some wear clothing that shrouds from head to toe whilst others
insist their ankles are always bare. Many believe that knee-length is
modest enough, whilst some are daring enough to flash a little of
thigh. Some wear a nikaab (full face veil), some a hijab (headscarf),
some a dupatta Benazir Bhutto style; some prefer a bandana or even
a half-shaved head. Some show neck, others tease with a little glimpse
of cleavage, and some let it all hang out.

They shop at Tesco, Sainsbury, Asda, watch for deals at Lidl and

Netto; the posh ones even go to Waitrose, whilst the busy and tech-savvy use Ocado. Some even buy their meat there, whilst others insist on Mr Ali, the halal butcher, and a few won't eat their chickens until they know for sure they've been killed the 'good way' by slaughtering them on the quiet in their back garden. Some only trust their brother the kosher butcher to guarantee halal. They love a good bargain, are fans of BOGOF; the young adore the voucher websites, and the elders still prefer the old-fashioned way: 'I know someone who can do it cheaper.'

They choose private schools and grammar schools and fight like mad for good state-school places. Some get fed up with bad schools and start free schools and faith schools and some even home school. Some attend the mosque five times a day, others once a day, some only on Fridays and some only as a tourist when they visit exotic Muslim lands abroad.

Some use the Christmas break to go on pilgrimage to Mecca because the Saudi weather is at its best; others throw the biggest Christmas parties – tree, crackers and all – and those who don't celebrate Christmas still have turkey over the festive period. Many use Easter to justify ditching the 'no chocolate' diet, some even give up coffee for Lent in solidarity with their Christian brothers and sisters, and those who don't do any of the above still love a great bonfire and fireworks, we are as fascinated with explosives as the rest of Britain.

Some are writers and campaigners for free speech, others just read. Some read half a dozen languages, most read at least two, and a very small number can't read at all.

Most speak up to three languages and listen to music in many more. Some act, play instruments, sing and dance. Some denounce fun, and some, like most Brits, have two left feet.

Most worry about job prospects, the housing ladder and finding a compatible other. They use dating sites – singlemuslim.com does a roaring trade – some rely on friends and family to arrange a match. They fall in love, they marry, they divorce. Some are divorce lawyers and judges, some accountants, and lots are doctors, and those that aren't wish they were. They make pizzas better than the Italians, stir-fry better than the Chinese and sell Bengali food as Indian; one even baked a cake for Her Majesty the Queen. They drive taxis and tubes and buses, they collect your bins and they sweep the streets. They teach your kids, they cure the sick, they fix your teeth, they bank your money and fix your central heating. They police our streets, they gather intelligence both at home and abroad to keep us safe,[1] and for over a hundred years they've been giving their blood and sweat in our armies to defend the values we all hold dear.

They are boy-band heartthrobs and excel in Great British Bake Offs; they run faster than the world and win Olympic golds; they are football heroes and cricket legends; they are elected members of parliament and members of their Lordships' house, and one of them is the most influential person in London, our main man, the mayor.

Yes, they are everywhere, all 3 million of them and counting.

And of this 3 million, less than a tenth of 1 per cent over my lifetime have wanted to cause us, all of us, some really serious harm.[2]

They, the Muslims, are individuals with individual cares, concerns, issues and moans, individuals with individual views and politics who, like people in most communities, spend more time on focusing on differences between themselves than on differences between themselves and others.

Yet rarely a day goes by without a so-called expert on a news channel telling us who 'the Muslims' are and what 'Muslims' are thinking.

Indulge me and allow me to give you an insider's track.

We are hard to define because we are so diverse. But there are 'types', and I have taken my descriptions from real people, real communities.

Some Muslims have taken the Ravenous Bugblatter Beast of Traal from the *Hitchhiker's Guide to the Galaxy* as their inspiration. They've wrapped a towel around their heads, some quite literally, and assumed that if we can't see them, they can't see us. Separation and isolation are seen as the only way to preserve Islamic morality, ethics and lifestyles. Isolation is the first line of defence against assimilation. I grew up in a community in Savile Town where many believed this: that as long as we kept ourselves to ourselves and kept our heads down we could potentially live, work and pray without having much contact with the morally bankrupt world of the non-Muslim.

Some from these communities venture out to work, indeed have risen in lucrative professions, but always return to the bosom of the small, closed community, and many, despite their improved financial circumstances, raise their children in more isolated circumstances than their own upbringings, opting for faith schools for their children having attended state schools themselves and favouring jubbas for their kids having grown up in jeans.

We Muslims (like followers of other faiths) have our moralizing, self-righteous lot too. They have an unshakeable belief that they are the chosen ones, irrespective of their conduct or behaviour, and display a cultural and religious superiority that the EDL would relate to. Indeed they are so right that to them most fellow Muslims are beyond the pale. These Trunchbull-like characters live on sanctimonious island and talk consistently of Islamic virtues but possess few.

Then there are those who have ventured out to the suburbs and emulate the urban middle class: nice home, nice cars, nice holidays and, most importantly, nice schools. They enjoy friends from a variety of backgrounds, hold diverse dinner parties and feel comfortably British until the media, the government or even a well-meaning friend tars them with the same brush as some terrorist, at which point they are reminded that they are not 'us' they are still 'them'.

Then there are those who decided many moons ago that, irrespective of where they lived, they would reach out, play their part in wider society, run charities, become governors of schools (although Trojan Horse[3] proved that that backfired for some), volunteer and become beacons of interfaith work. Many engage daily in this predominantly pro bono world, though sadly in recent times many have been seen as suspect simply for engaging in democratic life.

There are also those who have either left the faith or have at least stopped hanging out with the Muslims. They hide or reject their Muslimness. Some simply walk away, whilst others take great effort to tell everyone they meet that they are not practising, non-believing. Some go further and vilify the faith and the community; some actually refer to themselves as ex-Muslims to make super sure that their new-found identity is completely clear to the 'non-Muslims'. Some of these have sadly had some individual bad experience with Islam and Muslims and deal with that experience by imposing it on the whole faith and community of faithful. Some of these are fêted by the media and policy-makers.[4]

But all of these are, mostly, like the rest of our fellow citizens, trying to earn a crust, bring their kids up well and survive in an environment of rising house prices, global competition for jobs and expanding waistlines.

Most of us dread breaking news, *Panorama* and *Dispatches* exposés and front-page headlines in the *Daily Mail*.

Most in private tell inappropriate Muslim jokes, the types that would send the politically correct brigade into a tailspin; lots still call themselves Muslim but can't necessarily recall when they last hit the prayer mat, and, as is often the case with religious types, those who shout the loudest about what they know often know very little.

And, yes, some are very devout, pious and deeply thoughtful, although there is no correlation between these types and lengths of beards or headscarfs. And some are very, very conservative, rejecting musical instruments like the Church of Christ,[5] wearing clothes that seem to belong to foreign lands, like Haredi Jews, holding deeply illiberal views on homosexuality like some Evangelical Christians and Baptists,[6] and having the potential to be deeply sectarian, like supporters of the two Old Firm Clubs, Celtic and Rangers.

Most of us simply want to get on with our lives. We love Britain; it's where most were born and the only home we know, and we continue to choose it as a home even though with British passports we could pretty much live anywhere in the world. We enjoy our faith and the principles, practices, culture and community it inspires. We haven't quite worked out how we've managed to get into this mess where we have become the bogeymen of the far right, the media and government. Most of us are like rabbits caught in headlights, staring, waiting, frozen, still not sure how to react. We just want to wake up to a news day which is not another bad-news day about bad Muslims; we want the government to engage with us on issues that matter to our daily lives like schools, the NHS and property prices; we want to stop being held collectively responsible for the actions of terrorists across the globe and want someone to switch off the bright, glaring, ginormous LED spotlight that seems to follow us everywhere.

So with all our differences there is one thing we agree on: it really annoys us when we are collectively and individually held responsible for each, every and any individual around the world who just happened to be born into or has adopted the same religion that we were born into.

Most Brits, thankfully, are unlikely to ever experience terrorism, but most Brits are very likely to meet fellow Brits who are Muslim. Among them may be your doctor: British Muslim doctors number in the thousands, the terrorists are in the hundreds, and yet the ad hoc life-takers are used to define British Muslims, not the daily life-savers. If the prism through which individuals, society and policy-makers view British Muslims is set by a terrorist act, if we see our Muslims not as the diverse, complex and varied lot that they are, with the same concerns, anxieties and joys as the rest of us, if we see them as some-how responsible for the actions of terrorists rather than as likely as the rest of us to be victims of them, then we are telling 3 million people that they are part of the problem. And that makes the chal-lenge of fighting the real issue of terrorism more problematic.

To face the challenge together we need to understand them, 'the Muslims', who they are, and 'us', who we are, and how both fit in to the mosaic that is modern-day Britain.

The Muslims are not new to Britain, nor Britain to them. And although Muslim migration to Britain in any significant way is just over half a century old, an awareness of Islam has been in Britain almost since the inception of the faith in Arabia in the sixth century.

By the early eighth century Islam was already in Europe, eventually ruling most of modern-day Spain, Portugal, parts of France and Italy, Malta and Gibraltar. Tariq ibn Ziyad, the Berber Muslim general who to this day gives his name to Gibraltar – Jabal Tariq, the rock of Tariq – assisted by the dispossessed sons of the recently deceased Visigothic King of Spain, Vitiza, and Spanish Jews who had been persecuted under Christian rule, quickly took territory in Europe and established Muslim rule under the Umayyad caliphate. The Muslims were definitely coming, and had it not been for Charles Martel, a French general who defeated them at the Battle of Tours in 732 near Poitiers, a place less than 350 miles from Dover, we may well have become the United Islamic Kingdom some 1,300 years ago.

This 'hero of the age' and 'champion of the Cross against the Cres-cent', a Frenchman, saved the English from the Muslims, and they, led by the Black Prince, Edward, Prince of Wales, chose to ignore this favour some 600 years later by defeating the French in the same spot in the Battle of Poitiers (1356) during the Hundred Years War between the English and the French.[7] Now, if the good but not always well-briefed folk of Pegida UK have suddenly freaked out because they've just worked out how close we came to being 'taken over' by 'the Muslims', let me add to your nightmare.

The Anglo-Saxon King Offa of Mercia, who ruled most of modern-day England from Northumberland to Dover, including East Anglia, during his reign from 757 to 796, commissioned a gold coin bearing the Islamic declaration of faith, 'There is no God but Allah alone'.[8] And in 1213, King John of England dispatched the country's first diplomatic mission to Morocco to make contact with Morocco's Sultan Mohamed Ennassir. King John, having been excommunicated by the then Pope, hoped he could secure the Sultan and the Almohad dynasty's support to quash internal uprisings and threats of invasions from other Europeans. According to some sources, in return for an alliance against France and support against his enemies within England, King John offered to convert to Islam and turn England into a Muslim state. The offer was refused and ironically precipitated the Magna Carta, the oft-quoted basis of British values and the settlement of power-sharing in the UK.[9] And in 1588, acknowledging the growing strength of the Ottoman Empire in Europe and with Protestant England at war with Catholic Europe, Queen Elizabeth I offered to enter an alliance with the then Ottoman Caliph, Murad III. Both disliked the idolatry of the Catholic Church and had a shared enemy in Hapsburg Spain and both saw the benefits of trade from strong and preferential trade links. Elizabethan England became enchanted with all things Islam. With spices, dried fruits and exotic nuts, with fabrics, jewellery, carpets and ceramics from Persia and modern-day Morocco and Turkey becoming fashionable must-haves for the well-heeled.[10]

It was during this time that a ragtag of Muslim adventurers, political outcasts and traders started to make journeys to these shores. Some settled, others passed through but left a mark on British homes, dinner tables, fashion and that great Muslim favourite, personal grooming and hygiene. The first Turkish bath opened in London in

1679, whilst Sake Dean Mahomed, an Indian Muslim who came to England in 1784 with Captain Baker of the East India Regiment, took halal hygiene to a whole new level when he was appointed 'Shampooing Surgeon to his Majesty George 4th'.[11]

And more recently Queen Victoria, whose loyal subjects included many millions of Muslims in what is modern-day India, Pakistan and Bangladesh and who granted the then Ottoman Sultan Abdul Aziz the Order of the Garter, developed a keen interest in Islam through her close and trusted relationship with her munshi, her valued and respected servant, Abdul Karim from Agra. She supported him in bringing his extended family to England, had a cottage, named Karim Cottage, built especially for them at Balmoral and arranged for meat to be slaughtered for him according to the Islamic tradition. Indeed the monarch's over-reliance on and interest in the ways of her munshi raised eyebrows and concerns in her court.[12]

Despite these 'near misses', with us potentially becoming an Islamic nation, some Brits over time were quite taken with Islam and in small numbers from about the sixteenth century started converting. John Nelson was recorded as the first Englishman to become a Muslim, having converted some time during the mid 1500s.[13] A 1641 document refers to 'a sect of Mahomatens' being 'discovered here in London'.[14] Further conversions came in the mid 1600s, and 1649 saw the first English version of the Qur'an, by Alexander Ross.

In the eighteenth and nineteenth centuries there were a number of high-profile converts to Islam amongst the English upper classes, including Edward Montagu, who served as a member of parliament and was the son of the British ambassador to Turkey. Indeed, some of these converts attempted to spread the faith amongst their countrymen and women. Academics, politicians, mayors and aristocrats found in this exotic religion an alternative religious life.

A significant few stand out.

William Quilliam, later known as Abdullah Quilliam, was a solicitor born into a wealthy Liverpool family. After his own conversion to Islam in 1887 he converted hundreds of fellow Brits. His book, *Faith of Islam*, is said to have been ordered by Queen Victoria for her grandchildren. In 1894 the last Ottoman ruler, Sultan Abdul Hamid II, appointed him Sheikh-ul-Islam of the British Isles, the only grand mufti British Muslims have ever had, and he was recognized by the Shah of Persia and the Emir of Afghanistan as the leader of British Muslims.

He established the Islamic Institute, in Brougham Terrace in Liverpool, around the same time as the first purpose-built mosque was established in Woking in 1889. The Institute was eventually sold off and became a Council registry office for births, deaths and marriages, which included records of the marriage of John Lennon and his first wife, Cynthia. It eventually ceased to be so and fell into disrepair before being acquired by the Abdullah Quilliam Society. Its renovation and restoration once more as a place of worship and cultural centre is still underway, although the mosque formally opened its doors again in 2016.[15]

Henry Edward John Stanley, third Baron of Alderley, for whom formal Islamic funeral prayers were held, and Rowland George Allanson-Winn, fifth Baron Headley, also known as Shaikh Rahmatullah al-Farooq, converted to Islam in 1913 and became president of the British Muslim Society. Muhammad Marmaduke Pickthall, born Marmaduke William Pickthall, was someone whom I was aware of as a child because of my first English translation of the Qur'an, which was done by him; this made him a household name in Muslim homes around the world. The son of a clergyman, a Harrovian and a friend of Churchill, he declared his conversion to Islam in dramatic fashion after delivering a talk on 'Islam and Progress' on 29 November 1917 to the Muslim Literary Society in Notting Hill, West London. His translation, *The Meaning of the Glorious Qur'an*, was authorized by Al Azhar University, the world-recognized historic seat of Islamic learning, and praised by *The Times Literary Supplement*.[16] I recently had the privilege of discussing the influence Marmaduke Pickthall had on many British Muslims with his great-great-niece Sarah Pickthall, who feels modern Britain could learn much from his story.

Early British converts faced both outwards to new lands, fostering connections and serving as emissaries for and to Britain, and inwards, combining their English culture and heritage with their faith, despite the prejudice they sometimes faced. These founding fathers of British Islam proved what I have often said: that Islam is not ethnically, geographically or culturally specific, it is indeed 'a river which takes the colour of the bed over which it flows'.[17] It always has, it always will.

But Britain's relationship with Islam prior to the twentieth century wasn't merely the preserve of the travellers, adventurers and the converts but was woven through some of our most iconic pieces of literature, art and architecture. The dozens of references by Shakespeare to Islam, such as in *The Merchant of Venice* and *Othello*, are but some examples.[18]

For me it was Chaucer, an author I was introduced to during A-level English Literature, where *The Canterbury Tales* was a mandatory text. Once I'd worked out Middle English, I became fascinated with that intellect and wit that underpinned Chaucer's characters. His 'Doctour of Phisyk' draws on the knowledge of the Muslim intellectuals 'Razis', 'Avicen' and 'Averrois'.[19] His references to the Prophet Muhammad as 'Mahoun our prophete' and the Qur'an, 'the holy laws of our Alkaron', in 'The Man of Law's Tale' are further examples. Although the influence and knowledge of Islam is clear in his writings, his lead baddy, the evil mother of the Sultan, a Muslim trying to force the heroine of 'The Man of Law's Tale', Custace, to convert to Islam, probably reflects the anti-Muslim hostility in fourteenth-century England, less than a hundred years after the end of the Crusades.

The Crusades are probably the single most widely known period of Britain's contact with Islam, and they weren't pretty. Started under the Papacy of Pope Urban II in 1096, a series of 'holy wars' were fought by the western Christian allies both in defence of the Byzantine empire and their brothers and co-religionists the Eastern Christians and for their own economic and political ends against 'the Muslims'.

The next two centuries (176 years) saw successive attempts by European kings and clergymen to battle the 'barbaric' Muslims. Some battles were won whilst others, because of infighting, inadequate planning and ineffective troops, ended in compromise or defeat. In 1191, Richard I, the Lionheart, king 1189–99, led one of the most successful crusades against an enemy, the Kurdish Muslim political and military leader Saladin, or, as I grew up knowing him, Sallauddin Ayubi. Childhood tales told to us by Dad painted Saladin as a man who was perfect in all ways: learned, brave, compassionate and clever. At the height of his power he ruled modern-day Syria, Egypt, Yemen, North Africa and parts of Saudi Arabia, Turkey and Iraq and most importantly he captured and controlled the holy sites in Jerusalem. He was a man idolized by Muslims and westerners alike: Dante referred to him as 'a virtuous pagan' and King Richard called him his 'favourite opponent'.[20]

These two icons, the Lionheart and Saladin, grew to respect each other and even in battle amidst holy war found compassion and humanity. Saladin's sending of fruit and ice to assist King Richard's recovery when he fell ill and a replacement horse when Richard lost his in battle are two stories that take me back to my pigtails and rara-dress era.

During our childhood Islamic history was taught to us as fairy tales, stories of conquests, battle and strife, but always focused on compassion, generosity and friendship. The story of the very special relationship with Jews during the time of Saladin as during others, his choosing of the Jewish philosopher Maimonides as a personal physician and, on capturing Jerusalem, inviting the Jews, who had been excluded by the Crusaders, to return were lodged firmly in our young minds.

I learned about the 'Crusades' at school years later and recall not being able to make the connection between the school narrative of Richard the Lionheart and the baddies he was fighting and my father's story of the hero who could do no wrong, Sallauddin Ayubi. Maybe it was the way my history teacher pronounced the Muslim names or maybe it was the way he interpreted history, but whatever the reason I didn't make the connection until much later in life.

By high school I had not only made those connections but become political enough to challenge conventional wisdom. I opted to write about the British Raj for my O-Level History project and, upon realizing that the 'school version' of that period in history was remarkably different to the 'home version', set about making a nuisance of myself in class. I wanted my version to matter as much as the school version.

It was another example of how British Muslim kids can have two experiences in parallel, how they can be living two presents based on two pasts, where the two aren't brought into a shared narrative to create a single future. It is something we still don't do well and something which is needed in these times more than ever before: a teaching of history which is inclusive, an honest discussion of 'our version' and 'their version' and a commitment to value the heritage of all those that today make this island nation Great Britain. A shared history woven through school in our formative years would teach all children early on that they mattered and belonged, so that all feel that people 'like them' had made positive and negative contributions to the world we have today. It was therefore bizarre when the need of the time was for us all to know more history and from different perspectives that Michael Gove, the education secretary, suggested in 2013 a narrowed, myth-supporting version of history which was quite rightly criticized by teachers, academics and historians and labelled as insulting, offensive and dangerous.[21] A redraft followed, which included the study of Islamic history at Key Stage 2.

Centuries after the Crusades, we entered another period of history which today is more relevant than ever and still not taught well. A period where instead of the British and the Muslims being locked in holy war and facing each other across the battlefield, we stood shoulder-to-shoulder to protect King and country and defend what these days we like to call British values.

The Muslims, our Muslims, who fought with us during two brutal and bloody world wars, were recruited from across the globe. The need for manpower led to the allied forces recruiting Muslims from many continents. The wars introduced working-class Britain to Muslims, as both the poor in Britain and the poor from our colonies became the front line in our shared war effort. Men from different faiths, different lands, different cultures and speaking different languages fought and died together. Imminent death and patriotism proved a heady cocktail for probably one of our most successful cohesive community moments. Muslims formed a large part of the 4 million-strong British Indian Army contingent in both world wars and were mainly recruited from modern-day Afghanistan, India and Pakistan.[22] And had it not been for their timely arrival in France and Belgium in 1914 as the Germans advanced and overwhelmed British troops, 'the Germans may well have got through to [English]Channel ports . . . history might well have been different, their contribution was vital'.[23]

Thousands died. Amongst the youngest were three fifteen-year-olds, Amir, Gulab, and Mian Khan, who lost their lives in Italy. They originated from towns and cities close to the villages where my parents were born, part of the geographical belt where the Martial races – the tribes, casts and clans designated by the Brits as brave and loyal – hailed from and which were seen as a fertile recruiting ground. They proved themselves great warriors, soldiers who followed orders unquestioningly. They were well known for their reckless bravery, and one of them, Khudadad Khan, became the first Indian Army recipient of the Victoria Cross.

Hundreds of thousands were injured. Some of the injured were brought to Brighton, where the Royal Pavilion for two years became a hospital for the war wounded from the Indian subcontinent. The grounds of the Pavilion became a tented gurdwara for the Sikhs and the lawn an open-air Muslim prayer facility. Muslims who didn't survive their injuries were buried within a short distance of Britain's first purpose-built mosque, Shah Jahan in Woking. The mosque had been built in 1889 as a collaboration between Dr Gottlieb Wilhelm Leitner, a Hungarian-born British civil servant with a Jewish father, and Shah Jahan, the then Begum of Bhopal, the female Muslim ruler of a princely state in India. It has become the burial place of the early English converts to Islam, Muslim soldiers from across the globe and more recently deceased British Muslims, such as Dodi Fayad, who lost his life alongside Princess Diana in that fatal Paris car crash in 1997 (though his body was later exhumed), and the inspirational and amazingly talented, world-renowned architect Zaha Hadid. The burial ground, now recently restored, has stood through the centuries as a silent witness both to Islam in Britain and the loyalty of British Muslims and is the most poignant rebuke for twenty-first-century Islamophobes, who would love to erase and rewrite our shared history. In government I successfully pushed for government to support projects and events which highlighted these contributions. I wanted us to build our shared future by acknowledging our shared past.

So Britain's awareness of, and encounters with, Islam reach back over 1,400 years, but Muslim migration to Britain in any real numbers is less than 200 years old. Humayun Ansari, in his book *The Infidel Within*,[24] charts early Muslim migration from the mid nineteenth century as 'sailors, merchants, itinerant entertainers, servants, princes, students and a sprinkling of people from the professional classes'. Seamen mainly from Yemen, Somaliland and Malaya established a growing community in Cardiff, whilst Indian intellectuals and students started attending English and Scottish universities. The Inns of Court in London became an early favourite. Lincoln's Inn was where Mohammed Ali Jinnah studied, and it's where many a British Pakistani parent dreams of their 'little Ali' going. The Inner Temple was Mahatma Gandhi's choice of Inn and holds as much relevance for British Indians.

But even in those early days it wasn't all exotic and positive. The Muslims who came arrived in different forms and received different responses. The well-to-do, royalty and adventurers fascinated English society, whilst the Indian servants, maids, nannies and footmen of the well-heeled English returning from India, when abandoned, which they often were, had to resort to petty crime and begging and became a menace.

It was the exotic part of these Muslim arrivals that provided the perfect storyline for Julian Lord Fellowes, the creator of *Downton Abbey*. Lady Mary's scandalous encounter with the exotic Turkish diplomat, who dies in her bed in the midst of a passionate liaison, was based on a true story, when English high society, politics and the exotic Muslims came together in fact that made great fiction.[25]

In the early 1900s a number of seamen from Yemen and India docked in England and decided not to return home, instead forming early settled communities in Liverpool, Hull, Cardiff and South Shields. Many married white girls, usually from poor and broken families, and caused outrage in local communities and the media. The concept of 'shame', which today Muslim girls are all too familiar with as a tool of control, was invoked by local English communities to describe white girls who were considered 'shameless' for engaging in relationships with Arabs, Muslims or coloureds. Families, friends and indeed even officialdom felt it necessary to step in to stop this 'most difficult problem', which resulted in the depraved and immoral species of 'mixed breeds'. And despite evidence suggesting that many of the white women were treated better by the Arabs than by white men and their children were well behaved, well fed and well disciplined, it wasn't enough to convince the chief constable in Cardiff, who demanded legislation to criminalize relationships between 'coloured seamen and white women';[26]nor did it deter local authorities from urban planning which resulted in Arabs 'living in a colony by themselves and not mixed up with white people'.[27]

Even though many of these early Muslim migrants intermarried or cohabited and practised little of their faith, they were still viewed as inferior and uncivilized; they 'smelled' different, looked different and were strangers, polluters or, in the more official word, aliens.[28]

Indigenous English communities felt they were not just taking their jobs but taking their women too. The settlers were too damn integrated, just couldn't keep themselves to themselves, their own sort and the locals didn't like them. Interestingly they were probably exactly the kind of Muslims which right-wing commentators today yearn for: intermarried, interfaith, mixed-race, non-practising and fighting to live in mixed communities.

As demand for labourers increased whilst our boys were away fighting in the First World War, Britain saw dramatic and visible increases in Muslim populations in small towns and cities near the shipping industry and docks. These labourers were tolerated while they were needed, but once the war was over they were expected to simply 'go back home'. Parliament obliged by passing the Aliens Order in 1920, but this was too late for many who, having returned from the war effort, found their jobs had been taken by foreigners. Race riots in 1919 led to white mobs attacking 'blacks and coloureds' and demanding their expulsion. Many sought to justify the violence: 'What blame ... to those white men who seeing these conditions (relationships between Arabs and white girls) ... and loathing them, resort to violence' and that 'such consorting or ill assorting ... is repugnant to our finer instincts in which pride of race occupies a just and inevitable place'.[29]

These sentiments, taken from articles in mainstream British newspapers at the time, would not be unfamiliar today amongst some Muslim preachers and recruiters who seek to radicalize the young and justify violence.

A Conservative home secretary, William Joynson-Hicks, went further, by bringing in the Special Restriction Order 1925, early immigration control, to stop England being 'flooded with the whole of the alien refuse from every country in the world',[30] with his under-secretary of state singling out 'the Arabs' as being particularly problematic.[31] The order remained in place for nearly two decades, until once again a wartime need for migrant labour took precedence over racism and thuggery.

However, the discriminatory practices, ill treatment and deportations in the interim both reduced the numbers of Muslims here and discouraged others from arriving. Although some Turkish Cypriots migrated to London alongside Greek Cypriots in the 1930s, and Indian Muslim intellectuals continued to come to British universities, immigration of Muslims generally halted until the 1950s, when a need for labour once more resulted in Muslims from the old colonies coming to work. It was during this period of migration that my family and my husband's families first started their 'in-country' relationship with Britain, having already been part of the empire and served in the British Indian Army.

My maternal grandfather arrived in 1958, my father in 1962, from the Punjab in Pakistan. Some from a nearby village in the Punjab had left in the early 1950s, and the chain reaction of geographical and family connections led to others following. The Commonwealth Immigrants Act 1962, which restricted automatic UK entry for certain Commonwealth citizens, including those from India and Pakistan, and the introduction of the 'voucher' scheme, which enabled those already in Britain to arrange jobs and vouchers for friends and relatives 'back home', resulted in concentrated migration from small village districts, clans and families.

My husband's grandfather arrived in 1962, and my father-in-law in 1965, from Kashmir. Many of the early migrants from Azad Kashmir, the bit of Kashmir on the Pakistani side of the line of control, came from Mirpur and were families who came as part of either the general voucher scheme or a specific voucher scheme negotiated in the early 1960s by the British constructor of the Mangla Dam in Mirpur for displaced families as compensation for the loss of ancestral land needed for the construction of the dam.

Both areas in Pakistan contributed to large levels of migration during the 1950s and '60s, as older heads of households and young, mainly single men flocked to the mill towns to work in the steel, textile and car manufacturing mills. They never intended to stay; that's why they left their families behind. Britain was familiar territory because of the colonial experience; it needed workers, and they needed work. However, controls introduced by the 1962 Act didn't include dependants, who still enjoyed restriction-free travel to join spouses and fathers in the UK, resulting in wives arriving accompanied usually only by their sons. Many of these early women settled in the boys and 'went home'.

Both my mum and mum-in-law were part of an early cohort of wives who arrived and settled in the late 1960s. They didn't go home. And the rest, as they say, is history.

Alongside these Pakistanis and Kashmiris during the same period a number of mainly Sylheti Muslims arrived from the newly established state of Bangladesh after the 1971 Pakistani civil war. And although the Muslim community in the 1970s and '80s was a significant minority, a large majority of the minority was made up of a handful of different origins: Pakistani and Kashmiris, Indians, Bangladeshis, Cypriot Turks and East Africans.[32]

But just as Britain was getting to know its now increasing Muslim community, which at that time was still defined through the prism of race and origins, Asian Muslims were getting to know other Muslims and finding both unity and difference through culture, theology and politics. The need to organize as a community to deliver basic needs and specialist services around births, marriages and deaths saw 'community organizations and leaders' starting to emerge. Muslim organizations began to develop and reflected both a unity of purpose on practical issues but also the differences within the Muslim communities based on race and origin and also geographical location in the UK.

Before the Muslim migration of the 1950s the home of British Islam was in the south of England. Its main centres were the Shah Jahan Mosque in Woking and its offshoots the Muslim Society of Great Britain, established by Muslim convert Lord Headley, and the Islamic Cultural Centre in Regent's Park, which sat on land donated in 1928 by

George VI in return for land in Cairo provided by King Farouk of Egypt and Sudan for the building of an Anglican cathedral.[33]

These early institutions had little impact on the ordinary lives of Muslim migrants based mainly in northern England and in Scotland. For those communities a local network of menfolk from similar backgrounds started to establish informal organizations and mosques. Most were small house conversions in residential areas where Muslim communities lived in large numbers. These house mosques still form something like 87 per cent of all mosques in the UK.[34] But eventually a need to influence, lobby and engage with officialdom led to the emergence of the more formal community leaders and community organization.

These individuals and groups hit the national conscience in 1988–9 during the scenes of book-burning as Britain's Muslims reacted to Salman Rushdie's *The Satanic Verses*, the first political moment in my lifetime when religion became a point of difference. Up to this point 'the Muslims' were simply part of a larger group of 'the Asians', mainly first-generation arrivals from India, Pakistan and Bangladesh as well as East Africa, including the Asian victims of Idi Amin's ethnic cleansing of Uganda. And Asians were themselves a part of the larger group of 'coloured' people.

Although while I was growing up racial discrimination was overt and at times brutal, religious discrimination was simply not a feature. 'Asian', 'black', 'coloured' and, for the less sophisticated, even 'Paki' were familiar terms to describe my lot during the 1970s and '80s, but 'Muslim' was rarely if ever used. My identity was rooted in the colour of my skin; it's what made me and others like me different. It was a difference which led to many misunderstandings and at times blatant racism. And it started early. Dewsbury had an immigrant centre when I was growing up. Kids like me were sent to it. I'm sure the centre was well-intentioned: it was a stepping stone to proper school for non-white kids, to make Asian kids school ready. But my father insisted we, that is, my sisters and I, were not immigrants: we hadn't arrived from overseas, we were born in Britain and therefore would go to school, proper school, like others our age. We never went to the immigrant centre but heard many a story about what went on there. One that stuck in my mind was the story about kids being fed stew and dumplings which contained non-halal meat. It was perceived by my parents and their friends as a deliberate act to sabotage their practices, but it may simply have been a lack of awareness about religious dietary requirements at a time when 'Asian', not 'Muslim', was the identifying 'other' feature. But it represented a world I did not want to be part of. To do so would mean that I was an outsider. And I wanted to belong.

High school had its own complications, not least hitting puberty, a moment which most starkly marked Asian girls out as different and thus more likely to be in the firing line for racist insults. Puberty was a moment when a huge red flag went up which said to my parents: the girls are growing up and need protecting. We needed protecting from any exposure to sex and relationships: hence the TV was switched off at 9 p.m., *Dynasty* and *Dallas*, the long-running US soaps, were off limits. We needed protecting from inappropriate, immodest clothes, so a compromise was negotiated between local schools and Asian parents to enable trousers to be worn under the school skirt so ensure no bare legs. Hitching the school skirt just doesn't have the same effect when you simply reveal more polyester. And summer brought its own challenges, when my mum, who was an excellent seamstress, decided that a beautifully stitched silky Pakistani shalwar kameez in the school colour, maroon, was very fetching. Not only was it too cold for British summers but it led to a phrase which I heard often: 'You smell of curry.' Dressing differently, not having the mainstream teenage girl's TV experience and a universal ban on socializing like the white girls defined me as 'the other'.

Quite a number of the other Asian girls at the school wore a similar uniform, and a few even wore the fine, see-through headscarf known as a dupatta, either wrapped around the neck as a scarf or pinned perfectly Benazir Bhutto style. But there were few hijabs, no prayer rooms, I don't recall halal food, and we just took the day off school for Eid without any formal fuss. So yes, there was a point of difference, but it was race, ethnicity and culture, not religion.

The racism I encountered was never brutal, and the attitude at home was never defensive enough to mark out the lines of 'us' and 'them' in my own life. I believe it's much harder now, where bullying doesn't stop at the school gates but goes on through social networking, meaning there is no respite. The 69 per cent rise in Islamophobic bullying in schools, according to ChildLine's annual report in 2013, should concern us all.[35]

Dad would occasionally end up on the receiving end of abuse and even violence while out cabbing on a Friday or Saturday night, but I saw that as fare-dodging yobs, 'bad uns' rather than race attacks. Yes, invariably the attackers were white and the victims Asian, and yes, the term 'Paki' would be used, but to me it didn't feel like a broader battle.

The real victims were a community more 'coloured' than us: the black community. It was they who were always on the telly in the middle of some trouble; it was they whom Britain didn't seem to want; it was they who still seemed to be second-class citizens in the US; and it was they who still didn't have freedom in Africa. And it was they who inspired me: Trevor McDonald, the iconic *News at Ten* presenter; Floella, now Baroness, Benjamin. The vivacious *Playschool* host was my heroine, and my connection of colour with John Barnes made me a lifelong Liverpool FC supporter.

I sensed the blacks had it tough. News coverage of the riots in the 1980s showed housing which appeared many worlds away from our small but tidy semi-detached home. The police action appeared brutal, and the stories always appeared to suggest something inherently wrong about black people, their culture and their values: they weren't like the rest of us. They had, as my colleague Oliver Letwin, current MP for West Dorset and policy adviser to Margaret Thatcher in the mid 1980s, put it, 'bad moral attitudes'.[36] Today these lazy and insulting stereotypes are reserved for 'the Muslims'.

The day of Nelson Mandela's release from Robben Island in 1990, his dignified and determined walk from the prison – the first time I had seen live footage of him – and the subsequent scenes of jubilation will always be one of my memorable political moments of my youth. I was nineteen, and it felt like real change.

So in the 1970s race seemed the political issue both domestically, with civil unrest, a demand for equality and the development of race relations laws, and internationally, with the black civil rights and the anti-apartheid movements. As a teenager what radicalized me was the colour of my skin. It's what motivated me to protest, to become a part of local action with the Racial Equality Council, to become involved in setting the tone through years of volunteering with the Joseph Rowntree Trust, racial justice work and engaging people in democracy through Operation Black. As the '80s gave way to the heady '90s, with many an Asian comfortably yuppified, I could not have predicted that Muslim was slowly to become the new black.

Racial inequality, racism and the deficiencies of racial justice are still problems, and we are far from living up to the equality of opportunity mantra we all trot out. Black boys are still over-represented in school exclusions, underachievement statistics and prison populations, although many of these are Muslim too.[37] But what had, certainly before the EU referendum, changed was society's slow drumbeat of acceptable racism. Politicians using race as a convenient headline and newspapers selling copies off the back of a good anti-black story are now thankfully less acceptable and quite rightly vociferously condemned. Instead, religion has become the new race, the point of difference, the basis of radicalization, the reason for politicization, the other, the problem.

This journey – from race to religion – came in waves, with high-profile events bringing the Muslim communities to the attention of the media, politicians and public. The seminal pre-September 11 Muslim moments in British domestic policy were the Salman Rushdie affair, the protests immediately after and the subsequent 2001 riots in Lancashire and Yorkshire mill towns. Alongside this sit foreign policy moments such as the anti-Soviet Afghan War of the 1980s and its fallout in Pakistan, the genocide of Muslims in the Balkans war of the 1990s and the first Gulf War. All these events gave rise to a sense within British Muslim communities that their sentiments didn't matter and in the world of policy-makers that Muslims were starting to become troublesome.

The Salman Rushdie affair, the reaction of Muslim communities across the world to a satirical piece of fiction, *The Satanic Verses*, highlighted a number of flashpoints which had been developing for years and the consequences of which we still see playing out today. Firstly it reidentified British Pakistanis, Indians and Bangladeshis from the Muslim faith as British *Muslims* rather than British Asians. British Muslims not only formed a group identified by their faith rather than their origins, culture, race or class, but were also identified with a wider group of Muslims around the world who at this moment were all collectively incensed, angered and united in opposition. The Rushdie affair also identified the target of this anger. Yes, Salman Rushdie, a man born a Muslim from South Asia, had written the book, but it was 'the West', 'the colonialists' who were not responding in the way British Muslim communities expected. The issuance of the fatwa, a religious legal ruling to kill Rushdie, by Ayatollah Khomeini of Iran in February 1989 came within weeks of a number of book-burning protests both in the Lancashire town of Bolton and the Yorkshire town of Bradford. The message from the fatwa signalled to British Muslims that, where their government, the British government, didn't understand or, worse, didn't care about the sincerely held beliefs and values of the British Muslim community, a power overseas did. And, worse still, it started to implant the belief that, however successful the community became, it would never be treated the same, as equals to white Brits.

Britain at this time still had blasphemy laws on the statute books, and even though the last public prosecution dated back to 1922 the courts did issue a fine against *Gay News* magazine in 1977 for the publication of a poem about Jesus which was deemed blasphemous as a result of a private prosecution by Mary Whitehouse, a staunch Christian and socially conservative campaigner.[38]

The response from politicians in Britain by today's standards was both measured and considerate, with a clear underlying attempt to calm and reconcile. As the then foreign secretary, Geoffrey Howe, said

> the British government, the British people, do not have any affection for the book . . . It compares Britain with Hitler's Germany. We do not like that any more than the people of the Muslim faith like the attacks on their faith contained in the book. So we are not sponsoring the book. What we are sponsoring is the right of people to speak freely, to publish freely.[39]

But Muslims wanted the blasphemy laws extended to them, and they wanted the state to prosecute. They wanted British laws to protect Islam and indeed other religions as they did Christianity. When neither demand was met the government was accused of hypocrisy by

British Muslims. These accusations, I believe, stemmed both from misjudged and misunderstood positions and statements both around the blasphemy law and its evolution over the last century. The law was seen by most in politics and the judiciary as a relic of the past and at the time of the Rushdie affair hadn't been used by the police and the state for nearly seventy years. Britain had become increasingly tolerant of intolerance towards Christianity. Britain's attitude to all things religious had started to change, and that attitude was simply being reflected in the government's approach to Islam.

The private prosecution of Rushdie by British Muslims for blasphemy and the subsequent drafting of the particulars of blasphemy by some barristers who themselves were from the Muslim faith showed a number of deep misunderstandings: the failure of the Muslim community to see how Britain had moved on from its historic outrage against all things against God; the failure to comprehend and come to terms with the liberal commitment to freedom of speech; and mostly the failure to read the damn book to enable genuinely informed discussion meant that British Muslims spectacularly failed to be heard.

In reverse, Britain hadn't even started to understand the depth and sincerity of belief within Muslim communities, and with the exception of some senior figures from faith communities such as the then archbishop of Canterbury, Robert Runcie, and the then chief rabbi, Immanuel, later Baron, Jakobovits, Britain failed to grasp what Muslims rightly or wrongly would find deeply offensive and interpret as a personal attack on them. Most notably, the government failed to recognize that if Britain didn't hold its Muslims close, if it didn't show them that they mattered and treat them like they belonged, then there would be others more than happy, on this occasion the Iranians and Saudis, to befriend them and shower them with concern and moral support. The more the liberal elite of Britain shouted freedom of expression, the more the Muslims raged about freedom of religion.

As the Rushdie affair played out domestically, an altogether different battle – one with an international dimension – was starting to develop: the battle for who would speak for the Muslim world. Whilst much of the early condemnation was from Saudi Arabia and groups in Pakistan, India and Bangladesh, the homelands of the majority of

British Muslims, by issuing the fatwa Iran took pole position, ready and willing to come out leading the collective Muslim sentiment.

The Rushdie Affair resulted in civil unrest across the UK, with over seventy arrests taking place at an anti-*Satanic Verses* demonstration in London in May 1989, which saw 20,000 men, women and children gather to voice their anger at Rushdie and demand a change to the blasphemy laws.[40] More serious attacks and even bombings took place across the globe, and even today the fatwa and the bounty on Rushdie's head stands.

The seeds of distrust had been sown, and the fallout set the Muslims on a journey of simmering resentment and a narrative of grievance.

A growth of towns and geographical areas with single faith communities, local tensions about homes and schooling and challenges of underachievement both in Muslim communities and white working-class communities formed a bonfire of problems into which the Rushdie Affair threw a match. In the summer of 1989, in the midst the Rushdie affair, Dewsbury experienced a British National Party protest which turned into a riot. The protest by the far right was a show of solidarity towards families who had taken their children out of the local middle school, complaining it had too many Asians in it.[41] The BNP chants of 'Rushdie! Rushdie!' during the protest had the desired effect and riled local youth.[42]

A counter-demonstration was organized, and local youths from the Muslim community in Savile Town were only too happy to respond to the rally call. It was a weekend, the weather was good, and this was a moment to be a hero. I was eighteen and at the end of my A levels. Dad was out, but Mum made sure all five of us were securely inside: the streets were not safe for her girls. I recall being scared and excited at the same time. The phone rang a lot, and although I was relieved at being safe I also wanted to be out.

A friend of mine was in town. He had heard the BNP were coming into town to fight the Asians, and at a time before mobile phones and social networking when you needed to know what was going down you went to find out. He recalls being in a large group of Asians, hearing chanting from the 'others' but never seeing them. They were pushed into Savile Town, and it took him a number of hours finally to find his way back to Staincliffe, where he was to receive a rollicking from his parents for firstly getting involved and secondly being out so late. He, like many other Asian youths, felt they had been treated like the troublemakers, whilst they felt it was the far right that had come to the town to cause trouble. The provocation by 'the whites' and the targeting of a local pub by local Asian youths when pushed back into Savile Town, damaging the premises and cars of locals who were drinking there that Saturday, caused deep divisions and resentment, which even today occasionally rears its head.

The proximity of the Rushdie Affair to the Dewsbury riots and the near single-faith identity of all the non-whites in Dewsbury redefined the Asians as Muslims. As a spokesman from the Muslim Council of Britain said at the time, '*The Satanic Verses* brought them [different ethnic communities] together and helped develop a British Muslim identity.'[43] A large majority of the arrests that followed were from the Muslim community; many fewer were from the BNP provocateurs, which left the community feeling it had been punished for defending itself.[44]

Grievance on both sides started to set in. The Muslim community felt they were being excessively targeted and punished, and white, mainly working-class communities, living amongst or on the edge of growing Asian enclaves, felt their way of life was being threatened. This mutual distrust could simply be viewed as the challenges of different races living ever-separate lives in the same towns, but this sense of mistrust entered an altogether more difficult phase as we entered the era of terrorism and the war on terror.

This narrative of grievance – of being excessively targeted and more harshly punished – once again became a major point of discussion a decade or so later during the court appearances, convictions and sentencing of those accused of taking part in the Bradford Riots during the summer of 2001. The riots, which started on 7 July 2001, exactly four years before the date of the London bombing, as a reaction to the far-right presence in the city centre and the stabbing of an Asian man, became a defining feature in a grievance narrative which pre-dates the more recent challenge of terrorism. The excessive sentencing was seen as 'one rule for the Muslims, another for the rest' and it's a narrative which has gained ever-increasing traction amongst young Muslims over the past eighteen years as they face the consequences of the war on terror and an increasingly hostile policy-making environment.

Much has been written about what triggered the Bradford riots,[45] but some facts are indisputable: the growth of the Asian community in Bradford, of which a large part was Muslim; the growth of segregated communities, with parts of Bradford being over 70 per cent from a single ethnic group; despite some success, large parts of the community both white and black still living in poor housing and engaged in low-paid work; deep resentment in both Asian and white communities about 'not belonging' in a changing world; a lack of trust between the community and the police and national and local decision-makers. For the white Bradfordians the space around them – the buildings, the businesses and the bureaucracy – had changed for the worse, and they felt shut out. As for the Asian Bradfordians, they had helped change the buildings, businesses and bureaucracy for the better, but they still felt they hadn't been let in. The spread of unrest was linked to an increase in racial violence; a long-standing mistrust of, and disillusionment with, the police; the overt and taunting presence of the BNP and other far-right groups; and the entrenched poverty and unemployment that existed within the cities.[46]

The underlying resentment and distrust between segregated communities was once again exploited by the National Front, the British National Party and other far-right groups, just as today terror is exploited. The Anti-Nazi League, with its long history of counter-demonstrations, sought and found recruits from a local community for whom this wasn't just political and ethical but personal.

Nearly 300 arrests were made, and 200 jail sentences totalling 604 years were handed out. These figures are unprecedented in English legal history, and many cases took years to conclude, as the long sentences were repeatedly appealed. Many felt the provocateurs, the far right, who had come into the city to rally support and show solidarity to the 'marginalized' whites, had gone unpunished. Sentences for white youths involved in disturbances the night before the riot were much more lenient, whereas a number of the Asian youth received heavy prison sentences for acts which in effect amounted to the throwing of a stone. During appeals against the heavy sentences given to the Asian youths it was accepted that the judge failed properly to take account of the trigger events and the climate of fear that had been created by the far right.[47]

Disproportionate, hypocritical and institutional racism were oft-used phrases that over time fed grievance, some justified, some not, and which even today inform debates on belonging. The rot had set in, and it set the lens through which future policy-making was seen. Grievance for many young people was a real reaction to a real challenge; for officialdom it became a view increasingly to dismiss, an approach that hasn't worked.

In the Rushdie affair Bradford's Muslims had displayed collective anger; in the 2001 riots they had displayed collective muscle. Each time they responded excessively – excessive anger, excessive violence – to an external trigger, and each time little effort was made by local or national government to understand – not condone, but understand – the underlying issues and grievance.

We failed as a country to recognize the collective call from white and Muslim communities in northern towns who were saying they felt like they didn't belong, we feel like we don't matter. And in a rush to find someone to blame we focused on the self-proclaimed community leaders, the mainly male 'gatekeepers', who quite rightly deserved some criticism, but in doing so we overlooked the large number of the elders, male and female, who, having been outraged during the Rushdie affair in 1989, did not support the violent anger of the youth during the riot in 2001.

The riot signalled a generational shift. No longer prepared to engage in passive protest and no longer prepared to carry on being grateful for being 'allowed' to make Britain their home, Asian youth, becoming increasingly Muslim youth, demanded the political value of equality, had higher expectations of education and the labour market and were increasingly disillusioned in the face of continuing race and religious discrimination and the first generation's compromises with what they viewed as the white power structure.[48]

These young Asians were critical of the police, fearful of the far right and resentful of the media, whom they viewed as stirring up trouble with one-sided reporting of racial attacks, only paying attention when it was suggested that most racially motivated attacks were by South Asians on whites. The rioting showcased the new generation, of young men in particular, shunning the acquiescent attitude of their parents and elders and demanding radical change.

This new-found assertiveness unsettled white communities, who felt that this aggressive demand for equality was a code word for dominance and thus pushed back with the 'whites' rights' mantra. Grievance was the new campaign, with both groups staking a greater claim to victimhood. The fight to be at the top was played out by laying claim to being at the bottom. This hasn't been addressed, nor has it helped us, as we've faced the challenge of terrorism, and the focus on difference has grown.

Years on, Bradford is better at responding to provocation but still resentful of a point in its history when the us-and-them divide wasn't just between communities but also between the authorities and the Muslim community. It captures how genuine grievances which remain unchecked and unanswered remain grievances years later.

With the attacks on the twin towers following within two months, in September 2001, the Muslims' fate was sealed. This violent and very visual attack defined 'the Muslims' worldwide, and, despite there being no Brits involved in the attack, British Muslims became part of the problem. Their Muslimness not their Britishness became their defining identity – perhaps the only identity they were going to be allowed. A community of people from different backgrounds, races, ethnicities, origins and colour became 'the Muslims'.

Despite the burgeoning Muslim middle class, its increasing numbers of entrepreneurs and millionaires – fifteen in the 2013 *Sunday Times* Rich List[49] – despite the thousands of medics and health professionals, lawyers, accountants, teachers and other professionals, despite starting to make their mark in arts, culture, media and sport, 'the Muslims' were seen through the prism of their faith. Their faith, Islam, was increasingly seen as the basis of a broader international cause of conflict and Britain was no longer at ease with either.

The 'war on terror', our support for the Bush administration's decision to go to war in Afghanistan in 2001 and Iraq in 2003 and the first terrorist attack on British soil by British Muslims in July 2005 further set the scene for a future relationship between Britain and its Muslims. A Britain that hadn't entirely reconciled race was about to have to reconcile difference on the basis of religion. My country was not comfortable with my religion, my religion was not at ease with my country, and neither was well informed enough to know our intertwined history, culture and language.[50]

We failed to understand 'our Muslims' but also failed to understand 'ourselves'. We set off on a path of policy-making and demanded that 'the Muslims' sign up to 'our values' and more, without truly expressing who we are and our journey to the Britain we live in today. In an attempt to build a more cohesive and resilient society we demanded that 'the Muslims' join what we believed we stood for rather than jointly charting a route to what we wanted to be. We set out to prescribe what it meant to be British by a series of statements we called British values.

2

What Are British Values?

'I may not agree with you but I will defend to the death your
right to make an ass of yourself.'

Oscar Wilde

Around 500 years ago we didn't like the Catholics much. We didn't
trust their 'divided' loyalty. We couldn't accept that they could reconcile their faith and their citizenship, that they could be both Catholic
and British. We institutionalized anti-Catholicism by passing the Act
of Supremacy 1534. We killed people because they didn't follow our
version of our faith; we didn't allow our Royal family to marry them;
we didn't allow them into those great British institutions Oxford and
Cambridge; and when 'the Catholics' wanted to marry we insisted
they did so in an Anglican Church.[1] Just over 200 years ago we finally
allowed 'the Catholics' to own their own property and some years
later allowed their well-to-do menfolk to vote.[2]

Women, however, had to wait a little longer, as 200 years ago we
believed married women were subordinate to their husbands and both
the wife and her property belonged to the husband. Married women
finally got the right to keep their 'wage' in 1870 and to own their
property in 1882, though didn't earn the right to be treated equally for
inheritance purposes until the Law of Property Act 1922. After much
bloodshed and strife all women acquired the vote in 1928, but female
civil servants had to leave their jobs upon getting married until 1954:
it was believed that a woman's place was in the home.[3] I'm pleased
that we've progressed since those dark days, but women still aren't
equally represented on boards or in the top professions,[4] the battle for

equal pay is still not won, and tragically two women a week are still killed at the hands of their partner or ex-partner, with 2015–16 seeing such violent crimes in England and Wales reach a record high.[5]

We weren't always compassionate towards people of colour. Over 200 years ago we thought it was OK to enslave black people. Britain dominated the slave trade during the seventeenth and eighteenth centuries, as we fed the colonies with workers. Many a respected politician and intellectual made persuasive arguments to support this position. Many a British businessman made good money off the back of selling blacks.[6] And it was only about fifty years ago that, commenting on the black civil rights movement in the US, the opinion of our embassy in Washington was that 'the Negroes wanted too much too soon'.[7] Closer to home, only thirty years ago it was suggested that schemes to get young blacks into business would result in them setting 'up in the disco and drug trade'. it is only a few decades ago that mainstream politicians, mainly in my party, found the idea of blacks in their own country being equal to whites quite novel, and so considered those fighting to end apartheid in South Africa were terrorists.

We didn't much like the Jews either. We burned and butchered them and about 600 years ago, in King Edward's Edict of Expulsion of 1290, got rid of all of them. We were early pioneers in ethnic cleansing. Those who were brave enough to return or remain secretly were finally acknowledged just over 250 years ago via the Jewish Naturalization Act, 1753. Such was the extraordinary uproar it provoked that the 1753 Act, designed to allow foreign-born Jews to naturalize as British subjects, had to be withdrawn after two months.

We eventually let them into our great institutions and even Parliament but made sure at least until 1858 that they nominally converted or pretended to be Christian to enable them to take the oath of allegiance and hence their parliamentary seat. It's likely that the oft-cited great Jewish Tory prime minister Benjamin Disraeli, who converted to Christianity in 1817, would not have made premier if he had still been Jewish at the time of his election.[8]

We questioned their loyalty during the British mandate in Palestine: were they Jewish or British first? They were the bogeymen for far-right fascists, the target of the blackshirts and the butt of bigoted headlines in the *Daily Mail*. Just over eighty years ago the *Daily Mail* shouted 'Hurrah for the Blackshirts' as it tried to convince fellow Brits that they were 'a well organised party of the right ready to take over responsibility for national affairs with the same directness of purpose and energy of method as Hitler and Mussolini have displayed'. And their headlines on 'German Jews pouring into the country' are not dissimilar to the way they write about today's refugee crisis.[9]

In the 1950s we officially sanctioned our police to persecute men who loved men and women who loved women. Scotland Yard led a witch hunt against lesbian, gay, bisexual and transgender (LGBT) people. We set them up using undercover police agents provocateurs; we hunted them down, prosecuted them and locked hundreds of them up. They, gay people, were deemed subversive and could not be trusted, and certainly not in government or the military.[10] The then home secretary, Sir David Maxwell Fyfe, a Conservative, had promised 'a new drive against male vice' that would 'rid England of this plague'.[11] Although in 1967 we partly decriminalized homosexual acts, notably between two men aged twenty-one and over in private, convictions of gay and bisexual men actually rose in the years following this limited reform.[12]

In 1971, six months after I was born, celebrities, politicians and even Royalty supported the Festival of Light, a campaign against a permissive, immoral society. The Festival vowed to protest against 'sexploitation' in the media and the arts and promoted traditional Christian morality as a remedy to the nation's malaise – and part of that 'malaise' was the LGBT community and their demand for equal rights.[13]

I was in high school before the whole of the UK decriminalized gay sex, and only then for over-twenty-ones, in 1982. It took a further nineteen years to make the age of consent for homosexuals the same as that for heterosexuals.

We sacked people for being gay, we treated them like social lepers, we chemically castrated them, we tried to 'cure' them through aversion and conversion therapies, we distrusted them and perceived them as a security risk, we saw AIDS as a gay disease only taking it seriously once it started affecting straight people, we rabble-roused the party faithful at conferences and meetings against them and enacted legislation to make sure we stigmatized them from birth. We created the environment where a loon took it upon himself to bomb a pub in London which was frequented by 'the gays', killing three and injuring dozens more.[14]

It was only in 2003 that we decided, at the insistence of that nasty, interfering lot from the European Union, that we could no longer legalize discrimination against gay people at work.[15]

Even in the mid-2000s, during my time as a Conservative parliamentary candidate, there was no real sanction, penalty or comeback from the party if you were homophobic. A friend with a formidable political CV and a long-term gay partner was advised that a 'single man' of his age may find greater success if he 'turned up with a woman'. Gay friends still took their 'girlfriends' along to selection meetings, and many a miserable Tory wife has dutifully played her part until her Tory man felt he could 'man up' and admit to loving another man.

The country and my party's views on homosexuality were in defence of our British values as we saw them then. In 2004 opposing civil partnerships was expressed as family values; today supporting gay marriage is supporting family values. So how fixed are British values? And how fixed should they be?

Today, we often talk of religious views, especially Muslim, as out of touch with British values. I too have been homophobic. It's something I am deeply ashamed of. My campaign literature from my 2005 campaign is toe-curlingly embarrassing and deeply offensive.

My faith, like all major faiths in the world, has a much-debated theological position on marriage, morality, gay sex and straight sex. And I've questioned whether my own homophobia was developed in the years of religious learning I was exposed to as a child. And yet in my conservative Muslim upbringing we didn't talk sex; forget gay sex – we didn't even talk straight sex. No mosque taught it, nor for that matter did school in what was the awful era of 1980s sex education. The school sex education videos which we watched as ten- and eleven-year-olds taught me nothing. Being forced to watch in mixed-sex groups meant any questions the girls had were drowned out by the testosterone posturing of the boys. It was the nearest most boys were going to get to a porn video, and one sanctioned as 'educational' at that. I just pretended I hadn't been there and hoped like mad that my mum wouldn't find out that I had. The other Muslim girls and I kept it as our little secret, the unsaid pact, because we all knew that if one spilled the beans to a mum the other mums would be told, and then we'd all be for it. We were coming to the end of middle school, and some of the girls knew that it could be the final straw which would break their parents' commitment to a western education and could result in them being shipped off to that containment centre that was the local 'Muslim school'.

So gay sex was not on the syllabus at school, the mosque or, for that matter, home. No religious book ever mentioned it, no imam ever preached about it, no madrasa teacher ever referred to it, no parent ever acknowledged it. And in a pre-internet age, where access to information was restricted to library visits. I don't recall a section on gay sex.

Naively I went through my teenage years and into an arranged marriage while still at university without having to engage with the gay issue. And then I discovered the Tory Party. Well, boy, were we obsessed with the gay issue. We protectors of British values of decency, family and honourable lifestyle choices came into our own on the subject of 'the gays'. From our political positions in 1994, rejecting lowering the age of consent to that of heterosexual couples, to the personal trauma many a gay Conservative candidate and activist faced over the years, to our moment of high-ground morality in introducing Section 28, which amongst other things forbade local authorities from 'teaching in any maintained school of the acceptability of homosexuality as a pretended family relationship', and large numbers of Conservative MPs expressing opposition to civil partnership in 2004, we have much to be ashamed of.

In a nutshell as politicians and as a country we have been sectarian, racist, sexist and homophobic, and each time our behaviour has in our view been consistent with our Britishness.

It can be hard, therefore, to hear politicians, media types and commentators trumpeting 'British values', insisting kids should be taught these values in schools and suggesting Muslims don't subscribe to them, when we in the not-so-distant past have done and said things which flew in the face of our current version of British values, which include individual liberty and mutual respect and tolerance. We speak about these so called 'British values' as if they have always existed in the way we define them today.

Allow me to take a deeper look at our history.

Let's start with that bastion of Britishness and values, the Magna Carta, the 'Great Charter', the world-famous document from the thirteenth century, whose 800 years of existence we all celebrated with great zeal during 2015. It is seen by many as the moment when we finally wrote down the values we stand for. Now, putting aside the fact that the Magna Carta wasn't really about protecting the little guy against the big guys, it was about protecting the big guys from the even bigger guy, we do gush about how June 1215 was a moment when the great rights, protections and liberties we all take for granted today were first born. Across the pond in the United States they based their Declaration of Independence and Constitution on the mythical values laid out in this great document, a constitution and values that in 2016 didn't prevent the country from electing disgusting views in the form of President Trump.

As centuries passed and we looked back with rose-tinted specs at this great moment, we decided to enshrine this cosy, fuzzy feelgood factor by drafting the Bill of Rights, 1689, which details many of the rights most believed or had been led to believe were in the Magna Carta: the limiting of power held by the big guys; the rights of ordinary folk, or at least those extraordinary enough to be considered ordinary enough to influence Parliament; the rights of the individual, although Protestant individuals were considered more important than Catholic ones; the right not to be treated cruelly and inhumanely, although we did carry on hanging and flogging people for nearly another 300 years until the 1960s and only eventually abolished capital punishment for all offences about eighteen years ago.

The Bill of Rights also gave us our now oft-quoted freedom of speech, although we couldn't use that freedom in relation to all things religious because of our blasphemy laws, which we only got rid of in 2008, and it didn't extend to anything the law forbade us speak about. So, yes, we had freedom of speech but we also made laws which restricted this freedom, ensuring we exercised the right responsibly. Even now, our right to freedom of speech currently enshrined in the Human Rights Act, 1998, is not absolute and can be, and indeed is, restricted to prevent crime or disorder, preserve national security and ensure child protection.[16]

Many of these 'British values' from the Magna Carta and the Bill of Rights were codified and thus more accessible to the ordinary man through the European Convention on Human Rights, 1953 (ECHR), itself inspired by the Universal Declaration of Human Rights, 1948. I'm incredibly proud of the British involvement in the creation and drafting of the ECHR and the enshrinement of these rights in a UK Act of Parliament in the now sadly much-despised Human Rights Act of 1998. We, Britain, stand proud, chest puffed, when we think Magna Carta; we swell with patriotism at the mention of the Bill of Rights and British values. But having seen what man can do to man, the Holocaust being one of the most extreme examples, we felt it necessary to once more declare the rights of human beings after the Second World War, despite Magna Carta and our Bill of Rights. Importantly, we felt it necessary to once again declare the universality of these rights. So, however much we dislike one another, we still afford each other the rights we hold dear for ourselves. We didn't feel confident enough to simply leave it to age-old religious principle of 'do to others as you would have them do to you',[17] or trust our belief that our western values are so unshakeably right that we in the West would instinctively get it right. It was, of course, other westerners who committed one of the world's most heinous crimes, the Holocaust, where both sides were fighting in line with their western values, even if many of those dying in the ditches were easterners like my grandfathers.

Each generation asserts its own 'British values', based on the society that makes up Britain at that time. Britain is on a constant journey where it redefines and reaffirms its values. The Rt Hon. Liam Byrne, MP, is a former cabinet minister and author of *Black Flag Down*, in which he argues that the 'problem with values is they often smack of the past'[18], a past, I would argue, which is often at odds with our so-called 'values'. He suggests a forward-looking, inclusive coming-together in what he calls 'ideals', future aspirations that we, wherever we come from, can build together.

The importance of this inclusiveness was what underpinned the value of 'multiculturalism'. In the 1980s and '90s the concept of multiculturalism was an expression of our Britishness, the acceptance of other cultures, faiths and practices, a belief in plurality and a respect for an alternative way, even if it wasn't a way we would choose for ourselves. More recently it has generated reams of newspaper column inches on why it has failed Britain and the current 'mess' we are in with 'the Muslims' is cited as the most striking example of this failure.

So what is multiculturalism? It can mean many things to many people. It can be a demand for equality of worth, a rebuttal to entrenched institutional racism, a slapdown of advocates of racial superiority, a humanitarian rebuff to supporters of ethnic cleansing, a sign of a comfortable global citizen, one who can be different and a part of the whole at the same time. It's an acceptance of equal value for different cultures. It can simply describe the practical manifestation and existence of multiple cultures living alongside each other in a defined space, it's the Chinese takeaway on one corner and the balti house on the next, it's the steel drums and carnivals alongside pomp and pageantry as we celebrate our Royals, it's saris blending effortlessly with cocktail dresses at nice dinner parties and it's modern menorahs in Muslim homes as pieces of art and decor. Multiculturalism can be the promotion of difference, an invitation to experience difference, a commitment to raise awareness of difference and not simply to tolerate but to celebrate difference.

But multiculturalism can also become a policy of segregation, division and siloing of communities so that each is engaged, supported and accommodated as a section of society rather than as part of a whole. It's the – thankfully rare – installation of squat toilets as a result of 'cultural awareness training', which makes for great headlines and destroys all that is positive about multiculturalism.[19] But a need to tackle a manifestation of multiculturalism is not a reason to reject the idea and many benefits of multiculturalism.

At its best, multiculturalism can create a society in which all feel as if they matter and they belong; at its worst it can leave majority communities feeling 'their way of life' is under threat and minority communities feeling ghettoized and left behind. It's why the debate on multiculturalism needs to be informed, evidence-based and conducted in language which explains in detail exactly what it is we mean.

The Conservative Party under David Cameron rejected multiculturalism, citing it as a doctrine that 'tolerated segregated communities behaving in ways that run counter to our values'. He saw it as the reason why we 'failed to confront the horror of forced marriages' and as being the root cause of radicalization, which leads to terrorism. He advocated a new approach that he called 'muscular liberalism', an approach that I define as the 'we need war to find peace' doctrine.

But this approach, this war on multiculturalism, can be traced back to the Tony Blair era.[20] The world after 9/11 and 7/7 was one of shifting political priorities, with the focus on anti-terrorism and protection, to which question Britishness and British values became the new answer. But what New Labour said and what they did were at odds. They spoke of liberty and yet proposed months of pre-charge detention in the name of anti-terror laws. They spoke of democracy and yet cosied up to dictators, Gadaffi being one of the most stark examples. They spoke of human rights and yet acquiesced to Guantanamo Bay. They spoke of the rule of law and yet found themselves answering questions about the UK's involvement in rendition flights. New Labour's commitment to equality on the one hand – championed via the Human Rights Act, 1998, the Civil Partnership Act, 2004, and the Equality Act, 2010 – didn't inhibit the then home secretary, Jack Straw, who felt it appropriate to tell women what they could and could not wear when they visited him in his constituency surgery.[21]

The Law Lords stepped in to strike down Labour's anti-terror legislation on the basis that it contravened the European Convention on Human Rights,[22] a move described as 'a much-belated judicial awakening' to ensure respect for the rule of law.[23] New Labour reacted by implementing the Prevention of Terrorism Act, 2005, which introduced control orders to replace detention orders. Once more the judiciary stepped in, with the High Court in 2006 finding the legislation to be incompatible with the right to a fair trial.[24]

So New Labour started to build a new policy rooted in the mantra of values and yet seemed consistently not to act in accordance with the very values they sought to champion.

Internal rumblings about multiculturalism had apparently been many years in the making in New Labour, with the likes of David Blunkett, Ruth Kelly and John Reid wanting to pursue a more muscular approach after the 7/7 bombings, which provided the perfect dramatic backdrop for Blair, who was never one to miss a media opportunity, to demand a duty to integrate.

In 2005, after his last election, Tony Blair abandoned Labour's long-held support for multiculturalism and set out a new deal, a new contract for ethnic minorities, many of whom had been here for generations. Blair's 'duty to integrate' speech in December 2006 called time on the multiculturalism project, arguing that it had led to 'a separation and alienation from the values that we hold in common'. He defined 'our values' as 'the belief in democracy, the rule of law, tolerance, equal treatment for all, respect for this country and its shared heritage'.[25] But the speech was flawed on a number of levels.

It painted a post-racism Britain which simply did not exist in all parts of the United Kingdom, and if we kidded ourselves into believing it did then the post-Brexit rise in hate crime demonstrates we were fooled.[26] Tony Blair spoke of media that are 'more sensitive', arguing that 'racism has been for the most part kicked out of sport' and that 'offensive remarks and stupid stereotypes have been driven out of conversations [and] basic courtesies have been extended to all people'. A decade on, these words seem naive at best and political platitudes at worst.[27] He spoke of these values as being values for us all, including those on the far right, and yet the duty to integrate was firmly aimed at the non-white folk: the 'adopt our values or stay away' comment was aimed at the foreigner, the outsider. In reality, it was a speech in response to 7/7 aimed at Muslims.[28]

The 7/7 bombing was a horrific coming-together of many issues from identity to exclusion, from poverty to a polarized community, from ideological interpretations of Islam to violence expressed as a form of political dissent which resulted in a tragic loss of life and terror on British soil. It also became the basis of bad policy, such as the outright rejection of multiculturalism and dangerous policy-making such as the extended pre-charge detention. It toxified good policy-making on integration by connecting all things integration to all things Muslims and terrorism, a flaw still present in government's thinking on integration as presented in the Casey Review in 2016.[29]

A debate on our responsibilities as Brits was long overdue. We have a duty to create a space for all to belong, and a discussion on the kind of Britain we needed to build together was welcome. But instead 7/7 was the start of a long walk away from historic freedoms enshrined in our laws, with politicians on both sides making announcements that allowed them to posture and look tough, and thus feed the very divisions that terrorists needed to exploit young minds.

Years of experience in negotiations in business, politics or even with my children has taught me that win-win solutions are the best ones, that public face-saving oils the wheels of agreement, and ultimatums rarely work.

I agreed with Blair's statement that 'no distinctive culture or religion supersedes our duty to be part of an integrated United Kingdom'. I resented his decision to direct it at 'the Muslims', to suggest that I was less British.

Britishness became a very popular theme within New Labour. Labour had traditionally had an ambivalent relationship with the concept of a 'British nation', many within the party viewing it as being synonymous with the Tory ideas of empire and 'reactionary-ism'. For Labour 'the nation' had been about 'the people', with the British nation sustained by the 'social democratic state': full employment, redistribution, social justice.[30]

A need to appeal to the splintering working-class vote in some of England's northern cities, to rebalance Labour's reputation of being 'soft' on immigration and to be seen to be fighting the war on terror at home as well as abroad saw a concept which had traditionally been a Conservative Party 'issue' adopted firstly by Blair and then by his Scottish successor, Gordon Brown, who additionally needed to be seen as a prime minister for the whole of the UK, a very British prime minister.

Britishness and British values allowed New Labour to grab the flag of patriotism which traditionally had been the preserve of the Tory Party. It allowed New Labour to redefine itself. It began the most recent process of defining 'values' in a way that was, as one Labour minister put it, 'inspiring as a dusty heirloom' and Britishness 'done to' communities rather than 'with them'.[31]

Gordon Brown took up the Britishness rallying call, choosing early on to flex his muscles at his first party conference speech as prime minister in 2007. The International Centre in Bournemouth, beautifully decked in patriotic red, white and blue, provided the backdrop for Brown's vision of Britishness, the place where he uttered those well-crafted, headline-grabbing but illegal and inapplicable words 'British jobs for British workers'.[32]

Politics seemed to have switched around: Labour using the language of the nationalists and the Tories being the party of inclusion. David Cameron's response at the dispatch box to this outburst, calling Brown out for his dog-whistle politics, was one of his finest moments on the issue of immigration, a glimpse of what David could be. His reference to the term as a phrase borrowed from the National Front and the British National Party[33] signalled a place where the Conservatives could have pitched their case for a truly inclusive Britain. I often wondered in government when and how we lost the Cameron of 2005–7.

The David Cameron of that era was talking about our shared values, which had over time evolved through our shared experiences; he spoke fondly of his time living with a family in Birmingham, the Rehmans, Abdullah and Shahida, who welcomed him into their home and gave him a glimpse into British Muslim life.[34] He spoke affectionately of Abdullah's mum and the multi-generational home she headed as a matriarch. He was inspired by the collective family effort to better lives and the notion of respect for the elderly, values, he said, all Brits could learn from and adopt: 'Not for the first time I found myself thinking that it is mainstream Britain which needs to integrate more with the British Asian way of life, not the other way round.'[35] He spoke of 'the British way of doing things … calm, thoughtful and reasonable', he insisted that we must 'never give the impression that this question of Britishness, this question of community cohesion, is all about terrorism, or all about Muslims'.[36] And yet by 2011 Cameron was talking about muscular liberalism and Christian values. The debate had moved away from how much we could accommodate in our nation through multiculturalism to how many we could exclude.

The Conservatives became as bad as Labour at inventing a post-multiculturalism narrative by attempting to write off the experience of multiculturalism as a failed project.[37]

We could have drawn communities together in an understanding of a shared past and the optimism of building a shared future. Sadly the 'British values' debate has achieved neither. Instead, it has made the challenges of divided communities worse and has on its journey sown a destructive path of policy-making towards British Muslims which has made neither them nor us any safer, or happier. I will discuss the many mistakes made on this journey in Part Two.

The British values debate has two major flaws. Firstly, there is a suggestion that 'the list' of values is exceptionally and exclusively British, and secondly, our history doesn't always support an adherence to these values. No one religion, race or nation has a monopoly over good or a responsibility for all that is bad. Progress has been the preserve of most races and religions over time and history. Let's not forget that great civilizations existed around the world thousands of years before we on these shores were introduced to Christianity, what we today profess to base our values on.

Let's also not forget that one generation's immorality is another generation's liberalism. The debate on homosexuality within British society, the Church and indeed the Tory Party has taken many twists and turns before settling where it sits today. Many western Christians, in line with their western Christian beliefs, still travel to Africa to preach to the natives and warn them against allowing their society to fall into moral ruin as they perceive the West has. As Roger Ross Williams a writer and producer of news and entertainment and director of *God Loves Uganda*, a documentary on the influence of conservative American Christians in Uganda, said: 'the anti-homosexuality [laws] would never have come about without the involvement of American fundamentalist evangelicals'.[38]

Our western Christian values took far longer to give women the kinds of rights that were enjoyed by women in other parts of the world, other cultures and other religions. Women in ancient Egypt, for example, enjoyed far greater rights than their sisters in ancient Greece and certainly more than in Christian Britain in the eighteenth century. Indeed, India, Israel and Sri Lanka had female leaders long before we did, whilst Pakistan and Bangladesh have had female heads of states on multiple occasions; the US in 2016 was still not ready to be ruled by a woman, instead preferring a man who thinks it's OK to grope women and believes in 'treating 'em like shit'.[39]

Every community, every generation, every individual is on a journey where views change: some become more conservative, some less so. To acknowledge that would be a good starting point. To go on to acknowledge our own positions, and indeed failings, of the past would give us the much-needed humility to ensure we got things right when trying to define British values and when trying to measure others against these values.

Britain is an amazing country which, despite some of her not-so-glorious moments of the past, has over time always found a way to accommodate those that come to these shores. As a British Muslim there have been moments when I've landed back in Britain from some faraway, sometimes Muslim, land and wanted to literally get down on my knees and in true eastern style kiss the tarmac at the airport. Not because I'd travelled budget airline for many hours and was grateful to step out of my chicken-coop seat in one piece and feel land underfoot but because I was grateful to the Almighty that I was born a free person in a free land, where difference isn't just protected but celebrated; where, despite all our challenges, the daughter of a penniless immigrant millworker could come to sit at the cabinet table, become a privy councillor and pay the higher-rate tax; where as a woman I feel safer than I've felt anywhere in the so-called 'Muslim world'; where I can be my opinionated self without official sanction or censure; where, despite our great love for animal welfare, we can 'understand' and 'accommodate' the dietary needs of Jews and Muslims with their very prescriptive slaughter methods; and where, if I want to pray, I can pretty much get my prayer mat out almost anywhere publicly or privately and check in with the Almighty, possibly even on the tarmac as I disembark.

But it was multiculturalism that made the above possible. It was the basis of what led to deep affection and pride-filled admiration from minorities all over the world who made this island their home. It has made Britain stronger. So let's not dismiss one of our greatest values, the value of equal worth. By all means suggest ways of improving it but don't throw out all that went before.

We have a duty to lay out what this country stands for whilst accepting that what it stands for will change and evolve over time, and that what we criticize others for today were 'our values' not so long ago. And just as we over time have changed our 'values', so will others. The election of Trump and the 'values' he espouses also shows that the direction of travel is not just one way: we cannot take our current values for granted.

Let's lay out a vision of a future, ideals upon which we can build a home together, as described by ex-Chief Rabbi Lord Sacks, a set of virtues that lay the foundation, the basis of belonging, and let's make sure we demand the same of all for whom Britain is home.

This shared home must have foundations formed from history, walls based on virtues evolved through our collective shared experience and a roof where all can feel sheltered. And these are laid block by block, brick by brick. It's something we build together. Britain never has been nor ever will be the finished product. It is ever-evolving and, whatever we say about Magna Carta and the Bill of Rights, today's Britain in gender, race, religion, ethnicity or sexuality is a very different place from what it was when these great documents were written. It is even a very different place from what it was after we signed up to Human Rights Convention obligations, a different place from when the Human Rights Act was born in 2008 and indeed a different place since we've decided to leave the European Union. It's a different place to the one my grandfathers fought for, my parents migrated to, and I was born into. Our so called unshakeable Christian British values have evolved and will continue to do so and should acknowledge and encompass the history of all communities that make up today's Britain, the diversity of faith practices and the journeys of those different faiths. This history is colourful and complex and unlike the British national identity that is based on generalizations that 'involve a selective and simplified account of a complex history', where 'many complicated strands are reduced to a simple tale of essential and enduring national unity'.[40]

And what makes the current-day debate on Britishness and British values even more problematic is that we have developed a notion which is neither clearly defined, nor honestly underpinned, nor transparently or consistently applied. We do not have an agreed single definition of Britishness and British values. There is no Act of Parliament, no debate in Hansard, no common-law precedent, no agreed guidance and no applied casework. It's a vague, abstract notion which has the potential to destroy reputations and marginalize communities, as I will discuss in Chapter 5.

The deeply worrying part of the debate about British values – in all its murky glory – is that it is often only directed at British Muslims. I've yet to see a politician go to a synagogue, gurdwara, temple or church and address the Jews, the Sikhs, the Hindus, the Christians or indeed any other group and talk British values. I've yet to see a policy announcement on British values which is directed at a specific ethnic or religious group other than 'the Muslims', despite the fact that many a Jewish girl in London isn't permitted to study beyond sixteen and her role is deemed to be to bear children and be subservient to her husband; many a Sikh girl has suffered physical and emotional abuse for simply daring to marry the man of her choice or forced into and trapped in marriage for years (indeed, much of the early campaigning against forced marriages was led by an impressive and courageous Sikh woman, Jasvinder Sanghera);[41] many a Hindu man has been told he is not as good as another Hindu in the workplace because of the caste/tribe he was born into;[42] many a child has been branded a witch and abused[43] with the Church's knowledge; and many a 'cure' has been developed by evangelical Christians for the immoral and sick gays.[44]

Now there are those who will argue, as Twitter trolls regularly remind me, that the reason these policies are aimed at British Muslims and not other communities is because they, 'the Muslims', are the ones blowing themselves up. Indeed, in Britain four terrorists who were Muslim have blown themselves up. But this 'Muslims are fair game because some terrorists claim to be Muslim' approach is flawed for two fundamental reasons. Firstly, because it's crazy negotiation tactics to assume we will get what we want from a community of 3 million by treating them all like they are viewed through the prism of the actions of a tiny number of them. And secondly, the moment we impose a set of rules, laws and demands on one community and not on others we have stepped away from our own supposedly inviolable values of equality, rule of law and sense of fair play. We must lay out what it is we find unacceptable and implement it consistently across communities. The duty to integrate must apply to all of us, all faiths, all races, and must target both religious and cultural separatists and white-flighters.

Sadly the modern-day debate on British values and Britishness is a yardstick with which we measure the views and conduct of a minority of a minority. A senior Catholic cleric described it to me as a 'loyalty test'. There have been rare examples of 'others', not Muslims, being caught in the net, but these are exceptions, rarely profiled in the mainstream media and rarely quoted, indeed often defended by politicians.[45]

'British values' has become the space where we police views and thoughts, where we punish opinions which do not break the law. It is government's version of what it, from its particular political and ideological perspective, finds acceptable at this moment in time. It's a criterion against which we measure what we today define as non-violent extremist views – so, not terrorism, not action, not even views that are inciting, encouraging or promoting violence or even hatred, because we have criminal laws which cover all this, but views which neither break the law nor incite others to break the law.

This issue was in the 1990s an abstract debate in right-wing think tanks, amongst neo-conservative writers and commentators predominantly in the US, and yet today, sadly, it has become an integral part of our children's lives through newly designed Ofsted inspections following the Trojan Horse affair.[46]

From September 2014 all schools – independent schools, academies, free schools and all local authority-run schools – are required 'actively to promote fundamental British values'.[47] This teaching of British values was rejected in 2016 by teachers, who passed a motion at the annual National Union of Teachers conference arguing that the approach set an 'inherent cultural supremacism, particularly in the context of multicultural schools and the wider picture of migration'.[48] A teacher speaking at the conference said that the term was both unnecessary and unacceptable and 'belies the most thinly veiled racism and a conscious effort to divide communities'.

It's a concept that children don't understand. When questioned, schoolchildren cited 'fish and chips', 'drinking tea' and 'celebrating the Queen's birthday' as manifestations of British values, whilst others ironically defined them as 'Pick on someone different to you' and 'We need to get rid of these immigrants, they're taking our jobs.'[49]

A report by Open Society Foundation suggests that the concept of British values could be alienating and counterproductive, with Scottish government officials cited in that report saying that they don't use the term because it could promote a 'them and us' thinking.[50]

If the notion of British values is revisionist in its view of history, if the teaching of British values does not acknowledge the real journey we took to get here, if it fails to balance our successes as a nation against our failures and if it isn't honest and inclusive it will not act as the glue that binds our nation. What binds us is a strength in who we are based on our past, good and bad, an acknowledgement that we got much right but others got it right too, an honesty in acknowledging the time and route we took to arrive at our current understanding of 'our values', an acceptance that some got to this destination long before others and some are still finding their way here, and an acceptance that the values we speak of today have been many years in the making with much contribution from others, either those whose lands we went to or those who came to our lands, others including 'the Muslims'. Championing values without following those values simply backfires and renders our values valueless. In promoting tolerance we can't be intolerant of others' views, experiences and contributions. As a nation, whenever we have found a view or type of behaviour or conduct intolerable we usually make it a criminal offence or a civil wrong. We have had laws to enforce what at any point we perceive as the standard of acceptable behaviour. We did it with race relations legislation, with disability protection, with laws against domestic violence, with gay rights and with human rights laws. Our laws, British laws, lay out what is acceptable and what isn't, and all of us as citizens of this nation are equal before the law and have equal rights of recourse to the law, which is applied equally to all of us. This is the rule of law, another cited British value.

Unfortunately the current debate on British values has done exactly the opposite. An intolerant view about others is viewed as non-violent extremism in government circles, but the only form of 'extremism' which is specifically and extensively defined is Islamist extremism.

No detailed definition and explanation was given of far-right extremism, animal rights extremism or even the everyday extremism and sectarianism we sadly still see in Northern Ireland.

The British values debate has most recently taken on a sinister tone, expressing a view that there are 'the others' amongst us who don't think like we do, don't behave like we do and don't believe in what we believe. They are unique, different, don't fit in, don't belong, need to be dealt with in a way quite different from ever before, because they are, as described by Trevor Phillips, the ex-chairman of the Equalities and Human Rights Commission, a 'nation within a nation'. Phillips wasn't talking about the cast of *Geordie Shore* or *TOWIE*, he was talking about your local corner-shop guy, your taxi driver, your dentist and your GP, the enemy within, 'the Muslims'.

In his documentary *What Do Muslims Really Think?*, Phillips tried to show that 'the Muslims' were uniquely out of step with the rest of Britain in their values,[51] a view subsequently contradicted in a report only months later which found that 'Britain's Muslims are amongst the country's most loyal, patriotic and law-abiding citizens ... upstanding members of society, who share many of the same ambitions and priorities as their fellow non-Muslim Britons'.[52] And yet Phillips suggested that not only were they not 'like us' now, but because 'the Muslims' were unlike anything we had encountered before they were never going to be 'like us', they were not going to 'join our values', as other comers-in before them had done. We couldn't sit by and hope that 'the Muslims' would simply join the values that we, whoever we are, had in the Britain of 2016. In other words, 'the Muslims' were exceptional and needed to be treated in a way we hadn't treated 'others' before them. He justified his views by referencing British Muslim views on homosexuality, on women's rights and on violence.[53]

Phillips' focus on points of difference and disregard for points of similarity between communities, his failure to refer to a plethora of polls conducted over the last decade or so which showed that Muslims have a strong sense of belonging and support for British institutions, more so than white Brits, damaged and muddied an important and necessary debate.[54] Indeed, polls after the Brexit vote showed that, where large numbers of white voters felt English and voted to leave Europe,[55] Muslims felt both British and pro-European in larger numbers.[56] So the approach in this documentary was both disingenuous and divisive. By using British values as a measure of belonging, we are undermining those values.

Viewers of the documentary were not told that the poll in its methodology had targeted those Muslims who were likely to be living in segregated, poor communities rather than those who live in less segregated and more mixed communities. It wasn't highlighted that the comparison of the 'Muslims' views' was not with those of the Jews or the Christians or indeed other faith groups but with those of the general public, which in large numbers identifies itself as having no religion or faith.[57] The documentary failed to tell the journey of how 'other communities', including white British Christians, had over time changed their views on homosexuality and women's rights and it failed to place the poll in any historical context. Had Phillips done so, he would have found that many in my own political party, the Conservatives, and many in evangelical Christian and orthodox Jewish, Sikh and Hindu communities probably held the same views now and indeed much worse in the not-very-distant past. Indeed, they are views that columnist Melanie Phillips in 2011 felt were very legitimate, lamenting that 'Anyone who goes against the politically correct grain on homosexuality or who has robust Christian views must be considered a bigot and thus have no place in public life . . . [this] obsession with equality has now reached ludicrous as well as oppressive proportions.'[58]

There is much anxiety amongst communities that a notion which all believed was about dealing with 'the Muslims' is now having much broader consequences. Indeed, other faith communities are starting both to feel the heat and to raise their concerns about the application of 'British values'.[59]

A British identity is more than a citizenship, it's a belonging. It's a shared identity around which the descendants of migrants from Africa and Asia, English patriots, Scottish nationalist and 'Muslims' of numerous varieties can coalesce. It's the space that belongs to all of us for whom Britain is home.[60] As Bikhu Lord Parekh argues, just as Britain 'has learned to respect the diversity of its four nations over time it should respect the diversity of its immigrants', others who now make up this nation.[61]

Values are transitionary; they are a snapshot of our sensibilities at a moment in time. Principles, virtues and historic truths are enduring, good travelling companions which root and anchor us, sustain and strengthen us in this journey our nation is on. Building a shared identity, forging ideals we all aspire to be true to rather than making demands to endorse values is the approach we need to adopt to build a resilient nation which lives out what it actually stands for rather than a nation that simply talks about what it thinks it stood for.

I am absolutely of the view that in Britain we can build such a resilient, cohesive nation, but to do so well let's start with admitting the mistakes of the past, especially the decade after 7/7.

PART TWO

The Errors of the Past

3

Terrorism

'If I had an hour to save the world I would spend 55 minutes thinking about the problem and 5 minutes thinking about the solution.'

Albert Einstein

Politicians are often accused of not answering the question. We do this because answering the question could compromise us personally, or the party, or indeed government policy. Sometimes we don't answer the question because we are acutely aware of the follow-up question, which we usually don't want to answer. Sometimes we hedge our bets in case the answer turns out to be the wrong answer, sometimes we don't know the answer; and sometimes we've simply not heard the question and aren't brave enough to say so. But most often it's because we've decided long before doing the interview 'the message' we want to convey, so whatever the question is we are still going to give you the answer we prepared.

The policy-making on terrorism is a little like that pre-prepared answer: we've decided what the answer is long before we heard the question. We've presented solutions to terrorism before understanding and unpicking terrorism itself. In Part Three I will be laying out my answers to the challenges we face, but I want to start by asking the question: what is terrorism?

In recent years for Britain it's 7/7. It's the day London experienced the worst single terrorist atrocity on home soil, the day fifty-two men and women lost their lives and hundreds more were wounded, losing limbs and receiving life-changing injuries. The victims were of all races, faiths and backgrounds. On that day four British men, all with connections to my home county, Yorkshire, and all followers of my faith, Islam, blew themselves up in a suicide mission; the capital's tubes and buses ground to a halt, and thousands walked home in silence. On that day terror struck at the heart of the nation's capital, and terrorism in Britain became truly synonymous with 'the Muslims'.

Sadly terrorism has become an intrinsic part of the British Muslim journey, the bit of the Muslim story that manifested itself as angry young British Muslim men publicly and horrifically turning to violence to make a political statement. To understand the journey of Muslim Britain we must understand terrorism, not just terrorism in the name of Islam but terrorism per se. We must understand its history, its many manifestations, whether what we face today is the same as or different from terrorism we've faced in the past and whether we have learned any lessons from the successes and failures of previous attempts to tackle terrorism.

That day, 7 July 2005, was a few short months after the General Election in which I had fought a parliamentary seat in my home town Dewsbury. It was four years after the Real IRA had killed seven in a car bomb in Ealing, and we once more experienced bombs on the streets of London.[1]

Britain tried to understand the shocking news that some of our own had done this: not people from faraway lands, not foreigners, not immigrants, but young men born and raised in Britain. This was not planned and performed from afar, as had been the terrorist attack on Pan AM flight 103, which exploded over Lockerbie, killing 270, this was terrorism made in Britain, and my home town Dewsbury found itself in the spotlight as the home of the ringleader, Mohammad Sidique Khan. I knew the family: Khan had lived a short walk from my parents' home; his mum-in-law was the happy, warm dinner lady in my junior school. All four bombers had been raised in Yorkshire, and three of the four were of Pakistani descent.

For me all this was too close to home.

Like me, the bombers were British-born Muslims of Pakistani descent; they were Yorkshire folk, ordinary boys from ordinary families; like me, two were graduates.[2] The young men launched an indiscriminate attack on Britain, seeing it as both high-value political propaganda for 'their' cause and revenge and punishment for Britain's military action overseas. Khan said this about their actions: 'Our words have no impact upon you, therefore I'm going to talk to you in a language that you understand. Our words are dead until we give them life with our blood.' 7/7 was the taking of innocent British life for what Khan described as the taking of innocent lives of 'our people', the Muslims. This was Khan's opposition to British foreign policy, this was his dissent; for him his act of terrorism was his outrageous way of saying he disagreed.

I refer to Khan because he is the only one we heard from in his words explaining why he did what he did. The others left no messages. They were silent participants in a horrific act of violence.

But, however horrific we found those acts on that day, terrorism is not simply defined by such acts. It is not just defined by the carnage it creates, the injuries it inflicts or the fear it features, as all these, when 'legitimately done', such as in war, are not defined as terrorism. The appalling moment of violence on innocent civilians on 7/7 was terrorism not just because it was a violent act but because it was an unlawful, unofficial and unauthorized violent act and one with a political end, a cause. Terrorism is defined through the prism of the intent and identity of the perpetrator, not just the atrocity of the act. And in modern-day Britain the terrorist perpetrator of our time is seen as 'the Muslim'.

On 7/7, 'the cause' of these terrorists, our fellow Brits, was not 'us' but 'their Muslim brothers and sisters in Muslim lands'. They had chosen to kill people at home as revenge for people killed in far lands. We felt their loyalty wasn't with Britain but with their fellow Muslims thousands of miles away. We felt that our fellow Brits had behaved like the enemy within.

And whilst we may have found it impossible to understand this mindset, it wasn't a new and unusual occurrence. We have faced, witnessed and been subjected to such arguments in the past; the Irish conflict and British Catholics is one such example.

This attack on London was a violent manifestation of a political position based on historic and current grievances. And it was justified as an Islamic duty. It was not dissimilar to Irish terrorism on mainland Britain as revenge for killings in Northern Ireland and violence used to support a demand to leave Irish lands. For my whole life Britain has faced a threat from Irish nationalists, some of whom felt the only way to secure political change was violence. The goal of an independent Ireland was intrinsically linked to an end to violence, as Bobby Sands, the IRA hunger striker,[3] argued, 'There can never be peace in Ireland until the foreign, oppressive British presence is removed, leaving all the Irish people as a unit to control their own affairs and determine their own destinies as a sovereign people, free in mind and body, separate and distinct physically, culturally and economically'.[4]

We heard similar words from the terrorists who murdered Drummer Lee Rigby: 'Muslims are dying daily by British soldiers . . . bring our troops back . . . leave our lands and you will live in peace.'[5]

Irish terrorism too relied upon a bond of brotherhood rooted in an identity of faith. The Fenian Dynamite campaign of the 1880s was an indiscriminate campaign of violence that led to a series of explosions in British cities including Glasgow, Liverpool and Manchester, and in London succeeded in targeting Mansion House, the Underground, the Metropolitan Police, the House of Commons and that bastion of Tory male life, the Carlton Club.[6] It was organized and funded by the Irish-American 'brothers', the Clan na Gael. Grievance and anti-colonial sentiment were exploited to justify the use of violence, and faith offered as a basis to unite. Irish-American Catholics connected with Brits through a cause, and violence became the expression of the frustrated Irish youth who felt that 'direct action', 'propaganda by deed', was the only way to get the British to pay attention to the Irish question.[7] This is not unlike the terrorists of today, who use grievance, historical and current, to justify violence as the only way to be heard.

Other religious communities too have been here. After the Second World War and during the creation of Israel, the use of violence against British armed forces and the support for it by British Jews made them appear to be the enemy within. Questions about British Jews serving in our armed forces and their connection to the Jewish resistance movement made us question the loyalty of our fellow citizens. We found it difficult to come to terms with the fact that our fellow Brits felt the need to use violence against us for their 'cause'.[8]

A connection, a brotherhood, an affinity and indeed a loyalty to 'them' rather than 'us' – these are neither new nor unnatural. Affinity keeps diaspora communities connected around the world; it's a sentiment that drives many ex-pat Brits who have lived overseas for decades to support their 'home teams' in football and to demand a right to vote in UK general elections. It's an emotion that means many British Indians, Pakistanis and Bengalis fail the Tebbit cricket test.[9] It's a pull that takes evangelical Christians around the world as missionaries in support of their co-religionists and many third- and fourth-generation British Jews to invest in and make Israel their home.

In the 1980s we celebrated and indeed exploited such connection, brotherhood and loyalty amongst the Afghan mujahideen, whom we in the West regarded as freedom fighters but who in the eyes of the Soviet Union were terrorists. 'Mujahideen' was a generic term that we, the UK and US, used for those fighting jihad, a holy war. We saw the mujahideen as our fighters in a positive and noble war against the government of the Democratic Republic of Afghanistan, which was supported by the Soviet Union. In this battle of the Cold War we supported the mujahideen to help to keep Afghan resistance alive and supported the provision of military equipment, 'including surface to air missiles'. We felt that 'one of the objectives of the West in this crisis was to keep the Islamic world aroused about the Soviet invasion [and] that would be served by encouraging a continuing guerrilla resistance'. In other words we supported and saw the benefits of violence in the name of Islam. Sir Robert, now Lord, Armstrong, cabinet secretary in the 1980s, said: 'So long as Afghans were ready to continue guerrilla resistance, and Pakistan was prepared at least to acquiesce in Pakistani territory being a base for such activity, the West could hardly refuse to provide support, where it could do so with suitable discretion.'[10]

This arousal of the 'Islamic world', which we directed to our advantage, helped create British mujahideen, who went on to become a source of recruitment for subsequent wars across the world, from Chechnya to the Balkans and beyond. Their talk of adventure and brotherhood is just as attractive today.[11] Many Brits who travelled to Syria at the end of 2011 and during 2012 to fight against President Assad's army felt they were simply continuing the work of the mujahideen of yesteryear and indeed, by joining the Free Syrian Army, felt that they too were in line with UK interests.[12]

The mujahideen were also the forerunners of Al Qaeda, which formed in the late 1980s to make jihad international. It was Al Qaeda who took credit for the 9/11 attacks, claiming them as revenge for Islamic 'humiliation and degradation for eighty years', for 'security in Palestine' and for 'the infidel armies to leave the land of Muhammad [Saudi Arabia]'

These are not unlike the words of 7/7 bomber Mohammad Siddique Khan, who 'justified' his attack as revenge for British foreign policy and the killing of Muslims around the world. [13]

The grievance on which Muslim terrorism was predicated stretched back to the end of the Ottoman Empire and the British/French carve-up of the Muslim world that became the 1916 Sykes-Picot agreement and ended in a rejection of modern-day 'western foreign policy'. More recently it has become a rejection of the very notion of the western world, in the creation of an 'Islamic state' where people can live out an 'Islamic life' and reject both western and national cultures, values and identities. Hundreds of Brits, some with their families, have responded to this call and travelled to Iraq and Syria, including young men from my home town, Dewsbury.

So the nature of terrorism in the name of Islam and British involvement in it have evolved over the last three and a half decades: from the Afghan mujahideen of the 1980s, to the 'freedom fighters' in Bosnia and Chechnya, to the post-Iraq War fighters that became Al Qaeda, including our 7/7 bombers, the 'home-growns', and the more recent ISIS recruits, 'the fourth wave of foreign fighters'.[14]

Our 'mujahideen' eventually came home to terrorize us, Frankenstein's monsters we created in the name of brotherhood. As Hillary Clinton said:

> the people we are fighting today we funded twenty years ago . . . it wasn't a bad investment to end the Soviet Union . . . we said let's go and recruit these mujahideen . . . But let's be careful about what we sow because it's what we harvest.[15]

Honest words from the ex US secretary of state and a good place to start to understand the latest illustration of terrorism.

Today the challenge all countries face in an interconnected, glo-balized world, where our citizens all carry multiple identities, is how do these 'connections', this 'brotherhood' and multiple bonds of 'loy-alty', play out in the face of conflict between our very many identities? For me it's simple: people pick a side that they *believe* they have a stronger connection to, and this isn't necessarily the side they actu-ally have the strongest connection to. It's something I will explore further in chapter 4.

The 7/7 bombers picked 'the Muslims' of Iraq, Afghanistan and Palestine, Muslims who practise and indeed preach a very different life and even faith than the one these young British men practised and preached. Much has been written about the four young men. They appeared to be adjusted, integrated and comfortably British. Indeed one played the very English game of cricket the night before the attack. *The Report of the Official Account of the Bombings in Lon-don on 7th July 2005* states the men displayed 'little outward sign' that their religious observance had escalated into anything danger-ous. Accounts from family members in the days preceding the London bomb attacks do not suggest 'angry young men' stereotypes. Moham-mad Sidique Khan was described as 'a role model to young people' while Tanweer Hussain was noted to have a character that 'did not stand out much'.[16] And yet they felt that they didn't belong to us, to Britain, but to an abstract cause overseas.

This again is not new for us in Britain. Many British Sikhs still spend much of their political energy on campaigning for justice for 'Operation Blue Star', the attack on the Golden Temple in 1984 by Indian troops. British Sikhs are still trying to get to the truth of what happened and whether there was any potential British involvement.[17]

British Tamils have won elections on the back of campaigns to highlight the plight of Tamils in Sri Lanka and to bring to justice those involved in their persecution. And many a person of colour and others were moved to protest and show support for their black sisters and brothers in America by shouting 'Black lives matter'.[18]

These are legitimate and understandable sentiments expressed via protests, petitions, parliamentary lobbying and media campaigns and not by bombs on public transport. To have a cause is British; to feel inspired to make the lives of others in faraway places better is

British, to have the freedom to dissent is British. To do so with indiscriminate and unlawful violence against fellow Brits is terrorism.

To fight for justice is Islamic; to protect the persecuted is Islamic; to demand freedom and dignity for fellow Muslims is Islamic. To do so with indiscriminate and unlawful violence against fellow Brits is terrorism.

Terrorism is a threat to my nation and my faith, and it's why it must be defeated.

Across the world there have been and remain movements for the right of people to run their own lives. The argument for the rights of the oppressed, the right to self-determination, of nationalist and separatist movements and the right of the state to govern and quell dissent is made on a daily basis in debates in parliaments across the world. Even in modern-day Europe from Scotland to Spain and Belgium to Bosnia politicians argue about the right of nations to determine their own futures and champion political causes.

The challenge of terrorism, however, arises when these causes leave the organized corridors of power and enter the mayhem of the theatre of war, from Sudan to Somalia, Kashmir to Palestine and Indonesia to Iraq, where violence becomes the tool and is seen as a legitimate way to achieve a political goal, and terrorism is justified in the interests of 'the cause'. This is not a new concept: allow me to give a little history of terrorism and how we've faced it.

The word terrorism today is pejorative, but it wasn't always so. The term originates from the Latin word *terrere*, to frighten, and it was first popularized during the French Revolution. Ironically, given its usage today, terrorism originally described a legitimate course of conduct by the state. It was a system, *régime de la terreur*, adopted by the new government in France in 1793 to restore and maintain order during the transient anarchical period of turmoil and upheaval that followed the Revolution of 1789.[19] The system's chief architect, Maximilien Robespierre, was a politician, a lawyer and an ardent campaigner against the slave trade. This man, described as 'an advocate for the poor and oppressed, an adversary of corrupt politicians and a prophet of a socially responsible state', was an influential figure in the Revolution. He declared the *régime de la terreur* to be 'justice, prompt, severe and inflexible . . . therefore an emanation of virtue'.[20]

But as with all good intentions cruelly implemented, it didn't end well for Maximilien, who, having seen the end of royal rule, the establishment of the French Republic and the execution of King Louis XVI in 1793, was himself executed by guillotine in 1794, aged thirty-six.[21] With his early death too died the early unquestioning 'virtuousness' of terrorism as a state tool.

Over the following years practitioners of terrorism sold the use of violence *against* the state or the current order to achieve change as a virtue.

Carlo Pisacane, Duke of San Giovanni in Italy, was born in 1818. He was killed in 1857 trying to establish republican rule in an independent and unified Italy. He was a pioneering advocate of the use of violence as a necessary element to achieve change. His championing of 'the propaganda of the deed' and his view that 'ideas result from deeds, not the latter from the former, and the people will not be free when they are educated, but educated when they are free' have influenced revolutionaries and rebels for over 150 years.[22] Violence, for Pisacane, was necessary not only to draw attention to and generate publicity for a cause, but also to act as a siren to inform, educate and rally the masses. In a Pisacane world peaceful endeavours such as protests, petitions, posters or pamphlets were just not effective.[23] Like the 7/7 bombers he felt violence was a legitimate form of political dissent. We have been here before.

Early adherents of 'propaganda by the deed' were the Narodnaya Volya or the People's Will, a revolutionary organization established in the Russian Empire in 1879. They felt that targeted violence against high-profile figures of the ruling classes was the wake-up call to trigger a mass uprising amongst the peasants, a necessary step for change. They were ruthlessly selective in their use of violence and, although they never made a virtue of terrorism, they did consider it a necessary evil. The group's assassination of Tsar Alexander II in 1881, a suicide mission, eventually led to their downfall and impacted European history in ways which led to mass bloodshed and persecution.[24] Terrorism as a tool of necessary reform became a trigger for no reform in Russia and beyond and a justification for further persecution of the poor and vulnerable, including anti-Jewish pogroms.

Despite this failure of outcome the assassination itself inspired revolutionaries across the world, including London, which became host to the International Anarchist Congress in July 1881, four months after the assassination, where the 'propaganda by the deed' approach that is terrorism was argued to be legitimate.[25]

The gathering fed the fear of a global anarchy movement with its central committee headquartered in London, and newspapers confused anarchists with foreigners, refugees and Jews, which eventually led to parliament introducing its first-ever immigration laws, the Aliens Act, 1905, to control the 'alien invasion' mainly from Poland and Russia, which was turning London into 'a foreign city'.[26] This media feeding of fear is something which we see again today, with terrorists being confused with refugees, refugees with settled visible minorities and ordinary law-abiding British Muslim citizens. We've been here before.

English newspapers of the time wrote stories of a global conspiracy, and Lord Salisbury, the then leader of the Conservative Party and later prime minister, argued that 'England is to a great extent the headquarters, the base, from which the Anarchist operations are conducted',[27] an argument that was made once again in more recent years by French officials when they coined the phrase 'Londonistan'.[28]

Even in the nineteenth century the concern about 'foreign terrorists' – who only ever managed to execute one, albeit unsuccessful, bombing in London, with the bomb detonating before it reached its destination – attracted much more political and media interest than Irish, 'homegrown' terrorists who were during the same periods achieving much more success through their Fenian Dynamite Campaign.[29]

This difference of approach and reaction to different forms of terrorism is today again a feature of policy-making and media reporting on terrorism.

Since 7/7 mainland Britain has seen three terrorist attacks which have resulted in the loss of life. Firstly the killing of an eighty-two-year-old great grandfather walking home from his mosque in April 2013 who was stabbed to death by Pavlo Lapshyn, a white supremacist and far-right terrorist who pleaded guilty to murder and to planting three bombs in mosques in the West Midlands. His cause was 'racial motivation and racial hatred'. He went out hunting for a victim on the night of the murder and taunted the police during their investigation with photographs of the hunting knife he used with the words 'white power'.[30] Secondly the murder of Drummer Lee Rigby, an off-duty soldier, outside his barracks in May 2013, who was stabbed by Michael Adebolajo and Michael Adebowale, two black British converts who killed him as a 'revenge' attack for the actions of our armed forces overseas.[31] And thirdly the murder of Jo Cox, a member of parliament and high-profile campaigner for refugees and other marginalized groups, who was stabbed to death outside her surgery in June 2016. Her killer, Thomas Mair, had links to the far right: Nazi regalia was found at his home and upon being asked to give his name in court he replied with the slogan 'Death to traitors, freedom for Britain', a slogan subsequently adopted by the now pro-scribed far-right terrorist group National Action.[32]

The first two happened during my time in government. At the time I was a minister both in the Foreign and Commonwealth Office (FCO) and the Department for Communities and Local Government (DCLG). It placed me in a unique position to observe and help shape the response from within both government and the British Muslim community. I saw how government, the media and indeed Britain responded to both murders. Both were terrorist acts, both involved the use of violence against an innocent victim to draw attention to a cause, a belief or an ideology or to pursue a political goal, and yet one hardly made it to the national media. For me both were the tragic loss of life at the hands of evil men.

Within hours of Rigby's murder the great and the good in government, the police and security services were in an emergency meeting. I was at this meeting, the COBRA meeting at 8.45 a.m. on Thursday 23 June 2013. The highly secretive-sounding meeting name is an acronym of the room within which these meetings were originally held, Cabinet Office Briefing Room A. It's a pretty nondescript room – bland, stuffy, with awful migraine-inducing fluorescent lighting – but it's where we meet at what are considered to be moments of national crisis or importance.

It was months before Mohammed Saleem's killer was caught and identified as a far-right extremist. When these facts came to light, there was no COBRA meeting or a prime ministerial statement, or a review of policy, or a new structure to tackle terrorism; Lee Rigby's murder led to the setting-up of the Extremism Task Force chaired by the prime minister. There were no calls to Saleem's family or local-area confidence-building visits by cabinet ministers. Neither the prime minister nor the home secretary nor indeed any other cabinet minister visited Birmingham for months after Lapshyn killed Saleem and planted three bombs at mosques.

Most of what we did in response to the brutal murder of Fusilier Lee Rigby, a brother, a son, a father and a soldier, was necessary. He was a man engaged to be married, he had his whole life ahead of him, he had joined the army to serve his country, he paid the ultimate price with his life. It was right we united in grief, it was right we showed our respect, and it was right we honoured him in death. It was right for government to both learn if the murder could have been avoided and take measures to try to prevent future attacks. It was great to see people of all faiths come together to remember, to pray and to pledge to fight terrorism together. And for me it was heartening to see British Muslims clearly, confidently and collectively condemn the murder that was done in the name of our faith, a response that wasn't lost on the PM and my cabinet colleagues.

So why was the response to Saleem's death so different? Are different forms of terrorism treated differently? Is the seriousness of a terrorist act determined not by the seriousness of the violence but by the identity of the perpetrator and the victim?

The lack of attention to the murder of eighty-two-year-old great grandfather Mohammed Saleem, also the victim of terrorist attack, played into the narrative of grievance for Muslims, the sense that we applied 'different standards' to far-right terrorism and terrorism justified in the name of Islam. Mohammed Saleem was described by his daughter as a hardworking baker who did double shifts at the bakery to support his family, a community man, a trade unionist, a fan of the late Tony Benn. He was killed as he walked home from prayers, a family man stabbed brutally in his local area. He received no memorial, no media tributes and no celebrity funeral attendees. For his family this, along with the questionable handling of the case both by West Midlands police and the coroner, means that they still do not have closure.[33] So many questions remain unanswered for them. Was Lapshyn a known extremist? What did we know about him? What connections did he have with far-right groups in the UK? And why, knowing his history as a fascist, did the British embassy in Ukraine support his application to come to the UK as an intern in a densely populated Muslim area? A man who had shaken hands with our British ambassador in Kiev had his hands on a hunting knife within five days of entering Britain and had stabbed a British citizen to death. Surely these facts merited a closer look from government in exactly the same way as we spent time, energy and resources on unpicking the murder of Lee Rigby.[34]

And the difference in approach wasn't just from policy-makers but from the media too. The obsessive focus quite rightly on the perpetrators of the Rigby murder was in contrast with the indifferent reporting of Saleem's death, which hardly made it to the national media and which was not even referred to as 'terrorism',[35] and the kid-gloves, 'sympathetic' approach towards Jo's murderer, who was referred to as a 'helpful and polite loner with mental health issues'.[36]

A member of parliament had been killed in cold blood in broad daylight, this was an attack on our democracy, our freedoms, our way of life, and yet there was no outcry, no dissecting of the groups Tommy Mair was affiliated to, no hunting-down of associates, no obsessive daily commentary of ideology and beliefs. A few brave journalists questioned the broader political environment that prevailed in Britain at that time in the middle of the Brexit campaign and its potential impact on inciting hatred but most simply focused on the perpetrator's history of mental health rather than his history of fascism.[37] His conviction for murder didn't even make most front pages.

Over the last century Europe has seen terrorists who are motivated by nationalism, communism, sectarianism, racism, fascism and religion. In the US too the terrorism space is diverse, from the Hutaree militia to the Unabomber, from Timothy McVeigh, the ex US soldier and Oklahoma bomber, who killed 168 and wounded over 600 more, to James Von Brunn, who killed a security guard during a suicide mission at the Holocaust Memorial Museum in Washington. Terrorists motivated by anarchy, white supremacy, fascism and 'Christian' patriot movement ideology.[38] But pick up almost any right-wing paper in the UK today and the picture painted about terrorism is that it's a Muslim issue, that the Muslims are uniquely violent, that the threat we face is new and unusual, and that it is an inherent part of the faith of Islam. It's an approach which the media seem to follow in the US too. In June last year a British man, Michael Steven Sandford, an illegal immigrant in the US, tried to shoot the then US Presidential candidate Donald Trump. Upon arrest Sandford said he'd been planning the murder for a year. Sanford sadly suffers from Asperger's. The story received little coverage, with Trump himself playing it down: a white British non-Muslim man did not fit his narrative of 'threat'.[39]

It's an approach in the media that is part of a broader approach towards all things Muslim, one that reports 'Muslim' stories differently from those involving other communities. The Rt Hon. Lord Justice Leveson, in his report following the Inquiry into the Culture, Practices and Ethics of the Press, argued:

> [T]he real point is whether articles unfairly representing Muslims in a negative light are appropriate in a mature democracy which respects both freedom of expression and the right of individuals not to face discrimination. The evidence demonstrates that sections of the press betray a tendency, which is far from being universal or even preponderant, to portray Muslims in a negative light. [40]

It's an approach which has been in play since before 7/7 and gathered much momentum since we set off on the 'war on terror'. Sadly, as I will explore in chapter 4, it's an approach that has fed both the push and pull factors that create the environment within which terrorism breeds.[41]

So both policy-makers and the media seem to treat terrorism and violence in the name of Islam differently from other forms of terrorism, but is the challenge we face today, the terrorism of our times, uniquely different to anything we've faced before? Should we treat today's terrorism differently from what has gone before?

The last century saw terrorism used mainly as a tool of nationalism. Both the left and right of politics adopted terrorism as a means to have their cause heard. The murder of Archduke Franz Ferdinand, the heir of the Habsburg empire, in Sarajevo, the capital of modern-day Bosnia Herzegovina, in 1914 by a Serb nationalist, Gavrilo Princip, was one such terrorist act which had the dramatic effect of triggering the First World War. It's a place I've visited often, an unassuming side street where the violent actions of one man changed the world. Terrorism worked.

Two world wars also saw the practice of state terrorism in Hitler's Germany and Stalin's Russia, a return to the French revolutionary concept of a regime abusing power and inflicting harm on its citizens. And as the world fell apart and was put back together again by men in grey suits many nations felt they hadn't been heard, that their right to determine their own futures had been overlooked and that their right to self-rule had been crushed beneath the bureaucracy of convenience. As deals were done, lines drawn across maps and the world divided up amongst the powerful, those that were too weak to be heard at the top tables used violence as a means to be heard. Communities across the world in Asia, Africa and Europe used terrorism to assert their right to a nation state against empires they considered alien or colonialists they felt had outstayed their welcome. We received our fair share of direct action both at home from Irish nationalists and overseas in Egypt, India, Kenya and Palestine.[42]

Violence was seen by nationalist movements as a legitimate course of action by citizens to achieve what was, according to the Atlantic Charter of 1941 signed by Prime Minister Churchill and President Roosevelt, their agreed right.[43]

And so, throughout the twentieth century, from Irgun and Lehi, Zionist paramilitary groups aiming to secure the state of Israel, to the FLN, the National Liberation Front in Algeria combating French colonialism, to the Mau Mau uprising and its brutal suppression in Kenya, to EOKA, the National Organization of Fighters in Cyprus, nationalist political movements employed terrorism in the struggle against colonial rule. Individuals and organizations, ideologues and revolutionaries, nationalists and the religiously inspired have reached for the gun, bomb, and sometimes simply the humble kitchen knife to make their point, to be heard and to change the course of history. And it often worked, resulting in nations becoming independent from colonial powers. Groups whom today we would define as freedom fighters, including the Muslim mujahideen of the 1980s, used violence to achieve our shared interests.

But herein lies the problem with terrorism: it's a concept and term that is difficult to define because it requires a moral and political judgement, a judgement on whether violence is a necessary ill to bring about good or simply an ill that can never be justified. For some it is a positive part of a struggle; for others it is a negative part of a negotiation. For some it is the weapon of last resort; for others it is a weapon of mass destruction. For some it is the journey to the ballot box and respectability; for others it is the basis for never being considered acceptable enough to be part of the power structure.

Much depends on who 'we' at any point believe are fighting a legitimate fight. Bluntly put, it's our judgement of right and wrong rather than an independent assessment of right and wrong. And because 'our' judgement is based on 'our' interests, 'our' friendships and 'our' version of history, it is unsurprising that there is no worldwide agreed definition of terrorism. The definition depends on who the 'our' happens to refer to.

Today the term terrorism is widely used. For the media it is shorthand for a wide range of 'events', from assassinations to bombings, violent targeting of civilians, sabotage, hijacking, sexual violence, arson attacks on laboratories and indeed any violent act, whether it's a sophisticated attack by an organization with a cause or simply an outburst by a lone individual. For the public it can include the actions of a government, and accusations have been made against politicians of engaging in 'state terrorism'. Tony Blair is the 'world's worst terrorist' was the emotional reaction by relatives of soldiers who died during the Iraq War at the publication of the Chilcot Report.[44]

Internationally, for politicians and policy-makers, as the definition of what terrorism is requires a moral judgement both about the perpetrator and the perpetrator's 'cause', what is considered a 'legitimate' cause by some countries is considered by others as terrorism. Our own experience in Northern Ireland divided politicians across the world: whilst we viewed the 'Irish struggle' as terrorism, politicians from the United States to Africa and the Middle East viewed it as a legitimate freedom struggle. And even where politicians and policy-makers agree that the use of violence is wrong per se they find it hard to reach agreement on the use of violence as a tool to resist state violence, colonization and occupation. It's a point made last year by Alex Younger, the current head of MI6, when he said, 'In defining as a terrorist anyone who opposes a brutal government, they alienate precisely that group that has to be on side if the extremists are to be defeated'.[45] Cherie Blair once famously got herself into hot water for suggesting that young Palestinians 'feel they have got no hope but to blow themselves up'.[46] A swift apology followed. To add a further challenge to this already difficult issue, historically politicians have often changed their position on the legitimacy or illegitimacy of different political causes. No mainstream politician today would refer to opposition to western colonization in large parts of the world as terrorism, even though that opposition often took violent forms.

And it is against this complex backdrop that we try to understand, define and defeat terrorism.

Terrorism is a relative term. It can be used in many contexts and has been known to have many meanings. In 2003 the US Army identified over 100 definitions of the term.[47]

The 'terrorism' experts industry is vast: from academics, to statisticians, writers to historians and commentators to politicians. We all seem to have an opinion on terrorism. And yet right now we still do not have one worldwide accepted legal definition or indeed a moral definition.

There have, however, been previous attempts to agree a legal definition at least. The United Nations started working on a draft in 2000; seventeen years on it has not reached agreement. The main sticking point is a lack of agreement on the need to draw a distinction between terrorism and the exercise of the legitimate right of peoples to resist foreign occupation. The view that terrorism should not be equated with the legitimate struggle of peoples under colonial or alien domination and foreign occupation for self-determination and national liberation is one favoured by numerous countries around the world, mainly those that have historically been colonized, but it's not a view successive UK governments have supported.

In the UK terrorism is defined under Section 1 of the Terrorism Act, 2000, as:

> the use or threat of action to influence the government or an international government organisation or to intimidate the public and the use or threat is made for the purposes of advancing a political, religious or

ideological cause. The action involves serious violence against a person, involves serious damage to property, endangers a person's life, creates a serious risk to the health or safety or is designed seriously to interfere with or seriously to disrupt an electronic system.

The UK definition does not make any allowance for legitimate freedom struggles.

It's an area of conflict that was discussed by the Supreme Court in 2013 in the case of R v. Gul.[48] The Supreme Court noted that, although the issue was one for parliament to decide, the current UK definition of terrorism was 'concerningly wide' and cited the concerns of David Anderson QC, the independent reviewer of terrorism legislation in the UK, that 'the current law allows members of any nationalist or separatist group to be turned into terrorists by virtue of their participation in a lawful armed conflict, however great the provocation and however odious the regime which they have attacked'.[49]

Although we don't have an agreed international definition, the UN has passed numerous resolutions to classify specific acts like hijacking as terrorist attacks and has managed to foster international cooperation on 'terrorism' without a definition. Within weeks of the 9/11 attacks the UN Security Council, in a meeting that lasted three minutes, unanimously passed UN Resolution 1373, which bound all UN member states to act collectively against terrorism despite not having a collectively agreed definition of the term. Members were encouraged to share their intelligence on terrorist groups and adjust their national laws so that they could ratify all of the existing international conventions on terrorism, establishing terrorist acts as serious criminal offences in domestic laws and reflecting the seriousness of such acts in sentences.

So whilst the world didn't manage to agree a definition of terrorism it agreed to work together to defeat terrorism.

The Terrorism Act of 2006 was our response to the 7/7 bombings. It created new terrorist offences of encouraging, training and preparing for and glorifying acts of terrorism. The passage of this Act was controversial. The debate between striking the right balance between security and liberty took centre stage, and a broad coalition including human rights activists, the ex-head of MI6 and the Tory Party all lined up against Tony Blair's proposals. Many raised the concerns about judging who was a terrorist and how this legislation had the potential to chill genuine opposition to oppression. The then shadow home secretary David Davis said:

> I want to see people who encourage terrorism either expelled or locked up. But we have got to be very careful on the one hand not to unnecessarily limit free speech or on the other hand give clever lawyers a way out by making it too wide.[50]

But the laws were passed and have not been revoked.

Our definition of terrorism has continued to cause much concern. David Anderson, the independent reviewer of terrorism legislation, in his 2014 report, found that the UK has some of the most extensive anti-terrorism laws in the western world and a definition of terrorism that is far broader than the various international treaties in this area. The definition covers acts in the UK and overseas and can be invoked even where there is no wish to spread fear or to intimidate. The definition, David Anderson argues, is broad enough to include a campaigner who voices a religious objection to vaccination or the racist who throws a pipe bomb at his neighbour's wall. He concluded that 'It is time Parliament reviewed the definition of terrorism to avoid the potential for abuse and to cement public support for special powers that are unfortunately likely to be needed for the foreseeable future.'[51] Or as Mike Harris, a writer and campaigner on freedom of expression, argues, our definition would make George Orwell a terrorist for travelling to Spain to fight General Franco's fascists as it would human rights activists who advocate for the overthrow of Robert Mugabe.[52]

Now you may ask: what's in a definition? Isn't arguing about the minutiae of phrasing and a detailed analysis of the words used simply a pastime of under-worked academics? I would argue not, because how broadly we define terrorism determines how widely we cast the net, and against which Brits we can use what are often draconian and punitive laws. And sadly what may have appeared as wild assertions about the abuse of the use of terrorism laws have been borne out by the way the legislation has been applied in real life.

THE ERRORS OF THE PAST

Let me give you some examples. In 2005 train-spotters at Basingstoke station were apprehended and questioned under anti-terror
laws: apparently noting down serial numbers and taking photographs
was akin to behaving like a reconnaissance unit for a terrorist cell.[53]
At the Labour Party conference in Brighton in 2005, an eighty-two-
year-old refugee from Nazi Germany who heckled and called the
then foreign secretary, Jack Straw, a liar, interrupting Straw's speech
on Iraq, was at the receiving end of anti-terror legislation when he
was ejected from the conference and refused re-entry. In 2008 a white
couple with a mixed-race child with cerebral palsy alleged that they
were stopped and questioned under anti-terror laws and questioned
on suspicion of human trafficking. Also in 2008 Gordon Brown
invoked anti-terror laws against Iceland,[54] the country not the frozen
food shop, to recover assets. In 2012 a former soldier with Parkinson's disease was arrested at an Olympic cycling event for not
smiling.[55] Anti-terror laws have been used against elderly peaceful
protesters: an eleven-year-old girl at an anti-war protest and even a
man with a cricket bat on his way to a cricket match.[56]

These are just a few examples which should convince us that it is
important we get this right. Laws designed to keep us safe should not
be so broad as to make the innocents fair game. Misquoting Ronald
Reagan's words poignantly said minutes before an assassination
attempt upon him in 1981, a 'Government's first duty is to protect the
people not ruin their lives'.[57] It's a phrase which is relevant when we
look at the number of people arrested under terrorism laws and subsequently neither charged nor convicted.

In 2015 there were 280 terrorism-related arrests. Only 34 per cent
were charged; nearly 40 per cent of those arrested were released
without any form of charge, terrorism-related or otherwise. There
were 49 convictions in that calendar year. Prior to that, between September 2001 and September 2015, 3,086 people were arrested for
terrorism-related offences. Of these 793 were charged, and of those
507 were convicted.[58] Now, you may argue that these innocent
people who are arrested and not charged are simply necessary collateral damage to keep us safe. As I will argue in chapter 4, these
individuals – usually young men and women who can have their

futures destroyed by a 'terrorist arrest' – are exactly the wrongly accused that become potential recruits for genuine terrorists.

This concern about the broader community being 'fair game', again, is nothing new. I have had many a conversation with Catholic friends on the pressures of life in England during the Irish 'troubles', friends in public life who found their loyalty being questioned, and friends who felt anger both at the violent actions of their co-religionists and the lack of understanding on the part of government as to the underlying causes that led individuals down the path of terror. Whilst there are many opinions on the men involved in the 'Irish struggle', whether they were heroes or villains, terrorists or freedom fighters, there can be no disagreement on the violence, victimization and vilification many Catholics faced growing up in Belfast. They had genuine grievances, even though their methods of expressing them were abhorrent and illegal. And there is no doubt that the broader Catholic community in Northern Ireland and the rest of the UK suffered as a result of the battle against Irish-related terrorism.[59]

We've been here before. During my lifetime thousands have died as a result of Irish-related terrorism on both sides of the divide: unionists and nationalists, paramilitaries, security forces and hundreds and hundreds of civilians – a total of 3,583 between 1969 and 2015.[60] But how does this compare to the threat from terrorism in the name of Islam? And how extensive is the current worldwide threat from all forms of terrorism?

Terrorism is serious and real; the threat from it is severe. But, as with all policy areas when government makes a choice between what it spends its time and money on, it's important that our assessment is based on fact. And when a nation holds a section of its society accountable for violence then it needs to do so on the basis of fact, not myth.

There is a plethora of words which others prefer to use to describe the current phenomenon of terrorism, some of which I will discuss later in the book, but all I believe carry challenges which stop us from both diagnosing and solving the issue. So however clunky my preferred choice, 'terrorism and violence in the name of Islam or other Muslims', it will be my long shorthand for describing this challenge that we face today, a good starting point for addressing the challenge.

The statistics on terrorism make for interesting reading, but I start with two caveats. Firstly, just as there is no single definition of terrorism, so there is no single up-to-date world tally of terrorist attacks. I have used some of the most authoritative. And secondly, terrorism is a changing scene, and therefore sadly and tragically one incident can quickly change the stats. We are constantly playing catch-up, but I hope that an assessment of the last fifteen years or so allows us to make assessments on overall trends.

The twenty-first century has seen a consistent rise in the number of deaths from terrorism, increasing from 3,329 in 2000 to 32,685 in 2014.[61] The majority of terrorist acts and deaths caused by terrorism occur in five countries – Afghanistan, Iraq, Nigeria, Pakistan and Syria – although there has been a steady increase in the number of countries which now experience some form of terrorism. In these five countries terrorism greatly increased after the intervention in Afghanistan, the war in Iraq and the start of the Syrian civil war.

Terrorism is most likely to occur where the use of political violence by the government is widespread – indeed 92 per cent of all terrorism between 1989 and 2004 was in such countries.[62] In the last twenty-five years 88 per cent of all terrorism has been in countries that are experiencing some form of violent conflict – either civil war, insurgency or western intervention and wars.[63]

In developed countries terrorism is more likely to occur in those places where socioeconomic factors such as high unemployment, a lack of faith in democracy and the media, prevalence of drugs and negative attitudes towards immigration are widespread.[64]

Nowhere in the world is immune from terrorism, but there are places in the world which have low or little impact from terrorism, such as large parts of South America and Central Asia, pockets of Africa, some Eastern European countries, and range from bustling, multi-faith countries such as Singapore to not-very-diverse New Zealand. We should study deeply where terrorism is widespread and where it hardly touches and from that try and understand why.

In reality the majority of terrorism is not targeted at the West. After 9/11 only 0.5 per cent of all terrorist deaths have occurred in western counties. Most terrorist acts committed by those purporting to be Muslim or acting in the name of Islam are against other Muslims.[65]

In the West the lone wolf attacker is the main face of terrorism, accounting for 70 per cent of all terrorist deaths since 2006. Eighty per cent of these lone wolf attacks were not primarily driven by terrorism and violence in the name of Islam but attributed to a mix of right-wing extremists, nationalists, supremacists and other anti-government elements.[66] In other words, we in the West are neither the main target of terrorism nor its main victims. And terrorism in the name of Islam is not the main cause of deaths from terrorism in the West: we are more likely to be killed at the hands of a terrorist with a far-right, nationalist or supremacist ideology.

Let me refer to another source, the Global Terrorism Database (GTD), an open-source database run by the University of Maryland, which provides extensive data on terrorist events around the world from 1970 through to the present day. The database, which is live and is updated from year to year, includes at the time of writing 150,000 terrorist incidents. As such, it is the most comprehensive terrorism database open to the public.[67] A review conducted by Global Research in 2013 looked at data for the US only and of the approximately 2,400 terrorist attacks on US soil between 1970 and 2012 contained within the database, it appears that approximately 60, or 2.5 per cent, were carried out by Muslims.[68]

According to the Global Terrorism Index (GTI) report on terrorism incidents in 2015, almost three-quarters of fatalities from terrorism occurred in the five countries mentioned above, four of which are Muslim-majority and in one of which, Nigeria, Muslims constitute almost half the population. As for perpetrators of terrorist violence, the GTI report shows that only four groups were responsible for 74 per cent of all these deaths; ISIL, Boko Haram, the Taliban and Al Qaeda. Moreover, of the 650 per cent increase in fatalities occurring in the twenty-one OECD countries which suffered at least one terrorist incident, the majority of deaths occurred in two countries, one of which is majority Muslim: Turkey (the other country was France).[69]

Closer to home, data from EUROPOL, the European Union's law enforcement agency, support the fact that few of the terrorist attacks carried out in EU countries are related to religious militancy. The specific year-on-year figures, which cover the broad picture by looking at 'failed, foiled or completed attacks', make for enlightening reading. In 2010, of 249 terrorist attacks, 3 were considered by Europol to be 'Islamist'.[70] In 2011 not one of the 174 failed, foiled or completed terrorist attacks in EU countries was 'affiliated' to or 'inspired' by Islamic terrorist organizations.[71] In 2012, there were 219 terrorist attacks in EU countries; 6 of them were 'religiously motivated'.[72] In 2013, there were 152 attacks, of which 2 were 'religiously motivated'. The latest figures, reported in 2016, show 211 failed, foiled or completed terrorist attacks of which 17 were 'religiously motivated'. In fact, in the last five years or so less than 2 per cent of all terrorist attacks in the EU have been 'religiously motivated', although these figures pre-date the recent Paris and Brussels killings.[73]

The data also helpfully provide a figure for failed, foiled or successfully executed terrorist attacks in the EU from 2006 to 2015, which is 3,096, of which 37, just under 1.2 per cent, were 'religiously motivated'.

In the UK even today the number of deaths attributable to the security situation in Northern Ireland far exceeds deaths occurring because of Islamic or Al Qaeda-inspired terrorism as it is defined in the statistics. Since 7/7 there have been twenty-nine lives lost as a consequence of the security situation in Northern Ireland, compared with two on mainland Britain, of which one has been in the name of Islam or Muslims. The vast majority of incidents have still been Irish-related, and indeed only last year the threat level to mainland Britain from such terrorism was raised to 'substantial', meaning that an attack is a strong possibility. For international terrorism, including terrorism in the name of Islam, the threat level is 'severe', meaning that an attack is highly likely, the same level applied to Irish-related terrorism in Northern Ireland itself.

The threat from far-right extremism too is a growing phenomenon in the UK, as it is in Europe and the US, where a report in 2015 warned that since 9/11 'more people have been killed in America by non-Islamic domestic terrorists than jihadists'.[74] More people around the world every year die from the consequences of climate change, natural disasters and poverty than terrorism, and thirteen times as many people globally die from homicide than terrorism.[75]

A few years ago in the US the National Counter Terrorism Center released its report into terrorist deaths, which led to a number of light-hearted comparisons to make the point about perspective and to emphasize that an irrational fear of terrorism is both unwarranted and a poor basis for public policy decisions. I found two of these personally interesting.[76] My dad's been making beds for over thirty-five years, and we still do it in the old-fashioned way in a factory in Yorkshire. I was surprised to read that Americans are more likely to be crushed to death by their furniture each year or die from falling out of bed than die in a terrorist incident. Not a great advert for the furniture industry but a good context for the scaremongers. In the UK you are more likely to die in your bathtub, in a road accident, at the hands of a current or former partner or even from being stung by 'hornets, wasps and bees' than in a terrorist attack.[77]

Or, as my friend and colleague Dan Hannan, MEP, recently said in his own unique style, you're more likely to die from 'unprotected' sex than at the hands of a terrorist.[78]

I cite these examples not to diminish the real threat of terrorism, or to minimize the loss and suffering of the thousands killed and injured around the world, but to set figures in context, to separate fact from fiction so that we can measure whether our response is both accurate and proportionate, a strategy based on statistics not scaremongering.

The terrorist threat we face in the UK is small compared to the rest of the world. Indeed terrorism is far greater in places around the world, where we have intervened in the recent past to bring about peace, places such as Afghanistan, Iraq and Libya.

In 2010 the then head of MI6, John Sawers, said we can never guarantee against terrorism. 'C', as he was known, in what was the first public speech by a serving head of MI6, also said that there was no single reason or theory to explain terrorism. I will explore this in chapter 4 but I quote 'C' because the reality is that we have been subjected to terrorist acts in the past, and sadly it is highly likely we will in the future.[79]

Terrorism is not an end in itself, it's a means to end. It's been used throughout history as a way of effecting change, to influence and exert political will upon others. Sometimes it's been crushed, such as the brutal purge of the Tamil Tigers by the government of Sri Lanka in 2009. Occasionally it's worked, resulting in the establishment of independent nation states such as Timor Leste in 2002 and South Sudan in 2011. But mostly it's been part of a process, with violent expressions of viewpoints eventually replaced with clandestine contacts leading to discussion, dialogue, and democratic engagement.

We in the UK today are lucky that our forefathers have been on that journey to democratic engagement and we have inherited the fruits of a mature and established democracy. At least every five years, through general elections, we as a nation are given the right to determine our future. Our revolutionary instinct is channelled through referenda, our dissent is funnelled through the petitions and protests, and our weapon is the pencil with which we mark a cross on a ballot paper. It's how we are heard. It's hard for us to imagine what it must be like to live under a dictator, a despotic regime or an occupation where the basic right to live, to work and to determine your own future simply do not exist.

Terrorism as a tool to make a point has no place in democratic nations such as ours, and terrorism thus can never be a tool to make oneself heard.

We are a privileged nation with the space to consider, think and respond. And nowhere is such an approach required more than in the battle against terrorism. Politicians owe it to the people to understand the problem well, as that will be the basis of responding well. But politics unfortunately does not always foster an environment for grown-up conversations. To suggest that we try to understand the history of terrorism, the diverse manifestations of it, to recognize when we have been at the receiving end of it and been accused of supporting, funding and promoting it is in politics unacceptable. To advocate that we speak to the angry young men who could be attracted to terrorism not to condone but to understand how they justify the use of violence is a crazy idea. To state the obvious, that most terrorist causes are eventually resolved at the table of diplomacy, and many terrorists become power brokers and some, like Nelson Mandela, international statesmen, is a novel idea. But these are all facts, a reality.[80]

It's an issue Jonathan Powell tries to unpick in his book *Talking to Terrorists*, a fascinating account of the why, when and how of engaging with terrorism. Powell is a civil servant with decades of experience. As ex chief of staff to Prime Minister Blair in Downing Street, he played a lead role in the Northern Ireland peace negotiations resulting in the Good Friday Agreement and now runs a charity which specializes in mediation and negotiations in complex conflicts.

He refers to a 2008 study which looked at 648 terrorist groups since 1968 and found that 7 per cent were crushed through military means, 10 per cent were successful, 40 per cent ended as a result of policing, but the largest number, 43 per cent, ended in a transition to a political process. These are facts, a reality.[81] Drawing on conflicts around the world, Powell argues that a definition of terrorism still escapes us. The world cannot agree on a set of words to define what are invariably complex, long-running and deeply entrenched positions of anger, grievance and violence. Powell argues that terror is a tool:

> used by governments to instil fear at home, or support the enemies of their enemies abroad, and by insurgent and separatist groups to attract attention when they are ignored or see no peaceful political route to achieving their objectives, or to scare the government into giving in to the demands of a minority.[82]

The UK historically has both been on the receiving end of, and accused of engaging in, terrorism. We have termed many an anti-colonial, anti-apartheid, nationalist movement terrorist and we've subsequently sat around the table with the terrorists as they became political leaders and statesmen. Powell quotes Hugh Gaitskell, the former leader of the Labour Party, who said, 'All terrorists, at the invitation of the Government, end up with drinks at the Dorchester.'[83] I had the fascinating experience of seeing up close attempts by us and our allies to bring the Taliban in from the cold as we withdrew our troops from Afghanistan. And yet despite this politics does not foster an environment for us to have these discussions. And from a practical perspective how can we start to fix a problem if as policy-makers we haven't given enough attention to unpicking the problem? Surely the fact that the world is struggling to find an agreed definition for terrorism suggests to us that this is a complex issue which merits a thorough analysis before we reach quickly for the solution.

Terrorism has been with us for centuries. Sometimes defined as virtuous, sometimes considered necessary, used both by the state and those fighting the state and almost always resulting in harming the innocent. During my lifetime the term terrorism in the UK has had two main faces, nationalist and religious. Irish terrorism encompassed both. The attacks on the twin towers on 9/11 brought Al Qaeda and its particular brand of terrorism to the attention of the world in shocking fashion. This was not the first Al Qaeda-inspired terrorist attack. An attack on a hotel in Yemen in 1992 which targeted US soldiers killed two civilians, the targeting of US embassies in Kenya and Tanzania in 1998 killed hundreds and injured thousands; and the bombing of a US Navy ship in 2000 killed seventeen sailors.[84] But it was on 11 September 2001, when they struck at the heart of 'western civilization', that the world finally took notice. Al Qaeda became the new enemy, and the 'war on terror' began.

Terrorism and violence in the name of Islam had arrived in the consciousness of us all. I felt the rules of the game changed overnight. The sense of unease between my faith and the West started to show, and the abstract and somewhat wild-eyed musings of the neo-conservatives who spoke of a clash of civilizations and a new world order suddenly gained mainstream traction.

It was the point at which I left Britain. Within a year of the attack, much to my family's horror, I had sold my legal practice and checked out of the UK. A disintegrating first marriage and an early midlife crisis made 2002 my very late gap year. I travelled to Pakistan, took up home in the capital, Islamabad, and travelled the length and breadth of the country. I spent time in Karachi and Peshawar on the India–Pakistan border in Kashmir, areas which today are considered too dangerous for westerners, and I even passed a few lazy days in Abbotabad, the place where they eventually found Osama Bin Laden.

(Now if at this point a few of you are vexed by this 'year' I disappeared from Britain, concerned about what exactly I was doing out there, unsure that I wasn't being radicalized, not convinced it wasn't my training time, my jihadi jaunt, the start of my life as a sleeper cell, the placing of me as an enemy within, to you I say: stop watching Fox News!)

By the time terror hit our shores on 7/7, I was back from Pakistan and knee-deep in politics.

Today terrorism presents itself in the consciousness of Brits as ISIS, the abhorrent death cult who torture, rape, pillage and murder their way to creating their version of an Islamic state. It's a terrorist organization condemned by Muslims across the world – even fellow terrorists Al Qaeda have distanced themselves from ISIS. It preys on the young and vulnerable and uses them as cannon fodder; a young man from Dewsbury, Talha Asmal, was one who brutally lost his life and took others' lives in Baghdad. Many around the world including Muslims in public life have been put on their 'hit list', including Congressman Keith Ellison and Huma Abedin, Hillary Clinton's political adviser. My own inclusion on that list last year was a stark personal reminder that 'they', the terrorists, abhor 'us Muslims' as much as they do the rest of Brits. They are the brutal thugs who lay claim to my faith, who claim to fight in the name of Islam by overwhelmingly targeting fellow Muslims.

There is much that has gone wrong in the war on terror, mistakes made and wrong turnings taken both by policy-makers and communities, but before we can analyse where we went wrong with the solution it's important that we analyse where we went wrong in understanding the problem.

The pursuit of security is a difficult balancing act between necessary measures to minimize risk of harm with sufficient individual liberty and open space to allow for the continued development of a free society in which dissent and disagreement is accommodated. In defeating terrorism we mustn't undermine the very freedoms and liberties that define us as a nation.

Understanding terrorism, its history, its manifestations, where it occurs and where it doesn't, when it rears its ugly head and when it disappears, and the stats and figures which separate media headlines from facts and myth from reality, and above all acknowledging the ability of terrorism to mean different things to different people at different times in history is the start of tackling and eventually defeating terrorism.

To defeat terrorism we must first define terrorism. We must learn the lessons of what worked and what did not when we faced these challenges in the past and be deeply aware of the nature and extent of the threat we face today.

Terrorism comes in many forms, and terrorists come from many communities, races and faiths, but to understand better the journey of British Muslims we must understand what makes a tiny minority of them terrorists.

4

The Making of a Violent 'Jihadi'

'One day everything will be well, that is our hope. Everything's fine today, that is our illusion.'

Voltaire

How do you spot a terrorist? How do you pick out a violent jihadi?
How do we identify an insurgent? How do we work out that someone
is of a type to have terrorist tendencies? Is there even a type? Is there
an identifiable pattern of behaviour we should look out for? Is there
a 'look', a style or manner we can easily identify with terrorist sorts?
Do they hang out in particular haunts? Do they live in specific places?
And, yes, let's address the big elephant in the room: do they follow a
particular faith, Islam?

Wouldn't it be fantastic if we could have a terrorist version of night-
vision goggles, where the darkness would part and reveal the terrorist
to us. Because if we could spot them we could then stop them.

The Muslims would love to be able to spot them, to pick out the
few hundred who brainwash our kids into becoming bombers, the
few for whom we, 'the Muslims' are as much, if not more, of a target
as you, 'the rest of Britain'. If we could hand over to the authorities
the bad apples who spoil it for the rest of us, the ones that cause carnage and leave ordinary Muslims to pick up the pieces as victims of
the Islamophobic backlash and the ever-intrusive policy-making
which invariably follows a terrorist attack, trust me, we would. For
us Muslims, the terrorists are the enemy within our faith.

But we, the British Muslims, all 3 million of us, like the rest of
Britain, like government and the whole police and security apparatus

THE ERRORS OF THE PAST

of this country, find it hard to spot the terrorist because there is no single road to radicalization, no identifiable journey to violent jihad and no specific identifiable type of Muslim that's on a terrorism trajectory.

Our domestic intelligence service, MI5, set out terrorist telltale signs in a document in 2008 which included, amongst other factors such as a history of criminality, experience of marginalization and racism, low-grade employment despite having a degree and religious naivety.[1] Another assessment, developed by Elaine Pressman, includes twenty-eight factors, including sexual orientation, marriage, age, past criminality, contact with violent extremists and extremist websites, to name a few.[2]

Simply put, the picture is not black and white.

We are now twelve years on from 7/7, and yet I believe government's understanding today of what makes a jihadi is less sophisticated, less evidence-based and, sadly, less honest. We have been on a slippery slope of bad policy-making that can be seen most starkly in the development of the UK's official policy response to terrorism, CONTEST, a publicly available strategy developed in 2003 by the Labour Government in the aftermath of the 9/11 attack and published for the first time in 2006 as a response to 7/7, a strategy continued by the Coalition and the Tories.

Today's government is worryingly less engaged with British Muslim communities than it was in 2005 and less trusted by them. Policy-making has over time shifted the focus away from the hard evidence of what makes a 'jihadi' and chosen instead to shine a spotlight on the abstract notion of 'ideology'. Counter-terrorism policy has extended the tentacles of officialdom into not just attempting to prevent violence but also preventing thought that the government finds unacceptable. Rather than doing counter-terrorism *with* British Muslims to defeat the menace of terrorism collectively, we have chosen to do counter-terrorism *to* Muslim communities. And through this approach we have both created an obstacle to confronting and defeating terrorism and alienated a large community of law-abiding citizens.

CONTEST is a strategy in four parts: Protect, Prepare, Pursue and Prevent.

Protect is the P whose purpose is to strengthen protection against a terrorist attack in the UK or against its interests overseas and so reduce their vulnerability. The work focuses on border security, the transport system, national infrastructure and plans for the protection of public places. It's looking at the potential weak links terrorists could exploit and putting protection measures in place – as politicians would say, getting ahead of the curve.

Prepare is the P that works to mitigate the impact of a terrorist attack where that attack cannot be stopped. This includes work to bring a terrorist attack to an end and to increase the UK's resilience so we can recover from its aftermath. This is about us making sure we are ready to deal with the aftermath when terrorists strike, which sadly they will.

Pursue is the P that attempts to stop terrorist attacks by detecting, prosecuting and otherwise disrupting those who plot to carry out attacks against the UK or its interests overseas. This includes the sneaky-beaky world of the security services, police investigations and having the right laws in place to find, capture and lock up those that want to cause carnage.

And Prevent is the P in the strategy with the stated aim 'to stop people becoming terrorists or supporting terrorism'. It was supposed to be the helpful 'upstream' intervention and yet it's the P that's managed to perturb the most people. The Prevent strand of the strategy was potentially a brave, dynamic and cutting-edge approach to counter-terrorism; it was committed to tackling terrorism by tackling the causes of terrorism. And yet now, a decade on, it is considered by a whole coalition of academics, lawyers, politicians, police officers and others to be not just ineffective but indeed counterproductive. Described as a policy 'to be remembered as a textbook example of how to alienate absolutely everybody', a policy designed to spot terrorists and stop terrorism has become a policy which has put on ice genuine policy work to understand the varied and complex causes of terrorism.[3]

The official purpose of Prevent in its first public outing in 2006 was to tackle the reasons which could result in people becoming terrorists and the milestones in the journey to the violent act. This first pillar of Prevent in 2006 was to tackle disadvantage, inequalities and discrimination. This thinking was an early acknowledgement that discrimination such as Islamophobia, racism and inequality of opportunity in education and employment feeds terrorism, something supported by research into terrorism in other developed countries, which shows a correlation between these issues and the prevalence of terrorism.[4] It was borne out in the academic studies looking at the numbers of Belgian Muslims joining IS and the increase of terrorist attacks by Belgian Muslims in Europe, which found that the education and employment gap between native Belgians and Belgian immigrants was higher than anywhere in Europe. It also found that an astonishing 50 per cent of Belgians of Moroccan origins lived below the poverty line.[5]

The second pillar of Prevent was deterring those who facilitate and encourage others to engage in terrorism by creating an environment where these ideas are subjected to civic challenge and debate.[6] And the third was engaging in a battle of ideas, 'challenging the ideologies that extremists believe can justify the use of violence primarily by helping Muslims who dispute these ideas to do so'. That is an intra-community struggle against violence.

I agreed with all four strands of the original CONTEST strategy, including the early thinking behind Prevent. For me the Prevent policy was, and still should and could be, a battle between violence and democracy, based on a belief that everyone has a right to their view, providing it does not break the law or incite or encourage someone else to break the law. Unsavoury views are something democracy, if it works, should be able to temper, although the 2016 US presidential election has left many questioning this notion.[7] Democracy is the process through which changing views are reflected. And, as we've learned from history, one generation's unsavoury view can become another generation's acceptable policy position. The promotion of homosexuality as a lifestyle of equal value and worth as heterosexuality was considered by the Thatcher government as an unsavoury anti-family view; for Cameron's Conservatives it was the cornerstone of his belief in family, although there is sadly nothing to guarantee that it won't swing back the other way. Democrats, those of us who are advocates and supporters of democracy as opposed to anarchists or terrorists, agree that democracy is the process that allows all views to be aired and tempered.

The battle of ideas about violence and the justification of violence is one in which government needs to be a player and quite rightly stand against groups such as Hizb ut-Tahrir and their offshoot Al Muhajiroun, who have condemned Muslims engaged in the political process. It is right that the battle of ideas and views on everything from tax to torture, farming to family to foreign policy, welfare to wind farms is debated and accommodated through our parliamentary democracy.

The battle of ideas was but one part of the Prevent work, alongside tackling discrimination, engaging communities and addressing grievances.

The Prevent strategy, however, over time from 2003 to 2015, slowly started to shift its emphasis. Concerns around discrimination and grievance were no longer the starting point and they moved from the first pillar under Prevent to the last. The process of understanding – not accepting, but understanding – why British Muslim communities themselves felt people were being drawn into violent extremism for politicians and policy-makers became a less important issue. The 'Muslim communities' views', which themselves were varied and broad on the drivers of terrorism, were sidelined, and we saw the start of a process of disengagement between government and British Muslims, an issue I will address in chapter 5.

Since 7/7 in the UK, as had happened after 9/11 in the US, discussions around the 'root causes' of terrorism became too difficult an area for policy-makers. The emphasis shifted from academic evidence, polling data and indeed the reasons given by the terrorists themselves to the abstract notion of 'ideology'. To discuss root causes was seen as an expression of disloyalty. Politicians were paranoid that to seek to understand would result in them being labelled as apologists. Politicians needed to be seen to be fighting these evil terrorists with raw force; 'shock and awe' was the order of the day. For politicians of Muslim heritage the policy space within which to operate was even narrower. And as the space to discuss root causes closed down, from around 2006 'radicalization' became the new buzzword for the discussion of all things that led up to the actual violent act of terrorism. Radicalization was defined as the process someone goes through in becoming a terrorist, not a reason or root cause. And with this shift of focus to process we could turn a blind eye to the reasons. We moved to the how of terrorism without sufficiently understanding the why. This was one of a number of early mistakes in tackling terrorism, because without understanding the why, without engaging with the root causes, we created a vacuum in the thinking of policy-makers who needed to prevent individuals from setting foot on the track towards terrorism.

I accept that a terrorist attack like 7/7, played out in the glare of a twenty-four-hour international media circus, triggered a political need to find a quick and easy answer to what makes a terrorist. But it is at times when our nation faces the greatest threat that we need our politicians to raise their game. The right answer was a considered and measured response, but the easy answer was a quick answer: we reached for ideology, the ideology of Islamism. Islamism became a quick, catch-all term, a reason that could encompass and explain radicalization in all its formats and manifestations, a term that would inform our thinking on how to spot a potential terrorist, a term that is now used in counter-terrorism policy-making across the world.

Islamism as the answer also allowed us to shift the problem of terrorism on to 'them', 'the Muslims', whose religion, Islam, politicians argued, was the basis of the 'ideology', albeit, as politicians would take great care to stress, 'a perverted version of the faith'. Terrorism became 'their problem' for them to fix as opposed to anything that may appear to be 'our problem' that we all needed to fix together. Civil war, foreign invasions, conflict, upheavals, strife in countries around the world are shared problems. As I explored in chapter 3, where we see these challenges is where we find the vast majority of terrorist acts and deaths caused by terrorism. These are our problems to solve.

Similarly, in developed countries where discrimination and disengagement are prevalent, terrorism is too. These too are our problems to fix, as a country, as a nation, to create more equal, more engaged communities where all feel as if they have equal access to opportunity and feel as if they belong. And yet in Britain we pushed on to the shoulders of a fragmented and challenged community of 3 million a problem which we as a country with all our resources could not easily fix.

But what exactly is Islamism, and what is Islamist extremism?

Islamism has been used in its modern sense as a shorthand for political Islam since the 1970s and '80s.[8] It is defined in the *Oxford English Dictionary* as 'Islamic militancy or fundamentalism'. In UK policy-making it been used as a term to describe the basis of extremism that leads to terrorism. I'm not a huge fan of Wikipedia but I would encourage you to read the Wiki page on Islamism, which gives a helpful dozen-plus definitions of the term, which starts to explain just how varied and broad its use can be.[9]

'Islamism' was originally used as a term in the 1700s and 1800s by the likes of French philosopher Voltaire and French philologist Joseph Ernest Renan simply to mean the religion of Islam. This was reflected in the 1900 version of the *New English Dictionary*, which defined Islamism as the 'religious system of the Moslems'. It was seen as the more respectable way to describe this religion, which was at that time regularly referred to as Mohammedanism. So for over 200 years and until less than a hundred years ago Islamism simply meant Islam. By the time of the completion of the publication of the *Encyclopedia of Islam* in English, German and French editions in 1938 the more recognizable term 'Islam' was being used to describe the religion.[10]

Decades later, when the West tried to find a term to describe a form of Islam which we felt was anti-modern or aggressive, or when we needed to project negative connotations on to a particular practised version of Islam, the preferred term was 'fundamentalism'. 'Fundamentalism' was used to describe Protestant Christians in America who asserted a literalist version of Christianity, but became a term to describe the Iranian revolution in 1979, with the followers of Khomeini described as Islamic fundamentalists.[11]

Many French scholars preferred the term 'Islamism' to the English term 'fundamentalism'. Some instead used *'intégrisme'*, a term which had been employed to describe a Catholic movement in nineteenth-century France which rejected the creation of individual state churches and believed the state to be subordinate to worldwide Catholicism united under the Pope. This pan-Catholic movement, which placed religion above state and the Catholic 'ummah' brotherhood identity above national identities, was seen as anti-pluralist and as a movement that sought to assert a Catholic underpinning to all social and political action, rejecting all alternatives. I believe this is a fair description which could be given to some Muslim thought today, and thus *'intégrisme'* may well be that elusive term that is missing in today's policy-making, a more accurate and politically less objectionable term than 'Islamism'.

My concerns about the term Islamism have always been that to ordinary people, Muslims or otherwise, it simply means Islam. It was exactly the same argument put by Maxime Rodinson, one of the most authoritative French historians of Islam. 'Islamism is often given as a synonym for Islam,' Rodinson warned. 'If one chooses this term, the reader may become confused between an excited extremist who wishes to kill everyone and a reasonable person who believes in God in the Muslim manner, something perfectly respectable.'[12]

These concerns on the use of language and descriptions were initially taken on board by David Cameron, who wrote in 2007, 'Many Muslims I've talked to about these issues are deeply offended by the use of the word "Islamic" or "Islamist" to describe the terrorist threat we face today,' and argued that efforts to fight terrorism 'are not helped by lazy use of language'. Indeed Cameron argued that 'by using the word "Islamist" to describe the threat, we actually help do the terrorist ideologues' work for them'.[13] In government this seemed to concern David less. It's a term I dislike, because to average Mrs Smith it means 'the Muslims' and to average Mrs Hussain it means 'her'. For the average Brit it simply means 'Islam'.

It's a term that even in its academic use has such a broad spectrum of meaning, encompassing at one end democratically elected parties in countries such as Tunisia, Turkey and Morocco, parties who are our partners, allies and business associates, to Al Qaeda and ISIS at the other. It simply fails to accurately describe the problem. This was an argument made by the then US assistant secretary of state Robert Palletreau Jnr in 1994, namely that:

> 'Islamists' are Muslims with political goals ... They do not refer to phenomena that are necessarily sinister: there are many legitimate, socially responsible Muslim groups with political goals. However, there are also Islamists who operate outside the law. Groups or individuals who operate outside the law – who espouse violence to achieve their aims – are properly called extremists.[14]

And the issue was explored in 2016 by the House of Commons For-eign Affairs Committee, in its report on 'Political Islam', where it recommended that the government 'devise a vocabulary that doesn't group these types together'.[15]

Some of my colleagues in government were unable to draw this distinction between 'Muslims with political goals' and those on a trajectory to terrorism. And thus they were unable to draw a distinc-tion between policy-making to tackle terrorism and policy-making towards British Muslims. This inability to differentiate is a problem in the media too.

I am a politician and I am a Muslim. I am a Muslim with political goals: a goal to have a low-tax economy; a goal to have a small state but one which always provides a safety net for the most vulnerable in our nation; a goal to have healthcare free at the point of need; a goal that a child's achievement should be determined by their ability and not by how much their parents earn; a goal that we preserve and pro-tect this planet that is our shared home; a goal that we treat all communities equally irrespective of race and faith; and a goal that we take our place in the world with humility and understanding rooted in history, ethics, and principles based on universal human rights.

Politicians with a faith or religion are not new. Many of our modern-day European political parties are rooted in faith, in Chris-tianity. The Christian Democratic Union, the CDU in Germany, the party of Angela Merkel, is probably the most well known, but there are similar parties all across Europe, from the Christian Democratic People's Party in Switzerland, to the Austrian People's Party and Christian Democratic Appeal (CDA) in the Netherlands.

Like Christian political ideology, Islamist ideology too has created a new generation of Muslim democrats from a plethora of parties which played a pivotal role in the Arab Spring, such as the Ennahda Party in Tunisia, the Justice and Development Party in Morocco and the AK Party in Turkey, which, as a centre-right party, presided over a period of unprecedented economic growth and with whom the Conservative Party are aligned as an international sister party.

In 2011, my party eventually adopted the term 'Islamist extrem-ism' to try and differentiate between Islamists, many of whom we had strong international relationships with, and those that we felt had a world view which involved imposing 'their' values on 'us'. But although the terminology changed, a little, the thinking did not, with many politically active British Muslims still seen as part of the problem. Policy-makers failed to understand and acknowledge that British Muslims who are deeply political didn't want to take over or Islamize Britain or impose Sharia law. There is no denying that young Muslim Brits are today politicized by their Muslim identity like my generation were politicized by the colour of our skin. This isn't a bad thing. It was after all politicized people of colour who pushed for the necessary equality laws we are all so proud of today. A politicized British Muslim is as important as politicized British Christians who fight for equality and freedom of religion and belief in Muslim-majority lands, individuals such as Lord Alton and Baroness Berridge, whom in government and since I am proud to champion as human rights defenders. Politicized British Muslims are as important as politicized British Jews who see Israel as a political expression of their faith.

Why should it be wrong to be angry at the vilification of your faith by the media, offensive headlines, being the target of the far right and on the receiving end of anti-Muslim hate crime? And is organizing as a community to lobby government to take these issues seriously an exceptional occurrence or simply British Muslims following in the footsteps of other communities who've gone before and tackled such issues via political engagement and influence? And is taking a position on foreign policy and trying to influence the government of the day to think like you think any different to what every diaspora in this country has done and continues to do? Politicized Muslims are not all Islamists, Islamists are not all extremists, and extremists are not all terrorists. To therefore suggest that one leads to another and use that as a basis of policy is simply flawed and isn't supported by evidence.

Let's take Sharia law. It has been argued that the ultimate objective of Islamist extremists is the merger of 'mosque and state' under Sharia law. This is not a position I recognize amongst the vast majority of British Muslims, nor is this borne out by polls.[16]

That is not what our British Muslim ancestors migrated to the UK for and it's not what they desired. British Muslims did not come to colonize, to impose their way of life on us nor reduce us to second-class citizens. They, like my grandfather, came as subservient, submissive, poor labourers. They kept their heads down and worked hard to crawl out of poverty.

Their descendants, at least the majority of them, just want to build a successful life in which they can combine faith, fun and finance. A few want to be left alone to live their conservative, closed lives, much like the Hassidic Jewish community of Stamford Hill. Only a tiny number want to live out their gangland fantasy of a takeover, a mirror image of the far right, and this last group hate the Muslims as much as they hate the rest of Brits.

But one thing I do see is a new generation of Muslims who are neither subservient nor submissive and, yes, they are politically engaged and aware, but that does not make them Islamist extremists, or the enemy within.

After much wrangling, the term 'Islamist extremism' was defined in a policy paper in 2013, prepared in response to the tragic murder of Drummer Lee Rigby. Extremism is now defined by the UK government as:

> Vocal or active opposition to fundamental British values, including democracy, the rule of law, individual liberty and mutual respect and tolerance of different faiths and beliefs . . . [and] includes calls for the death of members of our armed forces, whether in this country or overseas.

Islamist extremism in particular is defined as:

> an ideology based on a distorted interpretation of Islam, which betrays Islam's peaceful principles and draws on the teachings of the likes of Sayyid Qutb. Islamist extremists deem western intervention in Muslim-majority countries as a war on Islam, creating a narrative of us and them. They seek to impose a global Islamic state governed by their interpretation of Sharia as State law, rejecting liberal values such as democracy, the rule of law and equality. Their ideology also includes the uncompromising belief that people cannot be Muslim and British and insists that those who do not agree with them are not true Muslims.[17]

This definition of Islamist extremist ideology became the catch-all answer to explain what makes a terrorist. It was arrived at after a long and tortuous debate which had started in opposition with the policy paper *An Unquiet World*,[18] was further detailed in government by David Cameron in his 'Munich Speech' in 2011, the most comprehensive account of his thinking on this issue in his own words, and subsequently led to the publication of the definition in the Extremism Task Force policy paper in 2013, a paper that was deferred because Nick Clegg – the then deputy prime minister – and I continued to argue, with the prime minister, about the failings of the definition.

If the final definition is unworkable, the original one was explosive. The original arguments went something like this. The following groups are the most prominent Islamists: Tablighi Jamaat, Jamaat-e-Islami, the Muslim Brotherhood and Hizb ut-Tahrir. (This list is in itself flawed, as three of the four groups are democratically engaged both in the UK and overseas. We regularly deal with political figures overseas who belong or affiliate to, or identify with, the first three of these groups.)

The argument continued: all Islamists are extremists, some advocate violence, others are non-violent extremists. Those who are not violent provide the ideological climate or justification for terrorism. Even if these non-violent groups engage with democracy, that engagement should be seen as subversion, the individuals should be viewed as entryists, for whom MI5 should have a remit, and certainly these individuals should never have access to classified material. This argument too is flawed and indeed dangerous on many levels. Not all Islamists are extremists; politically engaged Muslims are not subversives or entryists; and disclosure of classified material should be based, as it is now, upon a full security clearance not on an individual's faith.

The argument was further built that the values of Islamists – despite there being no single set of agreed values that could be ascribed to all who even themselves self-identify as Islamists – are 'demonstrably subversive of modern British values'. Islamism manifested itself, the paper argued, as anti-western views, particularly anti-US or anti-Jewish rhetoric. Another example given was that the Islamists saw the world progressing towards a paradise that both is inevitable and justifies violence to bring it about. I agree, this is a view which is present amongst some Muslims, but it is also a view of some Christians, many in the US, and Jewish settlers in the West Bank. The original definition also made specific references to a number of Islamic scholars, including Mawlana Mawdudi.[19]

Now, leaving aside the political game-playing that went on behind the scenes in the drafting of this definition and the more extreme definition originally proposed by one of my colleagues in cabinet, even the tempered definition as a catch-all reason for terrorism in the name of Islam isn't supported by evidence.

Let's look at the facts. The security services, academics, the police, criminologists and indeed successive governments' own papers acknowledge that the evidence base of what makes a terrorist is weak, and there is no single driver of terrorism and no one recognizable road to radicalization. Indeed, evidence given by the Home Office itself admitted, in 2012, that:

> There is no standard profile of a terrorist and no single pathway or route that an individual takes to becoming involved in a terrorist organisation. Not all drivers will play a role in every instance of radicalisation. Rather, drivers and risk factors appear to be inter-connected and mutually reinforcing but exert influence on individuals to varying extents.[20]

A Home Office-commissioned paper found that

> The empirical evidence base on what factors make an individual more vulnerable to Al Qaida-influenced violent extremism is weak. Even less is known about why certain individuals resort to violence, when other individuals from the same community, with similar experiences, do not become involved in violent activity.[21]

The Home Affairs Select Committee in 2012 found that 'it is clear that individuals from many different backgrounds are vulnerable, with no typical profile or pathway to radicalisation. However, there is a lack of objective data, much of the evidence inevitably being anecdotal.' However, it then argued:

> One of the few clear conclusions we were able to draw about the drivers of radicalisation is that a sense of grievance is key to the process. Addressing perceptions of Islamophobia, and demonstrating that the

British state is not antithetical to Islam, should constitute a main focus of the part of the Prevent Strategy which is designed to counter the ideology feeding violent radicalisation.[22]

There is little evidence of these issues being addressed. But there are recurring themes which could help build a picture of a potential terrorist. Let me quote a few.

The Government's research has included work on the 'path to extremism'. MI5 have themselves been focusing on understanding the processes and psychology of radicalisation and extremism since 2004. They have found, for example, a high proportion (60 per cent) of terrorists are involved in other types of criminal activity, typically violent crime and fraud.[23]

This factor was borne out in the profiles of many, such as the brothers Ibrahim and Khalid El Bakraoui, the 2016 Brussels bombers, who had a string of criminal convictions between them, including amongst others armed robberies.

A European Parliament briefing in 2015 explained how 'Radicalisation can be viewed as a phenomenon relying on a combination of global sociological, political factors and with ideological and psychological aspects . . . ideology is not alone decisive.'[24]

And for me a fascinating insight from the UK government's own research is that 'a large number of those involved in terrorism do not practise their faith regularly and many engage in behaviours such as drug taking, drinking alcohol and visiting prostitutes'. The report goes on: 'many who become involved in violent extremism lack religious literacy and could be regarded as religious novices. Indeed there is some evidence that a well-established religious identity may actually serve as a protective factor against violent radicalisation.'[25]

There is a mountain of evidence from those who have studied the lives and backgrounds of these so-called Islamist extremist ideologically driven terrorists which shows that the 'Islamist extremist ideology' definition used now to determine counter-strategy and impacting on the lives of British Muslims simply does not fit them. A former CIA officer and forensic psychiatrist Marc Sageman, the political scientist Robert Pape and French professor and Islamism expert Olivier Roy are but a few. And the American-French anthropologist Scott Atran, who in 2010 gave evidence to the US Senate, said: 'what inspires the most lethal terrorists in the world today is not so much the Qur'an or religious teachings as a thrilling cause and call to action that promises glory and esteem in the eyes of friends, and through friends, eternal respect and remembrance in the wider world', and described these would-be terrorists as 'bored, underemployed, overqualified and underwhelmed' young men for whom 'jihad is an egalitarian, equal-opportunity employer ... thrilling, glorious and cool'.[26]

These expert opinions are borne out in the profiles of numerous terrorists. The 9/11 bombers indulged in drink, drugs and partying at strip clubs in the run-up to the attack on the twin towers. Neighbours of the 2004 Madrid train bomber Hamid Ahmidan remember him as 'zooming by on a motorcycle with his long-haired girlfriend, a Spanish woman with a taste for revealing outfits'.[27] Omar Mateen, the Florida gay bar terrorist, had a history of crime and violence, drug and alcohol use and was conflicted about his sexuality.[28] Mohamed Lahouaiej Bouhlel, the Nice truck terrorist, took drugs and, despite being married, used dating sites to pick up men and women.[29] None was, as our definition would suggest, 'rejecting liberal values'.

Few terrorists show a deep understanding or indeed a committed practice of religion. In 2014 would-be Birmingham terrorists Yusuf Sarwar and Mohammed Ahmed purchased *Islam for Dummies* and *The Koran for Dummies* online from Amazon before they set out for jihad in Syria. Both later pleaded guilty to terrorism offences. Didier François, a French journalist held captive by ISIS for ten months, said he and his fellow captives never saw a Qur'an; nor did their captors ever discuss it.[30] And Drummer Lee Rigby's murderers, Michael Olumide Adebolajo and Michael Oluwatobi Adebowale, are both British nationals whose families originate from Nigeria. Both were born and raised as Christians.

Adebolajo was an Essex boy from what neighbours described as 'a pleasant, ordinary, normal family'. He attended university and studied sociology. Adebowale too came from a good family: his mother was a probation officer, his father an official at the Nigerian embassy. Adebolajo had previous convictions for assault and possession of weapons. He had also been arrested in Kenya in 2010 and received consular support. He was known to the intelligence services and had been investigated by MI5 on five separate occasions; there is some suggestion that he was asked to work for them, and indeed both he and his family had complained about what they described as 'harassment' by the British Security Services, although a committee of parliamentarians found no evidence of this in their report.[31] Adebowale complained of being bullied at school as a child and had issues with gangs and drugs. He had been investigated by MI5 on two occasions and indeed at the time of the murder was considered a low-priority suspect.[32]

Neither fitted the 'issues of concern' that politicians cite when discussing extremism that leads to terrorism and makes someone a jihadi. They did not grow up in a segregated Muslim community, or go to the daily after-school madrasa that government is now keen to regulate. Neither seems to have the 'traditionally submissive' mothers, the types that David Cameron felt couldn't tackle extremism because they couldn't speak English. Neither had forced marriages or seemed to have been impacted by female genital mutilation. All these are so-called manifestations of extremism.[33] Neither appeared to be a scholar of Islam, or expert in theology. Nor was there any suggestion they had been radicalized in school or university. No reference was made to the writings of Sayyid Qutb; nor was there a rant about the rejection of British values in their post-murder street sermon.

I mention the above because it's a list that policy-makers quickly reach for when trying to understand those who commit terrorist attacks. These were two young men who had found a new gang, found like-minded men, found a cause through which they could vent their anger, frustration and criminality. They became part of a banned group, Al Muhajiroun, started by Omar Bakri Muhammad and rabble roused by the 'TV star' Andy Chowdry, who was finally convicted in 2016. Al Muhajiroun was a band of mainly young men who are as misogynistic as they are aggressive.[34]

The latest wannabe terrorists are those who have left Britain to join ISIS. Big guns, big cars, plenty of girls and the opportunity to play out computer-game violence in the real world is sadly attractive for bored young men, many of whom are seen as failures at home.

And as for the girls, the opportunity to have an adventure and marry a hunky European convert is a much more attractive proposition than their first cousin from a Sylheti village in Bangladesh. These young people are more the Snapchat and sheesha bars generation than experts in Sharia and the teachings of Sayyid Qutb. I did an impromptu poll of Muslim youngsters recently and asked them to tell me who Sayyid Qutb was, the man government has defined as god-father and key terrorism inspirer. The top three answers were: is he a rapper? Is he a cricketer? Sayyid who?

And yet despite all this information, including testimonies of returning jihadis and ex-extremists, we still insist, 'It's ideology, stupid' and continue making policy based on a premise that is simply flawed. If it blatantly isn't 'all ideology, stupid', it's stupid of us to keep saying it is.

If the analysis of the problem is neither comprehensive nor accurate, the solution will inevitably fail. This is dangerous territory, because the longer we fail to understand or acknowledge the root causes of terrorism, the longer we will simply deal with the symptoms, not the disease. The longer we fail to do the painstaking work of understanding what makes a terrorist, the longer we leave ourselves vulnerable to terrorism. And unfortunately the Coalition government of which I was a part from 2010 to 2015 made things a whole lot worse.

That of the many factors driving terrorism ideology alone was the one that policy-makers wanted to focus on was signalled in the then PM's speech in Munich in 2011. The speech was analysed by Dr Brian Klug, an Oxford University philosopher, expert in the study of Jewish/non-Jewish relations and one of the academics who submitted evidence to the British All-Party Parliamentary Inquiry into Antisemitism in 2006. In his expert dissection he makes a powerful point, which I repeat verbatim: 'not for one moment do I mean to minimize the gravity of attacks, planned or perpetrated, that put civilian lives at risk in the name of Islam. The issue is not one of minimization on my part but overstatement on the part of Cameron and others.'[35]

According to Dr Klug, the speech simply is not based on fact or backed by evidence and crumbles upon greater scrutiny. As he argues, he framed the issues in a tendentious way; appeared to grossly exaggerate the scale of terrorist acts carried out in the name of Islam, his distinction between Islam and Islamist extremism is not coherent and he perpetuated a discredited theory of causation. This is quite a catalogue of unreason.[36]

Let me quote what David Cameron defined as the problem in the Munich speech: 'We have got to get to the root of the problem, and we need to be absolutely clear on where the origins of these terrorist attacks lie. That is the existence of an ideology, Islamist extremism.'[37] And whilst casually acknowledging possible other factors, he went on:

Now, I'm not saying that . . . issues of poverty and grievance about foreign policy are not important. Yes, of course we must tackle them. Of course we must tackle poverty. Yes, we must resolve the sources of tension, not least in Palestine, and yes, we should be on the side of openness and political reform in the Middle East.

Having acknowledged these issues, he quickly cast them aside:

But let us not fool ourselves. These are just contributory factors. Even if we sorted out all of the problems that I have mentioned, there would still be this terrorism. I believe the root lies in the existence of this extremist ideology.

So, according to the prime minister at the time, if we addressed every grievance, from unemployment to discrimination, from mental health to the media's portrayal of Muslims to the injustices in the Middle East, and everything in between, we would still have terrorism in the name of Islam in Britain. I honestly think this is nonsense, but I'd rather we at least tried resolving all these 'other' issues and be proven wrong than not address them at all and find ourselves fighting the battle against terrorism for decades to come.

From 2011, Prevent also shifted its focus further. Its first pillar firmly became a response to the ideological challenge; the second pillar became appropriate advice and support to prevent people being drawn into terrorism; and the third was to work with sectors and institutions where there are risks of radicalization. At this point, we started doing Prevent to the community rather than with them. We went into the battle against terrorism in the name of Islam having alienated our most important troops: the community itself.

This was compounded by the introduction of policy which was predicated on the idea that many of them were influenced by what some have called non-violent extremists and they took their radical belief to the next level by embracing violence. The process of radicalization was seen as a linear journey, a 'conveyor belt' which starts with non-violent extremism. And non-violent extremists are individuals who do not sign up to the definition of current-day British values defined as 'democracy, the rule of law, individual liberty and mutual respect and tolerance of those with different faiths and beliefs'.

This conveyor-belt theory is a favourite of right-wing think tanks in the US and the UK. Like ideology alone, it has little evidence to support it and much academic and legal opposition.[38] As Arun Kundnani says, 'How a government makes sense of political violence directed at it usually tells us at least as much about the nature of that government as it does about the nature of its violent opponents.'[39]

This leap of faith, if you will pardon the pun, the tenuous evidence that those with unsavoury, unorthodox, radical or, dare I say, even conservative religious views are on a journey to becoming terrorists, has become a key plank of the UK's counter-terrorism policy. This is dangerous policy-making. We now have a counter-terrorism policy which casts its net so wide that it catches anyone whose views the government at this moment considers extreme, even if we ourselves in the recent past held such views on homosexuality or, in the more distant past, on women and race.[40] It should worry us all that government believes this is the best way of defeating terrorism.

And while you sit there worrying, try this little exercise. How many people can you think of, either in your personal life or in the public eye, who fit the following definition and are thus extremists who have set off on their journey to terrorism? 'Vocal or active opposition to fundamental British values, including democracy, the rule of law, individual liberty and mutual respect and tolerance of different faiths and beliefs.'

Here's my list: an office bearer of one of our very successful local Conservative Associations in the south of England with some dubious racist views; many an opinionated black cab driver; Christians who didn't abide by the rule of law and smuggled bibles into communist countries over the last 100 years; Christians who believe in the Old Testament edict that God's law is above man-made law; practitioners of civil disobedience like Martin Luther King; Dietrich Bonhoeffer, who 'did not accept the final authority of the rule of law – democratically passed in a democratically elected assembly – over issues of German Jewish citizens when the law was manifestly evil';[41] everybody in this country who is a communist, an anarchist or a racist. Hey, according to our definition, even that party-loving, non-voting eccentric Russell Brand, who believes 'it is a far more potent political act to completely renounce the current paradigm than to participate' and advocates a 'total revolution of consciousness and our entire social, political and economic system' is on the road to terrorism.[42]

Despite my reservations about the current definition of ideology, I do believe we must address religious ideology as a driver of terrorism. It's important for us to support scholars and activists within British Muslim communities and wider to push back theologically against those who selectively adopt verses from the Qur'an and twist interpretations to justify violence against innocents. This is necessary and important work, and this debate on theology has been part of the Islamic way for centuries and is already happening across the UK. What I take issue with is how we currently practically disregard the whole basket of radicalizing ingredients, from previous criminality, gang culture, mental health issues and the ones that are overwhelmingly cited – discrimination, marginalization and victimization – and focus simply on ideology.[43]

Unfortunately, in the past five years, the problem hasn't just been in failing to identify all the causes of terrorism but also ignoring the many ways to address it. Not only are we focused on only one kind of terrorism, but we're ill-defining it and tackling it in the wrong way. In Munich, Cameron laid out his solutions: 'Let us give voice to those followers of Islam who despise the extremists and their worldview.' Well, most British Muslims despise the terrorists, but what is 'their worldview'?[44] If it is that Islam and the West are at war, as intimated by the government's definition of Islamist extremism, then that's a worldview held by many a right-wing politician around the world, including the current US president.

And the rallying call goes out: 'Let us engage groups that share our aspirations', without clarity on what our aspirations are. In practice, this work simply became engaging with groups who tell us what we want to hear. This favoured group status, with access to ministers and handsome financial rewards reserved for those who simply repeat our policy back to us and pitting community groups against one other, is something I will cover in chapter 5. It is an approach that was raised starkly at the Home Affairs Select Committee in 2016 during the questioning of one such group, Inspire, which has received public funding from both central and local government. (It was challenged on its independence, with reference made to one of its co-directors being the sister of a civil servant.[45] Inspire disagreed that it was not independent, stating that it carries out its work as a voluntary organization.)

The Munich speech continues: 'We must build stronger societies and stronger identities at home . . . a lot less of the passive tolerance . . . and much more active muscular liberalism'. So this involves not just a belief in, but a promotion of, our values, which are espoused as 'freedom of speech, freedom of worship, democracy, the rule of law, equal rights regardless of race, sex or sexuality'. I could not agree more. The speech goes on to say: 'To belong here is to believe in these things.' I agree again. But if we really believe in these values – freedom of speech, democracy, the rule of law and equal rights – why does Prevent actually cut across this very approach?

The Counter-Terrorism and Security Act, 2015, made it compulsory for local authorities, schools, universities, NHS staff, and a whole range of other public-sector workers to police the government's definition of extremism. It has led to teachers, academics, medics and others raising their concerns about the challenge this presents to relationships like teacher and student, doctor and patient, and on university campuses this approach flies in the face of genuine and robust debate around controversial issues.[46]

Despite deep reservations amongst many of these professionals and indeed open rebellion from some, they are now officially the thought police and the frontline in our battle to cleanse hearts and minds. This Act, passed just before the 2015 General Election, with a Labour Party floundering under Miliband and a Liberal Democrat party exhausted from Coalition battles and bracing itself for electoral wipe-out, was the perfect opportunity to kick in an awful piece of legislation with little formal opposition. Colleagues from across the political divide sounded the sirens of concern in the House of Lords.[47] All political parties bear the responsibility for the corrosive fallout from Prevent stigmatizing young people and pushing debate and dissent into dark corners rather than under the shining light of a learning environment such as schools, colleges and universities, where it belongs. Censoring debate out of the public space doesn't make the debate go away, it simply masks the problem. Not allowing a space to discuss the tough issues of our time doesn't make us safer, it simply means we don't get to hear them until it's too late.

Let's look at what Cameron in his Munich speech suggests Prevent professes to protect and yet in its implementation it rejects. Take freedom of speech, a British value, a beacon of tolerance. This is not and has never been an absolute right: we have laws that determine what isn't acceptable and we quite rightly prosecute when those lines are crossed. But Prevent steps in to stop freedom of speech when no law is broken. It requires a whole range of professionals to police thought and controversial but legal views on university campuses, by banning speakers, not allowing public buildings to be used for legal gatherings and demanding pre-prepared written speeches to be delivered for censorship before events.[48] Prevent has had a chilling effect on freedom of speech, a freedom it sought to protect.

And politics too cut across the very approach Prevent espouses to preserve. Take freedom of worship. I know many a local councillor, often sadly Conservative, who has secured his seat at an election by opposing the building of a place of worship, in most instances, sadly, a mosque. Is this public display of intolerance and lack of respect for the beliefs of others an indication that these councillors are extremists on a journey to terrorism? Bigoted, yes; extremists, I think not.

The Munich speech also has a swipe at multiculturalism, or state multiculturalism as I defined it, as the reason why British Muslims had confused identities. It's a concept I discussed at some length in chapter 2.

I accept that in the 1980s and '90s a number of odd decisions were made at a local level which emphasized difference and segregation, but in reality by the noughties the message from the later Blair years, 'the duty to integrate' speech and constant posturing by us, the official opposition, had signalled change, and both local and central government had shifted its approach. Long before the Munich speech there had already been a shift away from single-group funding and the provision of community facilities which were unnecessarily divisive. The reason I know this is because every year in the run-up to Christmas the Conservative Research Department would be tasked to find 'Christmas stories' to brief the press which would embarrass the Labour government by exposing 'Winterville' and 'no tinsel in council offices' type stories. The annual scouring of newspaper articles and fast and furious FOI (Freedom of Information) requests that we the Conservative Party would engage in to 'expose' state multiculturalism and embarrass the government became harder every year as we approached 2010. In all seriousness the state multiculturalism project was over by the time we got into government, but we, including me, continued to politically exploit the term 'multiculturalism' for many years after. Again, this doesn't help.

Cameron in the Munich speech goes on: 'Each of us in our own countries, I believe, must be unambiguous and hard-nosed about this defence of our liberty.' Well, this liberty, this freedom which many of our allies are 'unambiguous and hard-nosed' about in their countries, sometimes results in Christians and other minorities not being able to build places of worship or proselytize. What we were advocating for in our own country didn't look great when our foreign allies implemented it in their countries. This blowback of a domestic policy which makes little sense in our foreign policy world is something I will return to in chapter 8.

Cameron continues: the answer is 'English language' for all, a 'common culture and curriculum', the 'National Citizen Service', a common purpose. Yes, yes, yes, I shout from the minaret, this is all fantastic stuff, but it's not counter-terrorism and it isn't Prevent; it's the P that's been missing from policy-making: it's Promote. Promote is the confident, sure-footed presentation of who we are as a nation, an inclusive shared identity, genuine two-way integration. I call it the sunny uplands of policy-making rather than grey skies that is Prevent: not the old-fashioned madrasa-style beat-them-into-learning that is Prevent but the inspirational environment of a chi-chi prep school.

It's not a demand to join modern Britain but commanding the aspirational high ground, so that people beat down the door not just to get into Britain but buy into what Britain is. It's what David Cameron in 2007, early on in his leadership, called 'inspiring loyalty by building a Britain that every one of our citizens believes in'.[49] It's a celebration of what we stand for rather than a denigration of what others might believe. It's a genuine, sincere and long-term political commitment from government to support and resource the promotion of a shared, inclusive Britain rather than short-term political posturing. It's work often called Community Cohesion and Integration in government, and in my experience it is badly funded and the first to face the axe in the face of austerity and budget cuts, in my view attracts some of our least-talented civil servants and is generally seen as low priority and not the serious work of government

It's the positive of Promote that I believe could eventually prevent terrorism, not the pernicious pursuit of ideas we don't like in UK plc. It's when all in the country feel as if they both matter and belong that the attraction to extreme ideas is diminished.[50] It's when the mainstream accommodates the overwhelming majority that the fringe no longer has a purpose.

In discussing the elements of successful counter-terrorism, Jonathan Powell refers to coercive policies and conciliatory policies and argues that 'Coercive policies should be restricted to the few actual perpetrators of the violence, while conciliatory policies ought to be focused on their potential recruits.'[51] It is this latter group that are the attention of Prevent, and it is why Prevent should be conciliatory and addressing grievances whether discrimination, inequality, life chances or foreign policy should be a key element.

The killing of Drummer Lee Rigby presented a unique opportunity for this new conciliatory approach. It was an opportunity to create a new, honest and robust partnership with community groups and activists who comfortingly had displayed a maturity in their response to the murder, which in many ways was lacking in 2005 after the 7/7 terrorist attack, and a clear, unequivocal condemnation of the terrorist attack by a British Muslim community that stood resolute in its fights against terrorism despite the Islamophobic backlash that followed in the days and months after Rigby's murder.[52] Instead, this new goodwill between government and community was wasted. It was a moment to unite all against the small fringe of potential terrorists but it was mismanaged, and government cast the net of who we defined as 'the problem' wider and deeper.

Prevent has been widely criticized. Dozens of cases have now been reported, some disputed, others not, where Prevent-trained teachers have overreacted to everyday school incidents and referred a child to a counter-terrorism process. A student accused of being a terrorist after he was seen reading a textbook on terrorism for his degree; children deemed suspicious simply for having a toy gun; the four-year-old child who couldn't pronounce 'cucumber', calling it 'cooker bomb'; the child who used the word '*l'écoterrorisme*' when speaking about climate change in his French class; and the much-reported ten-year-old Lancashire boy who misspelled terraced house using the unfortunate words 'terrorist house' are some of the most high profile.[53] It's what led to Rights Watch UK, a human rights organizations with over twenty-five years of experience in this area and leading lights such as Helena Kennedy, QC, and Michael Mansfield, QC, as its patrons, to conclude that Prevent has created a 'dynamic in which Muslim youth come to be fearful of the educational setting and distrustful of their teachers and classmates; [it's] counterproductive, discriminatory and a violation of the fundamental rights that are at the heart of the very civil society the government seeks to protect'.[54]

Muslim children are being singled out by a policy which fails to understand that 31 per cent of terrorist convictions in the UK from 2001 to 2010 were converts to Islam, who make up only around 3 per cent of the Muslim population of 3 million, individuals such as Lee Rigby's killers, who were Christian children who converted in later life, or European ISIS recruits like Raphael Amar, who was born to a Jewish father and Christian mother, and Jean-Michel and Fabien Clain, brothers and former Catholics, who became known as the voices behind the terrorist attacks in Paris in November 2015.[55]

A 2016 report by the internationally respected Open Society Foundations, founded in 1979 by investor and philanthropist George Soros, described Prevent as 'violating human rights, generating fear and distrust, and alienating Muslim communities while undermining their access to health and education'.[56] And most worryingly the National Police Chiefs Council released figures showing that 80 per cent of Prevent referrals were set aside between 2007 and 2014,[57] whilst the government's own 2015 CONTEST annual report says that 'several thousand' individuals were referred in 2015, but only 'several hundred' received support.[58]

The Home Affairs select committee in its report *Radicalisation: The Counter-narrative and Identifying the Tipping Point* stated: 'The concerns about Prevent amongst the communities most affected by it must be addressed. Otherwise it will continue to be viewed with suspicion by many, and by some as "toxic".'[59] And David Anderson, QC, the independent reviewer of terrorist legislation, said:

> the Prevent programme is clearly suffering from a widespread problem of perception, particularly in relation to the statutory duty on schools and in relation to non-violent extremism. It is also possible – though I am not in a position to judge – that aspects of the programme are ineffective or being applied in an insensitive or discriminatory manner.[60]

Everyone from the Tax Payers' Alliance to former extremists and Muslim communities now criticize Prevent. It has been a lose-lose policy, and 'other faith groups felt hard done by'.[61] And however well-intentioned Prevent may have been, it simply has not helped to address grievances or create a strong sense of belonging.

As a former Metropolitan Police chief superintendent said, Prevent is 'a toxic brand' run by 'mainly white officers with little understanding of faith, gender or race' and is 'hampering efforts to stop vulnerable young people joining Daesh'.[62] The Met has recently mounted its own charm offensive, with a Prevent social network presence only to be met by a counter-presence in the form of Prevent Watch and others which collates 'bad experiences' of Prevent.

Despite this damning indictment and extensive evidence to support it, the government continues to broaden its reach, both spending more and extending its scope. Ministers continue to insist it works, and government concluded after a secret Whitehall review in 2016 that the programme will be 'strengthened not undermined'.[63] And yet, despite the government continuing to exalt the virtues of Prevent and despite the decades-long and continuing threat from Irish terrorism and the thousands who have died as a result of that terror-ism, we've never implemented Prevent in Northern Ireland.[64] This issue was debated in parliament by Gavin Robinson, MP, a DUP member for Belfast East, who said:

> The Government recently published a counter-extremism strategy. When I asked why Northern Ireland, which has a fair number of extremists, was not included in the strategy, I was told, 'Don't push the issue too far. It is really a counter-Islamic strategy.'[65]

All things Muslim have become all things counter-terrorism, with much work on equality and diversity, including the teaching of Eng-lish to Muslim women, now rebadged by Prevent as counter-terrorism.

Over the years Prevent work has funded everything from football, cricket and basketball tournaments to a 'talk on prophetic medicine' to consular and healthcare support to British Muslims performing the Hajj pilgrimage to Mecca. Many were worthwhile endeavours, all well-meaning and indeed some necessary projects, but they are not counter-terrorism and should not be funded and badged with preventing terrorism work. This should be Promote.

This approach has also spread a sense of Muslims as the problem, both as terrorists and the beneficiaries of anti-terrorism funding, with far-right groups seeing 'the Muslims' as getting all the attention and indeed money for behaving badly. In the world of the far right extremist the brethren of the 'bombers' are getting the cash, whilst those that haven't been blowing people up are getting little support, the equivalent of the badly behaved child in class getting most of the teacher's time, and this is feeding resentment and racism.[66]

It has created a lucrative 'Muslim experts industry', individuals and organizations receiving large amounts of public funding where neither the funding nor the objectives nor the outcomes are transpar-ent or available to the public. Many offer 'training' to public-sector workers described by the general secretary of the Association of Teachers and Lecturers as 'poor quality ... sometimes factually incorrect'. Training material has been described as 'overdone stories of radicalisation filmed in black and white with emotive music'.[67]

'The Muslims', other than those making a small fortune from Pre-vent, are feeling 'singled out' and are generally sick of the attention,

the defining of what one can think and cannot think. This programme has left communities feeling paranoid and suspicious and
pitted groups against one another, with government determining the
version of Islam that one must follow as a Muslim. Despite the up to
£40 million per year spent on Prevent between 2011 and 2015,[68] a
YouGov poll in August 2016 showed that, whilst 25 per cent of those
polled in 2010 felt the terrorist threat had increased in Britain, by
2016 this had risen to 73 per cent.[69] We are not currently building a
more cohesive, equal society.

So if any other group wants this kind of attention, trust me,
Muslims are more than happy for you to have it: you are welcome
to it. Make your application to government to be the Prevent community, and Muslims will be happy to step out of the 'chosen ones'
category.

In Britain since 7/7 thankfully we have not seen any major loss of
life at the hands of terrorists. This is testimony to the work of our
intelligence and law-enforcement agencies. We are good at this. We've
been doing it for decades, mainly because of Irish-related terrorism.
We prepare well, we pursue well, we protect well, and it shows. In
2015 the number of people arrested for terrorism-related offences
went down, as did the number of people travelling overseas for terrorism.[70] But through Prevent we undermine much of the hard work.

We are aware of the series of issues that are the drivers of radicalization, so why do we pick and choose only one – ideology – to focus
on, speak about, invest in and tackle? Why is ideology more important than inequality, poverty, gang culture, Islamophobia, mental
health and the whole basket of reasons given by experts, including
our intelligence services.

This lack of comprehensive policy-making keeps me awake at
night, as it should you, because it is putting the long-term security of
our country at risk. I accept that for politicians it's easier to sell 'it's
their problem' than 'it's our problem' to the electorate. Focusing on
an abstract, difficult-to-define, confused concept such as Islamist
ideology as opposed to statistics on discrimination, social mobility,
criminality, mental health and the legality and success of our
foreign-policy positions is much easier. But by not dealing with real
issues in real communities I believe we are not only in the short term

making the matter worse but also prolonging the time we have to live with the scourge of terrorism.

Understanding the root causes of terrorism, the diverse and varied routes to radicalization and the journey to violence is the start of truly understanding the problem; and that is the start of fixing it.

Policing and preventing criminal acts should be the focus, not policing and preventing thought. In the UK democracy it is the route through which we flush out and flush away unsavoury views. The ballot box is always more powerful than a ban, and debate through bigger and better ideas puts bad ideas to bed. In the 2015 General Election we saw democracy at work. In Bradford, a city with a BME population of over 20 per cent, many with deeply held conservative views on gender, voters rejected both the politics of grievance and cultural bigotry by rejecting George Galloway of the Respect Party and electing a woman. South Thanet too, one of the 'whitest' constituencies in England with a large far-right presence, rejected the politics of fear and sent Nigel Farage the leader of UKIP off with his tail between his legs.

Population shifts and changes in the communities that make up the UK, whatever the perception of that change, something I will discuss in chapter 6, are never so dramatic, and democracy never so weak, in Britain for us to reach for draconian measures to protect ourselves from unsavoury views.

And the question we need to ask our politicians and those who influence policy-making is this. If what we are trying to do is fight terrorism, to kill 'the crocodiles', as one of my cabinet colleagues used to call them, then why in our counter-terrorism policy do we keep expanding the swamp and why are we in our approach possibly breeding more crocs? If we are committed to defeating terrorism in the name of Islam, then we must start by being committed to honest and evidence-based policy-making in which we acknowledge that 'the Muslims', our Muslims, are part of the solution. We must invest in community building. We must be connected to, trusted by and working with our British Muslim communities, not stigmatizing their kids, stifling them from being engaged in legitimate debate and alienating large sections of them. If we are to succeed in defeating the enemy, an enemy for all of us, then we mustn't treat our Muslims as the enemy within.

5

The Paranoid State

'When do the defense measures of a paranoid country become their own agents of self-destruction?'

Christopher Bollen, Orient

'Trusting no man as his friend, he could not recognize his enemy when the latter actually appeared.'

Nathaniel Hawthorne, The Scarlet Letter

In Britain we have a complicated but comprehensive set of laws and rules on rehabilitation. We believe in giving people a second chance even if they've committed some pretty awful crimes. In fact, in 2013 we changed the law to enable more people with longer sentences to be 'officially rehabilitated' more quickly.[1] In a nutshell if you get a sentence of up to two years in prison for a crime, and trust me you've got to do something pretty bad for the courts to give you two years' custody these days, then about four years after the end of your sentence you don't need to disclose it for most jobs, insurance applications and most other aspects of life. You've done the crime, served the time, and after a period are allowed to wipe the slate clean and move on. So you could steal a car, snatch a granny's handbag, even assault your partner and after a few years, providing you behaved yourself, move on with your life.

The rehabilitation periods for non-custodial sentences like fines, cautions and supervision orders are even shorter, whilst compensation and reparation orders are treated as spent as soon as they come to an end.[2]

I worked as a criminal defence lawyer before I entered politics. And whilst, like many criminal defence lawyers, I had my regulars, individuals who I knew would get themselves into some sort of trouble every weekend and for whom I knew I'd get that early Sunday-morning call to come and represent them during police questioning, I also met many for whom the foray into criminality was a one-off, and eventually even some of my prolific offenders managed to put the life of crime behind them and live drug-free, violence-free, crime-free lives. They were rehabilitated.

In politics the principle of rehabilitation applies too. I've yet to meet a colleague who hasn't at some time in his or her life done something, said something, been somewhere or met someone and lived to regret it. For me it was my terrible dog-whistle homophobic campaign literature on Section 28 during the 2005 General Election campaign. Politicians on the left are usually caught by their radical, anarchist views of a bygone era, something these days Jeremy Corbyn and some of his colleagues are regularly questioned about and confronted with, whilst on the right of politics we are usually embarrassed by our historical racism, anti-Semitism and homophobia. Many in cabinet today have form for stupid comments, actions and associations from the past. Politicians are humans who, like everyone else, can make the wrong calls.

Politicians can also be self-righteous, moralizing individuals who expect the public to accept their change of view and their apology and to acknowledge that they, like most Brits, are on a progressive journey and thus can be and indeed are rehabilitated. And yet politicians will merrily, for political advantage, hang the past around the necks of others.

Politics, amongst other things, is the art of debate and discussion, to persuade the other of your viewpoint, to reach out to those we disagree with to show them our way, the better way, to have our opinions challenged so we continue to grow as thinkers, to always strive to find solutions, to give diplomacy a chance, to disagree within the parameters democracy sets, to trust the ballot box, to passionately disagree with another's view but fight just as passionately for their right to have a say, and all within a commitment to the rule of law.

Fighting the General Election in 2005 as the parliamentary candidate for Dewsbury, I hadn't learned all these lessons. I was, and still am, on my political journey, constantly evaluating my views and opinions. That election campaign for me was an early lesson on how much both Britain and I still needed to learn and change. It was a campaign where I faced both overt and covert bigotry – overt from those who felt they couldn't bring themselves to vote for 'a Paki', despite voting Tory in the past. For them the lure of an active and high-profile campaign fought by the BNP was tempting. Some of my best campaign conversations took place with the 'overts'. The challenge of a doorstep racist whom I discovered after a lengthy and heated conversation was not a racist but just ignorant of difference was both worrying and comforting: worrying that people could be so ignorant, comforting that they could be persuaded to rethink. The challenge of a battle of ideas which left both them and me thinking differently was good, old-fashioned street politics.

And then there were the 'coverts', those within the conservative, orthodox Muslim community who had for decades stood proudly with a female Labour MP but for whom the thought of a Muslim woman wanting to step into a leadership position was a step too far. They were the types for whom gender trumped any conversations on policy – and indeed there were few policy conversations during these encounters. This covert bigotry troubled me more than the out-and-out racism. It was hard to pin down, difficult to get someone on record to talk about and deeply entrenched.

When I lost the election it would have been easy to vilify Dewsbury's orthodox Muslim men, who took it upon themselves during the campaign to discredit and dismiss me and ultimately rejoice in my defeat. The jeers and boos that I was met with outside the town hall in the early hours of the morning of 7 May 2005 as the counting of votes came to an end and the result was announced, leaving in the glare of the amassed media, is a moment that in its own way will always stay with me.

I had had the audacity to stand, I had had the audacity to want to represent my hometown folk in parliament as I had for years represented them in the local courts. I had wanted to herald a moment of progress when a woman from a very private community could take a very public stance. The noise from the crowd that morning wasn't your regular northern anti-Tory bashing, it was a very vocal manifestation of the judgement the community had passed that day: we are not ready for Muslim women to lead, we are not ready for this change.

So imagine my very bitter delight when exactly a decade later the very men who had led the campaign against women in politics, who had grasped at religion and morality to justify their position of bigotry and who had spent more time focusing on the length of my skirt than my slick multilingual campaign speeches, now proudly stood next to a young woman, the younger sister of a friend, as she became the first Asian Muslim woman to represent my old home ward at the tender age of twenty-five. The bitter pill for me was that, in winning, she ousted one of my closest friends and one of the Conservative Party's most decent and hardworking councillors.

But Savile Town had changed. In a period of a decade the unthinkable had become the possible, and those with unsavoury views had not only said they no longer held those views but also showed they'd moved on.

If those men in Savile Town can be rehabilitated, there is hope for everyone.

Yet time and time again, the message from government is that if you as a Muslim have ever believed, thought, said or even flippantly commented on an issue which could be seen as 'extremism', there was no road to rehabilitation. There was no redemption, no possibility for meeting, speaking to, sharing a platform, being associated or simply having a connection, however tenuous that might be, with someone who had believed, displayed, thought or suggested he or she had the aforementioned 'extremist' views.

So in your youth or in your heady days of activism or simply during your political journey, if you hadn't believed and said exactly what we the government say and believe right now on the issue of Islam, faith, women, minorities, homosexuality, you are persona non grata, not to be spoken to or engaged with, not allowed even to appear on the same platform.

This policy, which I term the policy of disengagement, started under the last Labour government under the leadership of the then secretary of state for communities and local government, Hazel

Blears, in 2007. John Denham tried to restore sanity when he replaced Hazel Blears in 2009, but months later, when the Coalition Government was formed in 2010, the policy returned. It continues to be applied today.

So for nearly a decade, firstly under Labour, then during the Coalition years and today under a Conservative administration, successive governments have adopted a policy of non-engagement with a wide range of Muslim community organizations and activists. And more and more groups and individuals have over time been seen as 'beyond the pale' for something they said or did in their past or someone they were associated with said or did in the past.

Not only is this policy ludicrously impractical at a time when the need for engagement and understanding our Muslims is greater than ever before, it is also dangerously counterproductive. Over half of British Muslims are under the age of twenty-five. They are in the media spotlight almost on a daily basis, they have access to more connections, information and travel than ever before, they are our frontline in the battle against terrorism and they are disengaged. The issues around terrorism can only be properly responded to with a 'whole community' response. This includes the government, the police and communities of which the British Muslims are an essential component.

A decade into this approach, I'm yet to be convinced that not engaging and not listening to a community gives us the best insight into 'them' and that not speaking to 'them' is the best way to convince 'them' of 'our' viewpoint.

The policy has been driven by a small number of politicians and commentators influenced by the now much discredited and failed neo-conservative thinking from the United States, although the election of Donald Trump has brought this divisive thinking back into the mainstream.[3]

The Coalition years saw regular battles in government about this policy, and the divide wasn't just along party political lines. Many a one-nation Tory with a strong commitment to civil liberties felt disturbed by this policy, not least because names of individuals they considered friends and associates started to be considered unacceptable by government. I recall a specific conversation with a senior cabinet minister about a young man with whom he had worked for a number of years but about whom the Home Office had concerns as someone with 'extremist views'.

There were a growing number of organizations and individuals who had said and done things which we felt were 'extremist', although not illegal, and thus were individuals and organizations that could not be engaged with by officialdom. So no meeting, no sharing of platforms with them, no photographs and certainly no funding or partnerships. The challenge was finding agreement amongst ministerial colleagues as to what or who counted as extremist and beyond the pale.

There were numerous occasions where one department would consider an individual or group persona non grata whilst another government department would engage. The annual Remembrance Day event in November at the Cenotaph on Whitehall was one such moment. The Muslim Council of Britain, an organization that ministers did not engage with, would still attend the Remembrance Day event at the invitation of the Department of Culture, Media and Sport to lay a wreath on behalf of British Muslims.

The quality of the Coalition government thinking on who was acceptable and who not was at best amateur, at worst dangerous. The evidence base, which appeared to be made up of Google searches, unsubstantiated accusations, old historic references and bizarre conspiratorial connections between individuals, was shockingly shoddy.

Many ministerial hours were wasted unpicking and questioning the 'evidence', and agreement between colleagues was rare.

Some ministerial colleagues who would have been incensed that they should be held accountable for the comments and actions of their ministerial mates were quick to impose 'whole group accountability' on others. The Muslim Council of Britain, for example, was considered beyond the pale because of comments made by Daud Abdullah in 2009, at the time one of the MCB's deputy secretary generals. His comments were criticized by the then communities secretary as capable of being construed as an attack on British troops, even though the MCB unequivocally condemned any suggestion that their organization supported attacks on British troops and distanced itself from the comments of Abdullah, who too confirmed that they were his personal views.[4] The 'do as we say not as we do' approach that sadly many a politician has become known for was dished out in large portions to community groups and activists. Group responsibility, guilt by association and collective punishment were the order of the day.

Government now has a fully functioning unit for this process called the Extremism Analysis Unit, which was officially launched in 2015 and described by the then home secretary as a unit that 'will help us to develop a new engagement policy – which will set out clearly for the first time with which individuals and organisations the government and public sector should engage and should not engage'.[5] It was described in 2016 by Home Office minister Karen Bradley as having 'a remit to analyse extremism in this country, and abroad where it has a direct impact on the UK and/or UK interests ... a cross-government resource, with government departments able to commission research and analysis'.[6]

The unit struck me as the extremism police run by civil servants[7] but argues that it 'engages widely with partners across government, academia and communities'.[8] Details of who these 'partners' might be are not published, and neither are the EAU's full remit and terms of reference. Its findings are not made public, its budget is not clear, and those who are 'discussed' are neither informed nor given the right to reply.

During my time in government we only ever 'banned' two groups: Hizb ut-Tahrir and, upon pressure from myself and mainly Lib Dem colleagues, the English Defence League. The Muslim Council of Britain, the Muslim Association of Britain and the Islamic Society of Britain were not, however, engaged with by ministers or officials. Personally, the policy of disengagement is one I consistently ignored because it is one I practically could never implement. I'm authentically ethnic. I live, work and play alongside Britain's Muslim communities. I attend birth celebrations, weddings and funerals within the community on a weekly basis. I shop where they shop, I eat where they eat, I meet where they meet. There is no way, unless I relocated to a nice cottage in a Suffolk village, that I could 'not engage' with individuals, members of organizations and community activists – in the way my white cabinet colleagues could.

After the murder of Drummer Lee Rigby British Muslim organizations and activists, from conservatives to liberals, women's networks to student bodies, were maturely united and clear, unequivocal and unconditional in condemnation of the terrorist attack. There were no ifs and buts in the communities' response and no 'justification' for the atrocity. Many from British Muslim communities who led this effort were the 'disengaged' and on the government's 'beyond the pale' list, individuals and organizations I had been advised not to engage with, advice which at that moment I was grateful I had ignored. At that difficult moment the lines of communication between community and government had to be opened, and I was relieved that I'd never closed them, including with the Muslim Council of Britain.

The Muslim Council of Britain was the most high-profile of a number of groups over which we never reached agreement, but one which nevertheless was never formally engaged with. Neither engaged with nor proscribed, they remained, as they do now, in no man's land. Unlike some colleagues, I never viewed the MCB as extreme or dangerous. My criticism, which I have on numerous occasions discussed with successive secretary generals of the MCB, is that, with a few notable exceptions, it has elected a leadership that is neither equipped to represent, nor is genuinely reflective of, the contemporary aspirations of large sections of British Muslim communities. It has until recently been dominated by mainly first-generation migrants; it has been overwhelmingly influenced by the more orthodox element of British Muslim thought; it has been almost entirely male in its senior leadership. The MCB has been late in accommodating change, often behind the curve, because in an attempt to take 'everyone' in the community with it, it has often been held back by the most intransigent of those it seeks to represent. But my experience of meeting 'faith communities' for over a decade in frontline politics both in opposition and in government has been that these traits are prevalent in most faith-based organizations. It was concerns about this issue, amongst others, which led to the setting-up of Nisa-Nashim, a Muslim–Jewish women's network for the many women from both religions who have at some point struggled with male-dominated faith-based organizations.

Of course, no one could argue that government should not have a set of people, a unit, a department who tell us who the 'dangerous folk' are and keep us safe. My argument is we do and have had for over

100 years: the intelligence services. We also have the police, experts in detecting, preventing and prosecuting the dangerous lot.

The fact that since 7/7 we have only seen only one murder inspired by Islam on the streets of London – the tragic killing of Lee Rigby – shows that, although our intelligence services have had some not-so-glorious moments in the recent past, the allegations of torture being one, on balance they do a very good job. In government often the most rational of arguments were made by intelligence officers around the table. I always found them more considered, informed and nuanced than politicians'. And often they were the only ones who would refer to the contribution made by British Muslims as members of these services in keeping us safe.

The police and the intelligence services relied on expertise to determine the plotters, planners and would-be terrorists,[9] whereas politicians' ability to make policy was clouded by personal ideologies and prejudices against those whom they do not like.

Politicians make policy in a 'paranoid state'. Policy-making which should have targeted the harm of 'terrorism' is increasingly simply targeting 'the Muslims'. I say this very specifically because I saw it at first hand. Let me give some very practical examples of the 'paranoid state' in practice.

A number of religious festivals are celebrated in No. 10 Downing Street each year: from Christmas through to Easter, Diwali to Vaisakhi, Hanukkah to Eid. And yet it was Muslim-focused events, such as the annual Eid reception, that had to be double-checked and cross-referenced. Invitations would often be held up until the last minute, causing much embarrassment. The potential political fallout of us getting it wrong was played out in an environment of frenzy and farce. An unacceptable view on the Middle East, a religiously conservative view on gay marriage or a historical less-than-PC approach to minorities could result in a 'no invite'. On a number of occasions an invite was issued and then 'revoked'. Imam Asim, the Ministry of Defence's Muslim chaplain, was obliged to embarrassingly 'disinvite' individuals to the RAF Northolt Eid reception in 2011. It did not appear that anyone ever deemed it necessary to check these apparently 'unacceptable' views held by individuals and groups of other faiths and communities, nor was this process ever condemned.

Another example is the refusal by government ministers and eventually civil servants to attend events where there might 'possibly', 'potentially', be a speaker whose views we might find unsavoury, even when attendance would itself provide the perfect opportunity to challenge these views.

In 2007, when he was leader of the opposition, I arranged for David Cameron to visit a mosque in the UK. It was six years before he returned to one, in 2013, as a confidence-building measure after the murder of Drummer Lee Rigby, when mosques up and down the country were targeted by far-right activists. My office was instructed to find a 'safe' mosque, one that was 'politically uncontroversial', one that was not theologically aligned to the more conservative elements of the community, one that was Barelwi or Sufi in its teachings and definitely not a Salafi, Deobandi or Tablighi Jamaat mosque – in other words, one that fitted the description of the government's version of acceptable Muslim belief. I didn't argue against the stupidity of the request, I was simply grateful the prime minister had finally agreed to visit a mosque: a show of solidarity in those troubled times was for British Muslims long overdue.

We chose the mosque where the imam and spiritual leader was the father of an ex-civil servant whom we had also recently contracted to deliver a flagship anti-religious hate crime project. We agreed to visit the day the mosque was holding a community event called the 'Big Iftaar'. This initiative was my baby, one we'd developed at the Department for Communities and Local Government and championed in response to the attacks on mosques in the wake of the murder of Lee Rigby. It was an initiative that encouraged mosques to reach out to their local communities during Ramadhan, the month of fasting, and invite them in to share the breaking of the fast meal. It was the British Muslim take on the 'Big Lunch', an Eden Project initiative which brings communities together to share lunch and has been running successfully since 2009.[10]

The mosque visit was a great success, and the prime minister managed to combine good photo opps – frying samosas in preparation for the iftaar – with substance – hearing directly from women who had been victims of anti-Muslim hatred. And yet a few months after the visit I was hauled in to No. 10 and rebuked for my 'choice of mosque'.

The prime minister's chief of staff, now Lord Llewellyn, told me, 'It was your job to protect David.' When I asked about what the concerns were, none was forthcoming. Frustrated by this cloak-and-dagger approach, I asked for concerns to be put in writing. Nothing was ever sent back. The issue was pushed around various political appointees within No. 10, each one 'unsure' what the concerns were and 'where' the concerns had been raised. This paranoid government-within-a-government approach was something that I'd come across over a number of years, and it wasn't just restricted to ministers and advisers employed by government.

When I was appointed to the job of minister for faith at the Department for Communities and Local Government in 2012, my then newly appointed political adviser, or SpAd, as they are known in the trade, was taken 'off site' to be spoken to by an individual who was employed by the Conservative Party. My SpAd was told that he had 'concerns' about me and was asked to keep an eye on me, especially whom I met with. This individual was not elected nor a government employee and yet thought it appropriate to instruct a paid government official to effectively spy on a minister who attended cabinet and occasionally the National Security Council and was a privy councillor.

Concerned by the inconsistent and murky approach to policy-making, I tested the system by writing to a cabinet colleague recommending that the Senior Officials Group on Extremism (SOGE) consider ruling on an organization which had extremist and intolerant views *about* Muslims. I was called in for a quiet conversation, and the referral was never made.

These were harsh personal experiences of an approach to policy-making which I consider dysfunctional and dangerous. This paranoid approach to all things 'Muslim' was in my experience, and to the best of my knowledge, not practised for any other community.

An interesting comparative case is the Global Peace and Unity Conference (GPU) arranged every few years by the Islam Channel at the Excel Centre in London. The GPU is a weekend of family-friendly entertainment, food stalls, ethnic fashion and the odd firebrand speaker. It's an opportunity for families to feast, charities to raise much-needed donations and businessmen to make deals. Attendance at the conference is in the tens of thousands. GPU started in 2005 and took place twice during my time in government. I attended and spoke at the event in one of its early years alongside ministers from the then Labour government and politicians from all parties. Speaking to an audience of 30,000 people was a unique experience.

But concerns emerged about GPU providing a platform for speakers who hold or have in the past held what can be described as either illiberal views or orthodox conservative views on gender and sexuality, views not dissimilar to those held both historically and currently by some Conservative politicians.

In government the debate about whether ministers should or shouldn't attend was split between those of us who felt that attendance was necessary and those who wanted to boycott the event. The former view was that to be absent from such a huge gathering of Muslim families was a missed opportunity to get our message out, and what better way to challenge illiberal views than to present the alternative view from the same stage. This view, amongst others, was a view held by my colleague Dominic Grieve, the then attorney general and now chairman of the Intelligence and Security Committee, and by Nick Clegg, the then deputy prime minister.[11]

The alternative view was to impose a boycott and ban ministers from attending because attendance would be viewed as an endorsement.

A compromise was reached: my party refused to allow me to attend, whilst the Lib Dems sent a junior minister. A moment where we could have made a real impact with thousands of British Muslims was viewed by Muslims as a snub from government. A white, male non-Muslim Liberal Democrat attended; the UK's first Muslim cabinet minister was told she must not. The banners and boycotters won the battle, the diplomacy and dialogue wallahs started to lose the war.[12]

However, there appeared to be no similar concerns when the prime minister attended the Festival of Light in 2015, by coincidence also at the Excel Centre. The prime minister met privately with Redeemed Christian Church of God (RCCG) general overseer Pastor Enoch Adejare Adeboye and received a rapturous welcome when he was introduced to the 45,000-strong crowd by Pastor Agu Irukwu, leader of RCCG UK, which has 732 churches worldwide.[13] Yet the festival, the umbrella organization and indeed the people he met have made controversial comments on gender and sexuality.[14] Pastor Irukwu is quoted as saying: 'But man marry man and woman marry woman. Then no need to stop global warming because soon there won't be newborn children. What's that they want to adopt, who will give birth to the child and how?'[15]

Pastor Irukwu had been one of the signatories to a letter 'on behalf of tens of thousands of black churches' addressed to the then Labour government about what were called 'anti-Christian laws', namely the Sexual Orientation Regulations, which outlawed discrimination in the provision of goods, facilities, services, education and public functions on the grounds of sexual orientation. The letter raised concerns about the promotion of the idea that 'homosexuality is equal to heterosexuality' and argued 'this is now we believe to be the truth'.

The RCCG, like most churches, like most faith communities, is on a journey, having said things in the past which they probably would not agree with now, and in some cases they still interpret scriptures literally and in a manner not in accordance with what we perceive today as modern British values. They too, like GPU, are a broad church, with individuals who may have unsavoury views that aren't shared by all, and they too have their firebrand speakers.

Many a Muslim group or individual has simply not been allowed to attend the Conservative Party conference despite being deemed 'safe' enough to attend the Labour, Lib Dem and SNP conferences.[16] The questions we therefore have to ask ourselves are these: are we defending our values per se or only defending our values against Muslims? Is an illiberal view only unacceptable when that view is held by a Muslim? Are historic statements on gender and sexuality only unforgivable if made by Muslims? Is collective guilt reserved for Muslims? Are conservative religious practices only problematic if the practitioners' faith happens to be Islam? Are we genuinely making policy 'where everyone plays by the same rules'?[17]

These are not easy questions for me to ask, and I have thought deeply before asking them. But when we reach a point when organizers of GPU write to government and ask them to approve or reject, clear or dismiss, and greenlight or ban the speakers we find acceptable and unacceptable, when they give us a free rein and government simply refuse to take it, we have reached a deeply worrying point.[18]

This setting up of the community and community events to fail, this 'not attending' whatever you do, this ' not playing' even if you let us set the rules is not in line with the oft-touted British values of fairness and mutual respect and tolerance.

Now I know that there may be extremists out there whose life ambition is to convince Muslims there is no place for them in Britain and who will seize on these comments and use them to poison young minds. To you I say this: I value and defend the values of freedom of speech, democracy and the rule of law, I want my nation to genuinely assert these values, I would defend them whether they worked for me or against me, unlike you, who simply use them as a convenient tool when it suits. It's because Britain has these values that I can make these difficult arguments so publicly.

To my colleagues in government I say, as I've argued for years: we must have transparency in policy-making and consistency in application of policy. There is nothing that feeds victimhood quite like treating some people differently from, and worse than, you treat everybody else.

In government I said the approach smacked of McCarthyism, a term named after US politician Joseph McCarthy, who in 1950, during the Cold War years, suggested communist and subsequently homosexual infiltration of the state and other government departments. The term describes Joseph McCarthy's approach to hunting down and exposing these 'enemies within'. His approach in 1950s America led to individuals having their reputations ruined based on defamatory statements made on little or flimsy evidence. Conspiracy theories were the order of the day, and many a homosexual was hounded out of office. Critics of McCarthy would be silenced with accusations of being traitors and communist sympathizers. His approach and party political positioning of the issue is widely accepted as hindering genuine counter-subversion work, and the term McCarthyism today is synonymous with making accusations without proper regard to evidence and using unfair investigative techniques to restrict dissent or political criticism. When I used the description in government I was shouted down. But surely, if it looks like McCarthyism, feels like McCarthyism, smells like McCarthyism, it's nonsense not to call it McCarthyism.

If we have decided to view ever-increasing numbers of Muslim organizations or individual Muslim activists with suspicion and to dangerously narrow engagement with British Muslims to a dozen or so people from a community of over 3 million, then let's at least have the decency to say that's the approach we've taken. Let's abide by our values and tell those whom we are not engaging with the reasons they are 'out in the cold'. Let them know the case against them and let them have an opportunity to defend themselves. The rules of natural justice, rules that have stuck in my mind from when I first studied law at the tender age of sixteen, *nemo iudex in causa sua* – no one can judge their own case – and *audi alteram partem* – the right to know the case against you – are fundamentally British values.

This approach of maligning through association seems all the more ridiculous when we look at the unsavoury characters around the world we have in the past and continue to not only talk with, but trade with, fight alongside and consider our friends and allies – 'friends' like Gadaffi, Hosni Mubarak, General Zia, Saddam Hussein and General Sisi to name a few, and of course President Trump, with whom the PM walked hand in hand. Yet it's an approach that we, the Conservative Party, used as a key plank of our campaign for London mayor in 2016. Time and again the party used dog-whistle messages to connect the Labour candidate, Sadiq Khan, to 'extremists'. The approach was both dangerous and disingenuous. The subtle message of the campaign was Khan is a Muslim and cannot be trusted to run London; the evidence paraded in aid of this message was 'connections' Khan had with extremists, a message that the then home secretary, now prime minister, Theresa May, disappointingly put her name to.

These 'connections' that the Conservative Party exploited were threefold.

Firstly, it was said that Sadiq Khan, during his time as a practising lawyer, human rights activist and chairman of Liberty, a civil rights organization, represented the likes of Louis Farakhan, the infamous leader of the US group Nation of Islam, and Babar Ahmed, who was extradited to the US by the UK government in 2011 to face terrorism charges. Khan's involvement with both was professional. I dread what the press could dig up about the clients I and many other lawyers – and there are lots of us in politics – have represented in the past. If we are to become a nation where a lawyer can be guilty of being an extremist because he represented people with extremist views, then how are we to judge those, including myself, who've represented paedophiles and rapists?

Secondly, apparently Khan could not be trusted to keep London safe because one of his sisters, one of eight siblings Khan has, had married and subsequently divorced – and that may be an important fact – a man who allegedly had or has extremist views.[19] So are we to assume that all politicians are now accountable for the views of men and women their siblings may choose to marry? The ex-chancellor George Osborne was also sadly a strong supporter of the 'guilt by association' approach; we had many a disagreement on it, and yet I'm sure he'd quite rightly be appalled if his ability as chancellor had been questioned because of the conduct of his younger brother, Dr Adam Osborne, who has courted his fair share of controversy, including being suspended by the General Medical Council for writing fraudulent prescriptions.[20]

And thirdly, Khan has shared platforms with local Tooting imam Suleiman Ghani. Ghani for sure has some dubious views on women, homosexuality and organ donations,[21] views for which he has been criticized by Sadiq Khan, but despite these views he was courted by and photographed with Dan Watkins, the Conservative parliamentary candidate for Tooting, in 2015, Conservative MP for Twickenham Tania Mathias, Conservative MP and financial secretary to the Treasury Jane Ellison and indeed even the Conservative mayoral candidate, Zac Goldsmith.[22] Khan had associated with the same man that the Conservatives had. Now members of parliament do numerous events in their constituency where local faith leaders too are invited, and it would be a worrying state of affairs if all future politicians would be maligned because their local imam, vicar or rabbi seemed both to hold some dubious views and enjoyed being photographed with his local MP.

For David Cameron to suggest, as he did at Prime Minister's Questions, that Khan had met Ghani 'again and again and again' without once clarifying that Ghani was Khan's equivalent of the embarrassing local parish vicar who opposes homosexuality, divorce, abortion and female bishops, and that Khan and Ghani had had a falling-out precisely because of these views, was wrong and not statesmanlike.[23] The prime minister's comments were covered by parliamentary privilege, something other parliamentarians too have used to make accusations which would likely be actionable in the 'real world'. When Cameron's comments were subsequently repeated outside the privileged environment of parliament by the secretary of state for defence, Michael Fallon, he was sued by Ghani and reportedly paid 'thousands of pounds' in compensation and legal costs.[24] Despite this unsubstantiated accusation, maligning of a citizen and political faux pas, Fallon continues to serve as secretary of state for defence.

I explore this matter in detail because it hit the public consciousness, whereas the maligning of less high-profile individuals goes unnoticed. The knitting together of the views of others, perfectly legitimate connections and a few untruths can so easily destroy reputations. The consequences for individuals can be as wide-ranging as losing jobs, declined foreign visa applications, extended 'random' checks at airports and online abuse. Some take legal action and succeed;[25] others, like most Brits, don't have the financial means to clear their name, but most in the interests of damage limitation simply keep their heads down and hope the media circus will move on.[26]

But perhaps the most worrying example of this was when a cabinet colleague in the presence of the prime minister suggested adopting the 'Al Capone approach', saying that if we can't get 'them' for their ideas and beliefs 'they' hold, let's do 'them' for health and safety, charity commission bureaucracy breaches and money matters. I was shocked at the conversation. But it was no surprise to me months later when the government announced its review into the Muslim Brotherhood, an organization which many of our foreign allies have issues with, the same phrase was used as a quote from a senior source close to the inquiry. The source said 'We cannot ban the organization, but that was never the intention of the review. We can go after single individuals, not for terrorist-related activity, but through the Al Capone method of law-enforcement. We cannot get them for terrorism, but I bet you they don't pay their taxes.'[27]

The 'Al Capone' conversation meeting was memorable for many reasons, but three stuck in my mind: firstly, the ease with which colleagues felt comfortable in using the levers of power to 'harass' communities; secondly, the boldness of a Lib Dem colleague when he suggested that Michael Gove, the then secretary of state for justice, sounded more anti-Islam than anti-Islamism; and thirdly, because it took place around the time self-confessed neo-conservative writer Douglas Murray, when writing of the government's response to the Lee Rigby murder, referred to me as 'the enemy at the table'.[28] I thought this concept of 'the enemy within' would make for a very good book.

Now one could argue that surely if people have views and ideas we don't like then isolating them and distancing them from decision-making is a good thing. It's what we did with the IRA and those associated with them in years gone by. But then as now we alienated a much larger group of Catholics than just the terrorists, we dismissed those who sought to highlight genuine Irish grievance as apologists for terrorists and we had an inconsistent approach to the way we treated communities, Protestant and Catholic. I would argue that the approach then as now was counterproductive, and one thing we can all agree on is that peace came about by talking to those we neither liked, nor trusted, nor agreed with.[29]

My view has always been that there are many groups and individuals whose views on a whole series of issues are at best conservative and at worst extreme, and government should not fund or take these groups or individuals as partners. As a country we absolutely have a right to state clearly what we feel is an acceptable and an unacceptable view on a whole series of issues. Let me take women's rights as an example.

Every woman in this country has a right to determine her own future, to pursue an education and career, to choose to spend her life with the person of her choice, to wear what she wants, to travel how she wants, to choose whether to have children or not. She should be free to make choices that are her choices. Of course, there are interpretations of all faiths which may appear to cut across what I have described above, from the issue of divorce and remarriage in Catholicism, to the status of, and discrimination faced by, widows in Hinduism,[30] to the value of female testimony in Islam, to the issue of female bishops in the Anglican Church and the very prescriptive role and responsibility of orthodox Jewish women and their impact on the pursuit of higher education.[31]

In a country committed to gender equality, even if we still have a serious problem with domestic violence, even if two women a week are killed at the hands of a current or ex-partner, even if each year we see around 1.3 million female victims of domestic abuse, even if we have a gender pay gap, and women are underrepresented at the top political and business tables, we cannot allow interpretations of faith or manifestations of culture such as forced marriages and female genital cutting to silence us. We must speak out consistently across all communities when we see women's rights being trampled upon, including being brave enough to call out misogyny, which we did not, in meetings with President Trump. We must exert our values.

And so groups or individuals who do not hold to the view that women and men, whilst different, are equal should not be funded to run government projects or considered as acceptable partners for government policy. They should, however, be engaged with, challenged and most importantly be given the opportunity to change their views, to travel a journey, to redeem themselves from their previous positions. So whether the historical unsavoury view was on gender or race, religion or sexuality or indeed any other issue, there must be a way back.[32]

Unfortunately, David Cameron's Conservative government continued in a paranoid state until its death. A stark example was the failure by government to consult a single Muslim organization during the development of its flagship anti-radicalization website, 'Educate against Hate'. This tool to be used by teachers and pupils amongst others was discussed with twenty-nine organisations but none representing British Muslim communities.[33]

Theresa May's government has yet to formally pronounce on this issue, though its approach appears to be the same. I urge them to reflect, think again and move on from the mistakes of the past. We need a rehabilitated approach, one with an ambition to bring more and more into Big Tent Britain and not, as the current policy is doing, push more and more to the fringe. We need to create a wider public space where we can shine a light on views we don't like or disagree with rather than creating a larger space on the dark side. We need to create the opportunity to change people rather than give them a free rein to rebel.

The rules of engagement must be clear, but engagement there must be, as a disengaged community is one that neither matters nor belongs.

And just as we have been quick to forgive and move on from President Trump's past, his distasteful and divisive comments and conduct, we must find it within ourselves to adopt a similar approach to our own citizens. If we are prepared to roll out the red carpet for someone like Trump, surely we can at least map out the route of return for many of these organizations and individuals who we need standing alongside us to create a Britain at ease with its Muslims and Muslims at ease with Britain, strong and united, especially when, and sadly it is a when, terror strikes our streets again.[34]

6

Islamophobia

'In time we hate that which we often fear.'
William Shakespeare, Antony and Cleopatra

A dislike of a group of people is not a new thing. The tendency to sweeping generalizations, lazy stereotypes and stigmatization of a community has reared its ugly and dangerous head at many moments in our history. And often when as a nation we find ourselves under pressure, usually economically, we have reached for a convenient whipping boy, often masked in the best of intents. So what I say in this chapter is neither new nor exceptional, it's just current.

It's sadly easier to blame rather than seek considered answers to complex challenges, and the current threat from terrorism is no exception. And whilst I understand, not condone, the 'fear' of Muslims that terrorists have been successful in instilling, I condemn the ever-growing reasons why people 'officially' say they don't like Muslims, reasons which over the years have changed. It's what clever folk would call an evolving narrative. I like to define it as the latest baloney to mask bigotry.

This approach is not new. Much justification has been provided for discrimination against black people. Historically many a European power, including Britain, felt 'native' Africans or Asians needed civilizing, needed to be prised apart from their native history and traditions and needed to adopt a western Christian lifestyle. Indeed, privileges including citizenship for these 'natives' in their own countries became linked to adopting 'western values' and lifestyles. We colonized them for their benefit, a sincerely held view, something that

Rudyard Kipling wrote about in his poem 'The White Man's Burden'. Imperialism became a humanitarian cause, and it was the 'responsibility' of the white man and Christianity to introduce the 'coloureds' to a more civilized way, our way. And in this approach was an inherent assumption that the 'white man' was superior and the 'coloured' inferior. Discrimination was ideologically and intellectually justified as being in the interests of those who were discriminated against.[1]

Many a rational intellectual in the past and even today has reasoned an anti-Semitic position too. Roald Dahl, a wing commander in the Royal Air Force and world-renowned author of books like *Fantastic Mr Fox* and *James and the Giant Peach*, books that in middle school fed my appetite for reading, said in an interview in 1983, 'there is a trait in the Jewish character that does provoke animosity, maybe it's a kind of lack of generosity towards non-Jews . . . I mean there is always a reason why anti-anything crops up anywhere; even a stinker like Hitler didn't just pick on them for no reason.' On the basis of this interview, Dahl seems to suggest that there is a justification for anti-Semitism, a reason for the hatred.[2]

And even that great British prime minister Winston Churchill wasn't averse to peddling conspiracy theories of Jews having a malign influence and a 'take-over' agenda. Of Jewish Bolshevism he said:

this worldwide conspiracy for the overthrow of civilisation and for the reconstitution of society on the basis of arrested development, of envious malevolence, and impossible equality, has been steadily growing. It has been the mainspring of every subversive movement during the 19th century; and now at last this band of extraordinary personalities from the underworld of the great cities of Europe and America have gripped the Russian people by the hair of their heads and have become practically the undisputed masters of that enormous empire.[3]

So even two of the nation's most loved heroes have at some moment found a 'respectable' reason to justify hatred of the 'other'.

It's always possible to rationalize racism and covertly couch bigotry in 'acceptable' arguments; it is this form of hatred that is the most dangerous.

Sadly, bigotry exists in all societies, communities and countries. We are no exception. And I have come to tolerate that some people are simply intolerant of others. But I believe that the large majority of Brits are at least tolerant, most often accepting of 'the others', and are repulsed by overt bigotry. After the last presidential election in the US, I am not confident I can say the same of Americans. Personally I can handle overt bigotry. In Britain if the 'overts' get enough exposure they will show themselves for the small-minded people that they are. It is why I was content to share a platform with Nick Griffin when we appeared alongside each other on *Question Time* in 2009, when many objected to him being given a platform. I knew that if you give racists enough rope they will hang themselves. Griffin's awful performance that evening, when he tried desperately 'to reach out to Britain', saying his appearance would give the BNP 'a whole new level of public recognition' but always with one eye on his 'core vote', was both pitiful and satisfying. Inclusive Britain took great delight in his sweating persona as he tried to justify his past associations with Gadaffi and the 'non-violent' branch of the Ku Klux Klan to one of the largest audiences to ever tune in. Griffin's resounding trouncing at the hands of fellow panellists and the audience was the beginning of the end of the BNP.

So if some Brits hate Muslims full stop, that's fine; it's the latest form of prejudice, the bigots need a bogeyman, and 'the Muslims' are a convenient 'other', someone to blame for failures and shortcomings in their own lives. We've been here before and no doubt sadly we will be here again in the future. These overt Islamophobes – the likes of the BNP, the EDL and Pegida – concern me far less that the covert ones, the ones who dress up their anti-Muslim bigotry in reasoned intellectual arguments.

But what exactly is Islamophobia?

The UK's leading thinktank on race and equality, the Runnymede Trust, defined it in 1991 as 'unfounded hostility towards Muslims, and therefore fear or dislike of all or most Muslims'.[4] The *Oxford English Dictionary* defines it as 'dislike of or prejudice against Islam or Muslims, especially as a political force', whilst the Center for Race and Gender at the University of California uses a much broader definition including referring to Islamophobia as a tool which 're-introduces and reaffirms a global racial structure through which resource distribution disparities are maintained and extended'.[5] The definition of the Center for American Progress deals not just with the hostility, but its purpose: 'an exaggerated fear, hatred, and hostility toward Islam and Muslims that is perpetuated by negative stereotypes resulting in bias, discrimination, and the marginalization and exclusion of Muslims from America's social, political, and civic life'.[6]

However, some argue that the term 'phobia' suggests that the fear of Islam is irrational, whilst many in Britain today believe that there is nothing irrational about fearing this very foreign religion. As Douglas Murray puts it:

> A phobia is something irrational, but there's a very rational fear in being scared of Islam today and wanting to act against it . . . Islam is not a race, it's an ideology. It's not bad to dislike someone for their ideology.[7]

Personally I believe Islamophobia is a bad term to describe bad behaviour. I prefer to use anti-Muslim hatred and sentiment.

The last decade had produced a plethora of commentators on all things Islam, experts who spend hours on news programmes and documentaries telling us all about 'the Muslims' – what the Muslims think, what the Muslims believe – and some even give detailed analysis on specific verses from the Qur'an. We seem to have become ever-greater experts on the Muslim problem with ever-growing analysis on why 'they, the Muslims' hate us, and yet little 'expert' time, attention and commentary is given to understanding and tackling why some of 'us' hate 'them', 'the Muslims'.

There are many, well-argued, intellectualized reasons for Islamophobia. I will be focusing on seven, the seven sins that rationalize hate.

Sin number one: there is no problem, Islamophobia doesn't exist. It's a view taken by many, from atheists, to academics, journalists to bloggers, who say Islamophobia is simply legitimate criticism of Islam and a response to the actions of followers of the faith. Criticism of a faith – any faith – should not be silenced; indeed, there is a great tradition within Islam of questioning, debating and disagreeing. But vilification of a community as the followers of a faith, if left unchecked, translates into the persecution of Christians simply for following Christ, anti-Semitism for being Jewish and Islamophobia for the followers of Islam.

What do the statistics show?

In 2016 the UK thinktank DEMOS researched Islamophobia on Twitter and found that, in July 2016, 215,246 Islamophobic tweets were sent; that's 289 per hour, every hour of July.[8]

Liam Byrne is the MP for Birmingham Hodge Hill. His constituency is home to one of the largest British Muslim communities. He ran a poll in his constituency in 2015 which found that 96 per cent of his Muslim constituents 'believed Islamophobia is on the rise in Britain and a staggering 87 per cent said that they or someone they knew had experienced Islamophobia'. He singles out the media as a particular contributor to the climate of Islamophobia with 82 per cent of those polled in his constituency citing it as the reason behind the recent rise in Islamophobia.[9]

A worrying report from the Open University in 2016 found that 39 per cent of Muslim pupils had personally experienced racial abuse. Most abuse was verbal – 'being called "terrorist" was frequently recounted in discussion, although 5 per cent also recorded instances of physical abuse'.[10] Young people raised concerns about negative stereotypes, especially of Muslims, and wanted more to be done, including 'organised events that bring young people together in a common activity such as inter-faith festivals or sporting tournaments' and 'better-informed teaching about Islam, in schools and in the media, to counter the assumed link between Islam and terrorism'. Young people didn't merely want to be 'tolerated' or to 'tolerate' others, but to respect and mutually understand others.[11]

I would highly recommend a *Dispatches* documentary by political commentator and journalist Peter Oborne called 'It Shouldn't Happen to a Muslim'. Aired on the third anniversary of 7/7, it investigated the rise of violence, intolerance and hatred against British Muslims. An ICM poll commissioned by *Dispatches* at the same time showed worrying results, with negative stereotypes of Muslims widespread. A pamphlet, *Muslims Under Siege*, was published alongside the poll and documentary which concluded, 'We do not treat Muslims with the tolerance, decency and fairness that so often we boast is the British way.' The report argued that it was time to end the 'culture of vilification against Muslims'.[12]

These findings were also three years after the Organization for Security and Cooperation in Europe passed a ministerial declaration at its

High Level Conference in Córdoba on 'Anti-Semitism and Other Forms of Intolerance', asking member states to collect and remit data on hate crime. We have been recording anti-Semitism since 2010. We are now trialling similar recording on Islamophobia, but definitive figures are unlikely to be available until 2018. I welcome this progress, but the discrepancy in the way in which we treat race, anti-Semitism or discrimination towards Sikhs on the one hand and Islamophobia on the other means that as a country we still fail to fully protect our Muslims.

The hatred of Muslims is real and growing, and incidents of unprovoked attacks on individual British citizens simply for being 'Muslim' are, sadly, despite being under-reported, on the increase.[13] Despite Britain's long history of tackling racism and anti-Semitism, on Islamophobia policy-making is still playing catch-up. These are not simply statistics, these are children bullied in playgrounds, women assaulted in the street, graduates not invited for job interviews, the media misreporting events and destroying reputations. Real people, real lives. So let's not fall for 'there is no Islamophobia'.[14]

Sin number two builds on one. It also fails to acknowledge Islamophobia, this time saying the challenge is hatred 'from' Muslims. It goes something like this: I don't hate Muslims. They hate us.

In chapter 3 I discussed the history of terrorism and its many manifestations both in the past and in the present. I presented data on how many terrorists are 'Muslim' and whether it's 'us' in the West who are the targets. Let me recap. Most terrorism is not targeted at the West. After 11 September 2001, only 0.5 per cent of all terrorism deaths have occurred in Western countries,[15] and in the US, as David Schanzer, director of the Triangle Center on Terrorism and Homeland Security, said at the launch of a report this year examining Muslim-American involvement in violent extremism, 'The data in this report contradicts two common narratives in our polarized discourse about terrorism . . . [I]t is flatly untrue that America is deeply threatened by violent extremism by Muslim-Americans; attacks by Muslims accounted for only one third of one percent of all murders in America last year.'[16] In the UK, since 7/7, we have had twenty-six murdered at the hands of terrorists; of them twenty-three were by Irish terrorists, two by far-right terrorists and one, Lee Rigby, at the hands of terrorists claiming to be Muslim.[17]

Most terrorist acts committed by those purporting to be Muslim or terrorism in the name of Islam are against other Muslims.

And yet against this statistical background we have an environment where all things terrorism are viewed as all things Muslims, and both broadcast and print media can perpetuate the myth that 'all terrorists are Muslims'. I'd urge people to watch the moment in 2010 when Brian Kilmeade of the US TV network Fox said, 'Not all Muslims are terrorists, but all terrorists are Muslims.'[18]

One could dismiss this as the uninformed rantings of a Fox News journalist, but sadly even mainstream politicians get caught up in this propaganda. The 2016 US presidential election campaign was a stark example, jumping to conclusions and reacting to world events from prejudiced positions based on stereotypical views that all terrorists are Muslims. The newly appointed foreign secretary, Boris Johnson, fell into this lazy thinking within weeks of his appointment in 2016 when in reaction to a terrorist shooting in Munich where nine were killed, he assumed the attack was 'in the name of Islam', calling the attack a part of a 'global cancer . . . incubated in the Middle East and around the world'.[19] 'The terrorist, Ali David Sonboly, turned out to be inspired by right-wing extremism, choosing the fifth anniversary of Anders Breivik's far-right terrorist attack in Norway to inflict his carnage. Sonboly was proud of sharing a birthday with Hitler, rejected Islam, hated Turks and Arabs, was obsessed with violent computer games and had a history of being bullied and mental health issues.[20] Muslims love to debate what Muslims in the past invented. We like to think we've made a positive contribution to the world. And personally I'm thankful for their pioneering work which led to soap and the humble toothbrush. Life would be pretty awful without either, as it would be without their other great export, coffee.[21] We Muslims, in classic *Goodness Gracious Me* style, like to take credit for a whole load of other stuff which is then disputed in endless papers, from algebra to astronomy and military marching bands to windmills. But one thing we can all agree on is that Muslims did not invent suicide bombing; that was the brainchild of the Japanese, with the missions of the Kamikaze pilots.[22]

But if you read the papers, watch the news or follow politics either in the US or Europe you'd be forgiven for starting to believe that 'Muslims are terrorists and they hate us.' Let's look at the evidence.

Polling by Pew shows that western Muslims are much more likely to have a positive attitude towards their Christian compatriots than vice versa.[23]

British Muslims have a strong connection to feeling 'British',[24] have a greater trust in institutions such as the police and parliament than other Brits, are more likely to want to live in mixed communities and have a positive attitude towards other communities.[25]

So no, 'British Muslims' do not hate us, and thus to try and use that as a basis of Islamophobia is not supported by evidence but is mere bigotry.

Sin number three is expressed by those who say, 'I don't hate Muslims per se, it's when they follow Islam, a uniquely violent religion, that I object to them.' It's an argument presented as the basis for suggesting that the problem is not the people but the religion itself.

It's an argument that crops up in many polls in the UK. One by COMRES in 2016 found that 43 per cent of people polled felt that Islam is a negative force in the UK, and 72 per cent agreed that most people in the UK have a negative view of Islam.[26] The 2012 British Social Attitudes survey found that only one in four people in Britain felt positively about Islam, with 55 per cent of people saying they would be 'bothered' if a large mosque was built in their locality. A YouGov poll conducted in 2015 found that 55 per cent of people agreed with the statement 'There is a fundamental clash between Islam and the values of British society.'[27] It's an argument that has even found its way into House of Lords debates, where UKIP peer Lord Pearson has asked for a 'national debate' on verses within the Qur'an which can be interpreted to support violence. There is a vast array of theological writings, opinions and fully argued fatwas explaining 'violent verses' in the Qur'an which conclude that the use of violence is not justified in Islam, from the internationally published fatwa against terrorism by Tahir-ul-Qadri, who in a 500-plus-page document argues the legal, moral and religious case against terrorism justified in Islam, to the ruling of leading British Muslim scholars, to the 'Open letter to Baghdadi', the self-styled leader of the so called Islamic State, which condemned both IS and its barbaric conduct.[28]

Just as ISIS are destructive individuals who draw religion close as a veil of respectability to justify their criminal behaviour, so too religious texts decontexualized and applied without reason make most religions appear bizarrely intolerant and violent at some point. As Madeleine Albright, the first woman in the history of the US to become secretary of state, said 'Both the Bible and Qur'an contain enough to start a war and enough to ensure lasting peace.'[29]

Anyone familiar with the main religions can find phrases in the ancient texts of these religions that aren't appropriate to modern life. 'An eye for an eye' is the advice from Exodus. 'If a man commits adultery with another man's wife . . . both the adulterer and the adulteress must be put to death' is what it says in Leviticus. And 'The false prophets or dreamers who try to lead you astray must be put to death' is what Deuteronomy says.

In 2015, two young Dutchmen conducted 'street experiments' in Holland called the Holy Qur'an Experiment in an attempt to show that the prejudice underpinning the view that Islam is uniquely violent is widespread.[30] It involved reading passages from the Bible but with a cover on it which said it was the Qur'an. The response was fascinating, with individuals responding to the passages on women's roles, homosexuality and violence by repeating stereotypical negative views of Muslims before being told and realizing that they were in fact passages from the Bible. The experiment has been repeated all over the world with similar stark moments of realization and acknowledgement of prejudice. It's one I would like to see politicians and media types take part in.

Now, even if we accept that our majority faith in Britain, Christianity, too, has the propensity based upon teachings within the Old and New Testament to be as violent as Islam,[31] we Brits believe that we would never condone violence in the name of our faith. However, I've yet to hear a history teacher or politician condemn the religious basis of the violent Crusades. Indeed often those who campaign against this 'violent religion of Islam' also employ the language, images and paraphernalia of the Crusades.[32]

No one faith has had a monopoly on mad, bad behaviour, and no one faith holds exclusive rights in the trade of terrorism, and yet, as Professor John Espsito at Georgetown University put it eloquently:

How come we keep on asking the same question [about violence in Islam] and don't ask the same question about Christianity and Judaism? Jews and Christians have engaged in acts of violence. All of us have the transcendent and the dark side . . . We have our own theology of hate. In mainstream Christianity and Judaism, we tend to be intolerant; we adhere to an exclusivist theology, of us versus them.[33]

Sin number four is a slightly tempered rational position. It's explained like this. I know not all terrorists are Muslims and I know that not all Muslims are terrorists and I know Islam is not uniquely violent, but why is it that Muslims don't condemn terrorists and say 'not in my name'? We've all heard the argument, haven't we? I've heard it from the far right and I've heard it from individuals whom I consider as friends. So let me explain.

Firstly, a terrorist act is bad news, to condemn a terrorist act is good news. Bad news makes good news and good news make no news. I hope you're still with me. So when terrorist thugs go out and commit carnage, it makes news. There is an expectation that Muslims, whether practising or not, of all backgrounds, of all races, from all professions, need to vocally, vociferously and unequivocally condemn the acts. And they do.[34] Indeed, there are community activists and organizations who now maintain lengthy historical records of 'Muslims condemning terrorism' to refute the constant allegation that 'Muslims don't condemn'.[35]

But the question I ask is this: why should they, 'the Muslims', feel obliged to, and why should they be vilified, as French Muslim Yasser Louati was by two CNN broadcasters, if they don't?[36]

Allow me to talk you through the sequence of thoughts for 'the Muslims' when a terrorist act happens anywhere in the western world or where westerners are targets. I specifically say 'western' and 'westerners', because terrorist acts in places like Turkey, Syria, Iraq, Pakistan, are usually of little interest to western media or indeed to us western politicians.[37] They are also of lesser interest to British Muslims, because we know we won't be under any pressure to condemn them as those who are killed are not 'us' westerners. Here's how it goes.

Breaking news – a terrorist act. Bloody hell, I hope it isn't 'the

Muslims'. This thought kicks in even before 'I wonder if any of my family were caught up in it'. If it is Muslims, is it in the West, or are westerners the target? If the answer is yes, then from here on starts the constant flow of Muslims being interviewed on radio and TV and providing quotes for journalists in the print media. Then there are local events, vigils, interfaith outreach initiatives, mosque invites to local communities, trust-building conversations on public transport with non-Muslims, specific conversation with work colleagues, all aimed at a very clear 'not in my name' message. We turn to Twitter, Facebook, Instagram, Snapchat, Tumblr – you name it, it is used to say loudly and clearly 'not in my name'. It's our phrase, special words for Muslims; we all know it, we all say it, we use the phrase so much we own it, we should copyright it. And just in case someone out there doesn't hear it on radio or TV, doesn't see it on the social network and doesn't have a Muslim friend who gives them a personal rendition, we, the Muslims, have even resorted to taking out adverts in national newspapers to get the message out – paying for the privilege of saying 'not in my name'.[38]

And after this huge collective effort two things usually happen. Firstly, some halfwit, usually in a robe and beard, goes on TV and condones or refuses to condemn the terrorist act and in doing so becomes the 'official voice of the Muslims'.[39] In a world made up of *Celebrity Big Brother*, *Love Island* and *Made in Chelsea* stars we shouldn't be surprised that the 'Muslim' wannabe celebrities want their thirty seconds of fame too. Then secondly, some other halfwit with some poncey-sounding organization and posh accent will ask the question, 'Why is it the Muslim community won't condemn these acts?' At which point thousands of British Muslims simultaneously scream at their screens, 'We do.'

So, for ease of reference and for all future references when there will be a terrorist act, and sadly there is likely to be one, I condemn all terrorist acts done in the name of the religion I was born into. Although I have more in common with the good folk of Yorkshire than my co-religionists in Afghanistan, Saudi Arabia or Tunisia, I am still prepared to apologize on behalf of those who put the planes into the twin towers, the bombs on the Underground and the bullets into sunbathers. They act as the criminals they are, with no regard for human life, and do not act on behalf of me or my faith. So once again: 'not in my name'.

Now, having said this, I ask the following question. Why should I or anyone else be held responsible for the actions of my so-called co-religionists? Are Protestants in the UK accountable for the actions of the Ku Klux Klan? Are Christians accountable for the actions of terrorist Scott Roeder, for the Christian Right, for the killing of Dr George Tiller, who was shot in 2009, or for the US-based Army of God, who advocate violence? Did Nick Griffin, Tommy Robinson or for that matter Policy Exchange and the Henry Jackson Society do a tour of the TV studios repeating 'not in my name' after the carnage caused by Anders Breivik? Would we ever demand a statement from Britain's Jews to apologize for the daily acts of violence, even murder, by the settlers in the occupied territories, and would Tony Blair ever write an opinion piece on how as a Christian he is appalled by the ideology that stems from his faith and is the basis of the conduct of the Lord's Resistance Army?

This divisive identity politics is what has led to widespread perse-cution of minorities across the world. British Muslims are not Iran's, Saudi Arabia's or Pakistan's Muslims, they are ours, just as Syria's, Egypt's and Iraq's Christians are not ours, they are rightful citizens of the lands in which Christianity was first born and practised. Those who argue, when discussing refugees, that we should take Christians only are as distasteful as those Muslims who interpret the concept of community or ummah as being an exclusively Muslim place.

Either none of us is responsible for the actions of our co-religionists or all of us are. There cannot be one rule for Muslims and another for the rest of us. There is no greater bond of loyalty between Muslim co-religionists than there is between Christians, Jews, Hindus, Sikhs, Buddhists or indeed any other religion. Brotherhood or indeed sister-hood stems from humanity and plays out in the form of the physical community in which you work, live and play. The concept of 'ummah', in Islam right from its early manifestations, means more than just Muslims. Terrorism is indiscriminate, that's why it terrorizes. No single group is the victim and no single group is the aggressor, and the followers of no single faith are collectively responsible. The argument that 'all Muslims' are responsible is popular on the far right, groups such as the EDL or Britain First, for example. So you can see the irony when Britain First, an organization that Tommy Mair, the convicted killer of Jo Cox, was photographed campaigning with, argued that they should not all be held responsible for the actions of one individual.[40]

Sin number five, an even more sinister version of this argument that 'the Muslims' do not condemn the terrorists, is that 'the Muslims' condone terrorists.

It's an argument that Prime Minister David Cameron felt necessary to make in a speech at a security conference in Bratislava in 2015.[41] The speech was a wide-ranging one that covered the ongoing crisis in Ukraine, the challenge to Europe of refugees and mass migration, European economies, NATO and the threat from terrorism. The threat from ISIS was but one aspect of the speech, and yet the 'catch-phrase' that was written into the speech and specifically briefed to the media was about views on extremism that are 'quietly condoned'.

The *Daily Mail* front-page headline 'UK Muslims Helping Jihadis' reporting this speech was very deliberate.[42] It fed into creating an environment of distrust, one which suggested that the outright con-demnation from British Muslims of ISIS was a lie, that Muslims were being deceptive, that the Muslims couldn't be trusted to inform authorities if they became aware of would-be ISIS jihadists, and the Muslims were secretly pleased with their young being groomed by a terrorist group and lured halfway across the world to sure death. Again the stupidity of the suggestion would be comical if not so dan-gerous. The vision of hundreds of Muslim parents across the country sat cross-legged on the floor with conversations with their kids over pakoras and chai, suggesting that ISIS jihadi fighter was part of a list of career options alongside doctor, lawyer or accountant, makes for a good stand-up sketch. It was not befitting of a serious speech by a prime minister.[43]

Many Muslim parents who in the past would have had the 'sex, drugs and clubs' pre-uni talk with their kids are now having the 'preachers, cults and robes' talk. It is our kids at risk.

This focus by the prime minister on potential 'community compli-city' came just twenty-four hours after the then home secretary, Theresa May, had made a personal plea to wannabe Isis jihadists, saying that, by leaving Britain to join ISIS, 'You will be subjecting yourself and your children to a life of war, famine and hardship. You will be hurting the families who brought you up and the friends who love and care for you,' shows how conflicted the government's policy-making was.[44] The cheap headline once again damaged the government's credibility on counter-terrorism and made the fight against terrorism that little bit harder.[45]

Sin number six is one based on the policy of controlled immigration, an argument by the intellectual Islamophobe based on population growth and its impact on our local culture and environment. It's what some commentators call the Islamization of Europe.

I am a firm believer in controlled immigration. I accept that we must control both our overall population and annual net migration. As well as ensuring that we meet our international obligations under the United Nations Conventions on the Status of Refugees and on Human Rights, we must be pragmatic and firm about migration. As the daughter of an immigrant and a Tory, I have no doubt that Britain must, as it has done in the past, remain open to the skills she needs alongside a firm and controlled immigration policy. Controls should be based on skills, professions, need and not religion. To suggest, as Trump does, that Muslim migration needs to be halted is institutionalized discrimination. To draw no distinction between a British doctor, a Syrian refugee, an Indian tech expert, a Canadian entrepreneur, an Egyptian diplomat, a Pakistani aid worker and an Al Qaeda operative is policy in the world of Trump; in the real world it's simply bigotry.

'Londonistan' was a term coined by DGSE, the French Intelligence Agency in the 1990s, as a way to explain the view that 'the Muslims are coming, they are out of control and attempting to take over'. They thought we in Britain were in denial of the attempt to Islamize Britain through terrorist violence and cultural creep. In retrospect they should have been looking at where France was going wrong with the way it accommodated, or rather didn't accommodate, its own Muslim communities, the way it was running Provincialism Paris. Interestingly, however, the Londonistan view is shared by both Muslim and the non-Muslim extremists. Just as the likes of Pegida and the EDL believe in the theory of the 'Islamization of Britain', so it seems do the bully boys turned terrorists who once made up the now-banned group Al Muhajiroun. The suggestion by the likes of Siddhartha Dhar, a Hindu convert also known as Abu Rumaysah, and now believed to be an IS leader, that they will fly the flag of Islam over Buckingham Palace, Downing Street and even the White House[46] would be comical if not for the current environment within which the debate takes place. How considerate of the excitable wannabe jihadis to keep the seats of power exactly in the same buildings as they are now after their takeover. The delusional, now-convicted extremist Anjum Choudry, of Al Muhajiroun, Islam 4 UK and poppy-burning fame, 'believes that such a takeover is possible'.[47]

Sadly this delusional view that the Muslims are taking over is not the preserve of the ignorant extremist. There is many a political commentator who bills himself as an expert who spouts similar nonsense, the famous Fox News interview with so-called 'terrorism expert' Steve Emmerson about Birmingham being a Muslim city that went viral being a case in point.[48]

But is an 'Islamic takeover' possible? Let's take a look at the facts

At the last census, in 2011, of a total population of 53 million Brits, 2.8 million, or 4.8 per cent, were Muslim. Nearly 60 per cent identified as Christians.[49] And yet in an annual poll by IPSOS MORI conducted since 2013, which asks the question 'Out of every 100 people in Britain how many do you think are Christian? Are Muslim?', Brits have consistently overestimated the number of Muslims in the UK and underestimated the number of Christians by a large margin, offering estimates of 15 to 24 per cent for Muslims and 34 to 39 per cent for Christians.[50]

Could it be the case, though, that the 'Muslims could multiply' so fast that they could take over in the near future? This was an argument made by Anjum Choudhry, to ensure a takeover by 2020.[51] It was also an argument made by Vincent Cooper, a journalist who cites his interests as 'philosophy, maths and economics', who claimed that 'by the year 2050 . . . Britain will be a majority Muslim nation'.[52]

It's an argument roundly rubbished by Channel 4's *Fact Check,* which finds that, while Muslim birth rates are higher, the gap between Muslim birth rates and birth rates among non-Muslim Britons will narrow over time, leaving less of a gap between respective birth rates in the future. So while the British Muslim population will certainly grow in number, they 'wouldn't bet on the British Muslim population *ever* topping 10 per cent, let alone 50 per cent.[53]

This argument of the 'Muslim takeover' moves from stupid to sinister when it seeps into more mainstream discourse, not in the clunky way of the BNP of flags over Buckingham Palace or the Queen in a burqa, but in a more sophisticated notion of the Muslims taking over by stealth, by entryism.

Entryism, the sixth sin of Islamophobia, is not a new concept. It is a term that has been used to describe Trotskyists, Marxists and communists throughout the 1900s and indeed even in modern-day Britain to discuss some aspects of Labour Party membership. Politicians, activists, lobbyists and even farmers have been accused of entryism, the practice of entering organizations and over time from the inside using the levers of power to implement a system more favourable to themselves. The theory is that the entryists engage in a long-term plan in which they work within an organization for decades with the ambition of gaining influence, power and perhaps even control.

It's a term which has been used to describe British Muslims, initially in more subtle tones and recently more overtly.

In July 2007, when I was appointed to the House of Lords and to the shadow cabinet as minister for communities, Conservative Home, a centre-right website run at the time by Iain Duncan-Smith's ex chief of staff Tim Montgomerie reproduced an article written by conservative commentator and Fox News contributor Niles Gardner for the Heritage Foundation which argued that my appointment sent 'the wrong signal at a time when Britain is fighting a global war against Islamic terrorism'. The article referred, amongst other things, to my opposition to the war in Iraq and described my demand of an apology from Blair as an 'extraordinary statement'. After Chilcott my statements are perhaps anything but 'extraordinary'.

The argument that British Muslims take up positions of authority and influence to implement some alternative agenda started as a view favoured by the right-wing press and neo-conservative commentators, but in 2015 became part of government policy. The Counter Extremism Strategy published by the newly elected Conservative government states as one of its aims: 'We will therefore carry out a full review to ensure all institutions are safeguarded from the risk posed by entryism',[54] which the paper defines as the practice 'when extremist individuals, groups and organisations consciously seek to gain positions of influence to better enable them to promote their own extremist agendas'. This policy response was as a result of the so-called Trojan Horse saga, the name given to an investigation into Birmingham schools in 2014 at the time when Michael Gove was secretary of state for education. The investigation was triggered by a 'leaked letter', now widely accepted as a fake or forgery, which purported to be a plot by Muslim terrorists to 'take over' state schools through the appointment of teachers and governors. Birmingham City Council and Ofsted decided to investigate matters, and former Labour cabinet minister Liam Byrne 'patiently tried to get to the bottom of what was going on', but, not content with this, Michael Gove 'put the school in the national headlines' and appointed Peter Clarke, a former senior Met officer and ex-head of Counter Terrorism Command, to head up the investigation.[55] Clarke's job was to investigate and present an analysis of 'evidence of extremist infiltration in . . . schools', the suggestion being that this was a terrorism issue, a police matter, despite Midland Police saying there was no case for them to investigate.[56]

The report duly found no 'evidence of terrorism, radicalisation or violent extremism in the schools of concern in Birmingham', but said that there was 'evidence that there are a number of people, associated with each other and in positions of influence in schools and governing bodies, who espouse, sympathise with or fail to challenge extremist views.'[57]

In a nutshell, a bunch of blokes with pretty misogynistic, conservative and intolerant views had decided they were right and everyone else was wrong, that their vision of the world was going to trump others and through the brown boys network had managed to keep power in the hands of themselves and their mates. I'm sure many a political party, including mine, could be accused of this.

Those with intolerant views should not be responsible for the care of our children. But I disagree with how this incident was used to lead a widespread change to policy, including the placing of the much-discredited and toxic policy of Prevent on a statutory footing.

The handling of the Trojan Horse affair has led to the vague and now much-questioned policy of teaching British values and has had a general chilling effect on the numbers of British Muslims who are prepared to put their head above the parapet and take part in civil society organizations and bodies. Many a successful professional British Muslim who has much to offer their local communities has spoken to me about the fear of 'getting involved' and 'speaking out', including in politics.

Accusations of entryism have been made by politicians, commentators and journalists such as Andrew Gilligan of the *Telegraph*.[58] It's a charge which has been levelled at many activists, campaigners and indeed even elected politicians in Britain who are from the Muslim faith. It's a charge levelled by Donald Trump against Hillary Clinton's adviser Huma Abedin and thankfully roundly condemned even by members of his own party.[59]

It's a charge Andrew Gilligan levelled at me.[60] In the now well-known 'nudge-nudge wink-wink' style of journalism, Gilligan suggested that I facilitated the entry of 'Islamic radicals' at the heart of Westminster, a suggestion that led to the headline 'Colossal Conspiracy in Whitehall as Sayeeda Warsi's Aftermath Assessed' and an accusation that I had 'crammed' my government department with 'the most disgustingly fanatical Islamic zealots who are trying to allow dangerous scum into our country and achieve other uncivilised goals'.[61] It was a charge specifically levelled at me for an initiative I set up to tackle anti-Muslim hatred or Islamophobia.

What, you may ask, was so worrying about such an anti-hate initiative that it led to an accusation of 'entryism'? What was so wrong about convincing government to take hatred and attacks against Muslims seriously? Why would anyone, least of all a government minister, consider doing it clandestinely? Why would it even be seen as negative? And why, in 2010, did I need to make it a priority?

The answer to these questions is rooted in history which I lay out in Appendix 2.

But essentially in 2011 I asked the prime minister to set up a cross-government working group on anti-Muslim hatred as a mirror image to the cross-government working group on anti-Semitism, and after much discussion and argument he agreed.

Choosing the community representatives on this group proved almost impossible. Practically any known activist within the Muslim community was considered by the Conservative members of the Coalition government as beyond the pale. It left me a very small pool of 'Muslim talent' from which to make appointments. It is the setting-up of this group and the appointment of its members that Gilligan cites as 'entryism'. A group set up in response to a real and pressing issue in which government seemed uninterested, which the media, in response to my speech in 2011 'Islamophobia Has Passed the Dinner Table Test', failed to acknowledge existed, which had little parliamentary support, which affected Britain's largest minority was, according to Gilligan, the practice of entryism.

The undertone to charges of entryism are that 'the Muslims' 'have an agenda which is not the same as Britain's agenda, that 'the Muslims' are like the Catholics of bygone years, who were held to be loyal to a papacy overseas, that their loyalty is in question, and that 'the Muslim' politician cannot be trusted. This suggestion of disloyalty is not new: whether it was the Catholics in Britain or Jews on mainland Europe, both have in the past not been 'trusted'. Indeed, specific laws were made to restrict Catholic rights and more recently Jewish rights; 1930s Europe saw laws on overcrowding in schools passed to expel Jewish kids from schools; laws which expelled Jews from the armed forces, the civil service and the judiciary; laws which excluded Jews from working in healthcare, charities and the media; and laws which took away citizenship. The Jews could not be trusted, and in parts of 1930s Europe measures were taken to make sure that they never got their hands on any lever of authority.[62] The Jews of Europe, then, like the Muslims of Europe now,[63] were increasingly seen as fifth columnists, subversive agents, an undermining influence, sabotaging the national solidarity, the enemy within.

This term, 'the enemy within', was originally used in 1930s Spain to describe Franco sympathizers in Madrid during the Spanish Civil War, the side which many English and Irish Catholics both sympathized with and supported. It was a term used by UKIP in the 2015 General Election to describe Muslims, with Nigel Farage arguing there is 'an increasing level of concern because people do see a fifth column living within our country, who hate us and want to kill us',[64] and more recently utilized in the Tory London mayoral election campaign.

So we are in a situation where Muslims who engage with politics or any other British institution are to be viewed as suspicious, and Muslims who don't engage and keep themselves to themselves are to be treated as suspicious for being separatist and disengaged from mainstream society. In polite terms, it's a lose-lose situation or, as Ian Birrell, former adviser and speechwriter to David Cameron and award-winning columnist and foreign correspondent, writes, 'whatever they do, Muslims can't win in our society'.[65]

The 'fifth columnists' theory could be dismissed as the crazy conspiratorial talk of the far right when it comes from the likes of UKIP, but once it starts to receive mainstream traction, then it becomes dangerous, intellectualized bigotry. It should worry us all when the lazy stereotyping of a community is couched in the argument that 'phobia' about Muslims is nothing to do with terrorists or terrorism but simply that Muslims aren't compatible with Britain because 'their' values fundamentally differ from 'ours'; that they are the 'others', an argument most recently made by Trevor Phillips, the ex-chair of the Equalities and Human Rights Commission, in his documentary *What Do British Muslims Really Think?* I dealt with this in detail in chapter 2.

The documentary was yet another step in the 'othering' of British Muslims.

And that brings me to the seventh sin, the seventh form of Islamophobia. We judge 'the Muslims' by a higher standard than we would other fellow Brits. Consider issues such as homophobia, women's rights, the practice of segregation and the recent high-profile cases of grooming of children in northern cities. These are all individually serious issues which are present in most of Britain's communities. And yet they are all issues that have regularly been used as a stick with which to beat 'the Muslims'. The fact that misogyny is not the preserve of Muslim men – indeed I saw it displayed around the top decision-making table in the land in cabinet – and the fact that most crimes of child sex exploitation in Britain are committed by white men, and that revelations in the last few years have exposed politicians, celebrities and highly respected members of the Catholic

Church as paedophiles does not seem to get in the way of some good old-fashioned bigotry.[66]

We are now over a decade on from 7/7, when the debate on 'the Muslim problem' first started to take shape in the UK. As I explored in chapter 4, the analysis of the 'Muslim problem' has changed over the years. It started with the view that a few of 'them' are terrorists and violent extremists because they are inspired by verses from the Qur'an which they pervert in interpretation. Commentators and politicians were keen to stress that the religion of Islam was inherently peaceful. Over time this 'individual perverted interpretation' theory became a 'group perverted interpretation' theory, which was discussed in academic circles as an ideology, Islamism.

Over time the academic term 'Islamism' crept into mainstream use with very little understanding of its history or context or breadth of interpretation. It became a favourite of Tony Blair and subsequently the Conservative Party too. It became so popular that even our friend Tommy Robinson, of ex-EDL fame, started using it following his 2013 'Quilliam, I've seen the light' moment, preferring it over his colleagues' term 'Muslamics'.

But even at this stage in the 'problem-solving journey' the general underlying theory was that some Muslims used Islam as a justification to commit violent acts of terrorism, the key word being violent.

The argument, however, then developed to say that, although only a small number of Muslims were violent and extreme, many more Muslims had views that were non-violent and extreme. This widening of the net of 'the problematic Muslims' was promoted in 2006 by Michael Gove in his book *Celsius 7/7*, where he described this 'non-violent extremism' as the swamp within which extremists feed, and he argued that to deal with the terrorists and the violent extremists we needed to drain the swamp. It's a definition Gove fought for and succeeded in making Conservative policy.[67]

This widening of the definition to non-violent extremism troubles me, and it 'alarms' the independent reviewer of terrorism legislation.[68] It doesn't sufficiently draw a distinction between conservative religious practices, which are present in all faiths, and intolerant views that religious types seek to impose upon others. It fails to appropriately balance our great British commitment to freedom of speech, belief, thought and conscience and security. It fails to focus on non-religion-based extremism. It fails to focus on communities other than 'the Muslims'.

And with increasing counter-terrorism measures targeting not the violent extremists but the broader community, this definition simply feeds, not drains, the swamp.

And finally we've moved on from our concerns about Muslims who are non-violent extremists to 'the Muslims' full stop, who, according to Trevor Phillips and others, simply do not think like 'us' and 'never will'. In other words they, 'the Muslims' are all part of the problem and will always remain so.

This is the dangerous point the debate has now reached. An approach that set out to unite us all against those who want to do 'us' harm through terrorism has become a policy that's pushing Britain's Muslim communities to the fringe. A policy aimed at terrorists has become a policy aimed at Muslims.

Six years on from my first keynote speech on Islamophobia, the only one to date by a national politician, government policy-making on Islamophobia has made little progress. I introduced a section on anti-Muslim hatred alongside anti-Semitism and racism in our annual Human Rights Report in 2012, which, amongst other areas, reports on equality and discrimination issues, and yet in 2015 the sub-section on anti-Muslim hatred didn't appear, despite the ramping-up of anti-Muslim prejudice and hostility in global affairs.[69] There has been little funding for work combating Islamophobia, little political interest in the issue, little enthusiasm to treating it as seriously as anti-Semitism or racism, and all the while, the list of acceptable, intellectualized reasons for why it's OK to dislike the Muslims continues to grow; the media headlines about Muslims are as vitriolic as they are misleading; the kind that would not be used for any other community; political discourse on Muslims is inflammatory; and ordinary lives, especially those of children, are blighted by the daily occurrence that Islamophobia has now become. This situation led to a damning indictment last year in a report from the Council of Europe, which described the situation for Muslims in the UK as an

intolerant political discourse . . . Muslims are portrayed in a negative light by certain politicians and as a result of some policies. Their alleged lack of integration and opposition to 'fundamental British values' is a common theme, adding to a climate of mistrust and fear of Muslims. The counterterrorism strategy, Prevent, may fuel discrimination against Muslims ... Hate speech in some traditional media, particularly tabloid newspapers, continues to be a problem, with biased or ill-founded information disseminated about vulnerable groups, which may contribute to perpetuating stereotypes.[70]

The dislike of all things Muslim is no longer a fringe practice. Nobel prize-winning democracy campaigner Aung San Suu Kyi was caught making Islamophobic comments about award-winning broadcaster Mishal Husain when she assumed she was off air after a BBC radio interview.[71] Nicky Campbell, presenter of *The Big Question*, received a barrage of abuse for a cheeky 'Inshallah' on signing off the show one weekend.[72] Hollywood heartthrob Riz Ahmed of *Bourne* and *Star Wars* fame is still profiled at airports.[73] And even our *Bake-off* heroine Nadiya Hussain has spoken out against the everyday anti-Muslim prejudice she faces.[74]

The fact that as a country we have allowed this scourge of Islamophobia to grow should worry us all.

For over a decade mistakes have been made which have not only made the fight against terrorism harder but also negatively shaped the story of Muslim Britain.

Part two of this book paints a bleak picture of the relationship between Britain and her Muslims. It's this gloomy outlook which leads me to wonder whether the country that both my grandfathers fought for, a country I had the privilege of serving at the highest table in the land, is a country that my grandchildren will call their home.

Part three will outline how things can be different.

PART THREE

Press the Restart Button

7

The Muslims

'In my generation, there was a single girl given the strength and skill to fight the spread of darkness . . . but in your generation, there are nearly two thousand with the powers of the slayer, and not all of them have chosen to use their newfound abilities conscientiously.'

Joss Whedon, Buffy the Vampire Slayer: No Future for You

'Life is change. If you aren't growing and evolving, you're standing still, and the rest of the world is surging ahead.'

Louise Penny, Still Life

Technology and I don't seem to get on very well. Two years into the purchase of our 'new' coffee machine, we still haven't bonded. I love coffee, but the coffee machine doesn't love me. Coffee is one of those Muslim things we can all agree on. The Mohammedan bean, as it's been called because of its Yemeni or Ethiopian origins, depending on the story you believe, is one of those discoveries we are all grateful for.[1] So whether the bean was used as a food of last resort by a man named Sheikh Omar who was living as a recluse in Mocha, Yemen, or discovered by his teacher the Sufi Sheikh Hasan ash-Shadhili, who used it as a means to stay alert and awake to worship, or whether it was the Ethiopian goat herder Kaldi who tried it after his goats seemed on quite a high after eating the little red berries, the bottom line is: thank Allah they did. Today this humble bean has become the world's second-most-traded commodity, sitting smugly between oil and gas, as well as in most kitchen cabinets in Britain. And around the world it is only trumped by water as a drink. In recent years we have taken this traditional bean and mechanized the making of this exotic beverage. Personally, I'd be more comfortable with an old Turkish hand grinder and copper pot over an open fire.

But whether it's the coffee machine, the steam iron splurging out water, the DVD player frozen mid-movie or my iPhone on autopilot randomly calling people as it sits in my handbag, my solution is usually turn off, reset, restart. I'm sure, like me, there are other technophobes out there who do a special prayer for the inventors of the restart button. It's the single stress-free way of starting again when things have clearly gone wrong.

Britain's relationship with its Muslims and the Muslims' relationship with their country are in that frozen, random-calling, overloaded, simply-splurging-out-stuff-it-shouldn't-be phase, and it's time to do things differently. It's time to use the restart button.

As a country, as a society, as policy-makers, as politicians and as a community it's time we started to look at what went wrong and how to start to make it right.

Since the Brexit vote, Britain is sadly an increasingly hostile place.[2] The worrying rise in hate crime has also seen an increase in anti-Muslim hatred,[3] and whilst the easiest reaction from Muslims would be to retreat, now more than ever we, 'the Muslims', need to step up and step out. This is our country, we are an intrinsic part of it and have been so for generations. Its future and ours are as intertwined as our histories. So it's time to take a deep breath, belt up and get ready for a rollercoaster ride. It's time to abandon the twirling teacups mindset of going round and round in circles at a gentle pace and slip into 'Velocity' mode. The amazing bike rollercoaster ride 'Velocity' at the zoo, theme park and children's heaven in the beautiful North Yorkshire countryside known as Flamingo Land, requires you to clench your abs and hold on tight. And just like you wouldn't take a ride on 'Velocity' without first making sure that the kids too young to ride were being looked after, your handbag was put away, your pockets emptied and you are dressed appropriately, it's time in this era of resetting the relationship between Islam and Britain to put the kids first, ditch the extra baggage and make sure our manifestation of faith is fit for purpose.

And just as velocity, accurately defined, is dependent on both speed and direction, so this reset period will only work if we head in the right direction at the right speed. We are going to a destination, an island nation at ease with its Muslims, the Muslims at ease with their homeland, and frankly we are going to have to get there fast. It's time for all of us to get on board bus brand Britain; it's time for us to carve out a very British Islam.

Let me start my conversation with my co-religionists with a very clear statement. What I am about to say has nothing to do with terrorism, as just a minuscule fraction of British Muslims have been engaged in terrorism. We are not terrorists; if we were then the 3 million of us would have killed them and us. What I ask of you is not to counter terrorism. What I ask is whether we are fit for purpose, whether we as a community could be better, and what internal community barriers are holding us back. I know there are those who will use this frank exchange as a stick with which to beat British Muslims. I hope you will see it as a necessary conversation in shaping the British Muslim journey. What I ask of you is whether we are brave and bothered enough to address these barriers. And what I ask is no different from what we should be asking of all responsible Brits.

So let's start by visualizing what British Muslims could be a decade from now. For me it's a confident, successful community which both acknowledges the reality of the challenge we face and is prepared to invest the time, energy, money and patience to overcome them. It's a community that doesn't shy away from the debates, that is proudly patriotic and isn't afraid to say so. A diverse community, a non-sectarian community, a non-judgemental community, an outward-looking community, optimistic about its place both in Britain and the wider world. A community that is prepared to face up to the challenges that lie within and out. A community entirely comfortable in practising its faith in its country, neither fearing life in Britain nor seeking favour in treatment. A community that owns the language of its faith and isn't reacting to the definitions given by others: from 'ummah' to 'jihad', from 'Sharia' to 'fatwa' and others – terms that have become lazy tabloid words and lost positive and visionary centuries-old meanings. A community in line with the great tradition of Islam expressing their faith for these times, their very own British Islamic identity.

And this starts with a single focus on the future, what is right for our children rather than what would be judged right by well-intentioned first-generation members of the community, clergy or indeed family. We need to ask ourselves this: are we preparing our children, in an ever more globalized, interconnected world, to be successful world citizens? Are we making choices for them that will ensure they both matter and belong in Britain? Are we expressing Islam in the words and needs of today's generation or are we locked in a particular world of a bygone era?

We are partly responsible for why our children rejected the pragmatic practice of our parents' generation, instead embracing an uncompromising and often dogmatic belief. Out-of-date cultural practices didn't afford them the freedoms they sought and so they used Islam to negotiate these freedoms. The freedom to study, to travel, to dress as they wished and to marry a partner of their choice were some of the areas where we didn't respond quickly enough, and through their version of Islam, a reactionary expression of identity, many of our young took a short cut. Islam became their uncompromising rights agenda against older generations.

We now need to respond and ask ourselves: is the education we choose for them diverse and outward-facing or limiting? Are we teaching them to learn and love difference or in the name of 'protecting' severing them from mainstream society, restricting their knowledge and encouraging division? And are we embracing the diversity of opinion, the Islamic way, so oft quoted as a blessing within Muslim communities?[4]

I am a strong advocate of knowing your roots, both cultural and religious. I've encouraged my children to learn the language of their grandparents, their grandmother tongue, as well as Arabic, the language of their faith. To appreciate Islamic and South Asian art, music and fashion as much as British. To tune their ears to Qawalli as much as Kanye West, to Nasheeds as much as Naughty Boy, feel as comfortable in their shirwanis as they do in their snapbacks and appreciate Muhammad Iqbal's 'Shikwa' and 'Jawab-e-Shikwa' as much as Shakespeare. To understand values rooted deep in the societies where their great grandparents set off from, neither dismissing their heritage nor rejecting their home.

For me, for them, for us, it is thankfully in Britain not an either-or binary choice; multiculturalism is the very essence of being able to adopt many identities and combine them in ever-creative ways. And those within British Muslim communities who suggest that this isn't possible are as bigoted as the advocates of the question 'Are you Muslim first or British first?'

Identities are complex and multi-faceted and in many ways much harder for our children than they were for us. Our line to the outside world was a family phone in the hallway or a long-awaited letter from a pen friend, where no call was a private call and no correspondence a private encounter. Our children connect to the whole world through their mobile, where multiple private spaces to socialize exist which, however hard we as parents try to understand, we will never be IT savvy enough to find. We cannot disconnect them from what we define as 'the bad, immoral world out there' but we can give them the skills of reason.

I am still shocked to find the occasional home where there is no TV, music or other form of entertainment. And whilst these parents feel good at having created what they believe to be a pure 'Islamic environment', their children simply access entertainment, music – possibly even porn and ISIS websites – through their mobile devices. So we must ask ourselves: are we teaching our children the skills of reason and are we training them in the art of reconciling revelation and religion with reason? It is the Islamic way.

I believe that those of us who reject the above will sadly eventually lose our children. Islam cannot exist, and historically has not existed, as an uncomfortable alien in the environment in which it lives. Even the most conservative and orthodox practice of the faith flourishes only because of the ultra-conservative environment in which it dwells – Saudi Arabia and Wahhabism is one such example. But what may be natural 'over there' in their culture is not necessarily right for us 'over here' in our culture. In Britain it's time for all of us, Muslims and others, to move from simply tolerating to accepting and understanding others' religions, cultures and lifestyle choices. We no longer have the luxury of isolationism. And even if we did, I believe it simply is not the Islamic way.

It's time to understand Islamic history in all its complexities, good and bad, and not resort to simple narratives rooted in an unquestioned history. It's time to end sectarianism, caste discrimination, tribe discrimination, racism and sexism and accept that believers of all religions believe they are the chosen ones, but that is simply a belief not a fact. To suggest, as some British Muslims do, that they are the chosen ones amongst religions, then chosen amongst sects, then chosen amongst practices and rules and then the favoured mosque in their city, town, street is an astonishing, small-minded, inward-looking practice of a global faith. We should practise what we practise and preach our version of the faith but we must stop preaching hate against another version of our faith or indeed any other faith.

It's time to view sectarianism and caste and clan discrimination as equally socially unacceptable as racism and Islamophobia. If we don't like it dished to us, then stop dishing it out to others. If it upsets us to be vilified simply for being Muslim, it's hypocrisy to vilify other Muslims for simply not being our kind of Muslim.

It's time to stop bringing tribal and territorial battles from across the globe to these shores. We need to get over partition, stop reliving the 1971 Pakistani civil war, the rivalries between Ethiopians and Somalis or Iraqis, Turks and Kurds. If you really want to fight, set up football clubs and play the ball not the man. There's enough of a challenge in simply being British and Muslim right now without reliving battles of the past or importing battles from afar.

Sectarianism is one of the most rapidly growing internal challenges facing British Muslims. I had the privilege of a diverse and plural religious upbringing. I didn't realize how diverse until years later when I discovered how many Muslims simply had not. I was into my late teens, indeed at the time of my first marriage, before I became fully aware of the meaning of difference within faiths. It was February 1991, and I was marrying my first cousin, my maternal uncle's son, who had arrived from Pakistan a few days earlier. We were not legally married until May that year, and the formal ceremony and celebration didn't take place until July, but in Islamic terms I was now married.

My parents had opted for a local Sunni imam affiliated to the local Barelwi mosque to perform the nikkah, the Islamic marriage. The imam followed the Sunni Hanafi school of jurisprudence in the form and footsteps of Ahmed Raza Khan, a scholar from the north Indian town of Bareilly, the town from which the term Barelwi derives. The nikkah ceremony was simple and quick. It was performed in exactly the same way as it would have been in the village in Pakistan where my parents originated from. They tried to replicate the kind of imam they would have turned to in the village, the language used was as it would have been there, and in many ways the chosen groom was possibly the one that would have been chosen had we never left the Punjab. The ceremony felt wrong on many levels.

Many years later, when I married my second husband, Iftikhar, the ceremony had two important differences: it was conducted in English and it felt right.

It surprised me that in 1991 none of my religious teachers from the local mosques where my sisters and I had received our Islamic education had been asked to perform the nikkah. And it was whilst the discussion of the 'preferred imam' was happening that I became aware of difference within Islamic practice.

Probably not unlike many young people, I grew up knowing there were different religions, but it didn't occur to be that there were quite pronounced differences within religions. As a child, as far as I was concerned, all Christians were the same, and all Muslims were the same. The only difference was religiosity. Some practised more than others. But in fact, there are numerous differences in Islam, from how one prays, to which practices are prioritized, to what is considered 'mandatory' in clothing, worship and prayer. This plurality of practice should be seen as a positive; instead, for sections of the British Muslim community, it has become a source of division, rivalry and deep-rooted animosity.

My parents both come from predominantly Sunni backgrounds, although both sides of the family have members of the family who are staunchly Shia. They grew up mainly in the practice of Sunni Islam from a Hanafi school of thought, loosely Barelwi, a practice which has its origins in India in the 1800s. Sufiism too was a strong influence through an association with the followers of Haji Waris Ali Shah, a Sufi saint (1817–1905), who preached love, tolerance and non-discrimination and was learned and well-travelled, reportedly having an audience with Queen Victoria on a visit to the United

Kingdom.[5] Warsi is the name his followers adopt as a surname. My mum's brother did so, as did his son, my ex-husband, and it's how I first got my surname, which has stuck.

On a visit to Pakistan in my mid-twenties I visited the local shrine of the Warsi followers, which was presided over by a scholarly gentle man whom we simply referred to as Bawa jee. It's where I took 'bayat', a practice popular in Sufi Islam. Bayat can be interpreted in many ways: it can be seen as a commitment to the teachings of Islam, or an oath of allegiance, or an acknowledgement of a relationship of guidance. I simply went through the motions because my ex-husband's family expected it of me. I found the practice of touching the cloth on the shrine, bowing and taking 'bayat' at the hands of Bawa jee uncomfortable. I think Bawa jee did too. It was a ritualistic norm expected in rural Punjab, and he appeared to tolerate it. But what Bawa jee appeared to thrive on was deep spirituality and firm faith. What impressed me about him then and on subsequent lengthier meetings I had with him on a visit to the UK was his knowledge, humour, tolerance, desire to question and be questioned and his flock of followers, which included Muslims from all walks of life, but Hindus and Sikhs too. I never took to the blind hero worship of some of his followers but I greatly admired him for his vision.

It's an experience I recalled in 2010 when I was appointed a privy councillor. Meeting Her Majesty the Queen, taking her hand to swear my oath of allegiance as a cabinet minister, kneeling and 'kissing' her hands in line with tradition felt like I'd taken 'bayat' from the monarch.

But the theatre of religion which as a child stuck in my mind the most was Ashura during my first visit to Pakistan in 1979. Ashura, the tenth day of the month of Muharram in the Islamic calendar, the month of Remembrance and mourning because of the loss of many members of the Prophet's family who were killed during a civil war, is observed mostly by Shia Muslims but also some Sunni Muslims. My father's sisters had strong connections with the local Shia communities. The deep respect and reverence that the local community felt for the Sayeds, the descendants of the Prophet, was apparent. No major event would take place at my paternal grandmother's home without the Shia Sayeds present. Indeed, my mother named me after the daughter of the local Shia Sayed family; she says she loved the way Sayeeda was pronounced.

So during Muharram for days we would travel in the evening to a place called Samote, about twenty minutes' walking distance from my parents' village. It was a village built on small hills and valleys, which gave it a mystical feel, as did the smoke from the cooking, the speeches and chanting, the baby cradle that depicted the tragic death of baby Ali al-Asghar, the youngest son of Husayn. Husayn was the son of Ali and Fatima, the daughter and son-in-law of the Prophet Muhammad. The symbolism of the large silver hand, which depicted the amputation of Abbas, the son of Ali, and the hand of Fatima and the self-flagellation, created a heady, almost carnival-like atmosphere that was exhilarating. And food never tasted so good.

Both experiences, the bayat and Ashura, would have been seen as completely unacceptable by the religious teachers who taught my sisters and me in Savile Town.

My parents were always clear that there were many ways to practise Islam. I know how over the years they have specifically condemned sectarianism. My parents have commented at Deobandi indifference towards celebrating the lives of the Prophet and his family and despaired at Barelwi cursing of Wahhabis.[6] I've experienced both aggressive Wahhabi sectarianism against other Sunnis and anti-Wahhabi sectarianism by Sunnis. A very respected and enlightened Sunni Barelwi friend of mine recently said that he'd rather his son became a sharabi (an alcoholic) than a Wahhabi.

Personally I've found the intolerance amongst some Sunnis towards Shias the most surprising because of my own upbringing, and the most worrying because of the strength of feeling. We must collectively change it.

The practical consequences of sectarianism are playing out in our daily lives – British Muslims celebrating Eid on two sometimes even three different days is one example.

The fixing of the date for 'Eid' caused me much excitement as a child. The Islamic calendar, and thus Eid, is based on the lunar calendar. Eid is determined by a moon sighting, and in the days before Sky TV, which now enables us to access news channels from Pakistan, the Middle East and Africa, which give out 'moon sightings', Eid would be announced at the mosque. As women were not allowed in the mosque, we would pester Dad to go and 'find out' about Eid.

Today, despite advances in science and astronomy, most schools of Islamic thought in the UK still do actual 'moon sightings'. This has for years caused both uncertainty and division within Muslim communities in Britain. Scholars continue to disagree on the method and rules for moon sightings, with some insisting that the moon sighting must be with the 'naked eye', which in the UK, with its unpredictable weather, is rarely possible. Other scholars insist that the sighting should be in a 'Muslim country'. Many disagree on 'which' Muslim country; Saudi Arabia, Morocco and Pakistan are the front runners for most British Muslims, but some simply revert to their countries of heritage and others just follow the whim of the chairman of their local mosque. Family members have been known to celebrate Eid on different days because mosques have disagreed on moon sightings. As a family we follow Islam's holiest sites: when it's Eid in Mecca and Medina, it's Eid in our homes.

These 'multiple Eid' dates are an outdated, embarrassing and impractical feature of British Islam. It perplexes schools and employers and divides families. It is time for us British Muslims to insist on agreed, scientifically supported, lunar dates and hold our scholars to that date. So many of us are tired of trying to explain why we don't know when it's Eid. In government I had terse exchanges with my then chief whip, who insisted I gave a firm commitment to attend the House of Lords to take part in a debate. But I thought it might fall on Eid. It's the one day I have marked as sacred family time. Having a firm date would ensure it remains that way for British Muslim families for generations. Not getting our act together on this will see many of us celebrating Eid without our children, our siblings and our friends because we don't all have the luxury of flexibility when taking time off.

But most worrying is the political dimension to this sectarianism. Politics has traditionally engaged the British Muslim community via the Labour Party. Most first-generation South Asian Muslims came to the UK as migrant manual labourers, and their first contact with politics came via the trade union movement. The Conservative Party's both perceived and apparent hostility to these newly arrived foreigners further pushed the community towards developing a lifelong affiliation with the Labour Party, something which the Conservative Party has still not managed to penetrate in any significant way.

And although the first councillor from the Muslim faith was elected even before I was born in 1970,[7] it wasn't until the demonstrations following the publication of Salman Rushdie's *Satanic Verses* in the late 1980s that the Muslim community started to emerge as a visible and opinionated block. Thereafter started the long journey of engagement between the British Muslim communities and successive governments which meandered from leader to leader, group to group and eventually sect to sect. All these forms of engagement had their shortcomings, as I will discuss, but none did as much damage as the sectarian approach to engagement adopted by government from about 2005 and the sectarianism that British Muslim communities employed to become the government's favoured 'Muslims' and diminish the space for other sects – other 'Muslims'. The battle of British Muslims to become the 'right kind' of Muslims in today's Britain should have been and needs to be based on tolerance and conduct, not theology and sect. And yet this is exactly what both the Muslim communities and government did. Sect squared up to sect, Wahhabis against Barelwis, Sufis against Deobandis, and Tabliqis against Shias. With a seat at the table and funding from government at stake, Britain took sectarianism to new heights. It allowed British Muslims to play out their own historic sectarianism against the backdrop of the war on terror with the added dimension of groups being paid through the public purse to further their version of the faith. The war on terror became a convenient vehicle for those with sectarian views to jump on the bandwagon and then use it to drive others off the road.

More recently the Arab uprising, the isolation and then thawing of the relationship with Iran, the making and then breaking of relations with post-revolution Morsi Egypt and ever closer, economically necessitated relationships with Saudi Arabia and the UAE mean this micro community sectarianism has played out on the world stage.

Government's mistakes in this area I will cover in the next chapter, but the point for British Muslims is that sectarianism is now a real issue, and there are no winners.

I was brought up in a wonderfully plural way of practice. The ease with which my parents transcended these differences and this constant conflict in our religious learning I believe left my sisters and me both sure-footed in our belief and confident and unconflicted in our religious identity.

My sisters and I have all taken our own very individual journeys in faith, at times deeply religious and overtly practised, and at other times less so, much like most people of faith, finding and refinding religion at different stages in our lives. Three of the five of us pray at least thrice a day, two at least once a week. Four of the five have worn a hijab – the headscarf – at some point, and two continue to do so intermittently. And I have even worn a chador with a partial face veil during my time driving and working in the rural areas of Pakistan in 2002. And like many others found it an immensely empowering moment. It freed me in Pakistan from censure or scrutiny and allowed me to take control of and determine an environment which was male-dominated and male-determined. I believed it was the right garment for that place at that time.

Our home town, Dewsbury, where we were all raised, is both the European headquarters of the Tablighi Jamaat and the headquarters of its Barelwi missionary equivalent Dawat-e-Islami and has a strong Ahl-e-Hadith presence. Conservative Islam is widely practised. The landscape is peppered with minarets, and women in full burqa are a common feature.

My formal religious education was in a Deobandi mosque with a strong Tabliqi Jammat presence. It was a politically disengaged community, one that felt that the Almighty would right wrongs, and pacifism was the best approach and that personal worship and self-evaluation were the most important aspects of Islam even at the expense of family responsibility. Many younger followers found this constant turning of the other cheek in the face of persecution and discrimination stifling and found Salafi and Wahhabi political ideas more attractive and relevant to their lives. The harsher, more political and aggressive positioning was for some more attractive.

Years of 'living' as a Muslim amongst many sects and years of involvement in policy-making in this area have convinced me of this: that no one sect is more likely than another to churn out an extremist or a terrorist; that bigotry and intolerance exists in all sects of Islam, as they do in all sects of all religions; and that political inactivism justified as a faith practice can be as much a driver of radicalization as political activism as the basis of faith. And it's a fact that Dewsbury and its religious institutions are as likely to produce a cabinet minister as they are a suicide bomber.

Broad and plural Islamic upbringings, an accepting of 'the other', the understanding of 'many ways' to worship allow one not just to tolerate but to understand and accept 'the other'. It leads to an open mind, an outward-facing attitude and a rooted sense of identity. It's an approach today lacking in many of Britain's Muslim communities, but one we must embrace and champion. It's time to stop playing the games of division, separation and oneupmanship. It's time to stop manipulating and being manipulated by policy-making to further a version of a broad and diverse faith and accept that even within families there can be differences in practice and approach. Not to judge but experience, not to reject but embrace, and not to condemn but celebrate this burst of difference within Islam.

Because an acceptance of the 'other' type of Muslim is the start of accepting many an 'other', whether that is race, religion, gender or sexuality. We must move from hatred and rejection to acceptance and hopefully even celebration of diversity.

Now let me turn to something I've fought for all my life. The equal value of women in Muslim communities. As a woman, as one of five girls, I declare an interest as I set out my demand to have equality of opportunity and equality of worth: there's something in it for me. For me, Islam is the faith that gave women a separate legal and economic identity, not simply as chattels of their fathers and husbands as they were in Britain until the 1800s. Women in Islam right from its inception played a major part in forming the faith, playing an equal role in business, in trade, in politics, as jurists, academics, scholars, physicians and even in battle.[8]

We have some fantastic female Muslim role models in Britain: Mishal Husain at the BBC, the nation's beloved Nadiya Hussain, the teen campaigner Malala Yousafzai, members of the Lords and Commons, women in finance and banking and even a deputy governor at the Bank of England, singers and rappers, athletes and artists, policewomen and members of our armed forces, medics and lawyers, teachers and the unsung volunteers in our communities. And across the world six Muslim women last year made it on to the Forbes World's 100 Most Powerful Women list.[9] But despite this success there are still women in British Muslim communities today who do not have access to higher education and employment. We still fail to reinterpret the great roles Muslim women historically enjoyed in the context of Muslim women in Britain in 2017.

And here's the interesting part: if, Muslim women do well, the whole community does well, and if the community does well, the country does well, and if . . . you get the picture. It seems obvious and simplistic, and for Muslims it should be, that these are teachings that have been part of Islam for over 1,400 years. British Muslims will all be familiar with the teaching 'educate a man, you educate an individual; educate a woman, you educate a family'. The multiplier from investing in a woman is far greater, so why do we continually fail to put money in our best stock? Why are women still being denied rights today that their religion gave them in the sixth century? So, my dear fellow British Muslims, start by celebrating the birth of a girl as you would a boy, invest in girls as much as your boys, give girls the same life opportunities as boys, value girls' contributions, opinions and rights as much as you do the boys, and most importantly learn to genuinely respect women – not the archaic, patriarchal 'we respect them by protecting them by hiding them away' respect, but the respect you demand for yourself, by seeing them as equals. And women, too, who subjugate and hold back other women and elevate their boys as little demigods need to stop. If we genuinely believe in equality we need to bring our boys up to respect women – not just their mums, all women.

Archaic practices which have no basis in Islam, from the forced marriage, curtailment of choice in marriage, control of women in the name of honour, the killing of women in the name of honour, the mutilation of women's bodies in the name of culture to the lack of worth and respect for women, must stop. One such case is one too much. We must challenge not just the practice but also the underlying misogyny which feeds such practices.

I believe it was this misogyny and lack of respect for women in the world of some men that led to the dehumanizing of young girls who were sexually groomed and abused during the high-profile child sexual exploitation cases of recent years. The men involved thought women were second-class citizens and white girls third-class. They thought children who were prepared to exchange sex for money, takeaways and taxi rides were consenting. They couldn't fathom that adults having sex with children wasn't OK, and no amount of family background, social services neglect, alcohol and drug abuse absolved them of their responsibility as adults. For me these cases have been sources of deep shame, but I have also witnessed real courage by British Muslims. I was ashamed that so-called 'respectable' members of the community who were lecturing their 'own women' about the bad, morally decadent western culture were themselves so devoid of any moral values but heartened at the way group after group, activists and professionals, took on the challenge, condemned the behaviour, firmly planted the shame on the perpetrators and reached out to victims. We need to do more of this reaching out.[11]

Misogyny isn't just the preserve of a section or a sect or a specific ethnic community. As in broader society it is widespread. Culture, tradition and religion are often misused to justify bad male – and it's most often male – behaviour. It's as repulsive as French mayors and presidential hopefuls grasping at secularism to justify treating women badly on the beach by demanding they remove their burkinis[10] and US President Trump hiding behind 'celebrity' status to justify groping women.[12]

Islam was a religion that championed gender equality and equal worth, and yet so often it appears to have lost its way. Let me give some British Muslim examples: the ill treatment of women in matrimonial matters, unregistered marriages, multiple marriages and financial, emotional and sexual abuse within marriages are a regular feature. Women who turn to Sharia councils, an alternative dispute resolution forum for some Muslims, for redress often face years of misery.

The government is currently conducting a review of these Sharia councils.[13]

Sharia council casework is mainly made up of couples who have no legally recognized marriage and thus no recourse to English civil courts. There is a role for government, and I will address that in the next chapter, but the community has to lead the way.

Marriage is a very public statement about the recognition of a relationship. It is in Islam a legally binding contract, and yet time after time Muslim marriages are conducted in a way that ensures the opposite, that is for them to carry no legal status. Used by young people to bypass proscriptions against sex, and by men – and it is mainly men – to 'test' a union without legal consequences, it has become the basis of much heartache and abuse. A religious marriage should be a legal marriage. That is not currently the case in the UK, and until the law of the land catches up with reality and recognizes it as such, we, the British Muslims, should ensure that the legal ceremony takes place either immediately before the religious one or at the same time. It's what our grandparents and parents did in this country for years. Why is it no longer good enough for our kids? Couples should have to be legally married to religiously marry. It is the Islamic way.

And then there is the practice of polygamy, a practice for which the conditions, many well-respected scholars believe, simply do not exist in the present-day UK.[14] It must stop. It causes much emotional and physical trauma; rarely are 'all parties' in agreement or indeed even aware, and it's simply supposedly religiously sanctioned 'having your cake and eating it'. Now before those in polygamous marriages get terribly excited and argue, as you do when I meet you, that it's better than the 'morally corrupt West', where people have a legal partner and then multiple affairs, and that multiple marriages are a better way forward, I say 'they' don't justify their indiscretions as a religious practice. I have spoken to many, many individuals, men and women, who are in polygamous marriages, and I've yet to meet a happy three-, four- or fivesome. The union is usually a convenient way not to pay the first wife what she is due as part of a divorce settlement, or to keep the first wife in place as a housekeeper for the parents, or simply to keep control over the kids and finances. If you disagree with me, please feel free to go on *BBC News* with all parties to the 'arrangement' and argue your case. I expect you will quickly discover you'd all be better suited to an appearance on *The Jeremy Kyle Show*.

And then there is divorce. Women in twenty-first-century Britain should not be held hostage in a broken marriage, we should not allow men to use it as a bargaining chip to get a favourable settlement on finance or children. It's an issue faced by both Muslim and Jewish women, and one which English law tried to alleviate in the Divorce (Religious Marriages) Act, 2002. It has proved helpful in 'releasing' some Jewish women from broken marriages but due to its limited application many Jewish women still remain tied to former partners, husbands who under Jewish law (Halaka) hold the power to grant a get (Jewish divorce).[15] It's an issue which for the sake of women in both communities needs revisiting.

The Muslim Women's Network published a comprehensive report last year dealing with some of these challenges; the Muslims and government would be well advised to engage with its recommendations.[16]

And to those who might argue that these 'rights' I demand for women are alien 'western rights' and out of step with Islam, you know little of your faith. This fightback is being led by brave Muslim women across the world.[17]

If we genuinely believe in equality, then that should be extended to all in our country. Muslim women deserve the same rights and protections as other women, and sadly both the government and the community are currently failing them.

While I'm talking about an equalities framework, let me touch upon gay rights. I've had many a discussion on gay rights with religious scholars from different faiths, including senior Muslim scholars. The debate between scripture and modern-day equalities legislation has been a fraught one for all faiths, and amongst Muslims the discussions have been broad, including the many interpretations of what was proscribed and the 'punishments' ordained.[18] But as someone who is deeply entrenched in Muslim communities socially, politically and in the past legally, I am absolutely sure that there are greater challenges facing us than what two men or women may be doing in a consenting relationship. And I'm convinced that the moral police and religious preachers could be kept busy for years trying to deal with the child abuse, paedophilia, incest, child sexual exploitation, marital rape and other non-consensual and abusive sex, which, like every other community, plagues British Muslims too.

Of course, abusive practices exist in all communities. It is a fact that most child abusers and paedophiles are white men.[19] But it is also a fact that 'the Muslim community' in Britain is not devoid of them.[20] I've dealt with such in my role as a solicitor. I have a GP friend who can tell many a tragic story of what passes through her practice in the heart of a large Muslim community. So let's sort out the harm that really matters, let's be outraged and let's preach about what's going on under our noses rather than attempt to pull back the curtains and reach into the private life of a homosexual couple.

Rights for minorities should be universal, whatever the race, religion, sexuality or other characteristics. As someone who prides herself on championing minority rights, I'm ashamed I chose which minorities mattered enough for me to champion. I'm not asking people to rewrite religious texts, I'm asking everyone to treat others as we would wish to be treated ourselves. Let compassion and understanding be what we reach for rather than condemnation and persecution.

Returning to 'Velocity', my rollercoaster ride, my mum, who has never been on a rollercoaster, always served as the scarf and jacket monitor as we queued to ride. My mum is someone who has spent a lifetime advocating modesty of dress – no bums, tums, cleavage, underarms, thighs on display. Skirts must be below the knees, necklines high, sleeves demure and no midriff ever. I've pretty much followed her rules most of the time, and her nagging voice in my ear has likely saved me from many a wardrobe faux pas on TV and at the dispatch box.

And yet she is no fan of the burqa, something neither she nor any of her six sisters born and raised in Pakistan wear, nor does she have any patience for the hijab/tight t-shirt/skinny jeans combo. And neither do I. As a feminist I will always defend a women's right to wear what she wants, as a Brit I will champion individual liberty, but as a Muslim I increasingly find myself questioning whether the burqa is the best manifestation of British Islam. It's an expression of identity I sincerely want to see the British Muslim community lead in bringing to an end. Mum is an advocate of modesty rather than prescriptive of what form it should take. And in her world the appropriate outfit for a rollercoaster ride is one that is not going to hinder the experience, has been risk-assessed and is fit for purpose.

Tests not out of place when assessing our religious leaders, campaigning groups and community representatives. Do they hinder, have they been risk-assessed and are they fit for purpose? Do they genuinely understand and represent the concerns of the communities they seek to speak for? Do our scholars have the understanding, language and skill set to respond to the needs of British Muslim youth of today? Are the so-called community leaders even aware of what the challenges are?

My experience is that we have a large group of well-intentioned but sadly not very competent community activists, a smaller group who are very competent but of dubious motivation and intent and a third even smaller group, often scholars, who are fit for purpose and engaged in pioneering and much-needed work. However, this is part of the journey. Other communities have been here too. And even today, when the British Jewish community is both well-resourced, well-informed, well-organized and well-intentioned, it is still accused by its own of not speaking for the community.[21]

The difference with us Muslims is that we don't have the luxury of not understanding, getting it wrong and not delivering. We don't have the time to keep failing. Today we desperately need Islamic teaching which gives not just answers but the tools and skill set to ask the questions, the ability to listen and an open and critical mind. We must stop interpreting Islam as a loyalty card that guarantees 'free' rewards as you accumulate stamps and points. We must stop the blind following of literalist sermons, and treating Islam as a series of calculations with only one right answer. It's not about symbols, dogma and straitjackets, it's about spirit, soul and submission to the will of God through values and practice. It is an attractive faith, and we must practise it as such.

And with an attractive faith must come attractive places of faith. Mosques need to become welcoming places, somewhere you would turn to at both times of distress and joy, they need to be open to women, accessible by the disabled and prepared to provide appropriate scarfs, gowns and hats in the event of someone turning up unprepared. All things I've experienced in mosques around the world. They need to be clean and tasteful and in tune with the local environment. They should strive to be eco-friendly, non-Muslim-friendly and welcoming to the poor and vulnerable. They should serve as hubs of community activity, as places of great debate and discussion and an integral part of their towns and cities. And they should be beautiful. I would love to see a quintessentially English mosque, with an old cobbled central courtyard, with on-site beehives, as they have at the East London mosque, a community vegetable garden, wifi, facilities for hot desking, a world food café, a well-stocked library and its own personal app and maybe even snapchat geo filter. And although it can, it doesn't have to have a minaret, as the purpose of the minaret as a vantage point for the call to prayer is not relevant to British Muslims.[22] It's time for mosque committees to genuinely reflect their communities. They need to appoint the brightest and the best to manage the mosque. Nepotism, clan and caste politics and financial self-interest have to be challenged. The young should be invited, encouraged and persuaded to take roles, not shut out and be forced to mount coups and takeovers.

I recently met a chairman of a mosque committee who proudly told me he'd been chairman for over thirty years. He was rather taken aback when I expressed my horror. Professor Tariq Ramadan is quoting an Islamic teaching when he says that 'Anyone who appoints to a position an individual from a community where there is someone else more competent betrays GOD.'[23] Let's follow that teaching and ensure our scholars and religious leaders are the best amongst us. We can start by ensuring scholars and religious leaders speak the common language of most British Muslims, English. Let's ensure that they understand that they are going to serve and preach in cities like Manchester, not Medina. They must be familiar with historical Islamic periods when Islam flourished both as a minority faith and as part of a multi-religious, multicultural environment. They have to be brave and be prepared to reason and rationalize the practice of the faith within the broadest parameters allowed by religious texts. From the privileged conversations I've had with scholars both in the UK and from across the world, who have provided important guidance and support to me in the writing of this book, I'm convinced that's pretty broad.

They must become approachable counsellors, articulate spokespeople, community champions and respected reformers. We must reject the era of sycophantic personality worship, the misplaced loyalty to imams from overseas and the underpaid, overworked maulvi who has to rely on state benefits to make ends meet. Most of us pay more per month for our Sky entertainment package than we do for the religious education for our children. This needs to change.

This work must be led by the community. The Mosques and Imams National Advisory Board (MINAB), a body that came about following a post-7/7 recommendation, was a good start, but lack of government engagement and funding has rendered it pretty much ineffective. Muslim communities need to reinvigorate it, and the government needs to bring it in from the cold. We need community-led organizations to assist mosques to strengthen governance, confront safeguarding issues and support them at times of difficulty, particularly when mosques are being threatened by hostile takeovers. A programme I was involved in while working with the Muslim Charities Forum might provide a template, even though the project became yet another victim of the policy of disengagement.[24]

Activists and community organizations need to do Islam rather than simply be Muslim. Too often people talk faith rather than do faith. And that means fighting for the rights of others as much as our rights. That in turn involves being part of a broader coalition of those who fight for equality, part of the wider civil rights movement and a member of the family who speak against injustice wherever it arises. It also means being at the forefront of social action, an inherent part of Islamic belief.[25] From rubbish picks to befriending the elderly, from helping the homeless to feeding the destitute, Muslims need to be there, doing what our faith teaches.[26] And in doing so let's follow the teachings of the Prophet of Islam, who didn't differentiate on race or religion when working to benefit humankind. So not just doing more but doing more for 'others'.

Practising Muslims are the most generous charitable givers, obliged by faith to give zakat, 2.5 per cent, of disposable income to charity, with most giving generously over and above this basic obligation.[27] Zakat is but one way in a list of many, including sadaqah, lillah, waqf, kaffarah, qardh hasan and others; Islam is a faith rooted in generosity evidenced in the array of ways to 'give back'.[28]

British Muslims have traditionally supported causes in their countries of heritage, and it's easy to see why. The levels of poverty, destitution and vulnerability in South Asia or Africa are far worse than most of us could imagine. But sadly in recent years the need in local communities can be just as acute. From the lonely elderly to the mistreated child, from the homeless to the hungry, it's time for

Muslims to take their responsibilities to their local communities seriously. It's time for local zakat investment. This has already started with the National Zakat Foundation, which is a campaign to keep zakat local and support the most vulnerable here in the UK, and organizations such as the Al Mizan Trust and the Muslim Charities Forum.

The most visible example of this approach was when Muslims – beards, caps and all – rolled up their sleeves over Christmas 2015 and aided their fellow Brits to deal with the devastating aftermath of the floods. The images on Sky News of 'the Muslims' in places like rural Cumbria and quaint York just getting on with helping families who had never met 'the Muslims' before was Islam at work. As in the 'Snow Patrol' of the year before,[29] individual British Muslims spoke without saying a word for British Muslims and did so well.

And this brings me to the most vexed question of recent times: who speaks for British Muslims? And right now this needs to be addressed more urgently than ever. It's an issue over which I clashed with Charles Moore, former editor of the *Telegraph*, on *Question Time* in 2009. Moore appeared to suggest Muslims' views were those as represented by 'the Muslim Council of Britain, which is the umbrella organization for all Muslim groups in this country'. To suggest that 'the Muslims' are some unique group who have a single view was, to me, patronizing and displayed a lack of understanding on Moore's part.

So who does represent British Muslims? And why does it matter? I've sketched the history and the landscape of British Muslim community groups and organizations in Appendix 1. As the appendix details, the plethora of groups and individuals who are or have been part of this 'Muslim industry', that profess to have the solution, the golden bullet which will fix the 'Muslim problem', is vast. Some have long histories and pedigrees, some are highly professional, some have grassroots support and others simply slick PR machines. But what they all have in common is that none of them alone can speak for Muslims. None of them alone can advise the policy-makers and none of them alone can respond to the diverse range of views, needs and challenges of Britain's Muslim communities.

What is needed is a focus amongst groups on the issues and not on each other and a sense that there is space for everyone. This is ever-more important as we try to protect our children from the poison that is terrorism.

We must let a thousand flowers bloom. There will never be a single voice for a super-diverse community of 3 million. No one group or individual or group speaks for British Muslims, as is the case with other minority communities, and both community and government must come to terms with this. Britain's Jewish community numbered 263,346 in the 2011 census (compared with 3 million Muslims), and yet they too do not coalesce around a single group. They have, however, somewhat succeeded in bringing together representatives from their main bodies to engage annually with government. It's something I would urge British Muslims to do too.

So, my dear co-religionists, let many voices speak and remember also to speak to each other. Challenge each other in the spirit of learning, jostle for space to be heard, not to silence the other, and if as community groups, activists and organizations you feel inspired to fight each other, do so on the battlefield of ideas not for pole position at the government funding trough. We must encourage and employ the brightest and best in roles where they 'speak for Muslims', men and women whom we headhunt into the 'Muslim industry', not those that frequent it as an economic resort. And we must make a push for more female representation – I'd love to see a female secretary general of the MCB.

I accept that religious organizations in all faiths are male-led. The annual meeting between the prime minister and Britain's Jewish community rarely has more than one woman, and the Church of England and its many affiliated bodies continue to struggle with gender parity. The Muslims are no exception. But sadly in recent years the press have sought to highlight the 'women problem' and issues such as segregation in Muslim communities only. It's yet another issue for which we are in the spotlight.[30]

I grew up in an environment where segregation was an accepted social practice, more at the insistence of women, who needed 'female space' to catch up when friends came round. Most Asian homes had a men's room and a ladies' room. To be more precise the men's room was the formal room, which would be used for guests who were not close family and friends and on those occasions would have male and female guests in it. It was also the room where my dad's friends would sit with my dad if they were not accompanied by female relatives. The ladies' room was usually the regular family room which was used by the family all the time and by guests on almost 90 per cent of occasions. The exceptions were either distant friends or the need to use two rooms to accommodate large families and traditional large Asian gatherings. From a fairly young age I never really took to segregation, moving effortlessly between the men's room and ladies' room.

I was a reader, I could spend hours reading mainly fiction, and as a teenager housework and cooking distracted me from reading. I had no interest in fashion or make-up and the only time I would agree to my mum's insistence to go shopping was to buy shoes and even then the deal was we would go on half-day Tuesday, when most of the town centre was closed but Clarke's was open, so shoes could be bought but hardly anything else.

Debate and discussion interested me, and from a young age I quickly realized that I could push the boundaries of debate so much further in the men's room: my mum would intervene on me much more quickly than my dad. It's a habit that has stuck, and even now during large family gatherings, where without any formal segregation men and women find themselves socializing in different parts of the house, I can invariably be found arguing politics, religion or business in the men's room.

I've never felt disapproval or censure for doing this. And neither should other women.

I was born, raised and lived in Dewsbury until my mid-thirties and don't recall ever going to a mosque in Dewsbury simply to perform my prayers. Other than the childhood attendance at mosque, my first experience of praying namaaz in a mosque was at the round mosque in Karachi and later at the Faisal mosque in Islamabad.

Most religious experiences were segregated in some part. Shia gatherings during Ashura were segregated, and so was the local Tablighi Jamaat version of Sunday school, 'Taleem'. The Bawa Jee shrine in the Punjab, however, wasn't, and neither, unusually, was my religious teaching at the local Deobandi mosque.

My first experience of communal mixed praying was in Saudi Arabia, during an early umra, a pilgrimage, to Mecca in 1996 with my parents. It's a practice which is not as tolerated in Mecca today except during Hajj, the annual pilgrimage. It was while performing Hajj with Iftikhar in 2010 that I felt the power of praying as a couple.

But segregation either in a religious environment or in more broad community activities never felt disempowering. I was grateful PE in school was segregated: hockey and netball was more fun, and cross-country running less embarrassing. Most of my madrasa education was co-ed. I'd chosen along with another eight girls to join the Hafeez class, where we memorized the Qur'an over three or four years. All classes were held jointly with the boys. At no point in those classes did I feel or was I made to feel second-class. The punishment, at a time when corporal punishment was still practised in madrasas and schools, handed out for failure to learn one's lessons, was harsher for the boys, so on many an occasion I felt lucky being a girl.

The only point of difference was a book, called *Behshati zewar*, broadly translated as 'Worldly Ornaments', which appeared to be exclusively given to girls. I owned a copy of it. I don't recall being taught it but do recall reading extracts from it which at that age seemed to deal with subjects that had until then been taboo, such as relationships. It talked a lot about dos and don'ts and at times it appeared to contradict itself. It insisted on blindly following a faith – to question was seen as wrong – and its teachings on women's education was deeply conflicted, appearing to both support and oppose.[31]

Years of indoctrination by my mother had left us in no doubt that we were not going to settle for a passive or a second-class lifestyle, and observing the strength of women like my maternal and paternal grandmothers, both whom clearly ruled the roost, made the stories in *Behshati zewar* more folklore than reality. It's a book we need to stop giving girls.

The occasional soft social segregation is a feature in some form amongst most communities and faiths, and Britain has always accepted and indeed at times promoted it in the sphere of education, health (the Tory Party was a great champion of single-sex wards) and sports. So segregation should be accommodated if it's out of genuine choice, but what concerns me is the growing number of British

Muslims who are taking it to levels which I believe is holding back women from leadership positions. From political events which are 'men only', to events where men and women sit separately and women away from the main speakers, to university campuses where some Islamic societies insist on segregated events, this 'hard segregation' is a phenomenon growing far beyond the segregation I experienced growing up. It's something I, amongst others, have challenged, but not enough has changed. Too many men and women are concerned by community censure if they step out. Let's not use segregation as a tool to limit learning and limit experience. Let's stop using segregation as a reason to hold back women and let's open up our mosques, madrasas, community groups, political campaigns and most of all our minds to ensure that we develop and promote a generation of community leadership amongst women. Let's do this not out of fear of a *Daily Mail* headline but because it will create a British Muslim community that is fit for purpose, embracing and utilising all the talent that makes up British Muslims.

What matters now is that we build rich lives based upon the spirit of Islam in its broadest traditions, an Islam relevant to today's Britain.

This is nothing new. Islam has always taken its cultural reference points where it lays down its roots. Professor Timothy Winters of the University of Cambridge beautifully describes it through the

> spectacular moment [of Hajj] when 4 million pilgrims [change] from the white robes which unified them during the earlier rites . . . back into their national dress, African colours, Indonesian batik sarongs, a riot of Uzbek ikats: this affirmation of . . . diversity in unity is . . . necessarily Islamic.[32]

I urge you, my co-religionists, to celebrate this diversity, to embrace the British cultural space in which Islam had set down roots. I urge you to become active citizens, engaged in politics, playing your part in presenting solutions to the challenges of our times, from the economy to climate change, education, welfare and foreign policy. I urge you to be strong, articulate citizens who champion democracy and reject violence as the way to dissent, not compliant and malleable, as healthy democracy needs dissenting citizens, a community that agrees with policy-makers because it believes in the policy and not simply to

gain favours, one that disagrees with policy-makers on points of
principle and not simply to feign grievance. All things government
are not good, nor are all things government bad, a statement, as polls
show, British Muslims agree with. Government is not the enemy.
It's our government, which we played our part in electing. And
when it acts in ways we find unacceptable we must play our part
in democracy in changing it. That is the British way and the Islamic
way.

When we disagree we must learn to disagree well, both within our
communities, with fellow Brits and with government. On our journey
in Muslim Britain we must learn to take responsibility for our 'wrong
turns' of the past and try not to make them in the future. The
over-reactions to *The Satanic Verses* was a wrong turn; the MCB's
historic position not to attend HMD was a wrong turn; the holding-
back of women in our communities was a wrong turn; the creation of
'the Muslim industry' in response to Prevent funding was a wrong
turn; and being caught unprepared as the Blair government consulted
after 7/7 and then never implemented 90 per cent of the agreed proposals was a wrong turn. We as a community have to take responsibility
for our mistakes too just as government needs to take responsibility
for its. Cohesion is a two-way dance, we must accommodate and compromise as we expect others to do.

There are, as I see it, three roads at this juncture, three ways forward. Which one we take will partly determine how future generations
tell the tale of Muslim Britain and the negative or positive role played
by today's British Muslims.

Firstly, more of the same. But the answers of the Islam we grew up
with and continue to be taught in many a mosque simply do not provide the solutions to the questions and challenges we face today. This
will mean we are consistently out of step and a 'problem' community.

Secondly, constant acceptance of all things British as espoused by
the state, with British Islam being done to us. This Anglican Islam
could simply become a non-practised, non-observant, part-time
extension of a historic identity which future generations will read
about in history books.

Or, thirdly, an honest and robust engagement with scripture, teachings, environment and history to find an accommodation – or, as

scholars like to call it, ijtehad. This is in line with the concept of universality of Islam, both geographically and historically, and thus it is right to read, reconsider and revisit the teachings of Islam for their application and expression in today's Britain.

This is not revolutionary, it's always been the Muslim way. It is proposed by many an intellectual, including Swiss academic, philosopher and writer Tariq Ramadan, who explores this approach in his book *Western Muslims and the Future of Islam*, Muslim identity is not rigid or inflexible; it has been and should be 'a constant dialectical and dynamic movement between the sources [of the faith] and the environment' it finds itself in to create harmonious living.[33]

Muslims in the West, if they want to retain their faith, need to find answers which are relevant to where they are, who they are and the way in which they want to matter and belong.

As my good friend the political journalist and broadcaster Mehdi Hasan writes, we don't need 'a Christian-style reformation of Islam', with all its injustices, persecution and bloodletting, but 'Muslims do need to rediscover their own heritage of pluralism, tolerance and mutual respect – embodied in, say, the Prophet's letter to the monks of St Catherine's monastery, or the "convivencia" (or co-existence) of medieval Muslim Spain'.[34]

From culture to dress, the arts to music, there are great Islamic traditions to draw upon to help accommodate our European Muslim identities. And we must explore the full range of possibilities.[35]

This would have been easier to do over time if it wasn't for events. Muslims failed to do this adequately in peaceful times only to find themselves having to at breakneck speed while being battle-weary.

And yes, that identity will be diverse, as British Muslims are super-diverse. The concept of a homogeneous, monolithic Muslim identity in Britain runs counter to history and evidence. It's why it's not going to be easy or quick to define.

Diversity within the faith, within ethnic communities who follow that faith and practice within those communities create a vibrant and varied tapestry that makes up British Muslims. It's not a label that does justice to the diversity of the community but it's one that encompasses our faith and our nation.

British Islam should be our project, a British Muslim project, not a

THE MUSLIMS

coming-together and appearing to homogenize as a community in resistance under pressure. British Islam should be a positive, optimistic project and not a reaction to the state and its policy-making towards 'British Muslims', which has invariably pulled many more Muslims into a united Muslim identity. There is nothing quite like being told you are a problem to encourage you to go out and find others who too are 'the problem' and form a 'problem gang'. This must not be the reason to carve out a new British Muslim identity. We should do so because it's what Muslims have always done. This evolution is the continuous journey, the fission and fusion and clash of fundamentalists of individuals and communities who imbibe, live and reject as they evolve in a pursuit to belong and become in new-found environments. It's the Islamic way.

There is no doubt a political consciousness amongst a younger British Muslim community, one because of successive world events which has created a more politicized European Muslim identity, a more active British Muslim identity. It's time to channel this consciousness, albeit triggered in part by a rejection of Islam in Europe and in Britain, into a process that creates, defines and is lived out in the form of Islam that is made in Britain, matters to Britain and belongs in Britain. It's time to forge a British Muslim identity that is neither hostage to the history, culture and tradition of our forefathers' homelands nor shaped in the bowels of Whitehall.

We are British and we are Muslim and we must take the best of both and fight the flaws in each, based on our heritage here, in tune with the nations we have made home, that runs with the grain of Britishness instead of jarring against it.

We will be responsible for what we do or fail to do.

We must define our own future as British Muslims. We owe it to future generations. We must be prepared to take the tough decisions and have the courage of our convictions to build a better community that will play its part in building a better Britain.

187

8

The Politicians

'You must learn from the mistakes of others. You can't possibly live long enough to make them all yourself.'

Samuel Levenson

Politicians have much to be proud of. It was political will that made the case against fascism, saw the need to lead the war efforts in the first half of the twentieth century and establish the NHS and a welfare state. It was political will which in the end abolished slavery, gave women, ethnic minorities, the disabled, homosexuals the right to be treated with dignity and shaped a Britain where all were equal before the law.

But we have also made many mistakes along the way, many in recent times regarding policy on 'British Muslims', where some policy has simply proved counterproductive because the how and why of policy-making has been flawed. Often led by naked politics, we have made decisions which are neither historically correct nor evidence-based.

It's time to rebalance policy-making and reboot Britain's relationship with its Muslims, because politics indicate a country's direction of travel.

To leave or not to leave Europe is a question that has plagued British politics, and the Conservative Party more acutely, for decades. So the referendum in 2016 was a once-in-a-lifetime opportunity to settle the question. And although the debate had its fair share of exaggerated announcements on both sides of the argument, which predicted doom if voters were to vote one way or the other, for me the most startling revelations were from Steve Hilton, David Cameron's long-term friend, godfather to his children and chief strategist for over seven years. The first revelation was this: that the numbers being used by government, most specifically the Treasury, were simply 'made up'; he knew this, he said, because he'd done so in the past, simply made them up. And the second revelation was the claim that David Cameron was a closet Brexiter, and had he not been prime minister he would have voted leave.[1] The allegation was, of course, denied by the prime minister, but the comments fed into a broader view that firstly politicians simply 'make things up' so the evidence fits their narrative and secondly that politicians don't actually say what they truly believe, or indeed even do what they say.

Do we say what we believe? Do we do what we say?

I can't profess that I could say yes to both questions at all times during my times in politics. There was many an occasion as Tory Party chairman I put my name to awful press releases about the then leader of the Labour Party, Ed Miliband, which would have been more suited to a primary school playground spat than so-called grown-up politics. But these two simple questions, these two filters, have the potential to act as a great check and balance against not just bad decision-making but also ruthlessly political decision-making. And they help us unpick the sins and inform the solutions to British Muslim policy-making.

The two questions seem most difficult to answer when it comes to Britain's approach to foreign policy.

Let me start with our armed forces, an issue which for me and many British Muslims is personal. Of the millions who fought for Britain during the two world wars nearly 900,000 were Muslims; two were my paternal and maternal grandfathers.[2]

In 2013 the two men who killed Drummer Lee Rigby claimed to be Muslim; they killed in the name of Islam. Legally they committed a murder, religiously they committed a sin.

I had the privilege of being the minister with responsibility for Afghanistan from 2012 to 2014 in the last two years of the Afghanistan War as we withdrew our troops. I had the opportunity to travel to Afghanistan on many occasions, including to Helmand. I travelled with our soldiers, ate with them, met and talked with them, ordinary men and women with extraordinary courage. We lost over 450 during that war, which in the end lasted fourteen years.

They do what few politicians would have the courage to do. They implement the decisions we make and sadly often without the equipment and support they need. They give up the best years of their life, and many return to civilian life again without the support and resources they need to reintegrate into local communities. Sitting alongside young men and women dressed for battle in the intense Afghan heat, knowing that some of them would not survive the operation, was a sobering moment.

When terrorists murdered Lee Rigby they struck at the heart of what Britain held sacred, its young men and women who put themselves in harm's way to protect us.

Fusilier Lee Rigby was twenty-five; he was a brother, a son and a father. From Crumpsall in Manchester, he had joined the army at nineteen and had served in Afghanistan. He was engaged to be married. His mother Lyn, when speaking of her loss and 'the pain (that) never goes away', put it in a way that only a mother could: 'I thought giving birth was the hardest thing to do in the world, but to bury a child. That is a whole complete person you will never see again.'[3] Lee's life was cut short by two men who felt hacking him to death was an appropriate and 'Islamic' response because they disagreed with British foreign policy.

In 2006 we lost yet another soldier in Afghanistan. He was Lance Corporal Jibran Hashmi, who was killed in Sangin in Helmand Province in a rocket attack. The town, a strategic centre for the Taliban and one where British troops suffered a large number of casualties, is now sadly once more on the verge of falling under Taliban control.[4] His family described Jibran as 'a committed soldier and a committed Muslim. He was fiercely proud of his Islamic background and he was equally proud of being British.'[5]

I met Jibran's mother some years ago. The years had not healed her loss. She quietly sobbed as she spoke of her son, but the pride she felt of her son's service to his country shone through. She was an unassuming woman, one who could easily, because of her demeanour and how she was dressed, have been mistaken for being 'traditionally submissive'.[6] Her son was a British Muslim soldier.

Lee and Jibran lost their lives serving their country. We owe it to them to get things right.

And that starts with our first solution: clarifying our laws on who Brits fight for.

The current war in Syria, and the young European men and women, the foreign fighters, who have travelled to fight in the region, has again raised issues we've faced in the past. Europeans who went out in 2011–12, early on in the conflict, to fight against the Assad regime were in their belief, if not in their action, in the same place as government policy. They, like the government, believed Assad was a brutal dictator who needed to be defeated. Like the mujahideen of 1980s Afghanistan, whom we armed and advised,[7] these young men simply implemented what we believed.[8]

It's a phenomenon we've seen before. The Spanish Civil War in the late 1930s, despite the UK's official neutral position, saw hundreds and possibly thousands of Brits travel to Spain to fight alongside the subsequently defeated republicans as part of the International Brigades. The prospect of fighting against fascism as their country kept quiet attracted a group of Brits who were made up of both educated middle-class and working-class idealists, socialists and communists, young men with a purpose who played their part in an international effort to uphold democracy against the right-wing threat and to live out an adventure. Some Brits even fought for the other side, the nationalists, who were supported by the fascist forces of Hitler and Mussolini.

Our intelligence services knew about these early 'foreign fighters' as they did the many that we not only knew about but also encouraged during the Soviet War in Afghanistan from 1979 to 1989.[9]

Like the International Brigades of the Spanish Civil War, the young men who first went out to help as the Syrian Civil War started simply felt they were stepping up because their government wasn't doing enough and they wanted to play their part. Some were aid workers and doctors who got caught up in Syria as the state collapsed, whilst others felt it their duty to fight injustice. The 'thug life' that ISIS offered came much later.

We currently have Brits fighting on all sides of the conflict in Iraq and Syria, some with anti-Assad groups, others for him, some with ISIS, some against them alongside the Peshmerga, but the only Brits we should have in the fight should be Brits in our armed forces. And yet some eighty years since the Spanish Civil War we still haven't set out what I believe is a clear and necessary principle that if you are British and wish to be a soldier then you fight for Britain. Our law in this area is vague. Fighting for Britain is one of the most public acknowledgements of a commitment to Britain and what she stands for. If you take the nationality and the passport, then you fight under our banner and no other. It may have served us well, as it did during the Cold War, to harness the power, passion, religious fevour and brotherhood to attract foreign fighters to our cause, our agenda, but we must now stop doing so. It was a bad policy decision and it back-fired. It's time for us to make it a criminal offence to fight for a nation other than our own. We live in a diverse, multi-ethnic country, and whilst it's natural to have multiple affections and affiliations to coun-tries around the world, it should not be acceptable to take up arms for another nation, friend or foe.[10]

The second issue is violent dissent. As a nation we need to learn the art of disagreeing well, and that includes how we dissent on foreign policy. Many people disagree with British foreign policy. In 2001 I had reservations about our intervention in Afghanistan. Our plan-ning, strategy and stated outcomes I felt were not sufficiently clear. In 2003 I was against the war in Iraq. As a lawyer, I had concerns about the legal basis of what we did and the reasoning behind the intervention.

These concerns were shared by millions across the UK, many of whom took to the streets: from the tens of thousands in September 2002 soon after Blair made the British case for war to the million who marched in London on 15 February 2003, as millions around the world too marched, expressing their opposition to the planned invasion of Iraq. Just over a month later the war started, the ramifica-tions of which we are still feeling today.

Muslims, like the rest of Brits, have a stake in Britain's future and in the welfare of our armed forces. They, like the rest of Brits, bear the consequences of the decisions our governments make, including on foreign policy. And they, like the rest of Brits, must be both mature about 'national interest' in foreign policy and passionate about hold-ing our government to account when it says one thing and does another. That is patriotism.

Brits of all backgrounds, including Muslims, should be at the fore-front of fighting persecution, discrimination and injustice anywhere in the world, but first we must hold our government to account, ensuring it remains true to the deep-rooted principles of fairness, human rights, the rule of law and international justice.

So let me be clear: attacks on our troops either here or overseas can never be justified; nor can an opposition to our foreign policy be seen as justification for inciting hatred against our soldiers. British Muslims owe it to our forefathers to remember the sacrifices that they and others made and owe it to their memories that live on through their medals to shout down the small number of bigots that think burning poppies or using violence is an appropriate form of dissent.

The responsibility and indeed culpability for those wars lies with politicians who made those decisions and not the thousands of men and women in our armed forces who simply follow orders. Such sentiments were expressed in emotional outbursts by families of soldiers on the publication of the Chilcot report into the war in Iraq. The decisions to go to war are made by politicians elected through the ballot box. Those decisions must be opposed through the ballot box. So strengthening democracy must be our second solution.

But just as British citizens, including Muslims, have a responsibility to dissent on foreign policy in line with our traditions and principles, so too politicians have a responsibility to make foreign policy in line with our traditions and principles. So thirdly, we need to tackle how we make foreign policy.

In an ever-more-connected world I believe we cannot have a domestic policy and foreign policy which send out completely different messages. To do so leads to charges of hypocrisy, a sin which toxifies the process of policy-making. I was one of the few ministers in recent years to simultaneously hold both a domestic and foreign brief. I explored the challenges of one rule at home and another abroad in 2015 at the Global Strategy Forum lecture:

> For a very long time, I have said that how we conduct ourselves over-seas reflects on who we are domestically, and the way in which we deal with our domestic communities has both positive and negative consequences as to how we are viewed in the world. Quite uniquely, as

a Foreign Office minister and a communities minister, every day I saw how that played out with practical consequences.[11]

Policy-making in the context of counter-terrorism has seen this 'difference in approach' operate at its worst and it's an approach that has a direct impact on Britain's relationship with her Muslims.

Let me go back to David Cameron's Munich speech from 2011, which I explored in chapter 4, in which he set out a number of tests which form the basis of sifting the bad guys from the good guys, the acceptable Muslims from the unacceptable ones.

Do they believe in universal human rights – including for women and people of other faiths?

Do they believe in equality of all before the law?

Do they believe in democracy and the right of people to elect their own government?

Do they encourage integration or separation?

Cameron argued that if individuals and organizations fail these tests then 'the presumption should be not to engage with organisations – so, no public money, no sharing of platforms with ministers *at home*'.

It's these last two, quite innocuous words that set the tone for a policy that says one thing and does another, one approach at home and a different one overseas. An approach and a policy which I thought, before her US visit, the current prime minister would distance herself from.

I took the 'Munich' tests and stress-tested them against the company the government keeps.

Do they believe in universal human rights – including for women and people of other faiths? What about women not being allowed to leave the country without the permission of men (Iran), not being allowed to drive (Saudi Arabia) or having what they wear proscribed (France)? Our domestic policy would suggest these 'views' are not to be engaged with. And yet we do. Do they believe in democracy and the right of people to elect their own government? If that were so, people who came into power via military coups would be out, and all democratically elected governments would be in. And yet we have regularly engaged with 'military regimes' throughout history in Pakistan, and more recently in Egypt. Do they encourage integration or separation? A wall separating communities, as in Israel, could be a pretty good indication of a separatist nation. And a lack of recognition of a minority, such as the Rohingya in Burma, should signal a 'no mates' stance. And yet they don't.

There are many more examples. I often raised them during my time at the Foreign Office, suggesting that we 'blind test' countries against our stated values and principles. Many a current foreign ally, friend and special relationship would fail such scrutiny.

British foreign policy makes increasing reference to 'ethics' and 'values': from New Labour's 'ethical foreign policy' to the use of the term 'values' four times during the Coalition government's Strategic Defence Review and a whopping thirty-one times in the Conservative government's National Security Review in 2015.[12]

Labour's ethical foreign policy was laid out by the late Robin Cook, a man for whom I had great respect, within days of taking office in 1997. Labour's policy, Cook said, would have 'an ethical dimension ... with human rights at the heart' and 'reverse the Tory trend towards not so splendid isolation'.[13]

Thirteen years later, the formidable William Hague, former leader of the Conservative Party and foreign secretary from 2010 to 2014, gave his verdict:

> the previous government fell into a chasm of their own making between rhetoric and action in large areas of foreign policy. Their tenure began, as one newspaper put it, with 'a sounding of ethical trumpets'. It ended with allegations of British complicity in torture, an Inquiry into the Iraq War, questions about the conduct of our Intelligence Services, a foreign policy machinery-of-government that had been run into the ground, piecemeal sofa-style decision making in Downing Street, accusations of hypocrisy and double standards in respect of international law and the epic Ministerial mismanagement of the finances of the Foreign Office and the Ministry of Defence.[14]

And that phrase, 'hypocrisy and double standards', was one that I was hopeful would not be used for the Coalition government.

It was the phrase that seemed most apt as Wikileaks started to publish confidential conversations from across the world. In the interest of national security I condemn the disclosure of classified material.

But what became apparent in the cases of Bradley, now Chelsea, Manning, the former US soldier convicted of leaking sensitive government documents to Wikileaks, and Edward Snowden, the former CIA employee who leaked classified documents to journalists, was not the compromise of national security, which, to quote a former US defence secretary, Robert Gates, was 'fairly modest' and hadn't really compromised intelligence sources or methods, but the fact we'd been found out, all of us: leaders around the world caught red-handed saying the things they dare not say in public. Showing our respective citizens that we neither say what we believe nor do as we say.[15] Our main ally and friend the US has over time simply become complacent over its inconsistent approach, and allegations of hypocrisy are simply brushed away. This has occurred not only in the 'war on terror', where the great defender of human rights shelves them when it comes to its own conduct on security; not only in its refusal, like Sudan and Israel, to ratify the Rome Statute, which has now been signed by 139 states, including Australia, Canada, France, Germany, New Zealand and the United Kingdom, which created the International Criminal Court in 2002 to try perpetrators of war crimes and genocide, especially when national courts are unable or unwilling to do so; but also on issues such as nuclear non-proliferation, where the US picks and chooses who can and who cannot have nuclear weapons, turning a blind eye to those who illegally develop nuclear if they are friends whilst insisting others endorse the Nuclear Nonproliferation Treaty. Indeed Trump seeks to make a virtue of such hypocrisy.

Over the last decade many a discussion with foreign ministers of other nations confirmed to me that Britain was viewed very differently from the US. We are still in many countries, thankfully, viewed as measured, informed and genuinely committed to human rights, but this view is by no means universal. We must try to maintain this reputation, as without it what does Brand Britain mean? Does it mean anything if it doesn't include a deep-rooted commitment to human rights and the rule of law?

Since 2003 successive British governments have produced an annual Human Rights Report, and each year the minister for human rights is questioned on it by the Foreign Affairs Select Committee. In government, I felt this was an occasion to showcase our stated values and how we act upon them. I quickly realized that it was seen within the FCO as an ordeal to survive. We went through the motions and hoped like mad we wouldn't get found out. So I laid out some ground rules. If we were going to 'do human rights', we were going to do them properly or not at all. Human rights are an intrinsic part of my previous life as a lawyer and an essential part of my faith. For me they are about who we are.

Unfortunately, the Humans Rights department at the FCO seems to me to be a parking lot for mediocrity. It is low-level, low-priority, low-impact work. The most honest public acknowledgement of this was in 2015 from the top civil servant at the FCO, Sir Simon McDonald, at the Foreign Affairs Select Committee when he said that human rights are no longer 'a top priority' and that 'prosperity was further up the list'.[16]

It's an admission which pains me, but I welcome it because of its honesty. It says what we believe, it does what we say. If we believe in human rights we should say so and we should do so. If we don't, which both my experience and the direction of travel suggest, then we should stop talking about them. Today, sadly, the talk of values and human rights in foreign policy-making is at best a fig leaf, at worst hypocrisy.

In the UK human rights is a dish served as a main meal at a very public banquet to our enemies. We shove it down their throat, force-feed them our values and make them sick by going on about their shortcomings. But when our friends come for tea we are happy to conveniently leave human rights in the back of the larder. To our foes we do human rights as public, loud and robust lectures alongside a stick of sanctions, bans and walkouts. To our friends it's an aside at the end of a conversation on issues that really matter simply so we can record it as 'done', or a broad discussion on reform without any specific reference to the specific violations, or outsourced to a low-level committee of officials, as we do with China.[17] Or, worse still, we make those awful diplomatic-speak statements that everyone knows mean nothing, like 'nothing is off the table in discussions', as we did during the state visits of President Xi Jinping of China and Prime Minister Narendra Modi of India in 2015.[18] We were warned by the Chinese that the president would not respond well if reprimanded on human rights during his visit. And there was no evidence that the appalling behaviour of the Rashtriya Swayamsevak Sangh, the RSS, a right-wing paramilitary Hindu nationalist organization, was raised with Prime Minister Modi.[19]

Or we say it's a discussion for another time, as the issue is too difficult at present, such as blasphemy with the Pakistanis, despite Brits being arrested under these non-Islamic, man-made British-inspired laws. Or we simply brush it under the carpet in the name of cultural sensitivity as we do with women's rights in Saudi Arabia. Or we compartmentalize human rights abuses and consider them irrelevant as we sign arms deals, selling as we have done in recent years record numbers to countries we list in our government's own annual human rights report as having questionable human rights records.[20]

In 2015 more than £3 billion worth of bombs, missiles, grenades and other weaponry made in Britain was exported to twenty-one of the Foreign Office's thirty 'human rights priority countries' – those identified by our own government as being where 'the worst, or greatest number of, human rights violations take place'.[21]

As minister for human rights between 2012 and 2014, I chaired a number of the FCO advisory groups on specific human rights, groups which harnessed the expertise of academics, lawyers, NGOs and others to inform our work on Human Rights. We had a learned and prestigious FCO advisory group on the death penalty and they did some tremendous work, often only to be let down by us politicians making our decisions based on whom we considered allies and enemies rather than on the issue. We talked a great talk on the death penalty, highlighting the numbers Iran hangs, whilst ensuring it was not an issue in our 'special relationship' with the US.

And then there is torture, that abhorrent practice which is against our law, against our numerous international commitments given through the numerous conventions we have signed and, of course, against our stated values. The prohibition on torture is a bedrock principle of international human rights law. It is absolute and allows for no exceptional circumstances – not war, not terrorism, not political instability or any other public emergency. And British law lays upon us a legal obligation to prosecute acts of torture, regardless of the place of commission, the nationality of the perpetrator or the nationality of the victim.

Our obligations are uncompromising and clear in an area where our conduct has certainly not been so. Take the recent, well-documented cases of British Pakistanis tortured by Pakistan with allegations of British complicity,[22] or the encyclopedia of British torture that is Ian Cobain's *Cruel Britannia*, a book described by the Reverend Nicholas Mercer (formerly Lieutenant-Colonel Nicholas Mercer) as 'a hand grenade in the heart of the establishment'.[23] Cobain's book charts the allegations of British torture from the Second World War through the colonial campaigns in Aden (now modern-day Yemen), Cyprus and the Mau Mau rebellion in Kenya, for which I apologized in the House of Lords during my time as minister,[24] to our conduct in Northern Ireland, until we were slapped down by the European Court of Human Rights, and the wars in Afghanistan and Iraq and our present-day war on terror[25] – constant reminders where we failed to live by our 'values'.

And then there's rendition, which in layman's terms is the kidnap, false imprisonment and the all-expenses-paid world tour of exotic torture destinations, something that led to a breakdown of relationship between our two spy agencies, MI5 and MI6. My colleague Andrew Tyrie, chairman of the All Party Parliamentary Committee on Extraordinary Rendition, has tirelessly tried to get to the bottom of rendition, but it still festers as a sore which successive governments fail to treat.[26]

It's against this backdrop that we announced once again in the 2015 Strategic Defence and Security Review: 'our core British values. Democracy, the rule of law, open, accountable governments and institutions, human rights, freedom of speech, property rights and equality of opportunity, including the empowerment of women and girls.'[27]

Democracy is an often cited core value. And yet we struggle with democracy sometimes, especially if it produces a result we neither envisaged nor supported. But let's take credit where credit is due. Unlike the US, who too talk a good game on democracy, we, in July 2014, as the Egyptian military overthrew an elected government, at least expressed discomfort with this assault on democracy. Although we refused to call a coup a coup, we did ostracize the Egyptians for a few months to show our displeasure at their rounding-up and imprisoning of political opponents, activists and journalists, including former BBC journalist Peter Greste. The UK behaved like the awkward boyfriend as we looked down at our toes, not quite sure whether we had broken up with the last partner and not quite sure whether we were ready to date the new one, and this behaviour was not necessarily a bad thing, because in that shuffling of our feet in a way that other countries did not we showed that we were genuinely having a 'thoughtful moment' about what we felt was the right approach. Our dilemma of a commitment to democracy on the one hand and an eye on future interests on the other was clearly being played out in the public domain. We came to the President Sisi period slowly and in some ways reluctantly, and in the long run this had a positive impact on our reputation as democrats and in our relationship with our own domestic communities. We were trying to say what we believed.

In the summer of 2014 the Gaza incursion was a particular flashpoint in conflicted and confused foreign-policy-making.

In a war that resulted in 2,139 dead and 11,000 injured Palestinians and the death of 6 Israeli civilians and 64 Israeli soldiers. Britain's role in supplying arms into that conflict was put under the spotlight with a legal challenge on government policy mounted by the Campaign Against Arms Trade.[28] As concerns were raised about the proportionality of action by the Israeli government and the commitment of potential war crimes, the UK government was eventually forced into taking steps to revoke some licences as a 'precautionary measure', a move which was reversed within the year, with the Conservatives having won an election and those pesky Liberal Democrats with their obsession with human rights firmly out of the way.[29]

But why is this all relevant? Why does our approach to foreign policy matter in the tale of Muslim Britain? Because time and time again, in terrorist videos, suicide notes and the words of the terrorists themselves, our approach to foreign policy is cited as a reason for the violence. Academic sources and indeed even government acknowledge it as a driver of radicalization.[30] So it is right to examine what policy-makers are doing or perceived to be doing that triggers this accusation.

I do not believe that any individual community, faith or organization should determine British foreign policy. I believe that Britain should determine its foreign policy in accordance with our stated principles and values. And yet time and time again we do not appear to be doing so.

In government one of the most anomalous, inexplicable and morally indefensible positions I had to take related to the 2014 Gaza conflict. Human rights positions I had advocated for as an activist, lawyer and politician were being dismissed with no rational 'national interest' reason. At that time, I had, amongst other ministerial roles, responsibility for the United Nations, including the Human Rights Council in Geneva, the International Criminal Court and the human rights brief. I was also the government's spokesman on foreign affairs in the House of Lords. I was thus having to answer questions sometimes daily on the unfolding crisis in Gaza.

A cabinet reshuffle had taken place during the Gaza conflict. The Foreign Office had lost the visionary William Hague and gained the perfectly competent accountant Phillip Hammond. Hague had led the campaign on gender equality and fought the scourge of sexual violence in conflict. In my first conversation with Hammond as foreign secretary, he was dismissive of the department's human rights work, picking out the anti-death-penalty work for specific disdain. He appeared to see our worldwide support for the campaign against capital punishment as a distracting fringe issue. This set the tone for all future discussions. The last time we spoke was on the morning of 4 August 2014, the day of my resignation. In a discussion on rebuilding Gaza after the conflict the ifs, buts and caveats being laid out by Phillip Hammond were so extensive that it was obvious there was no political will on our part to make it happen, and that has since been the case.[31]

I did not resign because of what the Israelis were doing to the Palestinians, I resigned because of my government's reaction, or more accurately put inaction, to it.

The world is full of both dictators and elected leaders, brutal regimes and appalling armies who persecute their own citizens; Israel is not an exception. From Afghanistan to Iraq, Libya to Syria, Sudan to Sri Lanka, we have taken a stand against leaders and regimes that brutalize their own populations. We have employed condemnation, high-profile visits to support the persecuted, as David Cameron rightly did with the Tamils in Sri Lanka, support for independence movements, as we did in South Sudan, where we continue to play a key role as part of the troika alongside the US and Norway, ostracism, as in the case of Pakistan and its exclusion from the Commonwealth during military coups, sanctions, such as those that lasted over a decade in Iran, invasion and war, as in Afghanistan, regime change, as in Libya, and we keep repeating in relation to Syria: 'Assad must go, he is part of the problem not the solution.' We generally seem, at the very least, to find some words with which to show our displeasure, and yet during Gaza we couldn't even find the words to condemn the daily massacre of civilians, starting each government statement with the robust defence of Israel's right to defend itself.

I agree, Israel, like any other sovereign state, has a right to defend itself. But as a member of the international community it has an obligation to do so within the parameters of humanitarian and international laws and norms.

During the crisis a resolution was presented to the UN Human Rights Council in Geneva which condemned and called for a halt to the violence on both sides and asked for the establishment of a process of accountability at the end of the war for any war crimes committed by either side. It was a resolution which was in line with our values of accountability, no impunity for war crimes and support for international justice. We are a founder member of the International Criminal Court and one of its biggest funders, and believe in international organizations such as the UN. And yet we abstained on the motion.[32]

The resolution did pass, and a year later a UN report found credible the allegations of war crimes committed in 2014 by both Israel and Palestinian armed groups. It reported that the 'devastation and human suffering in Gaza was unprecedented and will impact generations to come'. Israel neither responded to repeated requests for information nor allowed access to Israel and the Occupied Territories, but the commission did conduct over 280 face-to-face interviews via Skype and VTC and considered 500 written submissions, concluding that 'impunity prevails across the board for violations allegedly committed by Israeli forces both in Gaza and the West Bank' and arguing that 'Israel must break with its lamentable track record in holding wrongdoers to account'. The report was balanced in its findings, saying 'accountability on the Palestinian side is also woefully inadequate'.

We, in abstaining, sent out the message we didn't want to support accountability. Our argument went something like this: we know it's wrong, and the loss of civilian life is tragic, but we have to be seen to hold the line and show support for Israel to bank goodwill for another day when we will use the influence gained to get Israel to shift its position on issues like settlements. On one level this appears to be a good argument, sensible diplomacy. But I have yet to witness it happening.[33]

For me it felt like yet another moral cop-out. It was not a solution.

At the time of my resignation I was accused by a senior colleague of not being a team player. I dispute that. I accept I stopped playing for the team, but that's because the team stopped playing for Britain. We should be at all times team GB, not team Israel, nor for that matter team Saudi, Pakistan, India or anywhere else in the world. Team GB's policy should be made in Britain, and not at the behest of any country, community or religion; no tail should wag Bulldog Britain.

A united sense of purpose for our country, a national interest which is rooted in our stated values and a government acting in line with those values, I believe, will lead to a stronger Britain. Citizens are more likely to feel they belong when those in power act in the interests of the country and not at the behest of foreign powers.

And the Gaza 'experience' is not an exception. The 'Muslim Brotherhood' review of 2014 is another foreign policy faux pas that does not satisfy that test. The Muslim Brotherhood (MB), also known as the Ikhwan al-Muslimeen, is an international political, religious and social movement. It started as a pan-Islamic movement in Egypt in 1928 as a reaction to secularization and westernization, which they saw as the root of all contemporary problems of Arab and Muslim societies, and felt that Arab nationalism was not the answer. There are many versions of the group in public life: from charitable outfits that provide life-saving healthcare, water, sanitation and education to legitimate political parties that performed strongly in elections in Tunisia (2011), Morocco (2011 and 2016), Eygpt (2012), Libya (2012), Iraq (2014) and Jordan (2016), to being considered a terrorist organizations since 2015 by Syria, Russia, Saudi Arabia and the UAE. They held the presidency in Egypt between 2012 and 2014, and before President Morsi was overthrown in a coup we were midway through organizing a state visit for him, including a Ramadan reception.

The Muslim world is divided on the Muslim Brotherhood. Qatar and Turkey, both strong UK allies, are seen as sympathizers, and the UAE and Saudi Arabia, again both strong UK allies, officially declare them terrorists. We define them as Islamists who follow the ideology of 'Islamism', which we argue is the basis for terrorism, an assertion I challenged in chapter 4. The Foreign Affairs Select Committee concluded: 'The vast majority of political Islamists are involved in no violence whatsoever . . . and because of their broader status as a firewall against extremism, political Islamists have suffered criticism and attack from ISIL.'[34]

The MB and its various offshoots worldwide are politically challenging to the status quo. Sometimes they are the only form of welfare provision locally. Monarchies in the Middle East are fearful of them. And, yes, there have been cases where they have 'inspired individuals to commit violent acts'.[35]

It's entirely right for the UK to review their activities in the UK and assess whether they pose a threat to us, but the review should have been our review, not, as was subsequently reported, a review at the behest of the UAE, a foreign government.[36] We should be team GB, not team UAE.

The report found that the MB 'had not been linked to terrorist related activity both in and against the UK', and yet the report was used as a means to discredit a number of British Muslim charities and organizations operating legally in the UK – again, a foreign policy position taken by the UK government, not to benefit other Brits but foreign states, having a negative impact on the relationship between Britain and its Muslims.

UK governments need to stop becoming pawns in other people's wars. Let's not be used to settle their scores, let's stop outsourcing our foreign policy to foreign nations. Let's make sure British foreign policy is made in Britain for Britain.[37]

The UK has much to be proud of, and it would have even more if we simply put into action what we say are our values. But the more we simply say and not actually follow, the more we stand accused of hypocrisy. The more we shout values and not play by the rules we have set, the more we lose our moral standing, our reputation and our influence.

I understand that we have to further our commercial interests. I support the FCO as it champions Brand Britain, as an ever-roving trade ambassador, but surely we must find ways to do both: champion interests and remain true to our stated values. If we truly are values-based, let's hold both friend and foe accountable, measured against the same human rights to the same standards. To do otherwise is both damaging our reputation and in the current war on terror merely feeding the problem. Or, if we are simply a market place and a nation of traders and no more, if we have genuinely decided to draw our self-interest this narrowly, then let's stop preaching principles. Laissez-faire is better than hypocrisy.

One approach at home and another overseas is not new. Evelyn Baring, the 1st Earl of Cromer, was a British diplomat in Egypt. He preached for the liberation of Muslim women, fought for them to be freed from the clutches of the backward practices of the veil and segregation and yet at home argued against granting women the vote.[38] Today such behaviour has consequences, and in Britain this approach to policy-making is having a disproportionate impact on our relation with 'our Muslims'.

Domestically, for example, we will not engage with Salafi-, Deobandi- and Wahhabi-inspired groups, mosques or organizations. These theologies are seen as the problem, supporters of the violent and the so-called 'non-violent' extremism the government is trying to tackle. And yet internationally we engage with all these groups, paying special homage to the home of Wahhabi Islam, Saudi Arabia. The message government sends to young disengaged British Muslims in, say, Birmingham who might identify as Salafi or Wahhabi is this: your views are not acceptable within government circles, and we will not engage with you, as you are the 'problem', but we have no issue as your elected government about showing affection and reverence for the home and heart of Wahhabism, our allies, our friends, Saudi Muslims. When Saudi Muslims become more important to the British government than British Muslims, it's time to rethink policy-making.

This domestic non-engagement strategy and its political dimension has resulted in a gulf between our domestic approach and our foreign policy approach. We regularly display our credentials as an open and transparent government; indeed we have branded the notion, developed expertise in this area and sell it to others around the world.[39] We regularly take the belated moral high ground on paedophilia and celebrity and establishment sex scandal cover-ups from the 1980s and '90s, on policing at Hillsborough, at miners' picket lines and policy decisions in Northern Ireland, but taking the moral high ground in hindsight is easy. If we genuinely regret these mistakes then let's adopt principled policy-making for now, for the future. And that starts with challenging the sin of dishonesty in policy-making and policy-making rooted in myth.

So, and this is our fourth solution: we must make policy based on evidence and experts. The Brexit campaign was a lesson in post-truth politics, as was the presidential campaign adopted in the US by Donald Trump. Both were worryingly successful. We've entered a space in politics where truth and fact are irrelevant, evidence is not required to support a claim, and 'experts' are belittled as an unnecessary distraction.[40]

If politicians run destructive campaigns to win office, how can we possibly trust them to be constructive in office? It was a trait allegedly attributed to Michael Gove by David Cameron when he said: 'The thing that you've got to remember with Michael is that he is basically a bit of a Maoist – he believes that the world makes progress through a process of creative destruction!'[41] It's an approach that I witnessed in government on the policy around counter-terrorism.

As I discussed in chapter 3, policy-makers must set the current war on terror within the context of history, be open to solutions from the past, mindful of the mistakes of the past and acknowledge that we've all been here before on many occasions. Counter-terrorism policy should be rooted in an honest understanding of terrorism, its manifestations and how we've tackled it successfully before. I'm convinced that if we put the politics and the obsession with ideology to one side and base our policy on evidence, data and science, policy-making in this area would be both more rational and more effective.

It was a point raised once again in 2016 by parliamentarians on the Home Affairs Select Committee in their report *Radicalisation: The Counter-narrative and Identifying the Tipping Point*: 'there is no evidence that shows a single path or one single event which draws a young person to the scourge of extremism',[42] a finding supported by academics, medics, intelligence services and the testimonies of terrorists, and yet government policy continues to insist it is ideology. This is a flawed position, as I argued in chapter 4, and one that I believe makes us less safe. This view was supported by the HASC: 'government's broad brush approach fails to take account of the complexities . . . that would be counterproductive and fuel the attraction of the extremist narrative rather than dampening it'.

Some FCO officials attempted to go back to policy-making rooted in evidence and reality in 2013 after the murder of Lee Rigby. They measured the accuracy of the 'Islamist ideology' theory against our foreign policy. The interpretation and definition fundamentally failed. We found, for example, states governed by strict interpretation of Sharia law with a harsh criminal penal code and restrictions on women and minorities such as Saudi Arabia which are not seen or defined as Islamist extremists by the UK, and on the other hand we have states such as Turkey, whom we consider to be inspired by Islamist ideology, but where Sharia punishments are not implemented through criminal law and women enjoy rights and liberties as elsewhere in Europe.

After the Rigby terrorist attack we set up the Extremism Task Force and had an opportunity to root our counter-terrorism policy in evidence and fact. But we failed to do so. Without assessing the 'problem', my colleagues were keen to move to solutions. We didn't discuss the two terrorists, their profile, their history; we didn't discuss or try to understand their road to radicalization or journey to violent jihadism. We didn't even take on board their own reasons, the words they spoke after the attack, or the note Adebolajo handed over as an explanation. A starting point to understanding, not excusing, would have been examining the two terrorists. As I argued in chapter 3, the first step to fixing the problem is knowing the problem.

This attack had been the second terrorist incident in mainland UK after 7/7, and the response from policy-makers was an inward-looking government-centric conversation dominated by ideologies, no community engagement, no genuine exploration, no call for evidence, no fact-based decision-making, no moment to reflect and no assessment of what had and hadn't worked in the past. It's no wonder that in 2016 a poll found that 96 per cent of Brits think the policy is failing.[43]

This issue is too serious to second-guess, and getting it wrong is having damaging ramifications for both our security and our relationship with British Muslims. It's time to finally turn to the experts: 'a cross section of academic institutions' is recommended by the HASC.[44]

Sadly, over the last decade or so, initially under Blair and latterly under Cameron too, much has been in the hands of the chumocracy: friends and friends of friends who have direct access to ministers and special advisers in No. 10 and the Home Office, interest groups, lobby groups and individuals pursuing their own agendas. I saw this in operation during my time in government, and sadly it still continues. It's the 'politics' behind the policy-making, the game-playing that is putting Britain's cohesive future at stake.

The politics of the domestic war on terror started over a decade ago, although it was 2008 when I first worriedly started to see the methodical sowing of seeds which in the end became a wisteria-like approach to counter-terrorism policy-making, slowly taking over and choking out alternative views. It resulted in a British Muslim community becoming ever more disengaged and marginalized and a blurring of lines between general policy-making and an exceptionalized approach to policy-making when it related to Muslims, something I explored in chapter 5.

It was present in both the right and left of politics, finding champions like Hazel Blears in Labour and Michael Gove and eventually David Cameron in the Tories. At the time of 7/7 it certainly hadn't taken hold of the Tory Party.

The 7/7 bombings happened while Michael Howard was leader, and I had the opportunity to work closely with him. 'Responsible' and 'measured' are the two phrases that best describe Michael's response. Within days of the bombings, Tony Blair called a meeting of the 'great and the good' in the Muslim community. Michael was invited as leader of the opposition, and he asked me to accompany him. Sadiq Khan described that meeting as Blair pushing the responsibility of the attacks on to Muslims.[45] His version has been disputed and questioned by Labour colleagues Khalid Mahmood, MP for Perry Bar, and Shahid Malik, former MP for Dewsbury, who recalls the meeting ending with 'a unanimous agreement on the need for unity in the fight against terror and the crucial role for Muslims'.[46]

Personally, I left with three distinct impressions. Blair's consultation with the community was more show than substance; he needed to be seen to be doing something. Secondly, it was an absolving of responsibility, firmly pushing the issue into the community's court. And thirdly, the community was torn and divided between individual British Muslim politicians, who saw this as a moment to make their mark, and the broader Muslim community attendees, who were keen to keep the root causes of extremism at the table. Michael Howard wanted a pragmatic and inclusive response, logical and non-ideological. Unlike Blair, Michael showed no religious zeal or any desire to link this to a broader international project. He saw it as a domestic issue which needed a proportionate domestic response, and I firmly got the impression that he did not and would not play politics with the issue.

Immediately after this Downing Street meeting, a task force was announced, set up and the first meeting called. I was at the initial meeting, at which a series of sub-groups were established. The groups reported back in October 2005. The Preventing Extremism Together report made over sixty recommendations, covering everything from appropriate language to grassroots counter-terrorism work, women's involvement, youth activism, online deradicalization material and better and more confident partnerships with the police.[47]

Less than six were fully implemented by the Labour government. The Muslim Women's Advisory Group, the Muslim Youth Group and the Mosques and Imams National Advisory Board (MINAB) were the most high-profile. Of these three, the first two were dismantled by the Coalition government in 2010, whilst the third limps on but is never engaged with by government.

It was the Labour government's response to terrorism, and although not perfect it was a very good start. And yet despite a further five years in government it simply wasn't implemented. It was during this time that the rift between the ideologues like Hazel Blears and the pragmatists like John Denham apparently started to play out.

Two years later came the first serious piece of policy thinking by the Conservative Party in the area of foreign policy, counter-terrorism and extremism in a paper, which was authored by Baroness Neville-Jones just months after both she and I were appointed to the House of Lords.[48] The paper, *An Unquiet World*, from 2007, appears informed and thoughtful. A focus on balancing liberties with security, a critique of 'contaminated . . . anti-terror legislation', a focus on prosecutions through the normal legal system rather than 'extra legal measures such as control orders', a focus on violent extremism, on building resilience and strong societies and a call for an inclusive British identity were all in the report. But in the specific area of counter-terrorism and Muslims it simply incorporated an earlier policy paper, *Uniting the Country*, published earlier in 2007, and a paper that started the process of discrediting many Muslim organizations and introducing the concept of 'ideology'.

Uniting the Country was heavily influenced by the thinking at that time of right-wing thinktank Policy Exchange. Policy Exchange was set up in 2002 by Nick Boles, the MP for Grantham and Stamford, who destroyed early attempts to set up an APPG against Islamophobia, Michael Gove and Francis, now Lord, Maude. It has been described as David Cameron's 'favourite thinktank'[49] and since its inception has had a close, indeed often indivisible, working relationship with the Conservative Party.[50]

In October 2007 Policy Exchange produced a report, *The Hijacking of British Islam*, which claimed to uncover 'extremist literature' being promoted in mosques and other Muslim institutions. By way of evidence it produced receipts of purchases of this 'extremist literature' from various mosques and institutions. Two months later, BBC *Newsnight* reported on the findings, alleging that amongst other concerns it appeared that the receipts were in fact forged, and the extremist literature could not have been bought from some of the mosques the Policy Exchange report cited. There followed a war of words, allegations and counter-allegations, which resulted in a partial retraction of the story in *The Times*, which had run the report on their front page, and the *Guardian* saying, 'Cameron must rein in these neo-con attack dogs'.[51]

This Policy Exchange episode is not a one-off. The thinktank has form in this area: earlier in 2007, the methodology and reliability of another heavily publicized report on Muslim separatism came under heavyweight academic attack. But it was still used by David Cameron to rubbish multiculturalism.[52]

There were questions about its financial sources, described by Transparify as 'highly opaque', its ideological links and the roll call of its employees and researchers, which include Dean Godson and Andrew Gilligan, and the platform they provided for Douglas Murray, a man who has been heavily criticized for his controversial views on Islam.[53]

Policy Exchange shaped that first intervention by the Conservative Party. On policy-making towards British Muslims it was then and is now an axis of influence that is part of the problem.

Our report, *Uniting the Country*, was criticized by a number of British Muslim organizations,[54] possibly because so many of them were criticized in it. Neither the evidence nor analysis was robust but despite this I felt that it had some good recommendations, including its very first recommendation that 'Government should combat the incorrect and damaging popular misconception, revealed in public opinion polls, that Islam as a religion per se is a threat to democracy' and 'make clear its intention to protect the right of Muslims to freedom of worship on the same basis as other religions'.[55] A decade on, I've yet to see the Conservative party fully embrace this first recommendation.

In hindsight the most worrying aspect of this report has been its selective implementation. The 'anti-Muslim' bits took centre stage in a future Conservative government and have become the basis of today's counter-terrorism policy whilst the more 'pro-Muslim' bits have simply been shelved. Had we simply implemented *all* its recommendations, both the ones acceptable and those unacceptable to British Muslims, then counter-terrorism and integration policy would be in a better place than it is now.

Not addressing this destructive direction of travel early on in 2007–8 is one of my failings. Unfortunately, the alternative view was well resourced by Policy Exchange, while I relied on a young and talented campaigner, Naweed Khan, who subsequently became my SpAd in government, and Eric Ollerenshaw, a party stalwart with decades of experience but who at that time was fighting a marginal seat in Lancaster.

A senior civil servant working in counter-terrorism policy whom I turned to for advice assured me that much of the toxic thinking would be tempered by the 'bureaucracy if [we] ever formed a government'.

In this policy area I was relieved that in 2010 the country delivered a Coalition government, where liberal thinking might prevail over an increasingly authoritarian streak.

So fifthly, we need to curtail the axis of influence in government. The many scandals involving the influence exercised by lobbyists, party donors, trade unions and big business have marred the reputation of politics and successive governments over the last two decades.[56] Private calls on private numbers, communication via text rather than formal write-round, social gatherings used to influence policy, friendships formed in donors' groups which led to visits to Chequers, private meetings in the flat above No. 11 Downing Street[57] – all these forums for policy to be influenced outside the proper channels must be replaced by civil-servant-led, academic-informed, evidence-based papers which inform politicians to make judgements. It's time for calls to ministers and SpAds, calls to No. 10 and 'private conversations' to be logged. It's time for transparency and public oversight of the axis of influence.

And that brings me to the sixth sin – policy-making not for the greater good but for the greater electoral result, the political analysis of who we feel will and will not vote for us and the slanting of policy-making accordingly. One such example was our 'triple lock' on pensions, which strengthened Tory support from the grey vote but didn't necessarily make good economic sense, a point made recently by my Conservative colleague Ros Altmann.[58]

This approach in counter-terrorism has had devastating impact on the tale of Muslim Britain. In 2012 The Conservative Party decided that Muslims were unlikely to vote for them, and thus 'the Muslims' didn't matter. At the time polling by Lord Ashcroft appeared to support this, but my experience and that of a number of parliamentary colleagues such as Andrew Stephenson in Pendle showed otherwise. The party decided to cement the Jewish vote and court the Hindu vote and, as Lynton Crosby colourfully put it, stop worrying about the 'fucking Muslims'.[59]

Campaign meetings increasingly focused on the 'Hindu vote', as polling showed us it was the 'softer' one to target. This thinking started to translate into divide-and-rule politics and dog-whistle messaging, something we saw play out in its worst form during the 2016 London mayoral election campaign.[60]

Policy-making for all things 'Muslim' revolved around counter-terrorism and extremism. Every engagement with Muslim communities from religious festivals to community events became an opportunity to discuss extremism, whereas other communities were engaged on business, entrepreneurship and other positive messages. The battle to engage the Muslim community on 'normal' issues or indeed any issue other than terrorism became a daily grind.

Language in speeches at Jewish and Hindu events was constantly referencing the 'others', the war on terror, praising our 'electorally relevant' communities and dismissing the others.[61]

The space for Muslims within the broader Conservative family too began to close. Conservative Home, a website run by the former chief of staff of Iain Duncan Smith, went as far as publishing a ten-point list that all Conservative political candidates of the Muslim faith should satisfy before they were considered sound.[62] And even Conservative Party conferences increasingly became a no-go zone for British Muslim groups, with many being turned away, not allowed to exhibit and refused permission to hold fringe meetings.[63]

This unwelcome approach alongside a disturbing policy agenda that exceptionalized 'Muslims' left many, including members of the Conservative Party, feeling that the party was not the one for them. On the one hand we raged against the politically correct brigade and especially 'the Muslims, whom we felt wanted exceptional treatment, and on the other hand we exceptionalized them, sending out the message to British Muslims that they didn't matter to the Conservatives and increasingly didn't measure up to our 'British values': they didn't belong.

This naked political aspect of policy-making and its impact on

Britain's minority communities isn't something new – the exploitation of the politics of race and minorities runs through all political parties – but sadly my party, the Conservatives, seems to have the worst history. 'The Muslims' may be the latest on the receiving end of this hostility, but, as I discussed in chapter 2, they are simply in a long list of 'others'. Oddly, despite our history, the approach towards 'the Muslims' started well under Cameron's leadership, and we have much to be proud of from those early years. Appendix 3 sets out some history and key moments in that journey.

But over time a combination of policy-making in the area of counter-terrorism and a Conservative Party uninterested in 'Muslim voters' has played a large part in how the Conservative Party is now viewed by British Muslims. It's shaped the tale of Muslim Britain.

I've often said to British Muslim communities who feel under attack by the government and feel there is a grand plan against them that, although there are and have been individuals in government with a deeply disturbing political ideology which is anti-Muslim, most politicians from all parties are well-intentioned. Despite the odd few who have over a period of around a decade engaged in a well-orchestrated but destructive policy agenda, much of what we see is either cock-up, complacency or, most often, politics and self-interest. Another time, another place, it could be, and indeed has been, another community.

Politics is defined in the *Oxford English Dictionary* as 'the activities associated with the governance of a country or area, especially the debate between parties having power'. Politicians are defined as people professionally involved in politics. An alternative definition suggested is 'a person who acts in a manipulative and devious way'. I urge my fellow practitioners of politics to focus on the former, not the latter – the professionalism not the manipulation – to use their status as policy-makers to create ease not angst, to unite not divide, and to find solutions not simply shout. It's time to take the politics out of policy-making on counter-terrorism; we owe it to the security of our nation.

And this means genuinely re-engaging our Muslims both politically and in government. Let's recognize the many hands within British Muslims that are extended in friendship, individuals keen to help, eager to play their part, more mature than before and accepting of their unique role in the challenges facing Britain, but also feeling vulnerable and isolated, battling the daily Islamophobic abuse and attacks that have sadly become all too common. As *The Economist* described them, they are 'pious, loyal and unhappy'.[64] And let's do so before it's too late. And let's do so sincerely and not as part of another counter-terrorism response.

In 2015, after the *Charlie Hebdo* terrorist attack in Paris, the government in a clumsy and mistimed attempt tried to reach out to Muslims. It failed miserably. A well-intentioned letter from the then secretary of state Eric Pickles backfired. I was not surprised: 'there was a trust deficit, a questioning of motive to a letter sent with the best of intentions. For too many, the hand of friendship felt like an admonitory finger that was once again pointing at Britain's Muslims.'[65] A further half-hearted attempt was made in October 2015 called the Community Engagement Forum. This meeting was hastily arranged, badly managed and not reflective of a broad range of British Muslim opinions, but at least it was finally an acknowledgement that the policy of disengagement had failed and government once again needed to start to engage British Muslims. The status of this forum is now unclear. It is uncertain whether the initial attendees were permanent members or one-off attendees. A subsequent meeting involved women only and was once again chaotic, with one attendee recounting to me that she 'was invited at short notice to a meeting with no agenda, no format, no clarity of purpose, no outcomes or follow-up'.

It's time for government to put in place a formal process of engagement. We have a blueprint for it: heads of all major Jewish community groups have an annual meeting with the prime minister. I have had the privilege of attending alongside David Cameron. The meeting was hosted in the cabinet room at No. 10 Downing Street. I've argued for a long time that all prime ministers should hold a similar meeting with other major faith communities. This would be a start.

At the time of writing the new Theresa May government has yet to make any major domestic intervention on 'the Muslim issue'. May's speech at the Republican conference in Philadelphia and subsequent press conference do not bode well.

This 'pause' in counter-terrorism policy-making was much needed after the Cameron years. So the seventh solution is to take stock, assess what has worked and what has not; to call time on policy failures and be brave enough to try another way; and to implement both the menu of solutions that we already have statutes on our books for before we call for more legislation.

And this starts with calling time on Prevent in its current form. The Prevent strand of the CONTEST strategy, which started as a policy 'for hearts and minds' and is widely now seen as a 'securitization' of a community, 'an array of mechanisms for the disciplining of Muslim subjects',[66] must stop. Let's start by having a thorough and transparent review, as recommended by David Anderson, QC, the independent reviewer of terrorism legislation. Let's acknowledge that Prevent as a brand is 'toxic' and at the very least needs to be reworked and reworded.[67]

The Coalition government tried to heed the advice of the parliamentary inquiry into Prevent by separating community cohesion from the hard-edged disciplinary aspect of Prevent, but in practice not much has changed. We have a well-resourced Home Office practising Prevent and a severely under-resourced Department for Communities playing at cohesion. Prevent, from the so-called science that underpins it,[68] to its hit-and-miss approach, to how it's interpreted and implemented locally, to the complete lack of transparency on where and how the funding is spent, is irreparable.

It's time for 'Promote', a concept I discussed in chapter 4. The work of Promote is too important to be an odd add-on in the Department for Local Government, where too often it has become the sacrificial lamb offered to the god of austerity. Promote needs its own space, with its own experts and most importantly its own resources. The fallout of the EU referendum, the diversity of the country that we now are and the fracturing of the UK between the British nations, the north and the south of England, the city regions and the centre due to ever-increasing devolution means the need for unity has never been greater. These times need a new approach: it is time for a Department of National Identity and Integration (NII), a proposal we considered as a party in 2008–9 as we put together a programme for government. The work on identity and integration is as important as national security. The NII should be as necessary as the NSC (the National Security Council). The secretary of state should have the remit to work across the United Kingdom, something that the current Department for Communities cannot do. We are either serious about the unity of the United Kingdom and we should show we are or we are not and as such should stop talking about it. National resilience is an essential element in national security.

Let's tackle inaction and implement the laws we already have rather than simply talking up an issue. Talking as opposed to implementing has been a feature of policy-making, which has had serious consequences for British Muslims and the security of Britain. The sorry sagas of Abu Hamza, Omar Bakri, Abu Qatada and Anjum Chowdry are but a few cases in point.

Abu Hamza, famously known as 'The Hook', arrived in the UK in 1979. We finally convicted him in 2012 and then extradited him to face trial in the US. This man poisoned young minds for twenty-three years and in the end he was convicted for, amongst other crimes, crimes under the Offences Against the Person Act, 1861, on evidence which he had publicly promoted.[69] He now serves a life sentence in the US for terrorism-related offences. We could have taken him off our streets earlier – a view apparently held by Her Majesty too.[70]

Omar Bakri arrived in the UK in 1986 and after building Hizb-ut-Tahrir and subsequently Al Muhajiroun, the source of many an extremist, he left the UK within weeks of the 7/7 attacks. The Home Office banned him from returning, saying his presence in Britain was 'not conducive to the public good'. In nearly two decades, despite his praise for terrorists, terrorist acts and terrorism, he was neither arrested, nor charged, nor convicted. He is now in Lebanon serving a prison term for terrorism.

Abu Qatada arrived in the UK in 1993, and, despite being responsible for sermons that radicalized many a future terrorist and fatwas calling for violence, it took twenty years to finally deport him. His preaching at Finsbury Park mosque inspired many a young man to commit terrorist acts.[71] He now lives in Lebanon.

The domestic, delusional, destructive force that is convicted extremist Anjum Choudry of Al Muhajiroun and Islam 4 UK fame was born here. The son of a market trader who failed his first year at university because of his preoccupation with drugs, drink and porn, he pronounced on live TV that I was not a Muslim because I didn't 'dress like one' and believes that a Muslim takeover is possible.[72] He is now behind bars. Most British Muslims have always viewed him as a dangerous, attention-seeking TV caricature of the *Daily Mail*'s idea of a Muslim. We loathe the amount of attention the media has given this man over the years, and after the murder of Drummer Lee Rigby I publicly challenged Channel 4's obsession with using him for comment. He was a darling of the media, who helped build his profile and made him more relevant than he was in reality. He inspired many an associate who went on to commit terrorism. The media need to consider their responsibility in giving him the oxygen of publicity. The media's constant billing of him as an example of British Muslim thought infuriated British Muslims, who neither saw him as a genuine, authentic or respected voice for British Islam nor supported his 'vision' of British Islam. The outpouring of joy from Muslims at his conviction was widespread.

There are numerous theories amongst British Muslims about Al Muhajiroun, its many manifestations and Chowdry, from the conspiratorial to the more believable: he is a terrorist honey trap, he has a 'deal' with the police about his 'remit', he is incredibly shrewd at staying within the limits of the law, and, as one police source suggested following Chowdry's conviction, he was a useful intelligence tool.[73]

Al Muhajiroun and its various aliases have operated in the UK since the mid-1990s. Successive governments since 2006 have banned their various incarnations, but the individuals involved have largely remained at large to continue their destruction, such as the gang of men who 'egged' me in a confrontation in Luton in 2009.[74] They took issue with how I dressed and my decision to enter politics. And they are the same gang that for three decades has attacked Muslim British politicians who have called for political engagement.[75]

British Muslims, including members of the Lords and Commons of the Muslim faith, have for two decades been calling for their removal from our streets, indeed from our country. And communities were pushing for a crackdown on them long before government got its act together.[76]

Hate preachers on our streets, the pop-up mosques of the 1990s and a gang of robed agitators caused unease between communities. They preached hatred in the name of Islam. Hamza, Bakri and Qatada were all foreigners, and yet for years we allowed them to poison young minds on the streets of London and create a broader movement for violence. We allowed them to shape British Islam.

And it seems ironic that the very community who suffered at the hands of these preachers, who lost its kids to terrorism because of these groups and who felt let down by the authorities who didn't confront these gangs, is today seen as a suspect community.

Policy-makers need to take responsibility for the mistakes of the past and act more quickly in apprehending and convicting those who sow division. The inability to arrest, charge and convict the hate preachers, some of whom still roam our streets and have become rent-a-quotes for the media while in the meantime government stretches ever deeper into ordinary British Muslim lives through an ever-increasing demand for legislation and surveillance powers, is not just bad policy-making, it's also naive and perilous. It can feel as though shaking the whole tree and losing good fruit through our ever-intrusive counter-terrorism policy we deem better than simply picking off the rotten apples that are rotten for all to see.

In policy-making let's implement the plethora of recommendations which successive governments have detailed as solutions in policy papers and simply never used. The vast majority of the recommendations in the Preventing Extremism Together Working Group's report in 2005 still hold true today, including recommendations on opportunities for young British Muslims to be leaders and active citizens and to instil a more faithful reflection of Islam and its civilization across the entire education system, including the National Curriculum, further education, higher education and lifelong learning.

It's a document I returned to after the Lee Rigby terrorist attack in 2013. We could at that point have simply looked at the response to 7/7, where there had been extensive community engagement, numerous recommendations, defined streams of work and expert assistance in the form of advisory groups, and actioned the recommendations which were published just over a decade ago and never fully implemented by Labour. But we didn't, instead setting up yet another task force, the ETF, extending the definition of the 'extremist', extending the flawed Prevent programme and drawing battle lines on the vague concept of 'British values'.

The practical solutions it did propose, such as communications support for groups that wanted to combat terrorism online, to legal and practical help for mosques at risk of extremist takeovers, to support for projects that highlight the shared British and Muslim history, were left to languish as civil servants and ministers failed to agree funding.[77] Each time solutions were offered but rarely implemented and certainly never supported long-term. And like the recommendations of the post-7/7 taskforce, the Conservative Party's policy papers from 2007 to the ETF, recommendations remained just that: recommendations.

In a policy area as serious as international and domestic security we can't afford to simply convince the public we are 'dealing' with the challenge when in reality through our policy positions and lack of implementation we simply are not. If we are serious about the fight against terror let's start by fully implementing our own damn recommendations over the last twelve years, which continue to gather dust as government policy papers.

Let's stop talking about forced marriages and fund genuine support for victims of this crime. Let's stop talking about FGM and start prosecuting perpetrators. Let's stop talking about Sharia councils and change the law to give Muslim marriages equal status and thus Muslim women equal access to the civil courts. Let's be brave enough to have that honest conversation with British Muslims. Let's work with them to get their house in order on civil marriage registrations. Let's give them a grace period, say three years, to implement the simultaneous religious and civil marriage ceremony, after which let's have the confidence to make it compulsory. Let's give civil courts the power to instruct a panel of approved scholars to grant women a religious divorce when an estranged husband is refusing to do so. These proposals have sat in 'policy papers' in government for over five years, and yet politicians simply announce another policy review. Let's stop talking it all up and get on with fixing the problem. Because, as history has taught us, politicians talking up matters does not resolve issues it simply greenlights bigots.[78]

Politicians are usually terrible historians. We have a great propensity to make the same mistakes over and over again. We find ourselves faced with political challenges faced by our political predecessors and sadly find ourselves making the same mistakes that they did.

As I outlined in chapter 2, we have a long history of making bad policy, and the right of politics seems to have particular form for getting it wrong when it comes to some of the most marginalized in society.

We've discriminated against communities in the past; it was morally wrong and we should learn from that. We've pitted community against community in the past; it backfired, we should learn from that. And we've marginalized whole communities in the name of fighting terrorism; it hindered, not helped, and we should learn from that. It's time to do things differently It's time to rethink the way we do foreign policy. It's time to say what we believe and do what we say.

It's time to make policy based on evidence and informed by experts, not influencers with personal agendas. It's time to have an honest fact-based discussion on the science of radicalization. It's time to use language which resolves challenges rather than riles communities. It's time to stop feeding the media monster which has become a large part of the problem. It's time to end the policy of disengagement, to call time on Prevent, to promote Promote.

Most politicians are on a journey, it's rare to see politicians take the same position decades after they first entered politics. Experiences and events shape us like they do everyone else. Regular moments of self-awareness are an essential part of good decision-making.

I'm not advocating midday yoga sessions or the contemplation suite or tranquility room created by the last Labour government in DCLG.[79] I'm suggesting a self-imposed filter which asks whether what we do as policy-makers is fixing or furthering the problem. Is our approach nurturing or destroying the journey of Islam in Britain? How will a generation of policy-makers be remembered?

Politics, like religion, is open to interpretation. It's a cocktail of ideology, pragmatism, national interest, public service, self-interest and a basic instinct for power. What may seem like the right thing to do may not be the right thing for oneself.

In policy-making the response to 'the war on terror' both domestically and internationally has seen the worst of this kind of behaviour. It's time for politicians to put naked self and party interests aside and, in forming our policies about our Muslims, start acting in the national interest.

9

The Rest of Us

'We should never forget those on whose shoulders we stand
and those who paid the supreme price for Freedom.'

Nelson Mandela

A decade ago ideas such as a 'Muslim register', a database to track
Muslims, 'a complete and total shutdown' of Muslims entering a
country, Muslim-specific immigration bans and Muslim internment
camps were the preserve of conspiracy theorists. Today they form the
policy platform on which US President Trump was elected.

After 7/7, conversations about life being made difficult for 'Muslims'
and the creation of a hostile anti-Muslim environment preoccupied
'Muslim activists'. It was a description I found absurd, a climate I
could not envisage and a journey I was confident would not be a part
of the tale of Muslim Britain. Today I do not believe any of us can be
so sure.

Democracy, an oft-cited British value, is the bulwark against arbitrary power, the place where extreme views are flushed out by the
good sense of the people, 'the considered view of the crowd [that
keeps] the mob from the gates', and which ensures we all continue on
our journey towards liberal values.[1]

But the narrow miss in the Austrian elections in May 2016, when
the far-right Freedom Party came within 1 percentage point of winning, the rise of far-right party Jobbik as an electoral force in
Hungary, the electoral success of the Front National in France and
the election of Donald Trump all show democracy in the West is enabling, not stifling, extreme views. And Denmark, Germany, Greece,

the Netherlands, Slovakia, Sweden and Poland are a growing group of countries where the far right are starting to take their seats in the nation's parliament. These times are stress-testing how we see democracy.

Each of these elections is a regressive step away from the plural, liberal, tolerant values we often cite as 'western values', values we've defined in the UK as 'British values' and which OFSTED measure our schools against. The victory of candidates who show an outright disdain for women, the disabled and LGBT rights, distrust religious minorities, demean blacks, Arabs, Mexicans and Latinos, despise Muslims, mock civil liberties, flout the rule of law, see knowledge and fact as an inconvenient distraction and display behaviour which breaches traditional boundaries of decency suggests that, as Britain fought to convince British Muslims of British values, large parts of the West appear to be giving up on the very values we espouse as sacred.

These elections demonstrate that democracy doesn't always deliver results in tune with our stated 'British values'. The fact that we have in Britain politicians who are prepared to overlook all of this and praise such victories is itself a defeat for 'British values', and a reminder that a simple reliance on 'our values', our innate good sense and even a belief in our laws no longer provide enough of a safety net to protect all within our nations.

Our values and our laws are only as good as public opinion, so it is we who must shape and lead it firmly on the path to a progressive, inclusive and tolerant future. As George Orwell poignantly said in his essay 'Freedom of the Park', 'If large numbers of people are interested in freedom of speech, there will be freedom of speech, even if the law forbids it; if public opinion is sluggish, inconvenient minorities will be persecuted, even if laws exist to protect them.'[2]

The way to ensure we aren't ruled by a tyrant is to ensure that public opinion isn't manipulated to elect one to office. This starts with politicians and the press taking responsibility for what they say and print.

Post-truth politics, pseudo-academics, a disdain for evidence, attacking judges, belittling the rule of law, discrediting hard-won human rights and those who defend them, dismissing equalities principles as political correctness, government policy-making reduced to Twitter-friendly 140-character messages, policy which doesn't even meet our stated values, shock-jock journos and 'alternative' news are now a part of the landscape that informs political discourse. And politicians and the media distort the truth and manipulate public opinion to win votes or sell papers. Describing women as sexual objects to either subjugate or vilify, mocking the disabled, viewing people of different races and faiths as inferior, gay-bashing, statements on race, religion, gender, sexuality and disability considered abhorrent only a decade ago today are normalized as the cut and thrust of political campaigning, as 'alpha male' behaviour which can be dismissed as a 'distraction'. Each statement of this type from those in authority gives permission to the public to say and do the same.[3] The chair of the Home Affairs Select Committee warned: 'In a democracy, political disagreement should never provoke violence, hatred or discrimination. Campaigners and political leaders have a responsibility to ensure their rhetoric does not inflame prejudice or become a licence for hate crime.'[4] The Equalities and Human Rights Commission (EHRC) urged politicians to engage in 'accurate information and respectful debate',[5] and my colleague Damien Green warned, 'It's become abusive, it's become personal, and it's not good for democracy.'[6] It started with spin, it's ended with strife and it must stop.

The politics of the last twelve months proves that we can no longer take for granted our hard-fought liberties or the direction of travel. All of us who value the liberal basis of today's Britain should, if not out of principle then simply out of fear, mount the fightback against bigotry, hatred and division. The alarms bells are ringing, and we must heed the words of those whose forefathers have been here before.[7] We must act now and we must do so collectively.

We must demand a quality of public discourse which pushes back against the emerging fashion of distorted political claims, falsehoods and emotively charged messages, campaigns targeted at appealing to primary instincts of fear and greed. Mainstream politicians need to stop serving up lies because, as they are starting to learn to their detriment, fringe politicians are much more effective in this form of campaigning. We let the genie out of the jar and we must firmly put it back. If we are worried about the direction of travel then we, as political parties, politicians and the press, need to stop and think how we contributed in laying this path. We need to ask ourselves why voter turnouts continue to fall, why voters are put off by our naked electioneering, why not acting in the national interest means people stay at home on election day whilst the marginalized and angry are incentivized to turn out only by extreme political messages. Campaigns which greenlight bigotry slowly destroy decency in democracy.[8] And it's why direct action is increasingly popular as referenda, petitions and protest appear to empower in a way parliamentary elections simply do not.

At the respectable end of the 'leave' vote in the EU referendum were the people who wanted to 'take back control' of their country; at the more extreme end were groups like Britain First, for whom direct action literally means physical confrontations. It's a view that finds advocates in the extremist ideology of groups like Hizb ut-Tahrir (HT), whose mantra is 'Elections are haram, bro.'[9]

This threat of democratic disengagement and a decline in public trust of democratic institutions should keep us awake at night. If we think people with a faith can occasionally cause us problems, our citizens losing faith in our systems will be catastrophic. The EU referendum was a stark and brutal example.

And as the post-referendum fallout continues to show politicians pitting community against community, manipulating the truth, legitimizing hate, raising expectations by campaigning on promises that will not or cannot be delivered means the angry and marginalized are once again disenfranchised.[10]

Much has been written about who voted for Trump and why. Some cite racism, others misogyny, while others point to the 16 per cent increase in the Republican vote amongst voters on incomes under $30,000 (less than £25,000), but the one thing we can all agree on is that over 40 per cent of eligible voters simply didn't vote; Trump was elected to the White House on the votes of only 26 per cent of eligible voters. When the masses are turned off politics, democracy serves extremism.[11]

And the ballot box is used to make extreme points, as a protest by those who feel neglected. As George Osborne wrote: 'Trump brilliantly captured the insecurity that so many [felt] . . . and turned their cry for help into an angry movement of change.'[12] This is a modus operandi also used by extremist groups like ISIS to recruit support.

People voted for Trump because they felt that they didn't matter or belong in the United States of 2016, and the election of an individual who seemed to follow no norms, no rules, indeed didn't even stick to basic civility, was their answer to the 'powerful'.

It's a mindset found amongst many a young violent jihadi, where a loss of identity, a need to matter and belong is found in the fold of extremist groups. Religious zealots and the far right are both manifestations of the same mindset.

Stephen Bannon, the controversial new chief strategist at the White House, believes the current crisis is caused by a loss of our 'Judeo-Christian Foundation', a 'crisis of our church, a crisis of our faith' and an 'immense secularization of the West'. And he makes the case for social conservatism, including giving voice to the 'anti-abortion movement' and the 'traditional marriage movement'.[13] Bannon doesn't argue that the West doesn't have enough religion, he believes that the West doesn't have enough of his kind of religion. This is an argument made by many far-right politicians. It's an argument made also by extremist groups such as Al Qaeda and ISIS, who too yearn for a world more Islamic, providing it's their kind of Islamic. Ironically, for all their commitment to religion, both Bannon and his ilk, like Baghdadi and his ilk, have little tolerance and space in their world for each other's faith, Bannon singling out Muslims as the problem other and Baghdadi persecuting Christians and others in their masses.

The far right and religious zealots have much in common. Both espouse a world view of us and them, both have a version of acceptable women – family types rather than a 'bunch of dykes' – both view anger and aggression as positive, both wish to overthrow established systems and institutions, both glorify hate and both ferment and perpetuate grievance. It is no wonder that ISIS were 'rooting for Trump'. They feed off each other's manic behaviour and hate. So whether they wear suits or swastikas, carry a Tasbih or a Kalashnikov, we should not be fooled. There is nothing respectable about this new form of bigotry, and we should not allow them to reach for religion to justify their creed of hate.[14] In Britain we must collectively challenge and condemn both the religious zealots and the new far right and its new narrative. And we must do so together, even if 'we' are not the main focus of their current attention.

The far right is a broad church. In the US it has tried to define itself as the 'alternative right', embracing much of the toxic bigotry which centre-right political parties have historically been trying to distance themselves from. The alt right in the US and Europe are often anti-black, usually anti-gay, occasionally anti-Semitic, currently anti-immigrant and, sadly, always anti-Muslim. Some today try to rebrand themselves as pro-gay, pro-women and even pro-Jewish. In a climate where anti-Muslim sentiment and fear of Islam is commonplace 'the Muslims' are useful political fodder to rouse the masses. But let us not be fooled. Hatred of any one of us should be fought by every one of us.

More than ever the famous and oft-quoted poem by Pastor Niemöller is relevant, and more than ever we need to remake the case for basic tolerance as a minimum requirement in a civilized society:

> First they came for the Socialists, and I did not speak out –
>   Because I was not a Socialist.
> Then they came for the Trade Unionists, and I did not speak out –
>   Because I was not a Trade Unionist.
> Then they came for the Jews, and I did not speak out –
>   Because I was not a Jew.
> Then they came for me – and there was no one left to speak for me.[15]

Other communities must not be lulled into a false state of confidence. They may be coming for 'the Muslims' today, tomorrow they'll come for you. 'Hail Trump' and calls for a 'White America' at an 'alt right' conference in Washington within weeks of Trump's win and a short distance from the White House should be a stark reminder.[16] Keeping quiet as 'they' come for 'the other' is bad enough, but befriending the fascist or his ideology, as some minorities do, is a deeply dangerous strategy.

I'm appalled how some of the most vile bigotry can come from minorities themselves: homophobia within the black church, Sikh and Jewish members of the EDL and anti-Semitism within British Muslims are but some examples. We need to challenge ourselves and all our communities on these issues. It's something I've raised on numerous occasions with other faith communities, most starkly at a speech at the Jewish Board of deputies in 2013.[17] And there are politicians and policy-makers who, despite taking strong and supportive positions on fighting one form of hatred, seem happy to promote another. Homophobes in the anti-Islamophobia world are one example, as are those who fight against anti-Semitism but often seem not concerned about anti-Muslim hatred.

I discussed this with a journalist from the *Jewish Chronicle* when the paper ran a 'soft' piece on EDL leader Tommy Robinson in which he combined his anti-Muslim venting with his pro-Israeli fawning.[18] It was uncomfortable and unacceptable, and personally I believe dangerous. We need to be collectively putting out fires, not lighting new ones.

Ethnicity, race, origin and, yes, religion are a great basis upon which to establish relationships, safe spaces within which to engage robustly and disagree. They are also great spaces to define agreed norms and values upon which to agree shared futures. They should not be used as tools to denigrate one community simply because that community is the 'other' of our times. And let's not judge the best of one community against the worst of another, we all have amongst our communities individuals who damage the community brand and with whom we would prefer not to be associated. Let's not 'other' those who are a part of the communities that make up today's Britain.

Our Muslims are our Muslims, not the 'other'. Our Muslims are not Pakistan's or Saudi's or Turkey's Muslims. Their Christians are their Christians, not our Christians, they are Pakistani, Sudanese, Syrian, Eygptian or others.

We must oppose identity politics that divide, and sentiments that underpin statements such as 'Let's take Christian Syrian refugees only' must not be the future. It is natural and instinctive to feel an affiliation with, and affection for, places and people you are connected to through race, origins or faith – the Anglican ummah or communion, the Catholic ummah or unity under a papacy or the Muslim ummah are attempts at unifying believers against schisms and heresies – but it is dangerous to make that connection the basis of an exclusive identity in which insiders of your own nation become the other. We have seen this approach lead to persecution of Christians across the globe and to the genocide of European Muslims in our lifetime in Bosnia.[19]

Understanding conflict and accommodating difference doesn't just require a dialogue of the West and the East but also requires advocacy from minorities in both too, the Muslims in the West and Christians of the East, for them to articulate on behalf of each other as minorities living in their own lands but increasingly 'othered' by the majority. We need to learn to disagree well and develop the space to dissent alongside the drive for respect. We need a homogeneous belief in the diversity of belief, a commitment to a battle of ideas through meeting and debating rather than by stifling the space for dialogue and discussion. We need to accommodate difference, and this requires us to understand who we are as a nation today.

To ask people to join a club, the club needs to have a clear idea of who it is. If we want 'the Muslims' to be more like us we need to know what the 'us' looks like. In understanding the place of a minority faith and its believers it's important to understand the majority faith and its believers.

The former archbishop of Canterbury Dr Rowan Williams said in 2009: 'faith is [seen] . . . as a problem, it's an eccentricity, it's practised by oddities, foreigners and minorities',[20] a statement that acknowledged the steady decline of faith and in the understanding of faith, specifically Christianity, in Britain. Britain's relationship with God has been on the move: from the historic trauma of the Reformation to the Anglican Church's accommodation of local beliefs, to diversity within Christianity, to forging the relationship between church and state, to the more recent development of a decline in religious observance, the rise in liberal attitudes, the jostling for space in the public space between secularism and religiosity and the influx mainly over the last fifty years of different faiths.

The data, polls and reports over the last decade broadly conclude that Christianity in the UK is in decline.[21] We are increasingly becoming a nation of non-believers. Despite this, the majority of believers in this country are still Christian, but many who still identify as

Christian neither believe in the teachings of the faith nor practise the faith or attend church.[22] What some would consider the fundamentals of Christian teaching around relationships and marriage, for example, are today no longer societal norms in Britain. In defining a British identity, being a Christian is becoming less relevant.

Despite this, we still have a notion of a Christian tradition which we believe underpins the values of our nation. We have an established church, bishops who influence the law by sitting in the House of Lords, a network of churches, parishes, land and buildings and preferential access to the monarch and the prime minister for the archbishop of Canterbury, the leader of the Anglican Church. We feel Christian in our heritage even if not actively engaging in it.

Britain is also less religious than most of the rest of the world. And what growth Christianity has seen in Britain in recent decades has been down to Eastern European migrants and the black Pentecostal churches. So ironically it's the comers-in, the foreigners, indeed many from black and minority ethnic communities, who are keeping Britain's Christian heritage alive.[23]

In 2013 the Woolf Institute convened a commission chaired by the, now retired, first female lord justice of appeal, the Rt Hon. Baroness Elizabeth Butler Sloss, to look at the place and role of religion and belief in contemporary Britain. It reported in 2015, finding what it describes as 'three striking trends': firstly, an increase in the number of people with non-religious beliefs and identities; secondly, a general decline in Christian affiliation, belief and practice; and thirdly, an increasingly diverse landscape of religious faiths in Britain.[24] All this is creating a confused British identity, no longer rooted in a unifying faith practised in a very English way.

For domestic policy-making the current situation is a challenge. If in policy-making we define ourselves through the prism of Christian values even if we neither follow the faith nor practise it, is there an inherent conflict between who we are and who we say we are? In making policy today, it's important that our understanding of faith and religion is informed, that we do not confuse our historical identity with current societal norms and the conversation about Christianity is a mature one that acknowledges its bloody past, its journey and its current accommodation with diversity within itself.

We need to consider whether the eastern church resurgence will impact on British Christian values, whether we will be able to accommodate this difference. And as the practice and values of British Christianity change over time, will minorities in Britain become the last bastion of religiosity, both Christian and others? Are we heading for a Britain that is not just uneasy with Islam but also uneasy with religion? And if the majority of British Christians are becoming Christian in name only and are non-observant, non-doctrinal and non-practising, does it follow that Britain will only be accepting of this type in other faiths: the intermittent Anglican-type Muslim, the secular Muslim, the non-practising, non-observant Muslim or the recently more fashionable cultural-heritage Muslim? If these are the only religious types we are comfortable with, we could find ourselves as a nation seeing people of any faith who say they belong to a religion and practise their faith a threat per se. And this places us at odds with a world which is more religious, more observant and more practising.[25]

So let's start by having an accurate understanding of religion and faiths in Britain.[26] And if the 'problem' is a secular state and policy-makers no longer comfortable with faith then let that be the starting point for discussion. An aversion to faith dressed up as an aversion to Islam is a dishonest basis for a discussion, and the demonizing of Muslims on the part of many a militant intellectual atheist such as Richard Dawkins, who has described Islam as 'one of the great evils in the world', serves no one except the haters.

As familiar norms and practices become less widespread, and the demographics in some of our major cities change, we need to both manage that change and continue to make the case for diversity. This diversity does not have to be at the expense of our traditions.

Growing up in Dewsbury, for me religion and faith came in three forms.

Firstly, there was the Easter eggs, Christmas cards, fairy lights variety, with large helpings of Christmas carols and school assembly hymns. My obsession with Christmas carols and hymns has stayed with me. In my crazy, busy Christmas diary carol services are my me-time. That uplifting feeling that I got as a child singing 'Give me joy in my heart' and 'He's got the whole world in his hands' and the sense of civic responsibility that was demanded by 'When I needed a neighbour' conjure the same emotions today as they did then. Hymns and carols are the two things from school I still remember word for word decades after I first started singing them there. Sadly, my singing voice is as embarrassing today as it was then.

The second form of religion was the daily madrasa attendance. It was studious, strictly managed and a world of knowledge interpreted and given a very personal slant by whoever was the teacher of the moment. The teaching was methodical, there were clear targets and progress levels, but much of it was rote learning with little given by way of explanation. The teachings were not contexualized to the world I lived in, and many of the stories felt like fables from a bygone mythical time.

The third form was the wonderful storytelling at home. My dad, now eighty-one years old, has the most amazing memory and talent for telling religious tales. He also has this insatiable passion for telling the same story hundreds of times and each time telling it as if it's the first. And whilst as kids we did get to the point where we'd heard the stories too often, the fact that it was about religion meant that, out of respect, we listened again anyway. In later years, robust debate about the stories, the basis of which were the Qur'an and the Hadith, stories describing the words, actions or habits of the Prophet Muhammad and Islamic history, allowed me to understand not just the 'what', which was the teaching in the madrasa, but also the 'why'.

It's the 'why' that has been the largest influence on my personal belief. I am a Muslim; I would describe myself as a pragmatic practitioner. I'm not content with simply 'doing' religion. There has to be a 'why': for me reason and religion go hand in hand. The lawyer in me needs to see the evidence, and the politician in me needs to hear the argument. And it's why belief for me is not a stagnant position, it's a journey not a destination, evolutionary not revolutionary and ultimately a source for daily reflection, self-evaluation at times of great success and a source of strength at times of distress.

My faith is about who I am and not about who you are. It's a rulebook for me, not a forced lecture series for you. Its strength is a source of peace for me not ammunition with which to fight you. It's a ruler I have chosen to measure myself against, not a stick with which to beat you. It allows me to question myself, not to judge you. And recognizing myself, being sure of who I am, being comfortable in my identity, does not mean having to downgrade, erase or reject who you are. I can only truly accept you for who you are if I am sure of who I am.

It's an argument I made in 2012 in a speech at the Pontifical Ecclesiastical Academy at the Vatican, when I had the privilege of leading the largest-ever UK ministerial delegation to the Holy See, which included a private audience with Pope Benedict XVI. I argued that strong, open faith identities are a good basis for understanding the 'other'. I reject the argument that somehow to create equality and space for minority faiths and cultures we need to erase our majority Christian religious heritage, as I reject the view that Muslims in Europe are a threat to our Christian heritage.

As I said in my speech, in Britain, in Europe, today, in order to encourage social harmony people need to feel stronger in their religious identities, more confident in their beliefs. In practice this means individuals not diluting their faith and nations not denying their religious heritage. And for me to be confidently accepted as a European Muslim, Europe needs to become more confident in its Christianity.[27] In other words, genuine understanding and confidence – not bigotry – in our heritage and identity allow us to be more accepting of the other.

Issues around identity and the strength of it are an intrinsic part of discussions around extremism. The BNP and EDL are unsure of the world in which they find themselves and yearn for the 'way it used to be', and this leads to insecurity of identity. Equally illustrative is the *Islam for Dummies* version of faith ordered online from Amazon and adopted by wannabe jihadists from Birmingham as they prepared to travel to Syria to fight.[28]

We must all strive for a better understanding of different faiths and religions, their teachings, their writings, their histories and their journeys. And for those in positions of authority with the power to influence policy, religious literacy in today's world is a must.[29]

It's important we allow faith a space in the public sphere and acknowledge the role faith and specifically Christianity can still play in the UK, as denying it creates grievance, a loss of identity, a sense that Christianity no longer matters.[30]

We must be prepared to manage this change, to explain it with fact, to address the alienation of our majority and minority communities and be prepared to deal with the underlying grievance.

So where do we start? The world of the expert is a good start – not commentators and talking heads but real experts, academics, statisticians, researchers, pollsters (despite their less-than-stellar performance in 2016), historians, sociologists and psychologists, and anyone else who can shine a light. For me the issues are too serious for us to take my colleague Michael Gove's approach of 'no experts, please', although ironically he considers himself a bit of an expert on 'the Muslims', despite his minimal contact with Muslims in Britain and almost non-existent experience of the Muslim world.

So step one must be an honest analysis of who we are and how we got here as a nation. It's time to get a full and transparent picture of that journey.

Step two is a no-holds-barred account of the lurch towards extremism and violence in all its forms. While policy-makers have focused on religious extremists, race hate and xenophobia have crept in through the back door; we have been caught napping. Race remains the largest motivator of hate crime – around 80 per cent of all hate crime is race-related.[31] Muslims account for a third of all black and minority ethnic communities.[32] They are consistently more likely to be victims of racist hate crime than any other faith. Indeed many individuals of other faiths, such as Sikhs, have been attacked because they've been wrongly perceived to be Muslim in Muslim revenge attacks.[33]

Referrals to Channel via Prevent[34] under the counter-terrorism framework have increasingly related to right-wing and anti-Muslim extremists.[35] Between 2012/13 and 2015/16, referrals about far-right extremism increased from around 170 to 560.[36] In 2016 Jo Cox, MP, was stabbed and shot dead in broad daylight by a man who shouted 'Britain first' and was described by the judge on sentencing him for murder as a man with 'an admiration for Nazism and similar anti-democratic white supremacist creeds, where democracy and political persuasion are supplanted by violence'.[37]

And yet the government has no specific policy to tackle far-right extremism.[38] Unlike Islamist extremism, it is neither defined nor explained. We are playing catch-up on extremism, only proscribing National Action, a neo-Nazi, white supremacist group, for the first time in late 2016,[39] and it is costing lives. Politicians need to be clear, loud and united in their condemnation of all forms of hate and need to resource policies and initiatives to tackle both the hatred and the drivers of radicalization.

What is feeding extreme views, what are the underlying grievances and how can we start to address them? We need to understand factors that can lead an individual to use violence to make his or her point. We need to determine what motivates terrorists and analyse in detail all the different drivers of radicalization, with sufficient weight given to each. From mental health to mullahs' sermons, from discrimination to community development, from political rhetoric to economic exclusion, from theology to foreign policy, we need to move on from the failed era of 'It's all ideology'. We need to have the courage to acknowledge the drivers of radicalization, all of them, and not just the ones that suit 'our' narrative, whoever 'we' happen to be.

We need to acknowledge where counter-terrorism, counter-radicalization and counter-extremism policy has done more harm than good and be brave enough to chart an alternative course.

This analysis would be the basis of a genuine debate from which solutions that work will flow. So politicians, the media, community activists and religious leaders should all speak reality and not myth and draw upon our own history, our previous experiences with other communities and the facts and figures about the extent of the problem.

The brave need to step forward. In government, the media and the community we need to see individuals who are prepared to challenge the current 'accepted norm': the journalist who will question an editorial bias, the writer who will be scrupulous about the quest for fact, the politician who will resist the temptation to grab a headline, the activist who will square up to ideas which are divisive and the masses who will demand transparency and truth and call out all those who seek to divide.

We must demand facts and evidence from those who seek to lead our nations and those who seek to inform our nations. Politicians and journalists who peddle false stories, perpetuate myth and feed and publish divisive headlines do so because we allow them to. Each time we vote for a politician who tells lies and each time we buy a paper that has published false stories we feed the monster that slowly swallows decency in society.

The third step is: we must challenge those who ratchet up the hate and challenge false stories about immigration, scaremongering about refugees and the now almost daily headlines tabloid papers and politicians reach for without fact and explanation.

Allow me to focus on a few.

Take Sharia law, words that conjure up a world of hanging, flogging, chopping off hands and at the end of the day retiring to a harem of four wives. For most Muslims it's about births, marriages and deaths. Male circumcision, a health decision practised by both Jews and Muslims, is an aspect of Sharia, as is getting your meat from the halal or kosher butcher, burying your dead quickly, having a nikkah, a religious 'I do' moment, during the marriage ceremony, having a non-interest-bearing account as an opposition to usury, getting a risk-sharing, non-interest-bearing mortgage, the UK borrowing money for its spending as part of a Sukuk, an Islamic bond, the financing of the building of the Shard, my 100 denier tights as opposed to the see-through ones, opting for a filet meal rather than the Big Mac and, yes, employing alternative dispute resolution which is faith-based, such as the Beth din or Sharia council.

So what, you may ask, is all the excitement? Firstly it's the sensationalist polls which tell us that 23 per cent per cent of Muslims want Sharia[40] without explaining that we already have it: Britain has been accommodating Sharia and religious practice for Jews, Hindus, Sikhs and others for decades. The polls make no distinction between what is everyday Sharia practice and a desire to have a religious-based rules system which governs the criminal and civil conduct in the UK. I am yet to be convinced that British Muslims think 'hang 'em and flog 'em' is the way forward, although if the poll was done at a UKIP conference there would be many a non-Muslim who I can guarantee would think so.

Secondly, the spread of the Sharia court. As a lawyer and a Muslim I've never attended one or represented at one or felt it a forum best suited for dispute-resolution, but for those without a legally recognized marriage it is still the only forum for recourse. We can fix this. If we are sincere in our desire to protect women then let's implement the recommendations I outlined in chapter 8.

And then there is the all-time favourite hot topic of politicians and tabloids: forced marriages. It was finally made illegal in 2014 under the 'British values' agenda, having been discussed for nearly two decades, and even today we still talk more and prosecute less. It is a cultural practice that has no basis in faith and indeed is practised by Sikhs, Hindus, Muslims and Christians, and yet it continues to be used as an example of the 'Muslim problem'.

We lectured Muslim women to learn English to stop radicalization despite having no evidence to suggest that non-English-speaking mothers were the cause of radicalization. Despite this, we massacred the budget for English as a second language in the name of austerity.[41] I reminded my colleagues that many mums of my mother's generation didn't speak great English but still managed to raise thousands of lawyers, doctors, accountants, pharmacists and engineers, whilst the number of terrorists of my generation didn't even get into double figures.

And then there is female genital mutilation (FGM), a pre-Islamic practice, prevalent in North African communities – Christian, Muslim and others – and officially forbidden in Islam. It can be traced back to pre-Christianity. References are made to it in Greek and ancient Egyptian writings as a method to prevent slave girls getting pregnant, and indeed it increased the value of little girls, who were seen as more chaste. In the western world gynaecologists in nineteenth-century Europe and the United States practised FGM to treat insanity and masturbation. Isaac Baker Brown, an English gynaecologist, president of the Medical Society of London and co-founder in 1845 of St Mary's Hospital there, believed that masturbation, or 'unnatural irritation' of the clitoris, caused peripheral excitement of the pubic nerve, which led to hysteria, spinal irritation, fits, idiocy, mania and death. He therefore 'set to work to remove the clitoris whenever he had the opportunity of doing so', according to his obituary in the *Medical Times and Gazette* in 1873.[42] So all in all it was used by many a man from many a religion, culture and community to control female sexuality and yet once again it is presented in the media as a 'Muslim issue'.[43]

These are all serious issues, but they are inadequately addressed and explained yet regularly used by politicians and the press to grab a headline.

And then there is the 'Islamization of Britain', a favourite theme of the far right, the scaremongering that instils the 'fear of a Muslim takeover' but without any factual basis. Only 5 per cent of Brits are Muslims, and less than 2 per cent of MPs are Muslim, and a number amongst these too would not define themselves as such. A takeover of 95 per cent of the population by 5 per cent of its citizens or a democratic takeover of 98 per cent of our parliament by 2 per cent of its MPs is simply implausible even for the conspiracy theorists. And yet the fear is peddled.

If it's the community leader types that scare you, the ones you see on your TV screens, the ones who appear to speak for the Muslim masses, let me again put you at ease: they do not. There is no single United 'Muslim community'. Whilst 'unity' has been the rallying cry since the late 1960s, the 'Muslim industry' survives because of disunity. The fight for 'the Muslims' is often a fight to be the chosen Muslim, the preferred one to be engaged by government and other officialdom, the media face, the well-funded jobsworth rather than an effective leader who has united 'the Muslims'.

And whereas right now it sometimes feels as if British Muslims are at war with Britain, this is a community that has been at war with itself even during times of peace.

The Leveson Inquiry was an opportunity to start to stem this tide of media bad behaviour. The inquiry agreed with evidence it heard:

> that Muslims, migrants and asylum seekers, and gypsies/travellers are regularly presented in a negative light in the mainstream media, and in particular the tabloid press, where they are frequently portrayed, for example, as being by definition associated with terrorism, sponging off British society, making bogus claims for protection or being troublemakers. ECRI is concerned . . . [about] the racist and xenophobic messages themselves that are thus propagated in the media.

Muslims, migrants, asylum seekers and gypsies/travellers as the targets of press hostility and/or xenophobia in the press, journalists being encouraged to write fictional 'Muslim stories', lies, phone-hacking, criminal activity and support for the far right were all explored, with the report warning that 'it is important that stories on those issues are accurate, and are not calculated to exacerbate community divisions or increase resentment'.

The inquiry concluded that:

> although the majority of the press appear to discharge this responsibility with care, there are enough examples of careless or reckless reporting to conclude that discriminatory, sensational or unbalanced reporting in relation to ethnic minorities, immigrants and/or asylum seekers is a feature of journalistic practice in parts of the press, rather than an aberration.[44]

Ratcheting up the hate has become a too-regular feature of our press, and yet years of dithering by politicians and a lack of implementation of key Leveson recommendations[45] means that four years on the environment is no better.

Those who manipulate public opinion through lies, fiction and skewed reporting, those who over-report migrant crime and under-report far-right activity, when negative Muslim stories are super-highlighted but positive ones are not reported, when terrorism in the name of Islam is given front-page coverage whilst the murder of an MP by a white supremacist is buried deep in the paper, are not informing our nation through a free press, they are creating and feeding the culture of hate.[46] When political journalists go soft in interviewing the far right,[47] when the BBC allows more airtime to a party with one MP than those with dozens,[48] when members of the press regulator strike out at those who seek to exercise their right to raise concerns,[49] when front pages of newspapers manipulate statistics to skew a story[50] or publish photos of a happy new Nazi, a Combat 18 activist, to capture a celebratory mood,[51] they are all creating the climate we now face.

We must not settle for this misinformation and divisive reporting. We must call an end to headlines deliberately designed to ratchet up tensions and appeal to basic instincts of fear, greed and hatred. We must not allow media moguls to disturb the nation's ease in order to sell a paper. Politicians must implement Leveson to stop the abuses it identified. We must challenge those who seek to divide either for politics or for profit.

As our fourth step, we must tackle the underlying causes of a non-cohesive society, the alienation felt by majority and minority communities and the grievances cited. We must address the economic inequalities that feed grievances, giving rise to citizens turning to extreme political or violent 'solutions'. It means reducing the gap between the haves and have-nots, those who can access opportunity and those for whom it is out of reach.

Income inequality in the UK is increasing: we are the third-most unequal country in Europe and the sixth-most unequal in a list of thirty OECD countries.[52] We have large variations geographically: the north–south divide in England continues to grow,[53] with children from poor homes in the north-east of England having little or no chance of going to Oxbridge.[54] The wealth gap has expanded: the top 10 per cent of Brits hold nearly 50 per cent of all wealth; the top 1 per cent hold nearly a quarter; social mobility has steadily declined; and we are experiencing 'the worst decade for [growth in] living standards since the last war'.[55] Where you are born determines your life chances; family income, not talent, increasingly determines educational attainment; and the top jobs in all professions remain overwhelmingly occupied by those from wealthy and privileged homes.

There are too many in our communities who feel like they simply do not matter. White boys from working-class homes, the group of young people least likely to go to university; families in northern towns such as Barnsley, where heavy industry and the mines declined decades ago only to be replaced with low-skilled, low-paid temporary and agency work; single parents who hold down multiple jobs but still need to visit food banks; all victims of a more unequal society but all for whom the solution is presented through a vilification of 'the other'.

In the UK the far right claim to offer a radical alternative to the mainstream parties who they claim have abandoned white working-class areas. Instead of any progressive alternatives, it presents 'racial' solutions to real problems. This is not new. The BNP saw the violence during the riots in northern towns in the summer of 2001 as its best opportunity in years to put its anti-immigration views on to the political agenda, asking for Belfast-style peace walls to divide Asian and white communities in Oldham and a boycott of South Asian businesses. Rather than tackle economic deprivation, the far right reaches for cultural separation. It seems we find it easier to blame the problem on Londonistan rather than to start to tackle Richistan.

But as many western nations lurch to the right, one, despite some challenges, has reaffirmed its commitment to the centre ground: Canada. It too has seen rising income inequality but fares better than us. In social mobility, life expectancy and all-round general well-being, it performs better than the UK and the US. Canada didn't bail out its well-regulated banks and cause resentment amongst the 'have nots'. They manage their immigration based not on race or ethnicity but on skills. Their refugee policy is compassionate, not reactionary, and they see diversity as a very Canadian value. And in 2015 they rejected the increasingly anti-Muslim Conservative Party, electing Justin Trudeau, the son of a former prime minister, in a landslide victory for the Liberals. Canada didn't the feel the need to rage against the establishment.[56]

Britain too has an opportunity to chart its own tolerant way, and the Scottish experience, despite its many economic challenges, is a good example. On economic inequality across many indicators it fares slightly better than England.[57] It remains a more tolerant nation than the rest of the UK. In its attitude towards immigration, its steady decrease in prejudice, its support for diversity, its support for LGBT communities and a willingness and desire to live in mixed communities, it is leading the way for what Britain could be.[58] Its strong leading female politicians may also be an important element, as could be availability of a free university education, a universal opportunity to get on.[59]

As our fifth step, we must as a nation remake the case for diversity. Detlev Peukert, a German historian writing about Nazi Germany and the values needed to push back against fascist ideology, talks of:

> reverence for life, pleasure in diversity and contrariety, respect for what is alien, tolerance for what is unpalatable, scepticism about the feasibility and desirability of chiliastic schemes for a global new order, openness towards others and a willingness to learn even from those who call into question one's own principles of social virtue.[60]

These ideals are as relevant today as they were then.

So, however twee it may seem, let's all try to implement these in our lives. Let's get to know our local communities better, become more than members of a group and interact as individuals. Let's understand the diversity that makes our nation, the nuance and detail of individual identities, rather than revert to lazy stereotypes.

Nadiya Hussain, the 2015 winner of *The Great British Bake Off*, made women in hijabs more than just women in hijabs. Her humour, her personality, her sharing of her deepest thoughts, her anxieties and tears of joy and her amazing ability to bake made her an individual. This is a two-way process, as individuals reach out across their differences and find both how much they have in common and how rewarding experiencing difference can be. And in meeting the other we will start to discover the very complex and multilayered identities that we in a globalized and interconnected world now hold. As Nadiya Hussain beautifully put it at the end of her amazing BBC journey through Bangladesh, 'I am British, I am Muslim, I am Bangladeshi and I am proud of all three.'[61]

Many Brits have these wonderfully complex and diverse identities. I am no exception. My parents originate from Pakistan. When I was in government, in response to a request from William Hague, the then foreign secretary, Pakistan was the first foreign place I visited. Pakistan and Pakistanis had celebrated my appointment to the cabinet. Attendance at my first cabinet meeting on that warm May morning in a pink shalwar kameez, a traditional Pakistani outfit, led to a frenzy of press interest in Pakistan and created the perfect backdrop against which to build a stronger and more honest relationship between our two counties. I was a British minister who also felt like one of their own. It cut across the 'us and them' narrative of East and West, victim and aggressor, colonized and colonizer, Muslim and other.

Pakistan was an important ally in our ongoing engagement in Afghanistan, the fight against terrorism and the control of the narcotics trade and was one of the largest suppliers of peacekeeping forces in the UN. Its young and large population and rich mineral base made it a potential trading partner, and our large British Pakistani minority community, who made more than 1 million annual journeys between the two countries, made it a country with which we were intertwined, not just historically, but also in the future.

On my first official visit I spoke about 'my country's values', Britain's values: the rule of law, equality of opportunity, the rights of women and the protection of minorities. I spoke of the values of my faith, Islam, which chimed with the values of my country, Britain, and yet those values, I felt and argued, did not seem to be the values of the Islamic Republic of Pakistan, a country created in the name of Islam. It was a tough, heartfelt message and one which was neither rejected as colonialism nor dismissed as western intervention. It was the kind of diplomacy needed in an ever-connected world. It was what I termed Heineken diplomacy – reaching the parts other diplomacy cannot reach. It was bringing two nations together through shared and individual heritage.

It's what we saw on display when Prime Minister Modi of India made his state visit in November 2015, even if we didn't challenge him on racism. The British Indian community, and more specifically the Hindu community, were intrinsically involved in the preparations and indeed made up the vast majority of the crowd in Wembley Stadium, where Modi received a rock-star welcome. He was speaking to Brits who dressed in Indian clothes, listened to a speech in Hindi, watched Indian entertainment, many of whom waved Indian flags. These were not enemies within, they were comfortable in their multiple identities and proud to display them, the bridge-builders and door-openers and practitioners of Heineken diplomacy.

I also know that many of the British Indians who cheered Modi that evening in Wembley would not have achieved the great success they've seen in Britain had they stayed in India. The poverty, lack of meritocracy and class and caste structure would simply not have allowed it. And I also know that, as one of five daughters of a poor man with no pedigree or family connections in politics, there is no way I could have become a minister in a Pakistani government.

This visit in 2010 was one of a number I made to Pakistan during my time in cabinet. And as well as addressing the usual security, economy and aid issues, I felt able to address the previously off-limits issues of blasphemy, corruption and minority rights. Today's Britain, this new multiracial, multicultural, multi-religious Britain, had made insiders of outsiders. I wasn't an exception: consider politicians like Priti Patel, now the secretary of state for international development in charge of Britain's worldwide aid budget and the prime minister's India diaspora champion, Baroness Patricia Scotland, a former attorney general and now secretary general of the Commonwealth, business leaders such as James Caan, Sir Anwar Pervaiz and the late Sir Gulam Noon, and civil servants such as our ambassador in Qatar, Ajay Sharma, ambassador in Indonesia, Moazzam Malik, and Anwar Choudhry, who was born in Sylhet and returned to Bangladesh thirty-five years later to serve as the British high commissioner. These, along with many others, are great bridge-builders and door-openers for trade and a great advert for global Britain and its place in the world, individuals who since the Brexit vote have become an increasingly vital part of our drive to set up new relationships of understanding and trade.

I celebrate these multi-faceted identities that so many of us in Britain have and I am sure that it is because we are Brits that we can have them. Britain has in the past created the atmosphere for individuals to feel they can embrace all that makes them, and it is this wonderful feature of Britishness that we must fight for and retain for future generations.

Diverse Britain has made us a healthier, wealthier nation, with immigrants responsible for founding one in seven of all UK companies,[62] and public services like the NHS functioning because of them. And the 'other' has proved invaluable for our security services, police and armed forces in the form of those who, because of their race, religion or origins, can provide policing and surveillance, both at home and abroad, in ways Anglo-Saxon Brits simply cannot. And then there are new and expanding markets: the halal food and lifestyle industry and the Islamic finance market alone are estimated to reach £2.6 trillion each by 2020.[63]

And it is this space, this diversity, the stage where we can proudly showcase difference, that we must all protect and preserve. We need a Britain where difference is seen as a source of strength, not as a source of suspicion, and where, in an ever-more globalized, competitive world, especially with Brexit, this difference gives Brand Britannia a competitive edge. We need a nation that that shouts 'Hello, world' rather than growls 'Little island'.

And in this changing world our ability to understand faith and religion, both the challenges and opportunities between religions and the challenges and opportunities within religions, will be crucial. Our minority communities are an essential aspect of this endeavour. They will be part of the solution; they will negotiate, build relationships and find solutions in an environment of agreed ideals. They offer an alternative space for diplomacy, Heineken diplomacy, utilizing which will both protect our security and enhance our economy.

We need to raise our vision to the horizon, to move on from the debate on British values, increasingly seen as a list of things that existed on these shores before the pesky foreigners came in. A single list of values which is reductively interpreted and mechanically applied is not only historically inaccurate, as I showed in previous chapters, but also paradoxical. To define an initiative to unite us in a divisive way undermines its purpose. We need to champion a pride in our country, a confidence, an identity and sense of 'we' that is broader than our specific ethnic and religious group, and this national identity forming should be for all that make up the 'us' and the 'them'.

So our sixth step is to articulate who we want to be: our British ideals. We need ideals that are explicitly stated, consistently applied and universally accepted, demanding of all communities the same level of behaviour to the same standard, measured against aspirations that we've all contributed to. A national conversation is required to underpin this. We must say what we believe and do what we say. If we preach human rights, we must practise them too; if we lecture the world on freedoms, we must implement them passionately at home and we must celebrate, not begrudgingly tolerate, our hard-won equalities framework.[64]

Let's adopt the first recommendation of the Woolf Institute Commission and 'create a shared understanding of the fundamental values underlying public life', a forward-looking identity rooted in the language of inclusion, formed not off the back of a one-off speech on yet another nondescript UN special day to celebrate minorities but a consistent and steadfast vocabulary that runs through everything that we do like words through a stick of rock, a language that ensures aspirations are realized and that is repeated and repeated again and implemented and re-implemented. We are not yet a truly inclusive community, but we can aspire to be one and work towards it.

Our ideals must be rooted in equal access to opportunity, a belief that no one is left behind, that nobody is exceptionalized because they belong to an 'unpopular' group, whether that's the vilified 'shirk-ers', the white communities in post-industrial towns in the north that are seen by some, including in my party, as takers not contributors; the vulnerable and destitute who seek refuge on our shores and whom we 'fear' and feel 'swamped' by; or the bogeymen of the moment, 'the Muslims'. We need to acknowledge and then push back against both this re-emergence of the politics of hate, bigotry and division and the more subtle politics of 'othering'. By scapegoating communities in law and institutionalizing suspicion of them, as has happened with Prevent, we not only kick the hard work of community integration into the long grass, we feed the beast of division.

Let's not be kidded by the veneer of respectability and the increas-ingly mainstream new form of fascism. The change of approach and target of far-right groups in the UK is documented by Professor Mat-thew Goodwin of Kent University. They may dress better, speak better, have a manual on which words to use and which not to use and talk not of racial superiority but cultural difference, but there is nothing respectable about the 'alt right'; they are still far to the right of what Britain stands for.

And we can continue to keep them there if each one of us is pre-pared to take a few small steps of friendship towards 'the other'. Here are a few practical steps to start with. Go visit a place of worship. Go see a Muslim/Jewish/Christian/Hindu comedian. Ask your 'other-race/faith' friend that burning question you've dared not to so far, and if you don't have an 'other' friend, make one. Celebrate an 'other' festival. Read a book by an 'other' author. Put yourself in the shoes of the 'other'. If an ethnic minority person moves into your street, don't white-flight out. And if you've got a moment, think how well you would do in the Qur'an experiment performed by the Dutch pranksters described earlier.[65] Integration must become more than a middle-class pastime in the fashionable suburbs of town.

The post-Brexit, post-Trump world has brought to the fore what many had been warning of. The phrase 'Islamophobia' has passed the 'dinner-table test': in 2011 it was seen as controversial and outspoken and vexed many a politician and journalist; in the world in which we live today, the statement is so tame it appears facile.

The outpouring of anti-immigrant, and specifically anti-Muslim, hate and rhetoric is of a scale I've never experienced or witnessed before. The interview by Ciaran Jenkins for Channel 4 on the Friday after the EU referendum was a chilling case in point, as a very reasonable-looking man from Barnsley, a town a few miles from where I live, where I regularly pop in for a sandwich or to go to the bank, said he'd voted leave because 'It was all about immigration . . . to stop the Muslims coming here . . . The movement of people in Europe is fair enough, but not from Africa, Syria, Iraq, everywhere else.' The argument he presented was a direct contradiction of the early Brexit campaign message that a leave vote would free us to take Africans, Syrians, Iraqis and people from everywhere else and not be forced into taking Europeans, as we are at the moment with free movement. Now it would be stupid to take the actions and words of one white person from South Yorkshire and present them as the view of all white people from South Yorkshire – unlike the far right, I'm not into collective accountability and, unlike the media, I don't demand that people take responsibility for the actions of their co-ethnics – but sadly this view in Barnsley wasn't isolated. With the threats, the abuse and actual anti-Muslim attacks in the hours after the Brexit vote, a disturbing picture emerged.[66] The jubilation at the Sunderland count as the overwhelming vote for leave was announced included worryingly aggressive jeers and cheers. It later emerged that one of the men punching the air with his fist was a Combat 18 activist, who celebrated having 'taken back control'.[67]

My husband often uses a saying which we have clung on to at many a difficult phase we have faced in public life: it's always the darkest just before it starts to get light. It's a statement that always gives me hope. He is a positive realist, insisting we see things as they are rather than as we'd wish them to be, the best solutions only flowing from the most honest analysis of the problem. Right now, for many British Muslims, it feels dark, certainly the darkest I've ever known it be. It could get worse, or we could be optimistically hopeful that it's the moment just before it starts to get light. We could start walking towards the light, that new dawn. It will require bravery on all sides. But if we reset and restart I am confident that the perceived enemy within will emerge as a misunderstood friend. And, as history has taught us, politics has taught me and the words of Bob

Marley put in a nutshell: 'Your worst enemy could be your best friend.'

This is nothing new, we have been here before. Only this time we have the benefit of hindsight, historical realities which remind us how it started and how it ends:

> Political behaviour marked by obsessive preoccupation with community decline, humiliation or victim-hood and by compensatory cults of unity, energy, and purity, in which a mass-based party of committed nationalist militants working in uneasy but effective collaboration with traditional elites, abandons democratic liberties and pursues with redemptive violence and without ethical or legal restraints goals of internal cleansing and external.[68]

I'd like you to consider and assess how much of this statement could apply to what we are seeing unfold today.

The fog of fascism is once more spreading across our continent, xenophobic views are drifting in from the east and west of us and beyond. It starts with words, and if the 'respectable' justification of hatred is left unchecked it ends with actions.

How Britain responds to this new environment will determine whether we succeed in remaining a tolerant, diverse, liberal inclusive democracy, and the canaries in the coal mine are British Muslims.

Appendix 1:
Who Speaks for 'the Muslims'?

The community leader wonderfully depicted by the sitcom *Citizen Khan* in his ever-failing quest to be relevant and respected first developed out of a genuine altruistic vision of community service in the 1970s. Many a non-English-speaking migrant needed help, from simple things like form filling to free translation assistance for appointments for jobs, housing, health and schools. The semi-educated community bod would take on these tasks mostly for free, although some were known to charge, and eventually became a regular face, a known entity for officialdom to use as a conduit to engage the Muslims. Some went on to serve on local quangos and some sought and won elected office, while others set up community organizations and sought to represent, speak on behalf of, lobby for and organize the Muslim community. These organizations dealt with everything from burial needs to parking restrictions outside mosques. They were well-intentioned and dealt with 'practical issues'. Most, if not all, were male, predominantly South Asian or East African, and mainly first-generation migrants. Few had any formal campaigning or organizing skills and even fewer had an understanding of policy-making and the media. They were effective at a local level but perhaps not as prepared for national political work.

But amongst these one organization stood out: the Union of Muslim Organizations (UMO), led by Dr Pasha, an educated man, a trained lawyer, with experience of organizing in the US, an understanding of politics, having been involved in both student politics and in national political engagement with senior political figures.

The UMO was established in 1970 at a meeting at the Regent's Park Mosque, London, as an umbrella organization for Muslim

Organizations across the United Kingdom and Ireland. Although Dr Pasha was politically engaged nationally, it only really rose to prominence during and after the Rushdie affair. The UMO was an attempt to bring together a community defined by its ethnicity into one defined by faith. Funded generously by the Saudi and Iraqi governments, it was well resourced and initially well led. It seemed in its activities to cater for a broad range of sects focusing on the Shia communities' important religious festivals as much as the more Sunni-focused ones and for the most part was interested in 'provision' of facilities, goods and services. Like most faith-based organizations, it was very conservative in its outlook.[1]

It was the UMO who demanded the use of the UK's old blasphemy laws to protect Muslims during the Rushdie affair and led a delegation to meet the then home secretary Douglas Hurd to convey the Muslims' 'strong feelings' at what was perceived as the continued inaction of the British government to ban the blasphemous novel.[2] And it was the UMO who urged the prompt enactment of a bill of rights for the protection of the Muslim community in the UK.[3]

Alongside the UMO a new more politically focused group launched in 1988: UK Action Committee on Islamic Affairs, born out of a growing frustration that the post-Rushdie era had created an environment in which British Muslims felt unheard. The desire to be heard, to influence, led to a flurry of activity amongst mosques, groups and individuals all united in the belief that the community needed to unite to organize and to create national bodies.

By the early 1990s Britain's Muslims had made progress in local politics, but both the Labour and Conservative parties appeared uninterested in their having national representation.

Some thought that the answer to not being engaged by British politics was to disengage from Britain's political system, an argument put most vociferously by Hizb ut-Tahrir (HT), a group that in the UK came to prominence in the early 1990s. HT had become fashionable as a political home amongst the British Muslim chattering class and newly emerging university types. It was originally a political party formed in the 1950s in Jerusalem, Palestine, as a response to the creation of the state of Israel. Its founder, Muhammad Taqi al-Din al-Nabhani, an Islamic scholar and jurist, envisaged a unitary

Muslim state ruled by a single elected Khalifa, with Arabic as the main language and the rule of law rooted in religious principles. This so-described utopia, which interestingly had never existed throughout the history of Islam, was the only answer to the many woes of Muslims worldwide. Much of the group's views were a deeply intellectualized fantasy, and in the UK it provided the perfect space to rebel against the perceived passive elder generation, as well as to socialize and find a future marriage partner.

My own encounters with HT members usually left me cynical. I came away with the view that most were men, with huge egos, misogynists, usually confrontational and never wrong. It was the group that created the self-confessed extremists of the noughties, now much publicized as ex-extremists. Although many who claim to be ex HT may have changed their views, I believe that many haven't mended their ways. HT was and is in many ways an old boys' network, where women know their very defined place. The head of state, chief justice and other heads of authority in their utopia would always be male, though they regularly profess that women are not seen as inferior.[4]

Whilst HT advocated disengagement from the political process altogether, awaiting a worldwide caliphate, a new group that emerged in the early 1990s, the Muslim Parliament of Great Britain, thought the answer was a very front-footed and confrontational demand for services and provision that would effectively allow for a separatist existence with Britain – or, as they described it, a 'non-territorial Islamic state' in Britain. The organization, although well-funded and vocal, lacked any depth of support amongst Britain's Muslims and faded away.

What was more palatable to most was the emergence of a discussion calling for wider, deeper and more sophisticated engagement which eventually resulted in the most widely known British Muslim organization, the Muslim Council of Britain, the MCB. Officially named in May 1996, inaugurated in November 1997 and electing its first secretary general in 1998, the MCB was over three years in the making. Its purpose was – and still is – to increase education about Islam, and to 'work for the eradication of disadvantages and forms of discrimination faced by Muslims'. It was well organized and had importantly reached out to try and build a genuine grassroots and accountable body through affiliates and elections. It fashioned itself

on organizations in Britain's Jewish community and both from structure to areas of interest copied much of what the British Jewish
community had done in decades gone by.

This was a smart move, not only because the issues of concern
from dietary requirements to health and school needs were similar
but also because Britain's Jews had proved that representative bodies
were effective in engaging lazy officialdom.

But the MCB found itself accused of promoting self-interest and
being unrepresentative, male-orientated and out of touch, the kind of
accusations levelled at everyone from the Church of England to the
Board of Deputies. Some of the criticism, as it is with other faith-based
organizations, was to my mind justified. Power did become concentrated in the hands of a select few, it did suffer with problems of
ethnic discrimination and it has consistently suffered from accusations of sectarian bias. It was accused of being Bengali-, East
African- and Indian-heavy as well as over-representing the more conservative elements within the community.

In my view it made some bad political judgements: from its desire to
invest time and energy in advancing overseas contacts with the Muslim
world, the beneficial result of which to the British Muslim community
at large is questionable, to its policy of non-attendance at the annual
Holocaust Memorial Day commemorations between 2001 and 2007.

Although professing to be party politically neutral, it became close
to New Labour early on. But then Labour was the party of choice for
large sections of the Muslim community, so one could argue it was
simply representing the majority view.

The golden era of the MCB was between 1996 and 2006. It was
courted by government and the media. Dominating both the airwaves
and government engagement, the MCB was seen as the answer to all
things Muslim, both representing Her Majesty's government overseas
as a tool to engage the Muslim world and being the conduit for politicians engaging on Muslim issues. And during this time, to its credit, it
produced some good reports on the needs of Britain's Muslims. But
despite lunches with cabinet ministers and hosting Prime Minister
Tony Blair at one of its events, the MCB was not reticent in its disagreement with the government's position on foreign affairs. Calling the
US decision to bomb Afghanistan and Sudan in 1998, in retaliation for

the bombing of its embassies in Kenya and Tanzania, 'the law of the jungle . . . and a violation of international law'.[5]

It's quite astonishing to think that it was as recently as a decade ago that Anas al-Takriti of the Muslim Association of Britain (MAB), an organization set up around the same time as the MCB and as New Labour took office in 1997, eyed the pole position the MCB occupied with envy. Although cracks started to appear between New Labour and the MCB during the time Hazel Blears became secretary of state for communities and local government, its accelerated fall from grace was during the the political changes of 2010–15. And this fall was less to do with its ability, which often did seem questionable, and more to do with politics both in government and in Muslim communities.

The growth of Muslim organizations, or the 'Muslim industry' as I refer to it, grew organically from the late 1960s but under more 'controlled conditions' during New Labour's term in office. New Labour started the revolving-door policy where organizations fell in and out of favour and where engagement, disengagement, government funding and withdrawal of funding was used to 'create' organizations it liked and 'kill off' those no longer in favour.[6]

Some, such as the Young Muslims and the Islamic Society of Britain (ISB), having been established in the 1980s, were very much social spaces where mainly young people and professionals could be Muslim and British. Their summer camp, which still runs, is a jolly boys and girls outing where culture and religion, art and academia rub alongside easily and for the oldies provides an opportunity to allow the youngsters to socialize under a watchful eye. Many a marriage has started with a smile at the ISB summer camp. And like many Muslim organizations the ISB became an affiliate of the MCB.

But one organization which pre-dates all of the above and is still going strong is the Federation of Students and Islamic Societies (FOSIS). Originally called FOISS (Federation of Islamic Student Societies), it was established in 1963 at a meeting hosted at the University of Birmingham. It is the umbrella organization for University Islamic Societies, although not all are affiliated. It was the organization I came into contact with during my student years and where the three things on the agenda seemed to be Middle East, meals and marriage. Set up as a support group for Muslim students, it has, as one would expect from students, been at times at the forefront of debate on Muslim identity, hosting Malcolm X at several universities in the 1960s.

As with most student bodies it has sometimes pushed the boundaries of debate. It is a broad church and over the years has been led by presidents with very differing political and religious beliefs and backgrounds. It has like many other 'Muslim groups' been accused of allowing platforms on campus for extremist views. Whilst some of these accusations are baseless, where it has come up short is its inability to attract and allow a platform for a wide range of speakers, both Muslim and others, its failure to see the many sides to a debate and to properly exercise its function as an umbrella organization. Many individual ISOCs (Islamic Societies) on campus are affiliated to FOSIS and yet often reflect views and practices not in line with broad national FOSIS thinking. Many ISOCs are too narrow in their representation of 'British Muslims', often judgemental and increasingly seen as spaces that many British Muslim students don't feel like they belong. To remain relevant to the broadest British Muslim student community FOSIS must raise its game. Sadly, twenty-five years on they, like the Jewish societies on campus, continue to perpetuate the same entrenched positions with little space for genuine 'new thinking' amongst a 'new generation'.

My own recent experience of FOSIS is both via my children on university campuses and my own time in government. For the most part FOSIS is neither politically savvy nor actually committed enough to effect real change. I found that action points agreed were rarely actioned and follow-up items were rarely followed up. The most memorable moment with FOSIS for me was an encounter with its top team and a refusal from one of their officers, a young kid around the age of my eldest, to shake my hand. Now I have no issues with deeply held religious beliefs that apparently forbid handshakes between the sexes; I've sat with many an orthodox rabbi or imam and engaged in constructive work without a handshake, but FOSIS are not a set of scholars, they are a student body. And I fail to understand the thought process of a young man who keenly puts himself forward to deal with third parties only to alienate half the country's population at the first meeting. If your personal religious beliefs are fundamentally in conflict with the basic requirements of the job, then my advice is don't accept the job. I'm sure plenty of others, hey, maybe even a girl, would have been prepared to accept the role. It would be like me getting a job in a pig abattoir only to insist on halal working conditions.

Like the ISB, FOSIS too is an affiliate of the MCB.

In 2005, a group of predominantly British Pakistani and Kashmiri Muslims, many of whom had felt unrepresented at the MCB, set up the British Muslim Forum (BMF). The BMF was the Sunni Barelwi fightback against what was perceived to be a Deobandi-, Tablighi- and Jamaat-dominated MCB. The BMF wished to speak for what they viewed as the 'majority of British Muslims', those from a Sunni Barelwi tradition of Islam. The BMF initially focused on spirituality and love for the Prophet. My ex-colleague Paul Goodman, MP for High Wycombe from 2001 to 2010 and currently editor of the web-site Conservative Home, was an early flag-bearer for the BMF,[7] and more particularly the pirs, Muslim religious leaders with large numbers of followers around the world, revered as saints and rooted in Sufism. Pirs, not unlike peers of the realm before we working-class folk joined the Lords and spoilt it, are considered to be of the highest social order in some Muslim traditions, with the rights and privileges to pronounce upon matters both religious and personal. Most are deeply devout, lead with humility and provide a much-needed community service, acting as therapists, councillors and offering spiritual guidance. Others have been known to abuse their position for financial and personal gain. And, like the occasional pervy priest, the pervy pir is sadly not entirely uncommon.

The BMF, however, came to prominence with their post-7/7 intervention, when they issued an unequivocal and unconditional condemnation, albeit twelve days late. It set a more conciliatory tone and presented a more palatable text than the version of the bombings put out in the MCB-led statement which the BMF had put their names to a few days earlier.[8]

The BMF, the new kids on the block, were neither as well funded nor as well organized as the MCB, but what they lacked in pounds they more than made up for in people. They had the potential to mobilize large numbers at short notice and, unlike the MCB, didn't feel threatened in allowing their congregations access to meetings with politicians. The social order and reverence for the pir meant the 'followers' wouldn't use an encounter with an influential politician to subsequently cut out the pir and engage directly. The MCB, on the other hand, built its reputation on being incredibly effective gatekeepers, and meetings with influencers were always limited to a very small select group, something that is still occasionally a feature of the MCB.

Like the MCB, the BMF too spoke of its affiliates but didn't necessarily speak to them when it mattered. And this approach spectacularly backfired during the 2008 passage of the Counter-Terrorism Act and the debate around the proposed forty-two days pre-charge detention for terror suspects. The then chairman of the BMF, Khurshid Ahmed, hailed as 'Britain's top Muslim' by the *Sun*, made a statement on behalf of the BMF supporting Blair's position.[9]

The Conservative party, led by David Davis MP, the then shadow home secretary, now secretary of state for exiting the European Union, opposed the legislation. The revised BMF position gave Blair some air cover of support from 'the Muslims'. The Lords rejected the proposal and dramatically defeated the government. The winners of this saga were undoubtedly David Davis and his fellow civil libertarian warriors. Khurshid Ahmed was awarded a CBE in the Queen's Birthday Honours list. Lord Ahmad raised the award in the House of Lords on 8 July 2008 and asked whether Khurshid Ahmed had been persuaded to come out with a statement in favour of detaining terror suspects for up to forty-two days in return for a CBE and funding for one of his projects. This was later dismissed by Khurshid Ahmed as nonsense.

Whilst the BMF made some real progress in pushing forward debates on issues the MCB had previously not engaged with, such as Muslims and their role in Britain's armed forces, the two groups very much operated in isolation of the other until 2010, when swords were drawn during the Zakir Naik affair.

Zakir Naik is the much-followed televangelist, a cross between the pirs who are adored by the masses and the US-style evangelical preachers who are more celebrity than theology.

Naik had been controversial in India, considered sectarian by some, an intellectual by others, an inciter of hatred by some and an enlightened orator by others. But one thing that is true for sure is that he has a large following in the UK. Naik was seen by the MCB as a moderate, by the BMF as an extremist. His banning from the UK by the then home secretary Theresa May was seen as a victory for the BMF and by the MCB as further evidence that the government was playing a dangerous game of choosing its favoured Muslims, an interesting and odd position from a group which until that time had been the favoured Muslims.

Cage Prisoners, later simply called CAGE, hit the headlines in 2005 as Moazzam Begg, a British detainee at Guantanamo, was finally released without charge. CAGE's role in campaigning for prisoners caught up occasionally in the excesses of state action in the name of counter terrorism has been important but is undermined by their unwillingness to find words of condemnation for those engaged in terrorism. In my experience this has set a tone and narrative amongst some young British Muslims which is destructive and dangerous.

The post-7/7 era also saw the emergence of British Muslims for Secular Democracy (BMSD), set up in 2006, unusually for a faith-based organization, by two women: Nasreen Rehman, an academic and writer, and Yasmin Alibhai-Brown, the writer and journalist. The well-intentioned intellectual basis of much of their thinking was the development of a European Muslim community. But due to a simple misunderstanding amongst British Muslims of the word 'secular' in the group's name and its liberal position on nikaabs and faith schools to name but a few issues, it was perceived by British Muslims out of step with the majority, which certainly at that time held very conservative views.

The year 2006 also saw the birth of the short-lived Sufi Muslim Council (SMC). The SMC was launched to a great fanfare, with government ministers praising what was effectively an organization that nobody in the British Muslim community had heard of, that had no affiliates, no visible grassroots support and an ideological leader, a foreign sheikh, little known to British Muslims. British Muslims saw it as a smokescreen body set up by government as a rival to the MCB.[10]

By 2010 the group was effectively defunct with a small handful of volunteers and administrators, and indeed government, left holding a financial failure.

Despite the political ambitions of its two co-founders and the political connections of its sheikh, SMC was sold as a non-political movement.[11] It was marketed as turbans, tasbees (prayer beads) and evenings of zikr (religious chanting). They were heady, hippy and happy, the nice lot who just wanted to get stoned on spirituality and not prissy about politics. It was an easy sell and a sweeter pill for politicians, as SMC neither asked the tough questions nor made any demands. They told us policy-makers what we wanted to hear.

Sadly the romance was short-lived, and, like most things that have no roots and haven't grown organically, the SMC withered, as did the relationship between the sheikh and Rafiq. The latter moved on to set up CENTRI, a counter-extremism consultancy, with Rashad Ali, and four years later he joined the Quilliam Foundation.

The Quilliam Foundation is a counter-extremism thinktank established in 2007 and is seen as one of Blair's last gifts to British Muslims. It was established by three men: Ed Husain, now a fellow at the Tony Blair Faith Foundation, Rashad Ali, of CENTRI fame and the least 'visible' of the three, and Maajid Nawaz, who ran as a Liberal Democrat candidate in 2015. All of them profess to have been linked to Hizb ut-Tahrir during their student days. All profess to have at some point 'seen the light' and turned their back on their extremist positions. They, along with a small but high-profile set of individuals, are the 'ex-extremists' popular in the right-wing press, and despite their self-confessed dubious pasts have been welcomed back into mainstream political life.[12] The name of this group comes from Abdullah William Quilliam, whom I wrote about in chapter 1. Quilliam swore allegiance to the Ottoman Empire and advocated for a global caliphate, not dissimilar to that of HT, the teenage ideological home of QF's founders and the very view the foundation today opposes.

Amongst British Muslims the Quilliam Foundation has been one of the most despised parts of the 'Muslim industry'. From accusations that QF is a tool of central government and receives shady sources of support from the US to a view that it has dubious links with organizations and individuals with Islamophobic form,[13] to the questioning by close family and friends of the ex-extremist stories of its founders,[14] it has had a controversial place in the tale of Muslim Britain.

QF has become a depository for British Muslim anger, distrust and ridicule and invokes the most extraordinary reactions from the most rational individuals, views that Nick Clegg was vociferously confronted with during the 2015 General Election, when potential party donors questioned Nawaz's selection and its impact on 'British

Muslim voters.' So QF within British Muslim communities has arguably become the mother of failed experiments, but in a wider context it has been a huge media success, dominating the airwaves on 'all things Muslim' and making 'red meat' statements to the red tops.

My view is that QF is a bunch of men whose beards are tame, accents crisp, suits sharp, and who have a message government wants to hear. Its analysis of the problem – 'it's an ideology called Islamism' – chimes with the government's narrative. It's a narrative set by Blair, promoted by QF, followed by Brown and Cameron and one which in chapter 4 I argued was fundamentally flawed.

Despite these concerns, I have had many a fruitful conversation with QF activists. Usama Hasan, a theologian at QF, is thoughtful and spiritual, and coffee with Maajid Nawaz, who was recently cited as an anti-Muslim extremist by the Southern Poverty Law Centre,[15] is always an entertaining if often combative experience.

The post-2010 Coalition government era saw the rise of a number of dynamic 'doing' organizations rather than simply 'saying' organizations. This posed a challenge to the traditional UMO, MCB and BMF types whose main focus was engaging with officialdom, photo ops and press releases. Younger and more professional British Muslims were less tolerant of campaigns that delivered little and meetings that appeared self-serving.

IEngage was an early attempt to 'do something tangible' and tackle Islamophobia systematically. But they were discredited by sections of the Conservative Party, including Robert Halfon, MP, who used parliamentary privilege to do so.[16] They also faced challenges from the likes of MCB, who seemed to feel their presence undermined their own position. By 2014 IEngage was no more, and out of the ashes rose Muslim Engagement and Development (MEND).

MEND has not been without controversy. It has been at the receiving end of a number of media hatchet jobs as well as facing the challenges of trying to appeal to a broad church and in doing so accommodating views that, although not illegal, are clearly illiberal. But it has matured, and I think it has the potential to achieve real change because not only is it grassroots-funded and run, it is also results-focused. It's a doer not a sayer.

Its main nemesis is an anti-Muslim monitoring organization called

Tell MAMA, which was born out of discussions at Tory HQ at a time when I was Conservative Party chairman. Fashioned on the community protection organization run by British Jews called the Community Security Trust (CST), its aim was to collect data and campaign for the proper monitoring of Islamophobic hate crime.

Tell MAMA started well, and my colleague Eric Pickles, the then secretary of state for communities and local government, was eventually persuaded to fund it. But a series of negative media stories questioning the accuracy and method of its data collection[17] nearly destroyed the organization in 2013. Tell MAMA's well-intentioned but highly emotional CEO Fiyaz Mughal was persuaded to engage CST help, which both resulted in administrative systems being put in place and provided the much needed political air cover which came with an association with the CST. Sadly a series of blunders, including becoming the source for *Telegraph* journalist Andrew Gilligan on a news story vilifying the cross-government working group on anti-Muslim hatred and some very respected members of the British Muslim Community, left Tell MAMA's credibility amongst British Muslims questionable and thus in many ways not fit for purpose.[18] The recruitment of the former Labour member of parliament for Dewsbury Shahid Malik as co-chairman in 2014 was an attempt to steady the community's nerves. It, however, unfortunately continues to invest too much time and energy in 'talking down' other Muslim activists and groups.

On the one hand Muslim community groups work to tackle Islamophobia and other challenging issues facing British Muslims and on the other sadly undermine each other in a bid to be seen as the chosen ones for government and other officialdom. As they fight to take credit for the meagre crumbs of policy concessions that the government has chosen to throw 'the Muslims" way, anti-Muslim hate crime continues to grow, in London alone rising by almost 60 per cent in the year to October 2016.[19]

The rise of ISIS has brought to the fore a series of smaller groups that have been involved in community work for many years, from Faith Associates to Active Change Foundation and more recently Imams online. These groups are trying to work collaboratively with government, putting out statements which are very much officially sanctioned and trying to mould the government's programme on preventing extremism. They are making an important contribution.

The most recent group, Inspire, was set up in 2009.[21] It is exceptional in that it is female-led – a positive – but because of its unexplained association with the governments anti-extremism agenda it has been kept at a cautious distance by large sections of the community. The co-founder, Sara Khan, was recently questioned by members of the Home Affairs Select Committee about Inspire's track record, project work and the funding it has received.[22]

These and others form Britain's 'Muslim industry', and all profess to speak for or about British Muslims and thus have played their part in the tale of Muslim Britain.

Appendix 2:
Party Politicking and 'the Muslims'

British Asians and Black Brits traditionally voted Labour, which was seen as the party of the poor and the coloureds. As Muslims were most often both poor and coloured, Labour became the party of British Muslims too. The Conservative Party was viewed by the blacks and Asians as 'the lot that don't like our lot'. It's a view still held today by many British Muslims.

Enoch Powell was often quoted, and little distinction was made between the views of the National Front and that of the Tories. A poll by Tory pollster Lord Ashcroft in 2013 found that:

> the memory of Enoch Powell remained strongest among black Caribbean participants, 64 per cent of whom said they had 'heard of him and know who he is or what he said'. 28 per cent of Asians knew who he was. Among the wider population, nearly three-quarters had heard of Powell and 58 per cent knew who he was or what he said. 90 per cent of UKIP voters fall into the latter category.[1]

The 'N' word was still widely used in the 1960s, and the Conservative Party was seen to have made it acceptable to use in the famous Smethwick election slogan 'If you want a nigger for a neighbour vote Labour,'[2] a phrase which UKIP returned to in the recent Stoke Central by-election, replacing the word 'nigger' with 'jihadi'.

Later, in the 1990s and 2000s, as the children of the immigrants grew up, the Conservative Party was seen as having moved from overt racism to covert racism. The party's approach to immigration was seen as deliberately structured to make life difficult for immigrants and the process of migration humiliating. The primary purpose rule of 1980 was one such example.[3]

Labour abolished that rule soon after the election in 1997. The move was popular in immigrant communities.[4]

An early government consultation by the Coalition government in 2011 raised concerns that the 'primary purpose rule was about to be brought in again via the back door'. Thankfully we didn't do this, but the suggestion we would didn't serve us, the Conservatives, well.[5]

The Labour Party was also viewed as the ones who were for the labourers. The migrants who had once worked in factories during the 1950s and '60s associated it with the trade union movement, the ones who kept them in jobs. It was also seen as the party that bought in anti-racism legislation and was the most vocal against the National Front – and of course as the party who provided protection by passing the Race Relations Act 1974.

This, however, is a simplistic narrative. For example, the Harold Wilson Labour government in the late 1960s gave grant aid to local authorities who faced pressures because of the presence of substantial numbers of immigrants. These funds were originally supposed to be directed at marginalized and discriminated black communities but didn't reach many, and 'the programme could be read as a compensatory programme aimed at whites living in multi-racial areas'.[6] And while there is no doubt Labour was the driving force behind the Race Relations Act, it was also broadly supported by the Conservative Party.[7] And Enoch Powell's views on race were at odds with many of his Conservative colleagues.[8]

However, there is no denying that there were some morally questionable positions taken by some members of my party. One Tory MP, Ronald Bell, who served as an MP from 1950 to 1982 and was a prominent member of the Monday Club, argued that to make the incitement of racial hatred an offence would curtail free speech and, by protecting a specific group, i.e. people of colour, was giving people special treatment and privileges. In other words it was a privilege not to want to be called a Paki and curtailed free speech if we made regular National Front chants such as 'Go back home, Pakis' illegal.

The question I have asked myself about the 1970s and '80s is whether the Conservative Party had a terrible racist streak at its core or whether much of its rhetoric and political posturing on the issue of race was just simply that: politics. Were we really, as the current prime minister described us when she was party chairman in 2002, the 'nasty' party?

There are many historical examples of Conservative members becoming involved with the National Front and the BNP, and indeed some of the language at times hasn't been too dissimilar. John O'Brien, the chairman of the National Front from 1970 to 1971, was a Conservative Party member and a supporter of Enoch Powell, and John Read, chairman of the National Front from 1974 to 1976, too was a Conservative Party member and chairman of Blackburn Young Conservatives, as were many activists and subsequently elected officials and councillors. The overlap between the far right and the Conservative Party over time diminished, and thankfully progress in the Conservative Party made it an increasingly less attractive offer to the fascists of the right. In the 2005 elections, for example, the BNP was more dissatisfied with the then leader of the Conservative Party, Michael Howard, than the National Front were with Margaret Thatcher in the 1980s. This would suggest that the Tories' appeal to the far right has over time diminished as it pulled itself into the centre ground. Personally, I believe it was more to do with an early and strong intervention by Michael Howard in the form of a hard-hitting anti-BNP speech in Burnley.

However, what is strikingly similar between the position of both the far right and the Conservative Party is that during the 2000s the focus of both the far right and mainstream right-wing politics shifted from a focus of difference on the basis of race to a focus on a difference in cultures and values. This became the basis of a new 'other', a feature also present in the more subtle positioning of UKIP, who, despite being described by David Cameron as 'fruitcakes, loonies, and closet racists', try hard to couch their arguments on race in terms of immigration and cultural difference. Unlike the BNP and National Front, they were not racists in suits, they never preached or practised violence, but some would probably satisfy what government policy would currently call 'non-violent extremists'.

This new positioning and alignment also spills over into the media. The right of politics receives more support from those newspapers that BNP voters are most attracted to and they are the same newspapers that regularly run anti-immigrant and anti-Muslim stories.[9]

The instinct of the political right is to conserve, and through that a suspicion of the new, the other, makes it more susceptible to attracting the respectable racist. I've encountered many examples of this. At a members' meeting I addressed in Croydon, an elderly member tried to explain to me that the use of the term Paki as in 'Paki shop' wasn't racist, it was merely a figure of speech. This caused my colleague Gavin Barwell, MP, much embarrassment; I simply took it as another frank question from a not very well-informed member. Whilst I'm convinced that the overwhelming majority of Conservatives are not racists or Islamophobes and genuinely believe that the odd embarrassing and inappropriate outburst from party members is more ignorance than malice, it could be argued that sometimes we, on the right of politics, can create the climate, the swamp, within which the racist feels comfortable. We have been the breeding ground for many an individual who eventually found his way to the soft far right such as UKIP or hard far right such as the BNP, individuals who went on to run a campaign of 'othering' during the Brexit referendum, one that translated into attacks on our streets.

Despite the mistakes of the post-9/11 period, the right of politics had a unique opportunity to define future race and community relations in the United Kingdom. Conservative thinking provided fertile ground for combining the strong message on security with the equally strong message on opportunity irrespective of background or origin. It was the perfect place to make the argument of a small state and a large society where individual liberties and community are precious. And it was the right party to understand religion with all its nuances and complexities.

I viewed the party as the space where a clear commitment to the rule of law, core principles around natural justice and a profound sense of a moral compass would be natural and instinctive. I felt that opportunity for all and a sense of fair play had the potential to drive an understanding that was fresh and realistic and that would allow us to look back and hold our heads high rather than in shame, as so often right-wing parties have to do on the issue of minority rights when history judges us as being on the wrong side. The 'Muslim problem' of the 1990s presented an opportunity for the Conservative Party to get it right and not make the mistakes of the 'black problem' or the 'Irish problem' they had got so wrong in previous decades.

Each of the last five leaders of the Conservative Party has in their own way had the tools to understand Britain's Muslims. William Hague, who was leader of the Conservative Party from 1997 until two days after 9/11, had Yorkshire experience, was a staunch defender of marriage and was respectful and understanding of religion. His Yorkshire roots and connection with key Tory activist Mohammed Riaz from Bradford, who himself was deeply rooted in the British Muslim community, gave him inroads, and he appeared to connect with umbrella groups like the Muslim Council of Britain.[10] Iain Duncan-Smith, with his understanding of faith and commitment to social justice, and then Michael Howard, with his own migrant history and minority religious roots, as the son of a Romanian Jewish immigrant, had personal insights into issues of race and religion.

David Cameron too started in a good place. He was open, prepared to learn, to ask the difficult questions, to understand the nuances and place himself in the shoes of others. During an early visit to Dewsbury in 2005, en route to party conference in Blackpool, when he made that historic note-free speech which convinced so many of the party faithful that he was the future, David went with his wife Samantha to visit a reading project for children of parents for whom English was a second language. As he sat eating biryani off a paper plate in the lounge of a working-class Muslim family and the children excitedly sought his attention, he seemed at ease with difference and comfortable with ordinary people despite his own extraordinary upbringing. In 2007, not long after David became leader, he spent time in the home of a British Pakistani Muslim family in Birmingham came away impressed with the sense of community, inter-generational living and family values. I was hopeful that he could be a man for today's Britain.

In both domestic and foreign policy speeches he was keen to stress inclusion, partnership and trust, inspiring people to be British, not demanding it, commanding loyalty from all who have made these islands their home.[11] In an early foreign policy speech in 2006 he spoke of a foreign policy based on humility, patience and winning the trust of the majority Muslim community.[12]

In 2007 he was the leader who, at the behest of David Davis, MP, now minister for Brexit, firmly planted the Conservative Party as the champions of civil liberties against a Labour Party onslaught. David Davis stood down from his seat in 2008 and called a by-election on the issue of civil liberties and Britain's increasingly draconian anti-terror laws. It was during this campaign that David Davis, at my invitation, came to Dewsbury on the third anniversary of 7/7 and at a community event gave a powerful speech on how Muslims felt unnecessarily targeted by arbitrary and unnecessary anti-terrorism laws.

So, by 2007 my party had distanced itself from neo-conservatism, was a champion of civil liberties and prepared to challenge Labour on how it was alienating Britain's minorities. From the oft-quoted Cameron's hug-a-hoodie moment to that resounding defeat of the Labour government's proposal to detain suspects for forty-two days without charging them, this felt like a new dawn for the Conservative Party and its relationship with its minorities.

And it was different to the platitudes and old-guard community leaders route that was the Labour way. We were not brown-nosing the brown folk, we were engaging on the issues. We were not thinking of how we could offer an alternative ethnic minority manifesto to the ones the Labour Party and the Lib Dems had offered.[13] We were focusing on the barriers to integration and committing to tear them down. From poverty to education, cultural barriers to political correctness, no longer were the minorities going to have to settle for the crumbs from the table: no, we, the Conservatives, were offering a stake in the cake.

It felt fresh and exciting, a new way, an honest way, a break from the past. It was substantial not showy, it was engaging and it was finding a balanced place between security and liberty. And we were engaged in serious discussions about fighting for the votes of British Muslims.

The Conservative Party has talked about engaging the non-white vote for nearly two decades. It's a vote we've traditionally not enjoyed, and ever since the days of Mrs Thatcher we have tried to make some overtures to the Muslims.[14] John Major as prime minister and Michael Howard as home secretary in the mid-1990s certainly tried to court the Muslim vote.

By the time I fought a seat in 2005, however, little progress had been made. Attempts by candidates like myself, Ali Miraj, who fought Watford, Sandy, now Baroness, Verma, who fought Wolverhampton, and Tariq, now Lord, Ahmad, who fought Croydon North in 2005, to reach beyond our core vote were seen as too little too late. This, along with the party's high-profile anti-immigration campaign and a refusal by Michael Howard to say that, if he had known then what he knew now on the dodgy dossier, he wouldn't have supported the war in Iraq, meant that the Conservative Party made few inroads either in the BME vote generally or the Muslim vote specifically. The Lib Dems picked up BME voters dissatisfied with Labour.

In 2005 the Conservative Party took approximately 10 per cent of the BME vote.[15] By 2010 the party had made little progress, taking only 16 per cent of the BME vote.[16] For me the BME vote was crucial to long-term electoral success, but despite my many efforts prior to the 2010 election the party seemed uninterested in engaging with the BME vote. Stephen, now Lord, Gilbert was head of campaigning. And despite numerous attempts to get him out of London to see BME community campaigning in action, his diary seemed never to permit it. Dates were arranged on three separate occasions, and each time he cancelled at short notice.

A meeting I had with Canadian Conservative MP Jason Kenney not long after I'd being appointed to the shadow cabinet in 2007 provided some early hope. His was a centre-right party that had taken the issue of BME votes seriously and had seen some success. I asked Stephen and others to study and learn from the experience; it took the party four years to get round to it, finally 'discovering' the Canadian campaign experience in 2012.[17]

Before 2010 we talked about extending our vote base but did very little practically to extend it in the BME community. We rarely attended 'ethnic' events and other than the customary handshakes and places of worship visits that made for good photos during the last few months before an election we didn't make any real effort as a party to engage. Individual candidates such as Gavin Barwell in Croydon and Paul Uppall in Wolverhampton made real inroads and took their seats in 2010, Paul sadly losing his after one term, but we failed to win in many other seats mainly because the national party didn't get its act together.

The Ashcroft poll and report of 2011–12 was a long overdue

wake-up call. The report, *Degrees of Separation, Ethnic Minority Voters and the Conservative Party*, was based on a polling of 10,000 people plus twenty discussion groups, as opposed to the more recent *British Future* report in 2015, which only polled 2,067. It found that voters who ordinarily fit the profile of 'Tory voters' based on criteria such as income, house ownership, profession, public or private sector employment and a whole series of other categories still didn't vote for us if they were 'not white'.[18]

The poll is significant both in its findings and the timings of its findings. It was conducted around the time the 'hard language' and policy towards Muslims, the Munich speech being one such example, was starting to take shape. It was also around the time that the party was very deliberately mounting a charm offensive towards British Hindus, including the setting-up of the Conservative Friends of India.

After 2010 I was appointed Chairman of the Conservative Party alongside Andrew, now Lord, Feldman. We both came from religious minority and migrant backgrounds: his Eastern European Jewish, mine South Asian Muslim. In Andrew I had someone who was as committed as me to extending the voter base of the Conservative Party. And by 2012 we had not only convinced the prime minister to push for broader engagement of cabinet colleagues with the BME communities but also established 'interest' groups within the party such as Conservative Friends of Pakistan, Bangladesh, India, Sri Lanka, Tamils, etc. They were very much modelled on Conservative Friends of Israel, which was widely regarded as the most effective group identity interest and lobbying group in British politics.

Alongside this sat the Conservative Christian Fellowship, which had been established in 1990, and the much newer Conservative Muslim Forum (CMF), an organization set up by Lord Sheikh, the Conservative Party's first peer of the Muslim faith, under the auspices of Michael Howard. David Cameron, however, for the most part viewed CMF and its chairman as an irritant, neither engaging them in policy thinking nor giving them real and meaningful access.

All political parties use sophisticated tools to identify and target individual voters. The targeted campaigning relies upon a sophisticated breakdown of individual voters by a number of key indicators including income, home ownership, employment status and sector, education, geographical location, etc. A racial or religious identity or affiliation as a key indicator provided a completely new dynamic. To woo these voters, we needed not only policies that resonated, but also to show them that people like them were made to feel welcome in our party, and our party understood the issues that mattered to them. It was, as David Cameron put it, not enough for us to leave the door open so they could step in, we needed to step out and welcome people in.[19] We needed to make them feel like they mattered and belonged in the Conservative Party.

The Conservative Party decided to focus its energies on certain groups only, and it paid off: these 'relevant' communities felt positive towards the Conservative Party as they believed the party felt positive about them. The reverse too was true. British Muslims felt the party over a number of years had distanced itself from them (the policy of disengagement), had unfairly discredited and demonized them (the Munich speech, the Bratislava speech) and had written off their votes and their community as collateral damage in the war on terror, a message I heard over and over again on the campaign trail during the 2015 General Election.

And although the 2015 General Election saw a modest rise in non-whites voting for the party in particular seats, the jury is still out as to whether any sort of breakthrough has happened.[20]

Appendix 3:
We Don't Like 'the Muslims'

In 1992 the race equality thinktank Runnymede set up a commission to consider anti-Semitism in contemporary Britain. Its report, entitled *A Very Light Sleeper*, published in 1994, found that anti-Semitism wasn't just in the form of violence or harassment by the far right but also in more subtle stereotyping and denial of the contribution of Jewish life to Britishness,[1] findings which could apply today in relation to Islamophobia. It made a number of recommendations, including a code of conduct for the media, the teaching in schools of the place of the Jewish community in British life, changes to legislation and a system of monitoring anti-Semitic incidents. It also recommended that Runnymede should set up a broadly similar commission to consider Islamophobia.

Despite concerns raised in the wake of the Salman Rushdie affair and the riots in Dewsbury, Bradford, Burnley and Blackburn, little progress was made, and it took a further five years for the issue to be taken up, once again by the Runnymede Trust, under the chairmanship of Professor Gordon Conway. The report, *Islamophobia: A Challenge for Us All*, was launched in November 1997 by the home secretary, Jack Straw.[2]

This was the first time that the subject of Islamophobia had been comprehensively tackled in relation to a British Muslim population which had had a significant presence in our major cities for at least a quarter of a century, was around 1.5 million in number and had hit the headlines for the wrong reasons. Sixty recommendations were put forward in the report targeted at government departments, bodies and agencies, local and regional statutory bodies and voluntary and private bodies. Recommendations included making criteria and procedures for providing state funding for religiously based schools more transparent, and permit appeals against decisions of the secretary of state; local education authorities to use their influence to ensure that local Muslim communities are appropriately represented on schools' governing bodies, particularly schools which have substantial proportions of Muslim pupils; applying consistent principles in the teaching of history in relation to Islam; scrutinizing measures and programmes aimed at reducing poverty and inequality with regard to their impact on Muslim communities; reviewing equal opportunities policies in employment, service delivery and public consultation and ensuring that these refer explicitly to religion as well as ethnicity, race and culture; guidelines on good employment practice on matters affecting Muslim employees; making discrimination on religious grounds unlawful; employers and unions to include references to religion in their equal opportunities statements and policies, and state their opposition to discrimination on religious grounds both in recruitment and in general personnel management; treating evidence of religious hatred as an aggravating factor in crimes of violence or harassment, as already with racial violence; reviewing legislation on blasphemy and including in this a study of relevant legislation in other countries; political parties to take measures to increase the likelihood of Muslim candidates being selected in winnable seats, and using their influence to increase the representation of British Muslims on public bodies and commissions; proposing the appointment of Muslims to the House of Lords.

It attracted wide interest and media coverage in both the UK and abroad. It also defined Islamophobia, focusing on four key words: discrimination, exclusion, prejudice and violence. A more comprehensive definition was later developed by the Center for American Progress in the report *Fear Inc.*: 'an exaggerated fear, hatred, and hostility toward Islam and Muslims that is perpetuated by negative stereotypes resulting in bias, discrimination, and the marginalization and exclusion of Muslims from . . . social, political and civic life.'

There has been much disagreement amongst commentators and academics about the term Islamophobia.[3] The arguments focus around what exactly it is we are referring to when we use the term. Is phobia an appropriate word to use or does the term shut down debate on Islam? I prefer the terms anti-Muslim sentiment and anti-Muslim hatred but like many others use Islamophobia as a quick and lazy term. Criticism of Islam, as of any other religion, is in Britain a legitimate and legal endeavour. Indeed, Islam itself has a long tradition of questioning, challenging and critique. Britain does not and should not protect Islam but we should absolutely protect individuals who follow a faith. But most importantly it lent its voice to the calls from the likes of the Muslim Council of Britain for the inclusion of a question on religion in the census of 2001, giving us accurate figures for British Muslims for the first time. And the emerging data from the census 2001 brought a new level of clarity to understanding and analysing the Muslim situation in the UK.

It also led to the setting up three years later in May 2001 of the Forum Against Islamophobia and Racism (FAIR), beginning the process of documenting anti-Muslim hate crime and responding to the changing policy environment after Runnymede and later, in readiness for the introduction of legislation which would outlaw discrimination on grounds of religion in the workplace.

As a follow-up to the commission and the report, and independently of the Runnymede Trust but led by a trustee of the Runnymede Trust, Dr Richard Stone, the Commission on British Muslims and Islamophobia was established, and it produced a report in 2004 at the launch of which Dr Stone made some damning comments: 'The only area where there has been major change is within Muslim communities themselves. Government has not taken on board, in a deep way, the anti-Muslim prejudice in this country.'[4]

These concerns, raised a year before 7/7 and over a decade after the Runnymede Trust raised the flag of concern, were no further developed six years on in 2010, when I first entered government.

The establishment of FAIR brought into being a body to record anti-Muslim incidents, but the activity largely remained within the Muslim community and didn't enjoy the level of political backing that work against anti-Semitism in the UK enjoyed. No formal process was set up within government and no schools initiatives existed to tackle it.[5]

But as my friend and ex cabinet colleague Eric Pickles, MP, once reminded me, 'The bloody Muslims need to help themselves and not always be looking to others to help them out.' These oddly phrased but robust words convinced me, as it had the Runnymede Trust, that the best template in dealing with religious hate crime was how the battle against anti-Semitism had been fought. That British Muslims needed to organize themselves and operate as professionally as British Jews if the issue of discrimination against them was to be taken seriously. I therefore used the work to combat anti-Semitism as a blueprint.

In 2005, the All Party Parliamentary Group (APPG) against Anti-semitism set up an inquiry into anti-Semitism in the UK led by the then, now disgraced, Labour MP Denis MacShane. The inquiry was 'established to investigate the belief, widely held within the Jewish community, that levels of antisemitism in Britain are rising'. It reported in 2006 with thirty-five recommendations, including that the Home Office provide support in addressing the security needs of British Jews especially at places of worship and faith schools, that all police forces record anti-Semitic crime as a separate category of hate crime, that the Home Office report annually to parliament on progress, with regard to Israel that a conversation take place with the media to ensure sensitive and balanced reporting of international events and for government departments to support more interfaith work and anti-racism initiatives in school later.[6] The government welcomed the report and responded comprehensively, agreeing to take forward many of the recommendations.[7]

I felt a similar approach needed to be taken in relation to Islamophobia. I felt an APPG against Islamophobia, followed by an inquiry, followed by a report, followed by a government response would bring much needed energy to an issue which seemed not to worry politicians. Little did I know what a storm I was about to create.

My private parliamentary secretary (PPS), the former MP for Lancaster and Fleetwood, Eric Ollerenshaw, persuaded Kris Hopkins, the MP for Keighley, a constituency with a sizable Muslim population, to chair such a group. He agreed. Eric at the Conservative Party conference in 2010 met with an organization called IEngage, a breakaway group from the MCB, who volunteered to act as administrators to the group in the way the Parliamentary Committee Against Antisemitism Foundation pays a member of staff to administer the group looking at anti-Semitism. The subsequent objections to this group, from the *Jewish Chronicle* to Lord Janner and the Community Security Trust, a charity working to combat anti-Semitism, led to the APPG collapsing before it started. The objections were based on allegations of anti-Semitism levelled at the trustees of IEngage. Indeed, Robert Halfon, MP, former Conservative Party chairman, used his parliamentary privilege to make such allegations of IEngage being 'aggressively anti-Semitic, homophobic and [having] extensive links to terrorism in Tunisia and the Middle East' on the floor of the House weeks after the launch of the APPG.[8] Bizarrely IEngage was also undermined and briefed against by the MCB, who were not at all happy at being outshone by a breakaway group. The APPG against Islamophobia was subsequently revived, with Stuart Andrews, the MP for Pudsey and a close friend of Eric Ollerenshaw, agreeing to chair. After the pain of its birth, it never managed to find a secretariat; nor did it produce anything which the government took seriously. Its hard-working chair Stuart Andrews and volunteer secretariat Hayyan Bhabha continued to run the All Party Parliamentary Group organizing meetings and briefings, which were always badly attended. Last year, when new officers were elected, I agreed to serve as vice chairman of the group, but the group's history is hard to shake off, and it is sadly all but dead in name. As my colleague and MP for Grantham and Stamford Nick Boles said to me, the plan to kill the group was 'a good plan well executed'.

Having failed to follow in the footsteps of the work on anti-Semitism, I called a meeting of a small number of activists and donors to see if 'the Muslims' could set up an organization similar to Community Security Trust, a Jewish charity that has been fighting anti-Semitism since 1994 and is the well-funded, well-run brainchild of someone whom I have great affection for, Gerald Ronson. This effort, too, failed, mainly through a lack of funding and inter-community rivalry. But some good came out of these conversations. One of the attendees at this initial meeting was Fiyaz Mughal, and out of the discussions was born Tell MAMA, an anti-Muslim-hatred monitoring body, which I subsequently supported through government funding.

Alongside funding Tell MAMA, we set up a cross-government

working group on anti-Muslim hatred, a group that Fiyaz Mughal served on but subsequently briefed against.

MEND is the latest and the only national grass-roots and community-driven group tackling anti-Muslim hatred.

Despite these groups and the long journey on this issue, Runnymede this year marking twenty years since the publication of *Islamophobia: A challenge for Us All*, the response to our dislike for Muslims is neither well organized nor well funded and is certainly not a government priority.

Acknowledgements

It's not often we get an opportunity to publicly acknowledge and thank those who have shaped your life, views, opinions and decisions. I'm therefore going to use mine liberally.

I start with my best friend, confidant and adviser – my husband. Iftikhar is my most honest critic, my unstinting support, who has spent years driving me around the country to attend political and community events, ensured my notes are in order, my hair is in place and a fresh latte and water appear at regular intervals and all the while pursuing his own career, caring for our children and running the business. He has been graceful and understanding as I've cancelled many a family holiday, romantic meal, birthday and anniversary celebration at short notice and has been the efficient back office to my very chaotic public life. But most of all, after a fraught first marriage, you taught me the real meaning of love: non-stifling, compromising, selfless, respectful and enduring. Thank you.

This book would not have been written if I had not served in government. So I owe this book first and foremost to Keith Sibbald, the Dewsbury constituency chairman who presided over my parliamentary selection in 2004. Keith, his wife Jennie, Colin and Bev Fretwell, Kath Taylor and James, Martyn Bolt, Khizar Iqbal, Salim Patel, Naeem Hashmi, Bhai Javed Iqbal and that dynamic trio of brothers Hamid, Khalil and Rashid-ur-Rehman were a small but uniquely formed core team of volunteers who were there at the start of my political journey, and I will forever be grateful for their support.

But mostly I am grateful to David Cameron, who appointed me to the Lords and asked me to serve in his shadow cabinet and cabinet. David and I agreed on most things; where we didn't is covered in this book.

He made possible the privilege of me serving my country at the top table. I will always value the opportunities he gave me, his infectious humour and his frank and open approach to discussions. I was alongside him as he started his journey as leader of the Conservative Party, and I'm pleased we were on the same side when he ended that journey. He is an intrinsic part of my tale of Muslim Britain.

I've had the benefit of working with some of the greatest brains and some inherently decent individuals both in government and the Conservative Party. It would be impossible for me to mention them all, but a few have had lasting impact. Michael Lord Howard of Lympne was an early mentor and remains someone whose intellect, reason and friendship I continue to value. Trish Baroness Morris talent-spotted me and was always there through the good times and not so good. Francis Lord Maude was the ultimate modernizing chairman. Ken Clarke, my political crush, was by far one of the cleverest and nicest people to work with. Dominic Grieve's commitment to the rule of law and basic decency, and Alan Duncan's unstinting support for fairness over political positioning, inspired me. I must also include my 'chum' Sir Eric Pickles, who taught me the art of the survival of the underdog; Andrew Feldman, my co-chairman, who alongside me fought many a battle to make our party more inclusive; Justine Greening, whose innate common sense made many a government meeting 'normal'; and the formidable William Hague, with whom I had the privilege of working at the Foreign Office.

My private office in both the party and government kept the wheels turning: Chief of Staff Richard Chalk, whose speech therapy and elocution advice serves this comprehensive-educated politician well to this day – his current role as Head of RICU (the Home Office Research Information and Communications Unit within the office for counter-terrorism) makes me sleep that little more easily at night; Ed Young and Jess Cunniffe, speechwriters extraordinaire; Jennie Gorbutt, who is by far the best PA, all-round office- and life-organizer I have ever worked with; Gulsum Aytac, who joined me as a timid new graduate and grew into a superb campaigner; private secretaries Ed 'Miliband' Roman, Anna Shotbolt, Steven Wignall, Kate Rudd, Ryder 'never flustered' Thomas, Nick 'simply amazing' Heath and Beth Dyson. I especially want to thank 'the team' who held it together in my last few agonizing weeks in government: Matt Forman,

Mandip Sahota, Nina Milne, Chris Freestone, Rosie Jones, Rhodri Jones, Will Johnson, Andrew 'sunshine' Davies and the brave Gillie Severin, who 'ran the gauntlet' to deliver the news of my resignation. I thank them all for their belief in my many causes in government, their support in the many battles which weren't easy but above all their loyalty and friendship in often difficult times.

I reserve my deepest gratitude for Eric Ollerenshaw, my PPS, and Naweed Khan, my special adviser. Their honesty, humour and friendship are as priceless today as they were over a decade ago, and I'm sure both their political careers could have been more fruitful had they been prepared to 'not support' me. I thank them for the sacrifices they both made.

I also want to thank Nick Clegg, my partner in crime on many an issue on human rights and civil liberties, and without whom government decision-making during Coalition years would have been less considered.

This book is the product of years of experience and hundreds of conversations with individuals, some with whom I profoundly agree and others with whom I disagree. But their input has been invaluable in helping form the arguments.

I'm grateful to the scholarly guidance and sounding board offered by the archbishop of Canterbury, Justin Welby, and the archbishop of Westminster, Cardinal Vincent Nichols, the time given by the Chief Rabbi and his office, the frank and enlightening discussions with Pir Imdaad Hussain, the visionary Qari Asim, Maulana Shahid Raza, Sheikh Ibrahim Mogra, Ajmal Masroor and the pioneering Syed Ali Rizwi.

I'm grateful to the many, many activists working on the 'Muslim issue', often as volunteers and often with little credit, who have given me historical context and have both questioned and helped inform my own thinking. I would need a whole book to mention you all, so I will mention the key individuals who gave up valuable time to discuss specific issues with me: Sir Iqbal Sacranie and Miqdaad Versi from the MCB; Sughra Ahmed from the ISB; Julie Siddique from Sadaqa Day; Maajid Nawaz, Haras Rafiq and Usama Hasan from Quilliam; journalist and commentator Yasmin Alibhai-Brown; Sufyan Ismail and his colleagues from MEND; Fiyaz Mughal from Tell MAMA with whom I have worked, agreed and argued with for over a decade; and Waqar Azmi, who delivered my vision of Remembering Srebrenica at a level I possibly couldn't even have dreamed of.

I want to pay tribute to Iftikhar Awan, Akeela Ahmed, Sarah Joseph, Mudassir Ahmed, Iqbal Bhana, Dr Chris Allen and Nick Lowles, who served on the cross-government working group on anti-Muslim hatred during my time in government and continue to fight a sadly losing battle on the issue of Islamophobia, often to personal detriment.

I'm grateful to the sisterhood, especially Shaista Gohir, CEO of the Muslim Women's Network, Hifsa Shaheen, Salma Yaqoob, Selina Ullah, Naheed Majeed, Sabbiyah Pervez, Koser Shaheen, Shazia Awan, Adeela Shaffi, and Shelina Jan Mohammed, for their support and guidance on difficult and challenging issues and their bravery in continuing to tackle many a taboo issue, and my two girl crushes the super clever academic and statistician Dalia Mogahed and the talented glass-ceiling-breaker Sapnara Khatun, aka Her Honour Judge Sapnara.

I also thank my parliamentary colleagues Yasmin Qureshi, Shabana Mahmood, Naz Shah, Roshanara Ali, Tasmina Ahmed-Sheikh, Merril Baroness Hussain-Ece, Pola Baroness Uddin and Haleh Baroness Afshar, women from across the political divide who have chosen to step out, often fighting battles on many fronts, both within and outside. I continue to be impressed by your bravery: you are part of a generation of amazing Muslims who convince me that the real powerhouse within 'the community' is surely the women.

Conversations with the 'brothers' too were vital in the writing of this book. I'm especially grateful to Mayor Sadiq Khan, Humza Yousaf, MSP, Ed Husain of the Tony Blair Faith Foundation, journalists and commentators Mehdi Hasan, Sarfraz Manzoor, Aaqil Ahmed, head of religion at the BBC, Jehangir Malik, CEO of Muslim Aid, Dr Hany El-Banna, Karim Sacoor and my ever-supportive friend and mentor Shabir Randeree, chairman of Mosaic and chancellor of the University of East London.

When I started this book I didn't realize just how much more time I would spend reading than writing. I had the luxury of immersing myself in amazing academic works. I'm especially grateful to Professor John Esposito of Georgetown University, Washington, DC, Professor Akbar Ahmed, chair of Islamic Studies at the American University,

Professor Khizar Ansari of Royal Holloway University of London, Professor Matthew Goodwin of the University of Kent, Professor Tariq Modood of the University of Bristol, Dr Francesco Ragazzi, assistant professor at Leiden University and Associate Professor Imran Awan of Birmingham City University, for what often became long and detailed debates. Their valuable insights prompted me to challenge my sometimes fixed and rigid views and provided the much-needed academic rigour, challenge and reflection a subject this serious required.

I'm indebted to a number of individuals who have provided me with their unique insight and expertise on specific chapters: Charles Clarke and John Denham for enhancing my understanding of the Labour years; Sir Jonathan Powell for his Northern Ireland and wider experience of tackling terrorism; Sondos Asem, President Morsi's former international media coordinator, for her helpful challenges and background information; Maz Saleem, the daughter of the tragically murdered Mohammed Saleem, for speaking so frankly and candidly about the loss of her father and how officialdom failed them as a family; and Mohammed Riaz, both for his continued support and historic experience of the Conservative Party; Owen Jones and Peter Tatchell for differing perspectives on how we fight the scourge of Islamophobia alongside other forms of bigotry, including homophobia; and Mark Gardner from the Community Security Trust and David Feldman for explaining and testing some of my thinking around both historic and current forms of anti-Semitism. I want to pay special tribute to the formidable Gerald Ronson, someone with whom I have more things in common than issues upon which we disagree and someone whom I admire as a staunch defender and protector of his community. Britain's Muslim communities would be lucky to have a Gerald Ronson of their own.

I'm obliged to Sir Peter Fahy, former chief constable of Greater Manchester Police; Liam Byrne, MP; Aiden Harris and Amrit Singh from the Open Society Foundation for their perspectives on the Prevent programme; and David Anderson, QC, both for his unique and informed insight and for agreeing to grace the cover of this book. David, along with Helena Kennedy, QC, and Peter Oborne, are individuals who continue to inspire me, and I feel humbled that they all agreed to both read the book and provide comment.

Sir Stephen Bubb, former head of ACEVO, has been a fearless

advocate for the charitable sector and provided much-needed support for many a 'Muslim' charity which has come under fire from many, including the Charity Commission. I am grateful for his courage and that of brave and principled civil servants at the Charity Commission who continue to inject reason in an often unreasonable debate.

And I want to especially thank Francis Campbell, vice chancellor of St Mary's University, who is convinced I am a 'shy Catholic'. His experience and enthusiasm were a necessary and much-valued tonic during government and remain so.

There were many I spoke to during the writing of this book to try to understand their different perspectives, from my former colleague Paul Goodman, Tim Montgomery, former editor of Conservative Home and columnist at *The Times*, Lord Pearson, with whom I've had fascinating conversations around the 'interpretations' of the Qur'an and his solutions to the current challenges, and Mohammed Khan from Prevent Watch. We may not always agree but I hope we will always fight for the other to be heard.

It it with sadness that I acknowledge 'Baba' F. D. Farooqi, a businessman, writer and adventurer who insisted I write. I promised him that one day I would. I wish you were still with us to see that I kept my promise. And the vivacious Ali Gunn: three years on I still can't believe you are no longer with us. A very bright light went out when you left us, and I will feel your absence most as I launch this book. God bless you both.

This book could have simply remained an idea if I hadn't been cajoled into writing it by the formidable human rights defender Shami Baroness Chakrabarti. Thank you for your years of friendship, for inspiring me to think in 'principles' and for introducing me to Tracy Bohan, my super agent, who allowed me to focus on the writing as she dealt effortlessly with the more mundane bureaucracy.

I'd like to thank my editor Helen Conford, who perfected the art of influencing me without appearing to do so – her guidance and regular suggestions made this a 'grown-up' book rather than a political memoir – her editorial colleague Shoaib Rokadiya, copy-editor David Watson, who injected order into the multiple drafts and citations, and the publicity team at Penguin, especially Penelope Vogler and Matthew Hutchinson.

And finally I want to thank those who make my 'real' life real: my 'school friends', aka the trenchcoat mob – I love the way you allow me a safe sanctuary to be me away from the very public and heady world of politics; the trustees, volunteers and employees of my 'charity world family', at both the Savayra Foundation and the BW Foundation – you are the stalwarts who support me in fulfilling my real passion: the fight for social mobility, women's rights and freedom of religion and belief. I want to single out Tariq, Lord Ahmad, the 'other sibling' with whom I have shared both my political and personal journeys: thank you for your unquestioning support and for being there during the highs and lows. I'd like to thank my amazingly clever, successful, hilariously funny and brutally honest sisters, Baji, Nasra, Naheed and Bushra, my best friends. What a wonderful adventure we've had together. You ground me, make me feel strong, anchor me, infuriate me because you understand me so well, but most of all your love continues to remind me that we were lucky to be 'all girls'. Thank you for your support in the many – and there have been enough – mad dreams I dream. My parents: Mum, the strong, driven and single-minded presence in my life who fought the battles for her girls to have the opportunities that shaped our lives, and Dad, my rock, a man of deep faith, with a huge sense of self-belief and determination, which he instilled in me, and the ultimate feminist who thinks 'his girls' should run the world as they would do so far better than the men. I am beyond lucky to have you as my parents. And finally my children. Aamna, who has and continues to be, much to my surprise, the 'perfect child', who, despite my many work absences throughout her life, has never judged, complained or guilt-tripped me. You continue to amaze me as you chart your own future career and you remain my greatest success. And our other children, Arfan, Naailah, Ayman and Zayn; I was lucky in later life to be blessed with you as my children and to receive the gift of a large, warm and loving family. All five of you have played your part in carving out a 'normal' family life for an 'unconventional' mum inhabiting a very unusual world. I was amazed by your maturity as you offered to live a 'social-network-free life' for many a month when we were hounded by the press and media – it wasn't easy for you as teenagers. Thank you all for your understanding, patience and love.

Notes

INTRODUCTION: BELONGING

1 Sunni and Shia are the two main denominations of Islam, after a schism that occurred shortly after the death of the Prophet Muhammad. The Barelwi movement originated in Bareilly in the Indian state of Uttar Pradesh, is based on the Sunni Hanafi school of jurisprudence and has around 200 million followers in South Asia. Sufism refers to a set of religious orders who emphasize the mystical aspect of Islam. Tablighi Jamaat is an Islamic revivalist movement that preaches a return to primary Sunni Islam, particularly in matters of ritual, dress and personal behaviour, and is part of the wider Deobandi movement, which was founded in India in 1867 in part as a reaction to British colonialism. Wahhabism is another highly conservative branch of Sunni Islam and is the dominant form of Islam in Saudi Arabia.

1. WHO ARE THE BRITISH MUSLIMS?

1 Speech by Alex Younger, head of MI6, 8 December 2016, available at: https://www.sis.gov.uk/media/1155/cs-public-speech-8-december-2016-final.doc.

2 Home Office, *Terrorism Arrests – Analysis of Charging and Sentencing Outcomes by Religion*, gives 175 terrorism-related convictions of Muslims in the period 2001–12. This equates to 0.006 per cent of the overall UK Muslim population; see: https://www.gov.uk/government/publications/terrorism-arrests-analysis-of-charging-and-sentencing-outcomes-by-religion/.

3 In late November 2013, a document that has since come to be known as the 'Trojan Horse' letter was received by Birmingham City Council. The letter described a strategy to take over a number of schools in Birmingham via the boards of governors and run them on strict Islamic

principles. This led to an investigation and report published in July 2014: https://www.gov.uk/government/uploads/system/uploads/attachment_data/file/340526/HC_576_accessible_-.pdf. The 'Trojan Horse' saga is discussed at length in chapter 6, below.

4 The two-part BBC2 documentary *Muslims Like Us*, broadcast in December 2016, was an illustration of this diversity; see http://www.telegraph.co.uk/tv/2016/12/12/muslims-like-us-wake-up-call-islamophobes-everywhere/.

5 Heidi Hall, 'Church of Christ Opens Door to Musical Instruments,' *USA Today*, 6 March 2015.

6 Linda Woodhead, 'Do Christians Really Oppose Gay Marriage?' *Westminster Faith Debate*, 18 April 2013.

7 Edward Gibbon, *The History of the Decline and Fall of the Roman Empire* (New York: Cosimo Classics, 2008), vol. 6, ch. 52.

8 The coin is held by the British Museum. See http://www.british-museum.org/research/collection_online/collection_object_details.aspx?objectId=1093298&partId=1.

9 P. G. Rogers, *A History of Anglo-Moroccan Relations to 1900* (London: Foreign and Commonwealth Office, 197[5]), pp. 1–5.

10 Jerry Brotton, *This Orient Isle: Elizabethan England and the Islamic World* (London: Allen Lane, 2016).

11 Humayun Ansari, *The Infidel Within: The History of Muslims in Britain, 1800 to the Present* (London: C. Hurst & Co., 2004), p. 31.

12 Sushila Anand, *Indian Sahib: Queen Victoria's Dear Abdul* (London: Duckworth, 1996); Elizabeth Longford, *Victoria R. I.* (London: Weidenfeld & Nicolson, 1964).

13 Nabil Matar, *Islam in Britain, 1558–1685* (Cambridge: Cambridge University Press, 1998).

14 Ibid.

15 Ron Geaves, *Islam in Victorian Britain: The Life and Times of Abdullah Quilliam* (Leicester: Kube Publishing, 2010).

16 Haifaa A. Jawad, *Towards Building a British Islam* (London: Continuum, 2012), pp. 43–73; Peter Clark, *Marmaduke Pickthall: British Muslim* (London: Quartet, 1986).

17 My speech to the Pontifical Ecclesiastical Academy, Vatican City, 14 February 2012.

18 Brotton, *This Orient Isle*.

19 Razis refers to Muhammad ibn Zakariya al-Razi (Rhazes or Rasis, 854–925), who was a Persian Muslim polymath, physician, alchemist and chemist, philosopher and scholar, a prominent figure in the Islamic Golden Age. Avicen refers to Ibn Sina (Avicenna, *c.* 980–1037), a Persian

Muslim polymath who wrote on a wide range of subjects, in particular philosophy and medicine, but also astronomy, alchemy, geology, psychology, Islamic theology, logic, mathematics, physics and poetry. He is regarded as the most famous and influential polymath of the Islamic Golden Age. Averrois refers to Ibn Rushd (Averroes, 1126–98), an Andalusian Muslim polymath, a master of Aristotelian and Islamic philosophy, Islamic theology, Maliki law and jurisprudence, psychology, politics, Andalusian classical music theory and the sciences of medicine, astronomy, geography, mathematics, physics and celestial mechanics.

20 Dante, *Inferno*, Book 4, cited in Brenda Deen Schildgen, *Dante and the Orient* (Champaign: University of Illinois Press, [1813] 2002).

21 'Michael Gove Redrafts New History Curriculum after Outcry', *Guardian*, 21 June 2013, available at: https://www.theguardian.com/education/2013/jun/21/michael-gove-history-curriculum.

22 Humayun Ansari, in *Remembering the Brave: The Muslim Contribution to Britain's Armed Forces* (Muslim Council of Britain, 2014), a pamphlet produced by the Muslim Council of Britain to commemorate the sacrifice of Muslim soldiers in the world wars, states that 1.3 million Indian soldiers served during the First World War, a large proportion of them Muslim, and 2.5 million fought in the Second World War. Again, a substantial number were Muslim. Moreover, Muslims were also employed in the British merchant navy: 50,000 by the beginning of the First World War, according to Ansari.

23 Military historian Gordon Corrigan in *The Muslim Tommies*, broadcast on BBC1 on 2 September 2009.

24 Ansari, *The Infidel Within*.

25 'Downton Abbey's Turkish Diplomat Sex Scandal "Is Not Fiction"', *Daily Telegraph*, 11 October 2011, available at: http://www.telegraph.co.uk/culture/tvandradio/downton-abbey/8819485/Downton-Abbeys-Turkish-diplomat-sex-scandal-is-not-fiction.html.

26 Lucy Bland 'White Women and Men of Colour: Miscegenation Fears in Britain after the Great War', *Gender & History*, vol. 17, no. 1 (2005), pp. 29–61.

27 Ibid., pp. 106–7.

28 R. Visram, *Asians in Britain: 400 Years of History*, 2nd edn (London: Pluto Press, 2002).

29 Ansari, *The Infidel Within*, p. 98.

30 Laura Tabili, 'The Construction of Racial Difference in Twentieth-Century Britain: The Special Restriction (Coloured Alien Seamen) Order, 1925', *Journal of British Studies*, vol. 33, no. 1 (1994), pp. 54–98.

31 'I am directed by the Secretary of State to inform you that he has recently had under consideration measures to facilitate the control of coloured alien seamen at present in this country and to prevent more effectively the entry of others into the United Kingdom without proper authority; and he has come to the conclusion that in order to deal with the problem presented by these aliens – *particularly those of them who are 'Arabs'* – it is necessary that they should be required to register in all cases, including those where the alien has hitherto been exempt under Article 6(5) of the Aliens Order, 1920, by reason of the fact that less than two months has elapsed since his last arrival in the United Kingdom or that he is not resident in the United Kingdom.' HO 45/12314, National Archives, Kew. The Open University, 'Making Britain Discover how South Asians Shaped the Nation, 1870–1950: Special Restriction (Coloured Alien Seamen) Order (1925)', available at: http://www.open.ac.uk/researchprojects/makingbritain/content/special-restriction-coloured-alien-seamen-order-1925.

32 *Understanding Muslim Ethnic Communities, Summary Report* (London: Change Institute and Department for Communities and Local Government, April 2009).

33 Despite its foundation stone being laid in 1937, it wasn't completed until 1977, when donations from King Faisal of Saudi Arabia and Sheikh Zayed, the then ruler of Abu Dhabi and president of the United Arab Emirates, finally got the project across the line. A half century passed for the journey from soil to minaret. And where today all too often local community objections and local planning committee bureaucracy can seem to make mosque building almost impossible, at least it doesn't take ten decades.

34 S. Saleem, *The British Mosque: An Architectural and Social History* (London and Swindon: Historic England Publishing, forthcoming 2017).

35 'Can I Tell You Something?', ChildLine review 2012/13.

36 'Oliver Letwin Blamed "Bad Moral Attitudes" for Widespread Rioting in Black Areas', *Daily Telegraph*, 30 December 2015, available at: http://www.telegraph.co.uk/news/politics/margaret-thatcher/12072129/oliver-letwin-race-row-rioting-comments.html.

37 Black Caribbean pupils were over three times more likely to be permanently excluded than the school population as a whole. (*Permanent and Fixed Period Exclusions in England: 2014 to 2015*, Department for Education, 21 July 2016.) The rate is consistent with periods 2012–13 and 2013–14. (*Permanent and Fixed Period Exclusions in England: 2012 to 2013* and *Permanent and Fixed Period Exclusions*

in England: 2013 to 2014.) If you were a black African-Caribbean boy with special needs and eligible for free school meals you were 168 times more likely to be permanently excluded from a state-funded school than a white girl without special needs from a middle-class family. (Cited in the report *They Never Give Up On You*, Office of the Children's Commissioner, 2012, p. 9.)

On education, a graph showing low attainment among black Caribbean and white/black Caribbean (mixed) 2004–2014 is available at: http://www.lambeth.gov.uk/rsu/sites/The_Underachievement_of_Black_Caribbean_Heritage_Pupils_in_Schools-_Research_Brief.pdf.

On prison, see Grahame Allen and Noel Dempsey, Prison Population Statistics, House of Commons Library briefing, Number SN/SG/04334, 4 July 2016. The number of blacks in prison at March 2016 was four times their size in the general population (12 per cent of the prison population is black, while blacks account for 3 per cent of the general population). Also, a study of one million court records by the *Guardian* found blacks more likely to be sentenced for certain types of offences compared to whites: black offenders were 44 per cent more likely than white offenders to be sentenced to prison for driving offences, 38 per cent more likely to be imprisoned for public disorder or possession of a weapon and 27 per cent more likely for drugs possession. See: 'Race Variation in Jail Sentences, Study Suggests', *Guardian*, 26 November 2011, available at: https://www.theguardian.com/law/2011/nov/25/ethnic-variations-jail-sentences-study.

38 Whitehouse v. Gay News Ltd v. Lemon, 2 WLR 281 (1979), AC 617.
39 'How One Book Ignited a Culture War', *Guardian*, 11 January 2009, available at: https://www.theguardian.com/books/2009/jan/11/salman-rushdie-satanic-verses.
40 'Muslims in London Protest Rushdie Book; 84 Arrested', *LA Times*, 28 May 1989, available at: http://articles.latimes.com/1989-05-28/news/mn-1613_1_london-protest-rushdie-book-blasphemy-law-satanic-verses.
41 Nigel Copsey, *Contemporary British Fascism: The British National Party and the Quest for Legitimacy* (Basingstoke: Palgrave Macmillan, 2008), p. 47.
42 A. Sykes, *The Radical Right in Britain* (Basingstoke: Palgrave Macmillan, 2004), p. 131.
43 'How One Book Ignited a Culture War'.
44 D. Lockwood, *Islamic Republic of Dewsbury*, 2nd edn (Batley: The Press News Ltd, 2012).

45 P. Bagguley and Y. Hussain, *The Bradford 'Riot' of 2001: A Prelimi-nary Analysis,* paper presented to the Ninth Alternative Futures and Popular Protest Conference, Manchester Metropolitan University, 22–4 April 2003, available at: http://pascalfroissart.online.fr/3-cache/2003-bagguley-hussain.pdf; T. Cantle, *Community Cohesion: A Report of the Independent Review Team* (London: Home Office, 2001); A. Kundnani, 'From Oldham to Bradford: the Violence of the Violated', in *The Three Faces of British Racism* (London: Institute of Race Rela-tions, 2001); V. S. Kalra, 'Extended View: Riots, Race and Reports: Denham, Cantle, Oldham and Burnley Inquiries', *Sage Race Relations Abstracts*, vol. 27, no. 4 (2002), pp. 20–30; C. Alexander, 'Imagining the Asian Gang: Ethnicity, Masculinity and Youth After "the Riots" ', *Critical Social Policy*, vol. 24, no. 4 (2004), pp. 526–49.

46 L. Ray and D. Smith, 'Racist Offending, Policing and Community Conflict', *Sociology*, vol. 38, no. 4 (2004), pp. 681–99.

47 A. Kundnani, *Four Sentences Reduced, Eleven Upheld, in Appeal for Bradford Rioters* (Institute of Race Relations, 2003).

48 Kundnani, 'From Oldham to Bradford'.

49 'London's Mecca Rich: The Rise of the Muslim Multi-millionaires Splashing Their Cash', *Evening Standard*, 30 October 2013, available at: http://www.standard.co.uk/lifestyle/london-life/londons-mecca-rich-the-rise-of-the-muslim-multi-millionaires-splashing-their-cash-8913153.html.

50 There are many words in the English language that derive from Arabic. Commonly used words such as *sugar, cotton, coffee,* even *alcohol* are words that have Arabic roots; *mattress* too, and, in our social media age, *algebra* and *algorithm*. We tend to forget how many words com-monly used in the English language have Arabic origins.

2. WHAT ARE BRITISH VALUES?

1 According to the Act of Settlement, 1701.

2 The provisions to purchase property were enacted in the 1778 Catholic Relief Act and the franchise in the Catholic Emancipation Act, 1829.

3 See https://history.blog.gov.uk/2015/05/26/a-perfect-nuisance-the-history-of-women-in-the-civil-service/.

4 See *Women on Boards: The Davies Annual Review 2015*, available at: https://www.gov.uk/government/uploads/system/uploads/attachment_data/file/415454/bis-15-134-women-on-boards-2015-report.pdf.

5 The number of offences against women, including domestic abuse, rape and sexual assaults, rose by almost 10 per cent to 117,568 in

2015–16. The scale of offences make up nearly 19 per cent of prosecutors' workload – more than any other single tranche of crime, including terrorism and fraud. See: 'Violent Crimes against Women in England and Wales Reach Record High', *Guardian* 6 September 2016, available at: https://www.theguardian.com/society/2016/sep/05/violent-crimes-against-women-in-england-and-wales-reach-record-high.

6 *Britain and the Slave Trade*, available at: http://www.nationalarchives. gov.uk/slavery/pdf/britain-and-the-trade.pdf.

7 See http://www.nationalarchives.gov.uk/education/resources/civil-rights-in-america/segregationists-us-troops/.

8 Cecil Roth, *A History of the Jews in England* (Oxford: Clarendon Press, 1964).

9 'Daily Mail Headline from 1938 Draws Comparison with Current Reporting of Calais Migrant Crisis, available at: http://www.huffing-tonpost.co.uk/2015/07/31/daily-mail-1938-jews_n_7909954.html.

10 Matt Cook, *A Gay History of Britain: Love and Sex Between Men since the Middle Ages* (London: Praeger, 2011).

11 Michael McManus, *Tory Pride and Prejudice: The Conservative Party and Homosexual Law Reform* (London: Biteback Publishing, 2011).

12 R. Rooney, 'Male Homosexuality in Britain: The Hidden History', paper delivered at Association of Journalism Education, Journalism the First Draft of History conference, London, May 2000, available at: https://www.scribd.com/document/26608050/Male-Homosexuality-in-Britain-the-Hidden-History.

13 The Festival of Light put pressure on churches to reinforce orthodox Christian theology on same-sex relationships. See: Andrew Atherstone and John Maiden (eds.), *Evangelicalism and the Church of England in the Twentieth Century: Reform, Resistance and Renewal* (Woodbridge: Boydell Press, 2014), pp. 193–6.

14 'London Nail Bombs: The Two Weeks That Shattered the Capital', *Independent*, 11 April 2009, accessible at: http://www.independent. co.uk/news/uk/crime/london-nail-bombs-the-two-weeks-that-shattered-the-capital-1666069.html.

15 The Employment Equality (Sexual Orientation) Regulations, 2003, and the Employment Equality (Religion or Belief) Regulations, 2003, came into force on 1 and 2 December 2003 and outlawed direct and indirect discrimination in employment on grounds of sexual orientation and religion or belief.

16 The incitement to racial and religious hatred is one such restriction on free speech. The offences of inciting violence overseas and glorifying

terrorism are encroachments on free speech under terrorism legislation; the removal of content from websites which is considered enabling
to terrorism, IS content for example, is an infringement of free expression, and the statutory duty introduced in the Counter-Terrorism and
Security Act, 2015, has been criticised for its 'chilling effect' on academia for its restriction on the exercise of free speech in education
settings. Child protection relates to the laws which curtail the display
of child pornography online and the Communications Act, 2003, and
Malicious Communications Act are both used to prosecute material
considered 'grossly offensive' that is circulated via a communications
platform.

17 See Luke 6:31.
18 L. Byrne, *Black Flag Down: Counter-extremism, Defeating ISIS and Winning the Battle of Ideas* (London: Biteback Publishing, 2016), p. 131.
19 'Controversial "Squat" Toilets Scrapped', *Manchester Evening News*, 7 August 2010, available at: http://www.manchestereveningnews.co.uk/news/local-news/controversial-squat-toilets-scrapped-895893.
20 Speech by Tony Blair, 8 December 2006, reproduced in *Runnymede's Quarterly Bulletin*, no. 348 (December 2006).
21 Jack Straw, 'I Want to Unveil My Views on an Important Issue', *Lancashire Telegraph*, 5 October 2006, available at: http://www.telegraph.co.uk/news/1530718/I-want-to-unveil-my-views-on-an-important-issue.html.
22 A and Others v. Secretary of State for the Home Department (2004), UKHL 56.
23 Adam Tomkins, 'Readings of A v. Secretary of State for the Home Department', Public Law (2005), pp. 259–66.
24 Secretary of State for the Home Department v. MB [2006] EWHC 1000 (Admin), [2006] HRLR 878.
25 'The Duty to Integrate: Shared British Values', speech by Tony Blair, 8 December 2006, available at: www.vigile.net/The-Duty-to-Integrate-Shared.
26 The number of racially or religiously aggravated offences recorded by the police forces in England and Wales in July 2016 was 41 per cent higher than in July 2015. See: H. Corcoran and K. Smith, *Hate Crime, England and Wales, 2015/16: Statistical Bulletin 11/16* (London: Home Office, 2016).
27 'The Duty to Integrate: Shared British Values'.
28 'Radical Muslims Must Integrate, Says Blair', *Guardian*, 9 December 2006, available at: https://www.theguardian.com/uk/2006/dec/09/religion.immigrationandpublicservices.

29 *The Casey Review: A Review into Opportunity and Integration* (Department for Communities and Local Government, 2016), available at: https://www.gov.uk/government/uploads/system/uploads/attachment_data/file/575973/The_Casey_Review_Report.pdf.

30 A. Aughey, *Nationalism, Devolution and the Challenge to the United Kingdom State* (London: Pluto Press, 2001), p. 90, quoted in Gerry Hassan (ed.), *After Blair: Politics after the New Labour Decade* (London: Lawrence and Wishart, 2006), pp. 75–94.

31 Byrne, *Black Flag Down*, pp. 131–2.

32 Gordon Brown's speech to Labour party conference, 2007, available at: http://news.bbc.co.uk/1/hi/uk_politics/7010664.stm.

33 HC Deb, 6 November 2007, vol. 467, column 22, http://www.publications.parliament.uk/pa/cm200708/cmhansrd/cm071106/debtext/71106 0004.htm#0711067000359.

34 A home stay with a British Muslim family was arranged to enable David Cameron to better understand British Muslims and neighbourhood renewal. Abdullah was at the time a 'capacity builder'; he is now chief executive at the Balsall Heath Forum, one of the most successful social action projects in the UK.

35 See: 'David Cameron: What I Learnt from My Stay with a Muslim Family', *Guardian*, 13 May 2007, available at: https://www.theguardian.com/commentisfree/2007/may/13/comment.communities.

36 Speech by David Cameron, 'Bringing Down the Barriers to Integration', 29 January 2007, available at: http://conservativehome.blogs.com/torydiary/files/bringing_down_the_barriers_to_cohesion.pdf.

37 I tried to prevent my party from going down the route of an out-and-out rejection of multiculturalism. The compromise I negotiated was one word, a word that I hoped would nuance the argument and prevent complete exposure of our naivety and lack of understanding. The deal was to insert the word 'state' before the word 'multiculturalism' in all of David Cameron's pronouncements. I sought to draw a distinction between society adopting a live-and-let-live approach, even if on occasions that led to segregated and separate communities, and the state encouraging division by policies such as single group funding. I didn't always succeed in ensuring that the fig leaf was used.

38 'How Uganda Was Seduced by Anti-gay Conservative Evangelicals', *Independent*, 14 March 2014, available at: http://www.independent.co.uk/news/world/africa/how-uganda-was-seduced-by-anti-gay-conservative-evangelicals-9193593.html.

39 'Donald Trump Sexism Tracker: Every Offensive Comment in One Place', *Daily Telegraph*, 9 November 2016, available at: http://www.tele

graph.co.uk/women/politics/donald-trump-sexism-tracker-every-offensive-comment-in-one-place/.

40 *Report of the Commission on the Future of Multi-Ethnic Britain* (London: Runnymede Trust, 2000), p. 16.

41 Founder of Karma Nirvana.

42 *Caste Discrimination and Harassment in Great Britain*, Government Equalities Office, Research Findings No. 2010 / 8, available at https://www.gov.uk/government/uploads/system/uploads/attachment_data/file/85521/caste-discrimination-summary.pdf.

43 ' "Witchcraft" Abuse Cases on the Rise', *BBC News*, 11 October 2015, available at: http://www.bbc.co.uk/news/uk-34475424.

44 ' "Gay Cure" Christian Charity Funded 20 MPs' Interns', *Guardian*, 13 April 2012, available at: https://www.theguardian.com/world/2012/apr/13/gay-cure-christian-charity-mps-interns.

45 Responding to a question put by Fiona Bruce MP about a Christian Union being 'banned from holding prayer and Bible study meetings' because of the newly adopted Prevent Duty Guidance in July 2015, David Cameron responded to say such reaction was 'clearly ludicrous' and called upon universities to apply 'common sense' to avoid misusing the guidance. *HC Debate*, vol. 611, no. 9 (8 June 2016), p. 1189; also 'Beth Din Safe with Us, Says Government', *Jewish Chronicle*, 26 March 2015, available at: https://www.thejc.com/news/uk-news/beth-din-safe-with-us-says-government-1.65844.

46 See note 3 to chapter 1 above. 'Trojan Horse', after the mythological Greek story of deceit, duplicity and dishonesty to win a war or the strategic genius of warfare planning, was the heading given by Michael Gove to chapter 8 of his book *Celsius 7/7*, which he published in 2006, after the 7/7 bombings. The argument he makes is that the UK has been duped by, or acquiesced in, a movement where individuals and organizations have over time both converted large numbers of Muslims to believe in an ideologically perverted and politically inspired form of Islam and sought positions of influence. His arguments about which Muslims are 'the problem' range from the seriously dangerous to the loud-mouthed attention-seeking TV clown, from academics to theologians and from the out-of-his-depth community leader to the ordinary, everyday British Muslim. In Gove's world few Muslims are part of the solution.

47 'Governors of New Academies and Free Schools Told to Abide by "British Values" ', *Guardian*, 19 June 2014, available at: https://www.theguardian.com/education/2014/jun/19/governors-academies-free-schools-

british-values-michael-gove; *Pupils Left Puzzled by the Term 'British Values'*, British Educational Research Association, 14 September 2016.

48 NUT annual conference, 25–9 March 2016, Final Agenda, p. 87.

49 https://www.bera.ac.uk/bera-in-the-news/press-release-pupils-left-puzzled-by-the-term-british-values.

50 Open Society Justice Initiative, *Eroding Trust: The UK's Prevent Counter-Extremism Strategy in Health and Education* (New York: OSF, 2016), p. 28, available at: https://www.opensocietyfoundations.org/sites/default/files/eroding-trust-20161017_0.pdf.

51 'C4 Survey and Documentary Reveals What British Muslims Really Think', Channel 4, 11 April 2016, available at: http://www.channel4.com/info/press/news/c4-survey-and-documentary-reveals-what-british-muslims-really-think.

52 *Unsettled Belonging: A Survey of Britain's Muslim Communities* (London: Policy Exchange, 2016), available at: https://policyexchange.org.uk/wp-content/uploads/2016/12/PEXJ5037_Muslim_Communities_FINAL.pdf.

53 Trevor Phillips used as evidence an ICM poll which found that 52 per cent of British Muslims polled thought homosexuality should be illegal. In 1960s Britain so did most Anglo-Saxon Brits, and as recently as 1999, 49 per cent of Brits thought homosexual relationships were 'always or mostly wrong'; 70 per cent of Anglicans and Catholics thought so in the early 1990s. (See: Ben Clements, *Attitudes towards Gay Rights, British Religion in Numbers* (2012), available at: http://www.brin.ac.uk/figures/attitudes-towards-gay-rights/; and Ben Clements and C. D. Field, 'The Polls – Trends: Public Opinion toward Homosexuality and Gay Rights in Great Britain', *Public Opinion Quarterly*, vol. 78, no. 2 (2014), pp. 523–47.) More recently, the lead organizations against same-sex marriage were Christian, and anti-gay-marriage leaflets in Tory-held seats during the 2015 General Election were from an umbrella organisation of Christian groups and activists.

Professor Linda Woodhead, who oversaw the ESRC/AHRC's Religion and Society five-year research programme, conducted a poll for the Westminster Faith Debates, which were policy debates designed to invite public discussion around some of the research outputs generated from the programme, on same-sex marriage and the attitudes among faith communities in the UK. The poll found that attitudes towards homosexuality and same-sex marriage were transforming within faith communities and that some faith groups had shifted more in their moral perceptions than others. Baptists and Muslims were the two groups most opposed to same-sex marriage with 50 per cent and 59 per cent respectively answering 'Should not' to the question 'Do you think same-sex marriage should be allowed?' To the question 'Do you think same-sex marriage is right or wrong?', 55 per cent of Baptists and 64 per cent of Muslims said 'Wrong', the highest among all faith groups and greater than the average across all faith groups (34 per cent). Interestingly, in the Religion and Society poll, which was conducted by YouGov in 2013, 13 per cent of Muslims said 'Don't know' to the question 'Do you think same-sex marriage is right or wrong?' but in a YouGov poll conducted in January 2016, 34 per cent of Muslims answered 'Unsure' to the question, 'Do you think same-sex marriage is right or wrong?'. In the same 2016 poll, a higher proportion of Evangelical Christians (63 per cent) than Muslims (52 per cent) answered 'Wrong' to the same question.

The ICM poll referred to by Phillips also found that 39 per cent of British Muslims polled thought a woman should always obey her husband. In 1950s Britain so did most Anglo-Saxon Brits; in 1970s Britain so did some in the Foreign and Commonwealth Office. Most British Muslims have been on their British Muslim journey for fewer than fifty years; Christians have been on their British journey for a millennium and a half; the Foreign Office has been around since 1782.

And then Phillips provided the 'shocker': the poll found that 4 per cent of British Muslims have 'sympathy for people that take part in suicide bombing to fight injustice'. In other words 96 per cent of British Muslims don't have this sympathy, a figure which bears comparison with a study from 2011, which found that 4 per cent of the general British public said 'suicide bombings' against a UK target were 'justified'. (See: A. Cousins, 'Muslim Opinion and the Myth of "Tacit Support for Terrorism"', *Counterfire*, 20 March 2015, available at: http://www.counterfire.org/articles/analysis/17732-muslim-opinion-and-the-myth-of-tacit-support-for-terrorism.)

See also: Press Release, 'Do Christians Really Oppose Gay Marriage?', *Westminster Faith Debates*, 18 April 2013, available at: http://www.religionandsociety.org.uk/events/programme_events/show/press_release_do_christians_really_oppose_gay_marriage; 'The Majority of Young C of E, Anglican and Episcopal Christians Agree with Same-Sex Marriage', indy100 by the *Independent*, January 2016, available at: https://www.indy100.com/article/the-majority-of-young-c-of-e-anglican-and-episcopal-christians-agree-with-samesex-marriage--ZkKps1IV6e.

54 Gallup Coexist Index 2009: *A Global Study of Interfaith Relations;* M. Wind-Cowie, *A Place for Pride* (London: Demos, 2011); Census 2011, which shows that more Muslims identify with a 'British-only' national identity than Christians. See *Who Feels British? The Relationship between Ethnicity, Religion and National Identity in England*, briefing by the Centre on Dynamics of Ethnicity, June 2013, accessible at: http://www. ethnicity.ac.uk/medialibrary/briefingsupdated/who-feels-british.pdf.

55 Lord Ashcroft Polls, 'How the United Kingdom Voted on Thursday . . . and Why', 24 June 2016.

56 Other polls show that British Muslims have a greater faith in institutions such as parliament, the police and the criminal justice system than white Brits, and a vast majority – nearly 80 per cent – are pro-integration and more likely to want to live in ethnically mixed communities. See: Gallup Coexist Index 2009: *A Global Study of Interfaith Relations.*

57 'People of No Religion Outnumber Christians in England and Wales – Study', *Guardian*, 23 May 2016, available at: https://www.theguardian. com/world/2016/may/23/no-religion-outnumber-christians-england-wales-study.

58 Melanie Phillips, 'Yes, Gays Have Often Been the Victims of Prejudice. But They now Risk Becoming the New McCarthyites', *Daily Mail*, 24 January 2011, available at: http://www.dailymail.co.uk/debate/article-1349951/ Gayness-mandatory-schools-Gay-victims-prejudice-new-McCarthyites. html.

59 Christian schools have complained about OFSTED's interpretation of British values and how they could conflict with Christian teachings on marriage, homosexuality and other aspects of the Christian faith (http://www.christian.org.uk/news/mp-faith-schools-are-being-damaged-by-british-values/). The Jewish Board of Deputies has argued that, although it 'believes that there is no contradiction between Jewish values and British values, it does think Ofsted may be overstepping the mark in its interpretation of the guidelines' (http://www.christian.org. uk/news/new-govt-standards-are-curb-on-freedom-jewish-critic/). Jewish faith schools have raised concerns about girls being questioned about homosexuality and relationships ('Faith Schools' Battle Over British Values', *Jewish Chronicle*, 23 October 2014, available at: http://www. thejc.com/comment-and-debate/analysis/124579/faith-schools-battle-over-british-values). As Daniel Blackman, an author writing on theology and ethics puts it: 'Yes, the government should tackle violent extremism – no one wants to live in a world where religiously-motivated suicide bombings, mass executions, slavery, and appalling cruelty towards

minorities are part of daily life. But this must not be used to impose Mr Cameron's idiosyncratic interpretation of British values on the rest of us' (D. Blackman, '"British Values" Prevent More Than Terrorism', *MercatorNet*, 16 March 2016, available at: https://www.mercatornet. com/articles/view/the-uk-government-is-preventing-more-than-terrorism/ 17767). The Christian Institute argued for the guidelines on respect for 'other beliefs' to be changed to 'other people' and claimed that inspectors had told a Christian independent school that it should invite an imam to take assembly to promote interfaith goodwill, to which they objected. ('Faith Schools' Battle Over British Values'). And my colleague Sir Edward Leigh MP blasted 'British values' as a 'classic bureaucratic response' that is 'damaging Christian schools'. ('"Faith Schools 'Damaged by British Values Curriculum", Says MP', *Daily Telegraph*, 12 March 2015, available at: http://www.telegraph.co.uk/ education/educationnews/11465380/Faith-schools-damaged-by-British-values-curriculum-says-MP.html.)

60 Tariq Modood, 'Multiculturalism Can Foster a New Kind of Englishness', *The Conversation*, 10 June 2016, accessible at: https://thecon versation.com/multiculturalism-can-foster-a-new-kind-of-englishness-60759.

61 B. Parekh, 'Being British', in A. Gamble and T. Wright, *Britishness: Perspectives on the British Question* (John Wiley & Sons, 2009), p. 37.

3. TERRORISM

1 'Ealing Bomb Was Planned as Massacre', *Daily Telegraph*, 4 August 2001, available at: http://news.bbc.co.uk/1/hi/uk/1474414.stm.

2 Mohammad Sidique Khan and Shehzad Tanweer both studied at Leeds Metropolitan University. See *Report of the Official Account of the Bombings in London on 7th July 2005*, HC 1087 (London: HMSO, 11 May 2006), p. 36.

3 Bobby Sands, a member of the Provisional IRA, died while on hunger strike at Long Kesh prison, where he was serving a fourteen-year sentence for possession of arms. During his imprisonment, he succeeded in being elected MP for Fermanagh and South Tyrone, but never attended parliament.

4 A. Arnove, C. Firth and D. Horspool, *The People Speak: Democracy Is Not a Spectator Sport* (Edinburgh: Canongate, 2013), p. 51.

5 'Woolwich Attack: The Terrorist's Rant', *Daily Telegraph*, 23 May 2013, available at: http://www.telegraph.co.uk/news/uknews/terrorism-in-the-uk/10075488/Woolwich-attack-the-terrorists-rant.html.

6 Dominic Janes and Alex Houen (eds.), *Martyrdom and Terrorism: Pre-Modern to Contemporary Perspectives* (Oxford: Oxford University Press, 2014), pp. 199–220.

7 S. Kenna, 'The Fenian Dynamite Campaign and the Irish American Impetus for Dynamite Terror, 1881–1885', *Inquiries Journal/Student Pulse*, vol. 3, no. 12 (2011), retrieved from: http://www.inquiriesjournal.com/a?id=602.

8 T. Suárez, *State of Terror: How Terrorism Created Modern Israel* (Bloxham: Skyscraper Publications, 2016), pp. 132 and 135.

9 The 'Tebbit test' takes its name from Conservative politician Sir Norman Tebbit, who in 1990 suggested that South Asians and Caribbean migrants were not loyal to the UK, and this was illustrated by the cricket team they supported. Tebbit argued most migrants failed his litmus test on loyalty because they were more likely to support the teams from 'back home' than root for England in a cricket match.

10 'National Archives: Britain Agreed Secret Deal to Back Mujahideen', *Daily Telegraph*, 30 December 2010, available at: http://www.telegraph.co.uk/news/worldnews/asia/afghanistan/8215187/National-Archives-Britain-agreed-secret-deal-to-back-Mujahideen.html.

11 Raffaello Pantucci, *'We Love Death as You Love Life: Britain's Suburban Terrorists* (London: C. Hurst & Co., 2015), pp. 45–6.

12 Award-winning documentary filmmaker Deeyah Khan explores this in *Jihad: A British Story*. The documentary was broadcast on ITV in June 2015.

13 '"Ordinary Yorkshire Lad", 17, Becomes Britain's Youngest Suicide Bomber', *Daily Telegraph*, 15 June 2015, available at: http://www.telegraph.co.uk/news/uknews/terrorism-in-the-uk/11674324/Ordinary-Yorkshire-lad-17-becomes-Britains-youngest-suicide-bomber.html.

14 http://www.egmontinstitute.be/wp-content/uploads/2016/02/egmont.papers.81_online-versie.pdf, pp. 4–6.

15 Akbar Ganji, 'U. S.–Jihadist Relations (Part 1): Creating the Mujahedin in Afghanistan', *Huffington Post*, 7 February 2014, available at: http://www.huffingtonpost.com/akbar-ganji/us-jihadist-relations_b_5542757.html.

16 https://www.gov.uk/government/uploads/system/uploads/attachment_data/file/228837/1087.pdf.

17 The issue came to the fore once again during my time in government in 2014, when some previously secret government documents were

mistakenly published, leading to the disclosure that the Indian government had requested advice from the SAS in the months leading up to
the raid. See: 'Margaret Thatcher Gave Full Support Over Golden
Temple Raid, Letter Shows', *Guardian*, 15 January 2014, available at:
https://www.theguardian.com/world/2014/jan/15/margaret-thatcher-golden-
temple-raid-support-letter.

18 'Black Lives Matter Rallies Hundreds in Second UK Day of Protest',
Observer, 9 July 2016, available at: https://www.theguardian.com/us-
news/2016/jul/09/black-lives-matter-rallies-hundreds-in-second-uk-day-
of-protest.

19 Bruce Hoffman, *Inside Terrorism*, 2nd edn (New York: Columbia
University Press, 2006).

20 Quoted in *Modern History Sourcebook: Maximilien Robespierre: Justification of the Use of Terror*, available at: www.fordham.edu/halsall/
mod/robespierre-terror.html. See also Albert Mathiez, 'Robespierre:
l'histoire et la légende', *Annales Historiques de la Révolution Fran-
çaise*, vol. 49, no. 1 (1977), pp. 3–31.

21 *Encyclopedia Britannica*, 'Maximilien Robespierre', available at: https://
www.britannica.com/biography/Maximilien-de-Robespierre.

22 Hoffman, *Inside Terrorism*, pp. 1–42.

23 Ibid.

24 Sue Mahan and Pamala L. Griset, *Terrorism in Perspective*, 3rd edn
(London: SAGE Publications, 2013), pp. 46–7.

25 Walter Laqueur, *A History of Terrorism* (New Jersey: Transaction
Publishers, 2001), pp. 50–51.

26 'The First Global Terrorists Were Anarchists in the 1890s', *New York
Times*, 29 April 2016, available at: http://www.nytimes.com/2016/04/30/
opinion/the-first-global-terrorists-were-anarchists-in-the-1890s.html.

27 Constance Bantman, *The French Anarchists in London, 1880–1914:
Exile and Transnationalism in the First Globalisation* (Liverpool: Liverpool University Press, 2013). pp. 143–4.

28 M. Radu, 'The Problem of "Londonistan": Europe, Human Rights
and Terrorists', 4 December 2002, in S. Gale, M. Radu and H. Sicher-
man (eds.), *The War on Terrorism: 21st-century Perspectives* (New
Brunswick: Transaction Publishers, 2009), p. 139.

29 S. Kenna, "One Skilled Scientist Is Worth an Army – The Fenian Dynamite Campaign 1881–85', 13 February 2012, available at: http://www.
theirishstory.com/2012/02/13/one-skilled-scientist-is-worth-an-army-the-
fenian-dynamite-campaign-1881-85/#.WEikZPmLRnJ. Martial Bour-
din, a Frenchman and anarchist, was discovered in 1894 in a gruesome

physical state in Greenwich Park on his way to the Royal Observatory, the target for the bombing).

30 'Ukrainian Student Who Murdered a Muslim Pensioner Before Planting Three Bombs Near Mosques Jailed for Life', *Daily Mirror*, 25 October 2013, available at: http://www.mirror.co.uk/news/uk-news/pavlo-lapshyn-jailed-life-after-2532574.

31 Neither Adebowale nor Adebolajo was convicted of terrorism offences; they were sentenced for murder. Lapshyn too was sentenced for murder. His bombing spree incurred charges under the Explosive Substances Act. He was charged with a section 5 offence under the Terrorism Act (preparing for acts of terrorism).

32 https://en.m.wikipedia.org/wiki/National_Action_(UK).

33 'Daughter of Mohammed Saleem Criticises West Midlands Police', *BBC News*, 24, March 2013.

34 It's an issue I raised with David Cameron in his final days as prime minister in the days following Jo Cox's murder – again at the hands of a far-right terrorist. I questioned the lack of a COBRA meeting, the lack of a focus on the motivation and ideology of the perpetrator, the lack of a serious response to the rising tide of far-right extremism and the failure of the broader 'right-wing family' to say 'not in my name'. I warned him that the difference of approach was causing resentment amongst ordinary, so-called integrated, moderate Muslims. He acknowledged that I had made a valid point. It signalled a potential shift in approach. It's a shame that a week later he had resigned as PM and a few months later had left parliament.

35 Bill Leckie, 'Terrorism Is a Monster With More Than One Face', *Sun*, 10 June 2013; 'Top Cop Attacks Media Coverage of Mosque Bombings and *Birmingham Mail*'s Report of Crime Rise', *Birmingham Mail*, 25 July 2013, available at: http://www.birminghammail.co.uk/news/local-news/west-midlands-polices-dave-thompson-5319513; 'Government Accused of "Double Standards" in Aftermath of Woolwich Murder of Drummer Lee Rigby', *Independent*, 28 July 2013, available at: http://www.independent.co.uk/news/uk/politics/government-accused-of-double-standards-in-aftermath-of-woolwich-murder-of-drummer-lee-rigby-8735665.html.

36 'Helpful and Polite Loner with History of Mental Health Issues', *The Times*, 17 June 2016, available at: http://www.thetimes.co.uk/edition/news/helpful-and-polite-loner-with-history-of-mental-health-issues-3sqjj3qp2.

37 Juliet Samuel, 'It's Time to Call the Killing of Jo Cox What It Is: "An Act of Far-Right Terrorism"', *Daily Telegraph*, 17 June 2016, available at:

http://www.telegraph.co.uk/news/2016/06/17/its-time-to-call-the-killing-of-jo-cox-what-it-is-an-act-of-far/; Glenn Greenwald, 'Why Is the Killer of British MP Jo Cox Not Being Called a "Terrorist"?', *The Intercept*, 17 June 2016, available at: https://theintercept.com/2016/06/17/why-is-the-killer-of-british-mp-jo-cox-not-being-called-a-terrorist/.

38 Matthew Taylor and Daniel Nasaw, 'Suspect in US Holocaust Museum Guard Killing Has Links to BNP', *Guardian*, 11 June 2009, available at: https://www.theguardian.com/world/2009/jun/11/holocaust-museum-shooting-bnp-von-brunn.

39 'British Man Pleads Guilty in Trump Attempted Attack Case', *CBS News*, 13 September 2016, available at: http://www.cbsnews.com/news/british-man-pleads-guilty-in-donald-trump-attempted-attack-case/.

40 *Report of the Inquiry into the Culture, Practices and Ethics of the Press*, vol. 2, ch. 6, para. 8.45, p. 671.

41 A. Saeed, 'Media, Racism and Islamophobia: The Representation of Islam and Muslims in the Media', *Sociology Compass*, vol. 1, no. 2, pp. 443–62.

42 Martha Crenshaw and John Pimlott (eds.), *International Encyclopedia of Terrorism* (London: Routledge, 1998).

43 Magnus Ranstorp (ed.), *Mapping Terrorism Research: State of the Art, Gaps and Future Direction* (London: Routledge, 2006), p. 60. (The United States and Great Britain were committed to supporting the restoration of self-government for all countries that had been occupied during the war and allowing all peoples to choose their own form of government.) See: https://history.state.gov/milestones/1937-1945/atlantic-conf; A. Cassese, *Self-Determination of Peoples: A Legal Reappraisal* (Cambridge: Cambridge University Press, 1995), p. 37.

44 'Iraq War Relative: Tony Blair Is "World's Worst Terrorist"', *Daily Telegraph*, 6 July 2016; available at: http://www.telegraph.co.uk/news/2016/07/06/iraq-war-relative-tony-blair-is-worlds-worst-terrorist/.

45 Speech by Alex Younger, head of MI6, 8 December 2016.

46 'Anger at Cherie "Sympathy" for Suicide Bombers', *Daily Telegraph*, 19 June 2002, available at: http://www.telegraph.co.uk/news/world-news/middleeast/jordan/1397696/Anger-at-Cherie-sympathy-for-suicide-bombers.html.

47 Cited in D. E. Pressman, *Risk Assessment Decisions for Violent Political Extremism* (Public Safety Canada, 2009).

48 R v. Gul (Appellant) [2013] UKSC 64, 23 October 2013.

49 For more on this, see: http://www.austlii.edu.au/au/journals/UNSWLawJl/2004/22.html; http://www.humanrightsvoices.org/eyeontheun/un_

101/facts/?p=61; https://ukhumanrightsblog.com/2013/10/23/supreme-court-considers-definition-of-terrorism/.

50 'Terror Detention Plans Outlined', *BBC News*, 15 September 2005, available at: http://news.bbc.co.uk/1/hi/uk_politics/4247638.stm.

51 David Anderson QC, *The Terrorism Acts in 2011, Report of the Independent Reviewer on the Operation of the Terrorism Act 2000 and Part 1 of the Terrorism Act 2006* (London: HMSO, 2012), para. 3.11, p. 37.

52 Mike Harris, 'The Legal Definition of Terrorism Threatens to Criminalise Us All', *Independent*, 24 July 2014, available at: http://www.independent.co.uk/voices/comment/the-legal-definition-of-terrorism-threatens-to-criminalise-us-all-9626325.html; https://terrorismlegislationreviewer.independent.gov.uk/wp-content/uploads/2014/07/Independent-Review-of-Terrorism-Report-2014-print2.pdf; 'UK Definition of Terrorism 'Could Catch Political Journalists and Bloggers', *Guardian*, 22 July 2014, available at: https://www.theguardian.com/uk-news/2014/jul/22/uk-definition-terrorism-political-journalists-bloggers-watchdog.

53 See: https://books.google.co.uk/books?id=h6KeBAAAQBAJ&pg=PT197&lpg=PT197&dq=trainspotters+basingstoke+station+terrorism&source=bl&ots=aywVQ5yZmG&sig=ZcDab8FW2VS3HfPrU14y3equwHw&hl=en&sa=X&ved=0ahUKEwjE5rqQxafOAhUHIsAKHUTICfoQ6AEIKDAD#v=onepage&q=trainspotters%20basingstoke%20station%20terrorism&f=false. Also, Philip Johnston, *Bad Laws: An Explosive Analysis of Britain's Petty Rules, Health and Safety Lunacies, Madcap Laws and Nit-Picking Regulations* (London: Constable, 2010), quoted in 'The Police Must End Their Abuse of Anti-Terror Legislation', *Daily Telegraph*, 2 October 2005.

54 'Terror Law Used for Iceland Deposits', *Financial Times*, 8 October 2008, available at: http://www.ft.com/cms/s/0/f86a290a-959a-11dd-aedd-000077b07658.html?ft_site=falcon&desktop=true#axzz4SvIIrmQd.

55 Lizzy Davies, 'Olympics Spectator with Parkinson's Wants "Exoneration" after Arrest', *Guardian*, 8 August 2012, available at: https://www.theguardian.com/uk/2012/aug/08/olympics-spectator-parkinsons-arrest-smiling.

56 'The Police Must End Their Abuse of Anti-terror Legislation', available at: http://www.telegraph.co.uk/comment/personal-view/3620110/The-police-must-end-their-abuse-of-anti-terror-legislation.html.

57 Speech by Ronald Reagan at the National Conference of the Building and Construction Trades Department, AFL-CIO, 30 March 1981.

58 *Operation of Police Powers under the Terrorism Act 2000*, quarterly update to September 2015, Home Office, 10 December 2015, available

at: https://www.gov.uk/government/publications/operation-of-police-powers-under-the-terrorism-act-2000-quarterly-update-to-december-2015/; *Operation of Police Powers Under the Terrorism Act 2000 And Subsequent Legislation: Arrests, Outcomes, and Stop and Search, Great Britain*, quarterly update to December 2015, Home Office, 17 March 2016, available at: https://www.gov.uk/government/publications/operation-of-police-powers-under-the-terrorism-act-2000-and-subsequent-legislation-arrests-outcomes-and-stop-and-search-great-britain-quarterly-u.

59 P. Hillyard, *Suspect Community* (London: Pluto Press, 1993).

60 'Deaths in the Northern Ireland Conflict since 1969', *Guardian*, 10 June 2010, # https://www.theguardian.com/news/datablog/2010/jun/10/deaths-in-northern-ireland-conflict-data.

61 Institute for Economics and Peace, *Global Terrorism Index 2015: Measuring and Understanding the Impact of Terrorism*, p. 2; available at: http//economicsandpeace.org/wp-content/uploads/2015/11/Global-Terrorism-Index-2015.pdf.

62 Ibid., p. 5.

63 Ibid.

64 Ibid., p. 68.

65 US National Counterterrorism Center, Annex of Statistical Information, 12 March 2012, p. 6. The report states that, where religious affiliation of victims of terrorism in the years 2007–11 is known, 'Muslims suffered between 82 and 97 percent of terrorism-related fatalities'.

66 Ibid., p. 2.

67 Global Terrorism Database, University of Maryland, is an online database covering terrorism incidents from 1970 to 2015 with updates added annually. National Consortium for the Study of Terrorism and Responses to Terrorism (START), Global Terrorism Database [Data file] (2016), retrieved from: https://www.start.umd.edu/gtd.

68 See also: 'Non-Muslims Carried Out More than 90% of All Terrorist Attacks in America', Washington Blog and Global Research, 13 June 2016, available at: http://www.globalresearch.ca/non-muslims-carried-out-more-than-90-of-all-terrorist-attacks-in-america/5333619.

69 Institute for Economics and Peace, *Global Terrorism Index 2016*, p. 4.

70 *EU Terrorism Situation and Trend Report*, 2010 (European Police Office, 2011), p. 9.

71 *EU Terrorism Situation and Trend Report*, 2011 (European Police Office, 2012), p. 8.

NOTES TO PP. 78–80

72 *EU Terrorism Situation and Trend Report*, 2013 (European Police Office, 2013), p. 8.

73 *EU Terrorism Situation and Trend Report*, 2015 (European Police Office, 2015), p. 8; *EU Terrorism Situation and Trend Report*, 2016 (European Police Office, 2016), p. 10.

74 Ryan Lenz with Mark Potok, *Age of the Wolf: A Study of the Rise of Lone Wolf and Leaderless Resistance Terrorism* (Alabama: Southern Poverty Law Center, 2015), p. 4.

75 Institute for Economics and Peace, *Global Terrorism Index 2015*, p. 4.

76 M. Zenko and M. Cohen, 'Clear and Present Safety: The United States Is More Secure than Washington Thinks', *Foreign Affairs*, March/April 2012.

77 David Anderson, *The Terrorism Acts in 2011*, para. 2.29a, p. 27, available at: https://terrorismlegislationreviewer.independent.gov.uk/wp-content/uploads/2013/04/report-terrorism-acts-2011.pdf.

78 'Horror in Paris: The Reason We Call It "Terrorism"', *Washington Examiner*, 14 November 2015; available at: http://www.hannan.co.uk/horror-in-paris-the-reason-we-call-it-terrorism/.

79 'Transcript of Today's First Public Speech by a Serving MI6 Chief, *Guardian*, 28 October 2010, available at: https://www.theguardian.com/uk/2010/oct/28/sir-john-sawers-speech-full-text. accessed on: 4 August 2016.

80 It was a conversation that I naively tried to have after 7/7. It was an early lesson for me in politics that I was stupid to assume that the media would be interested in a broader discussion on terrorism rather than just a specific 'Muslim politician's' response to 7/7. The example I used on TV was the decades-long war over Kashmir and the right to self-determination of the Kashmiris as enshrined in United Nations resolutions. Some British Indian members of my party took offence at my statement, threatened to withdraw support, including donations, and demanded an apology. The fighters were freedom fighters for Kashmiris under occupation but terrorists in the eyes of my British Indian colleagues. To this day I stand by the point I made: it is a fact that people in this country do not see conflicts around the world from the same perspective. The good guys and bad guys differ depending on individual political positions, ideology and history. But I was persuaded by Michael Howard to apologize and in typical political style I refused to apologize for what I had said but apologized for any offence I might have caused. A decade on from that attack it's a shame politics is still not the right forum for such a discussion.

81 Seth G. Jones and Martin C. Lebicki, *How Terrorist Groups End* (Santa Monica: Rand Corporation, 2008), available at: http://www.rand.org/content/dam/rand/pubs/monographs/2008/RAND_MG741-1.pdf.

82 J. Powell, *Talking to Terrorists: How to End Armed Conflicts* (London: Bodley Head, 2014), p. 10.

83 Ibid., p. 1.

84 Dan Lamothe, 'The USS *Cole* Was Bombed 15 Years Ago. Now It's a Floating Memorial to Those Lost', *Washington Post*, 12 October 2015, available at: https://www.washingtonpost.com/news/checkpoint/wp/2015/10/12/the-uss-cole-was-bombed-15-years-ago-now-its-a-floating-memorial-to-those-lost/?utm_term=.440f13bd25d9.

4. THE MAKING OF A VIOLENT JIHADI

1 'The Making of an Extremist', *Guardian*, 20 August 2008, available at: https://www.theguardian.com/uk/2008/aug/20/uksecurity.terrorism.

2 Elaine Pressman, *Risk Assessment Decisions for Violent Political Extremism*, Public Safety Canada, available at: http://publications.gc.ca/collections/collection_2009/sp-ps/PS3-1-2009-2-1E.pdf.

3 'The Prevent Strategy: A Textbook Example of How to Alienate Just About Everybody', *Daily Telegraph*, 31 March 2010, available at: http://www.telegraph.co.uk/news/uknews/terrorism-in-the-uk/7540456/The-Prevent-strategy-a-textbook-example-of-how-to-alienate-just-about-everybody.html.

4 Institute for Economics and Peace, *Global Terrorism Index 2015*.

5 Rik Coolsaet, *Facing the Fourth Foreign Fighters Wave: What Drives Europeans to Syria, and to Islamic State? Insights from the Belgian Case*, Egmont Papers 81 (Brussels: Egmont – The Royal Institute for International Relations, 2016), available at: http://www.egmontinstitute.be/wp-content/uploads/2016/02/egmont.papers.81_online-versie.pdf.

6 Christopher Baker-Beall, Charlotte Heath-Kelly and Lee Jarvis (eds.), *Counter-Radicalisation, Critical Perspectives* (London: Routledge, 2014), p. 195.

7 http://blogs.spectator.co.uk/2016/11/can-trust-people-trump-im-no-longer-sure/.

8 M. Mozaffari, 'What Is Islamism? History and Definition of a Concept', *Totalitarian Movements and Political Religions*, vol. 8, no. 1 (2007), pp. 17–33.

9 https://en.m.wikipedia.org/wiki/Islamism.

10 *The Encyclopedia of Islam: A Dictionary of the Geography, Ethnography and Biography of the Muhammadan Peoples* (Leiden: Brill and Luzac, 1913–38).

11 M. Kramer, 'Coming to Terms: Fundamentalists or Islamists?', *Middle East Quarterly*, Spring 2003, pp. 65–77, available at: http://www. meforum.org/541/coming-to-terms-fundamentalists-or-islamists.

12 Quoted by François Burgat, *L'islamisme au Maghreb* (Paris: Karthala, 1988), p. 14.

13 Cameron, 'What I Learnt from My Stay with a Muslim Family'.

14 Kramer, 'Coming to Terms'.

15 House of Commons Foreign Affairs Committee, *Political Islam and the Muslim Brotherhood Review*, HC 118, 1 November 2016, p. 47, available at: http://www.publications.parliament.uk/pa/cm201617/cm select/cmfaff/118/11802.htm.

16 'Vast Majority of British Muslims "Do Not Sympathise" With Suicide Bombers, Survey Shows', *Independent*, 10 April 2016, available at: http://www.independent.co.uk/news/uk/home-news/vast-majority-of-british-muslims-do-not-sympathise-with-suicide-bombers-survey-shows-a6977826.html.

17 *Tackling Extremism in the UK: Report from the Prime Minister's Task Force on Tackling Radicalisation and Extremism* (London: Cabinet Office, 2013), available at: https://www.gov.uk/government/uploads/ system/uploads/attachment_data/file/263181/ETF_FINAL.pdf.

18 Pauline Neville-Jones, *An Unquiet World: Submission to the Shadow Cabinet by the National and International Security Policy Group* (Conservative Party, 2007).

19 Interestingly, Syed Abul A'la Mawdudi was the subject of a glowing tribute in *Trends* magazine in the mid-1990s. The writer of the article now works at the counter-terrorism Research, Information and Communications Unit (RICU), illustrating that many are still on a journey on this complex issue.

20 Report of the Home Affairs Select Committee, *The Roots of Violent Radicalisation*, 21 January 2012, written evidence submitted by the Home Office, Ev88 94, p. 142.

21 Tony Munton, Alison Martin et al., *Understanding Vulnerability and Resilience in Individuals to the Influence of Al Qa'ida Violent Extremism: A Rapid Evidence Assessment to Inform Policy and Practice in Preventing Violent Extremism*, Occasional Paper 98 (Home Office, 2011), p. ii, available at: https://www.gov.uk/government/uploads/sys tem/uploads/attachment_data/file/116723/occ98.pdf.

22 Report of the Home Affairs Select Committee, *The Roots of Violent Radicalisation*, 21 January 2012, p. 12.

23 Report of the Intelligence and Security Committee, *Could 7/7 Have Been Prevented?: Review of the Intelligence on the London Terrorist Attacks on 7 July 2005*, May 2009, p. 49.

24 Anita Orav, *Religious Fundamentalism and Radicalisation*, European Parliamentary Research Service briefing paper, March 2015, p. 2.

25 'MI5 Report Challenges Views on Terrorism in Britain', *Guardian*, 20 August 2008, available at: https://www.theguardian.com/uk/2008/aug/20/uksecurity.terrorism1.

26 Scott Atran, 'Jihad's fatal attraction', *Guardian*, 4 September 2014, available at: https://www.theguardian.com/commentisfree/2014/sep/04/jihad-fatal-attraction-challenge-democracies-isis-barbarism.

27 Mehdi Hasan, 'What the Jihadists Who Bought "Islam For Dummies" on Amazon Tell Us About Radicalisation', *New Statesman*, 21 August 2014.

28 Nick Allen, 'Omar Mateen's 'Gay Lover' Claims Orlando Shooting Was Revenge against HIV-positive Partner', *Daily Telegraph*, 22 June 2016, available at: http://www.telegraph.co.uk/news/2016/06/22/omar-mateens-gay-lover-claims-orlando-shooting-was-revenge-again/.

29 Peter Allen, 'Nice Terror Killer Mohamed Lahouaiej Bouhlel "Used Dating Sites to Pick Up Men and Women"', *Daily Mirror*, 18 July 2016, available at: http://www.mirror.co.uk/news/uk-news/nice-terror-killer-used-dating-8440137.

30 'Isis Captors "Didn't Even Have the Koran" Says French Journalist Held Prisoner by Group for More Than 10 Months', *Independent*, 4 February 2015, available at: http://www.independent.co.uk/news/world/middle-east/isis-captors-didnt-even-have-the-koran-says-french-journalist-held-prisoner-by-group-for-more-than-10022291.html.

31 *Intelligence and Security Committee Report on the Intelligence Relating to the Murder of Fusilier Lee Rigby*, 25 November 2014, pp. 44–6, 166.

32 Ibid., p. 59.

33 'David Cameron: We Won't Let Women Be Second-Class Citizens', *The Times*, 18 January 2016, available at: http://www.thetimes.co.uk/tto/opinion/columnists/article4667764.ece.

34 Tom Whitehead, 'Lee Rigby Killers: From Quiet Christians to Islamist Murderers', *Daily Telegraph*, 15 November 2014, available at: http://www.telegraph.co.uk/news/uknews/law-and-order/10528365/Lee-Rigby-killers-from-quiet-Christians-to-Islamist-murderers.html.

35 Brian Klug (2011). 'An Almost Unbearable Insecurity: Cameron's Munich Speech', paper presented at the Cultural Studies Association of Australia Annual Conference 'Cultural ReOrientations and Comparative Colonialities', International Centre for Muslim and non-Muslim Understanding, University of South Australia, Adelaide, 22–4 November 2011.

36 Brian Klug, 'Fawlty Logic: The Cracks in Cameron's 2011 Munich Speech', *ReOrient*, vol. 1, no. 1 (2015), pp. 61–77.

37 Speech by David Cameron to the Munich Security Conference, 5 February 2011, available at: https://www.gov.uk/government/speeches/pms-speech-at-munich-security-conference.

38 A. Kundnani, *A Decade Lost: Rethinking Radicalisation and Extremism* (London: Claystone, 2015). As Ben Emmerson QC a UN Special Rapporteur on the Promotion and Protection of Human Rights and Fundamental Freedoms, said in his report in 2016, 'the path to radicalization is individualized and non-linear, with a number of common push and pull factors but no single determining feature' (*Report of the Special Rapporteur on the Promotion and Protection of Human Rights and Fundamental Freedoms While Countering Terrorism*, UN Doc. A/HRC/31/65 (22 February 2016), p. 15). As a European Parliamentary Research briefing from 2015 said, 'A recent approach to radicalisation suggests seeing it as a dynamic and non-linear process. Because the motivations driving radicalisation are personal and psychological, recruitment cannot be viewed as a logical chain reaction' (ibid., p. 3).

39 Arun Kundnani, 'Radicalisation: The Journey of a Concept', in Baker-Beall, Heath-Kelly and Jarvis (eds.), *Counter-Radicalisation*, p. 14.

40 In 1998, Theresa May and Philip Hammond voted against lowering the age of consent for homosexual couples from eighteen to sixteen, bringing it in line with heterosexuals.

41 Comments by the archbishop of Canterbury in the House of Lords, see: http://www.archbishopofcanterbury.org/articles.php/5815/archbishop-of-canterburys-speech-in-lords-debate-on-uk-values.

42 Russell Brand, 'We No Longer Have the Luxury of Tradition', *New Statesman*, 24 October 2013.

43 Similarly, Islamophobia, supported by plenty of evidence, wasn't considered. I saw this play out in government. Lord Carlile was the independent reviewer of terrorism legislation from 2001 to 2011, before David Anderson QC. In 2011 he presented us with a paper on Prevent in advance of the officially published Prevent review in which he cited Islamophobia as a driver of radicalization. He wasn't the first

person to raise this – there was ample academic evidence to support this position – but this was the government's appointee, an expert. And yet it took many battles with my colleagues for them to firstly acknowledge the problem and many more battles to convince them to do something about it, battles I will discuss further in chapter 6. See Tahir Abbas, 'The Symbiotic Relationship between Islamophobia and Radicalisation', *Critical Studies on Terrorism*, vol. 5, no. 3 (2012), pp. 345–58; Report of the Home Affairs Select Committee, *The Roots of Violent Radicalisation*, 21 January 2012, p. 12; M. Sageman, *Radicalization of Global Islamist Terrorists*, United States Senate Committee on Homeland Security and Governmental Affairs (2007), p. 3.

44 Maria Sobolewska, *Can We Ever Estimate How Many British Muslims Will Become Islamic Extremists?*, Manchester Policy Blogs, 26 August 2014, available at: http://blog.policy.manchester.ac.uk/featured/2014/08/can-we-ever-estimate-how-many-british-muslims-will-become-islamic-extremists/.

45 Naz Shah MP, written evidence to the Home Affairs Select Committee inquiry on Countering Extremism, CEX0037, 19 January 2016, available at: http://data.parliament.uk/writtenevidence/committeeevidence.svc/evidencedocument/home-affairs-committee/countering-extremism/written/27148.html.

46 Anjum Peerbacos, 'We Are Alienating Muslim Students – Terrorist Recruiters Can Use That Alienation', *The Times Educational Supplement*, 4 November 2016; Clare Gerada, 'Prevent Is Stopping GPs Like Me From Doing My Job', *New Statesman*, 3 November 2016; 'Counter-terrorism and Security Bill Is a Threat to Freedom of Speech at Universities', *Guardian*, 2 February 2015, available at: https://www.theguardian.com/education/2015/feb/02/counter-terrorism-security-bill-threat-freedom-of-speech-universities.

47 Baroness Hamwee, Baroness Smith, Lord Rosser, Baroness Kennedy of the Shaws, Baroness Manningham-Buller, to name a few of those who fervently opposed the government.

48 *Prevent Duty Guidance: for Higher Education Institutions in England and Wales*, HM Government, July 2015; *Revised Prevent Duty Guidance: for England and Wales*, HM Government, March 2015.

49 Speech by David Cameron 'Bringing Down the Barriers to Cohesion', 29 January 2007, available at: http://conservativehome.blogs.com/torydiary/files/bringing_down_the_barriers_to_cohesion.pdf.

50 Sarah Lyons-Padilla, 'I've Studied Radicalization – and Islamophobia Often Plants the Seed', *Guardian*, 13 June 2016, available at: https://

www.theguardian.com/commentisfree/2016/jun/13/radicalisation-isla
mophobia-orlando-shooting-florida-muslims-trump.
51 Powell, *Talking to Terrorists*, p. 13.
52 'Woolwich Attack: "Muslims Are Free of Guilt. We Had to Condemn
This Killing"', *Guardian*, 26 May 2013, available at: https://www.the
guardian.com/uk/2013/may/26/muslim-community-responds-woolwich-
killing.
53. See http://www.independent.co.uk/news/uk/student-wrongly-accused-
of-being-a-terrorist-after-he-was-seen-reading-a-textbook-on-terrorism-
for-10515669.html; https://www.theguardian.com/uk-news/2017/jan/27/
bedfordshire-local-education-authority-admits-racial-discrimination-
brothers-toy-gun-school-police; https://www.theguardian.com/commentis
free/2017/feb/01/children-detained-toy-gun-prevent-strategy.
54 *Preventing Education: Human Rights and UK Counter-Terrorism*
(London: Rights Watch UK, 2016), p. 5, available at: http://rwuk.
org/wp-content/uploads/2016/07/preventing-education-final-to-print-3.
compressed-1.pdf.
55 'Lee Rigby Killers: From Quiet Christians to Islamist Murderers', *Daily
Telegraph*, 15 November 2014, available at: http://www.telegraph.co.uk/
news/uknews/law-and-order/10528365/Lee-Rigby-killers-from-quiet-Christians-
to-Islamist-murderers.html; 'French Convert with Jewish Father Dies
Fighting for ISIS', http://www.israelnationalnews.com/News/News.aspx/
187418, 13 November 2014; 'Paris Attacks: Voice in Isis Propaganda is
"Probably" French Jihadist Fabien Clain', *Independent*, 17 November
2015, available at: http://www.independent.co.uk/news/world/europe/
paris-attacks-voice-in-isis-video-is-probably-french-jihadist-fabien-clain-
a6737736.html.
56 The Royal College of Psychiatrists in 2016 too raised concerns about
the 'quality of the evidence underpinning the strategy and the potential
conflicts with the duties of Doctors as defined by the GMC', warning
that there is a risk 'that Prevent could reduce the willingness of people
to access mental health services.' Royal College of Psychiatrists,
'Counter-terrorism and Psychiatry', Position statement PS04/16, September 2016, available at: http://www.rcpsych.ac.uk/pdf/PS04_16.pdf.
See also: 'Eroding Trust: The UK's Prevent Counter-Extremism Strategy in Health and Education' (New York: OSF), available at: https://
www.opensocietyfoundations.org/press-releases/new-report-calls-repeal-uk-
counter-extremism-reporting-obligation.
57 National channel referral figures published by the National Police
Chiefs Council, 2015, available at: http://www.npcc.police.uk/Freedo
mofInformation/NationalChannelReferralFigures.aspx.

58 CONTEST, *The United Kingdom's Strategy for Countering Terrorism: Annual Report for 2015*, London: HM Government, Cm 9310, para. 2.37, p. 16, available at: https://www.gov.uk/government/uploads/system/uploads/attachment_data/file/539683/55469_Cm_9310_Web_Accessible_v0.11.pdf para2.37.

59 *Radicalisation: The Counter-narrative and Identifying the Tipping Point*, Report of the Home Affairs Select Committee Eighth Report of Session 2016–17, August 2016, para. 55, p. 19.

60 Written evidence to the Home Affairs Select Committee (CEX0041), para. 7.

61 Y. Birt, 'Promoting Virulent Envy?' *The RUSI Journal*, vol. 154, no. 4 (2009), pp. 52–8.

62 *Radicalisation: The Counter-narrative and Identifying the Tipping Point*, p. 18.

63 'Prevent Strategy to Be Ramped Up Despite 'Big Brother' Concerns', *Guardian*, 11 November 2016, available at: https://www.theguardian.com/uk-news/2016/nov/11/prevent-strategy-uk-counter-radicalisation-widened-despite-criticism-concerns.

64 Gareth Peirce, 'Was It Like This for the Irish?', *London Review of Books*, vol. 30, no. 7, April 2008, pages 3–8.

65 HC Deb, vol. 604, no. 100, 579WH, 20 January 2016, available at: http://www.publications.parliament.uk/pa/cm201516/cmhansrd/cm160120/halltext/160120h0001.htm#16012030000590.

66 Birt, 'Promoting Virulent Envy?'

67 *Preventing Education: Human Rights and UK Counter-Terrorism* (London: Rights Watch UK, 2016), p. 10.

68 FOI Release, 'Home Office funding of the Prevent Programme from 2011 to 2015', published 28 November 2014. available at: https://www.gov.uk/government/publications/home-office-funding-of-the-prevent-programme-from-2011-to-2015.

69 'UK Terror Attack Expectation TRIPLES in a Decade as 84 Per Cent of Britons Fear Strike', *Daily Express*, 8 August 2016, available at: http://www.express.co.uk/news/uk/697709/UK-terror-attack-threat-triples-Brits-fear-strike-poll.

70 *Operation of Police Powers under the Terrorism Act 2000 and Subsequent Legislation: Arrests, Outcomes, and Stop and Search, Great Britain, Financial Year Ending 31 March 2016*, Statistical Bulletin 04/16 published June 2016, p. 1. See also https://www.gov.uk/government/uploads/system/uploads/attachment_data/file/539683/55469_Cm_9310_Web_Accessible_v0.11.pdf.

5. THE PARANOID STATE

1 England and Wales Order (2013) No 1198: Rehabilitation of Offenders Act 1974 (Exceptions) Order 1975 (Amendment) (England and Wales) Order 2013, available at: http://www.legislation.gov.uk/uksi/2013/1198/pdfs/uksi_20131198_en.pdf.

2 Guidance on the Rehabilitation of Offenders Act 1974, 10 March 2014, available at: https://www.gov.uk/government/uploads/system/uploads/attachment_data/file/216089/rehabilitation-offenders.pdf.

3 E. Love, 'Confronting Islamophobia in the United States: Framing Civil Rights Activism Among Middle Eastern Americans', in M. Malik (ed.), *Anti-Muslim Prejudice, Past and Present* (London and New York: Routledge, 2010), pp. 191–214; T. Mills, T. Griffin and D. Miller, *The Cold War on British Muslims: An Examination of Policy Exchange and the Centre for Social Cohesion*, Public Interest Investigations, 2011.

4 Hazel Blears, the then communities secretary, believed the Muslim Council of Britain deputy Dr Daud Abdullah had signed a letter bearing intent to attack UK armed forces during 2008/9 Operation Cast Lead and wrote to the MCB to demand his resignation as a condition for continued engagement with the government. She said the letter (the Istanbul Declaration) 'could' be construed as an attack on HM Armed Forces. ('Our Shunning of the MCB Is Not Grandstanding', *Guardian*, 25 March 2009, available at: https://www.theguardian.com/commentisfree/2009/mar/25/islam-terrorism.) Dr Abdullah denied the document expressed any intent to attack UK armed forces (the Royal Navy or otherwise) and stated as much in an open letter to John Denham (Blears' successor). Moreover, both he and the MCB affirmed that he did not sign in his capacity as deputy of that organization. (See 'Dr Daud Abdullah's Open Letter to Secretary of State, John Denham', 22 January 2010, available at: https://www.facebook.com/notes/middle-east-monitor/memo-alert-dr-daud-abdullahs-open-letter-to-secretary-of-state-john-denham/268576588835/.

5 Speech by Theresa May, 'A Stronger Britain, Built on Our Values', 23 March 2015, available at: https://www.gov.uk/government/speeches/a-stronger-britain-built-on-our-values.

6 Extremism Analysis Unit: written question 21752, asked by Alastair Carmichael MP, 11 January 2016; available at https://www.theyworkforyou.com/wrans/?id=2016-01-11.21751.h.

7 Theresa May, when home secretary, spoke clearly about the remit of the EAU: 'The starting point is, of course, the need for a better evidence

base for dealing with extremists and extremist organisations. The Government's new Extremism Analysis Unit is already up and running and helping to inform ... this strategy'; see: 'Speech by Home Secretary, Theresa May, "A Stronger Britain, Built on Our Values"', Royal Institution of Chartered Surveyors, London, 23 March 2015, available at: http://statewatch.org/news/2015/mar/uk-2015-03-23-theresa-may-anti-extremism-speech.pdf.

8 http://www.parliament.uk/business/publications/written-questions-answers-statements/written-question/Commons/2015-07-20/7943/.

9 'How MI5's Scientists Work to Identify Future Terrorists', *BBC News*, 12 December 2016, available at: http://www.bbc.co.uk/news/uk-38252470.

10 The Big Lunch, an initiative developed by the Eden Project aims to bring people together to have lunch one Sunday in June annually. It was started in 2009 and in 2015, brought together 7.29 million people for lunch. The next one will take place on Sunday 4 June 2017.

11 'Nick Clegg Attacks Policy Exchange for "Offensive" and "Underhand" Briefing', *Liberal Democrat Voice*, 24 October 2008, available at: http://www.libdemvoice.org/nick-clegg-attacks-policy-exchange-for-offensive-and-underhand-briefing-5064.html.

12 'Baroness Warsi Pulls Out of Muslim Conference Amid Claims of Tory Concerns', *Daily Telegraph*, 25 October 2010, available at: http://www.telegraph.co.uk/news/politics/conservative/8084340/Baroness-Warsi-pulls-out-of-Muslim-conference-amid-claims-of-Tory-concerns.html.

13 'Pastor of Brent Cross Church Welcomes Prime Minister David Cameron to Christian Festival', *Hendon and Finchley Times*, 23 April 2015.

14 Asonzeh Ukah, 'Sexual Bodies, Sacred Vessels: Pentecostal Discourses on Homosexuality in Nigeria', in Ezra Chitando and Adriaan van Klinken (eds.), *Christianity and Controversies over Homosexuality in Contemporary Africa* (London: Routledge, 2016), pp. 21–37.

15 'Pastor of Brent Cross Church Welcomes Prime Minister David Cameron to Christian Festival', *Hendon and Finchley Times*, 23 April 2015.

16 Peter Oborne, 'What's the Conservative Party's Problem with Muslims?', *Middle East Eye*, 7 October 2016, available at: http://www.middleeasteye.net/columns/peter-oborne-whats-conservative-partys-problem-muslims-1757982215.

17 Speech by the Prime Minister, Theresa May, to Conservative Party Conference at the ICC, Birmingham, 5 October 2016. The notion of one rule for the Muslims and another for the rest was explored by the High Court in 2016 on the issue of gender segregation and OFSTED's view that Muslims were discriminating by allowing the practice in a

mixed-sex school. The judge, Justice Jay, argued: 'Islamic faith schools were similar to some Jewish schools in this respect. Indeed, there is evidence before me of a particular Jewish school, operating on what is described as two campuses, which at its last Ofsted inspection in 2012 was rated outstanding across the board.' The judge noted: 'From brief internet research, I have gathered that a number of Christian faith schools have similar practices.' In other words, he implemented a uniform and consistent application of our values against the government's position argued by OFSTED. (See: 'Ofsted Wrong to Penalise Islamic School Over Gender Segregation, Court Rules', *Guardian*, 8 November 2016, available at: https://www.theguardian.com/education/2016/nov/08/ofsted-wrong-to-penalise-islamic-school-over-gender-segregation-court-rules).

18   I asked ministerial colleagues to take that moment in 2012 and shape GPU in a way that was acceptable to government and one that would enable senior government attendance at the event. My colleagues refused to do so: the response was 'Who they invite is a matter for them, and we will decide whether or not to attend once they've decided.'

19   'Exposed: Sadiq Khan's Family Links to Extremist Organisation', *Evening Standard*, 12 February 2016, available at: http://www.standard.co.uk/news/london/exposed-sadiq-khans-family-links-to-extremist-organisation-a3179066.html.

20   'Chancellor's Brother Adam Osborne Suspended as a Doctor – for Second Time', *Daily Telegraph*, 15 March 2015.

21   'The NHS Imam Who Opposes Organ Transplants but Has Been Employed in a Hospital for Three Years', *Daily Mail*, 23 March 2013.

22   'Zac Goldsmith's Extremist Attack Line Backfires', *The Spectator*, 14 April 2016, available at: http://blogs.spectator.co.uk/2016/04/zac-goldsmiths-extremist-attack-line-backfires/.

23   'MPs Shout "Racist" at Cameron after Comments on Sadiq Khan during PMQs', *Guardian*, 20 April 2016.

24   'Michael Fallon to Compensate Imam after False Islamic State Claim', *Daily Telegraph*, 23 June 2016, http://www.telegraph.co.uk/news/2016/06/23/michael-fallon-to-compensate-imam-after-false-islamic-state-claim/.

25   'Conservative Home Apologises to Sir Iqbal Sacranie, Carter Ruck, 16 December 2011', available at: http://www.carter-ruck.com/news/read/conservativehome-apologises-to-sir-iqbal-sacranie.

26   Sir Stephen Bubb, the ex-chief executive of ACEVO, has experienced this 'maligning of Muslims' in the charitable sector. He has seen at first hand the reluctance of British Muslims to take on the media and official bodies because of the increased potential of 'bad publicity' and 'reputation damage' despite a positive and favourable outcome.

27 'Downing Street Set to Crack Down on the Muslim Brotherhood', *Daily Telegraph*, 19 October 2014, available at: http://www.telegraph. co.uk/news/uknews/11171979/Downing-Street-set-to-crack-down-on-the-Muslim-Brotherhood.html.

28 Douglas Murray, 'After Woolwich, What Will Change?', *The Spectator*, 1 June 2013, available at: http://www.spectator.co.uk/2013/06/the-enemies-within/.

29 Paddy Hillyard, *Suspect Community: People's Experience of the Prevention of Terrorism Acts in Britain* (London: Pluto Press, 1993); Paddy Hillyard, ' "The 'War on Terror": Lessons from Ireland', in European Civil Liberties Network, *Essays for Civil Liberties and Democracy in Europe*, 3 October 2005.

30 V. Mohini Giri , *Living Death: Trauma of Widowhood in India* (New Delhi: Gyan Publishing House, 2002).

31 'Ultra-Orthodox Rabbis Ban Women from Going to University in Case They Get "Dangerous" Secular Knowledge', *Independent*, 22 August 2016, available at: http://www.independent.co.uk/news/world/americas/ultra-orthodox-rabbis-ban-women-from-going-to-university-in-case-they-get-dangerous-secular-a7204171.html.

32 A principle applied by George Osborne to Donald Trump: 'George Osborne Warns Theresa May She Must Work Closely With Donald Trump to Curb His Disastrous Ideas', *Sun*, 10 November 2016, available at: https://www.thesun.co.uk/news/2159155/george-osborne-warns-theresa-may-must-work-closely-with-donald-trump-to-curb-his-disastrous-ideas/.

33 Freedom of Information request to the Department for Education by Jenna Corderoy, 19 January 2016, response received 15 March 2016, available at: https://assets.documentcloud.org/documents/2779727/FOI-Educateagainsthate-Com-Consultants-and-Stats.pdf.

34 It would, however, be remiss of me to not address the one opportunity for reintegration, the one route to rehabilitation that is the route of the 'proper ex-extremist'. There are certain rules that apply. Firstly, you have to have been a real baddie. Not just someone who has some naff views on gays, Jews and women, but serious hardcore revolutionary stuff. You know the stuff I'm talking about: the Islamic takeover of Britain, a hatred for our democracy and institutions, a country run by religious laws, possibly even Arabic as the national language and preferably a few years' experience either in a 'war zone' or some 'academic learning / jihadi gap year' in an exotic Muslim place. So effectively you've got to have been a bit of a fantasist. I've met plenty of these types during my public life, and they are invariably male, well-educated

and charismatic, to my mind. Secondly you've got to have had, or manufactured, 'a moment' when you saw the light and recognized the error of your ways. Thirdly, in your thinking the pendulum has to swing from an extremist position based on religion to an extremist position based on liberalism, or preferably move to a position of non-belief. The one thing better than an ex-extremist in the world of rehab is an ex-believer. And providing you go through the above phases you can not only be deemed suitable for engagement but indeed even invited to advise government and funded to front counter-extremism work. If you follow this path you can be redeemed. If, however, you didn't go 'all the way' in your extremism phase but simply dabbled in the softer stuff, a cannabis user for social and recreational purposes rather than hooked on the Class A stuff, you are beyond the pale.

6. ISLAMOPHOBIA

1 D. Kumar, *Islamophobia and the Politics of Empire* (Chicago: Haymarket Books, 2012).

2 'Roald Dahl after 100 years: Remembering Beloved Author's Forgotten Antisemitic Past', *Independent*, 13 September 2016, available at: http://www.independent.co.uk/news/people/roald-dahl-antisemitic-100-years-remembering-author-forgotten-past-a7254266.html.

3 M. Ruotsila, *British and American Anti-Communism Before the Cold War* (London: Frank Cass, 2001).

4 *Islamophobia: A Challenge for Us All*, Runnymede Trust Commission on British Muslims and Islamophobia, 1997.

5 http://crg.berkeley.edu/content/islamophobia/defining-islamophobia.

6 W. Ali, E. Clifton, M. Duss, L. Fang, S. Keyes and F. Shakir, *Fear, Inc.: The Roots of the Islamophobia Network in America* (Center for American Progress, 2011), p. 9.

7 Douglas Murray, 'We Must Stop Avoiding This Discussion', available at: http://www.thejc.com/comment-and-debate/comment/108879/we-must-stop-avoiding-discussion.

8 C. Miller, J. Smith and J. Dale, *Islamophobia on Twitter: March to July 2016* (London: DEMOS, 2016).

9 Byrne, *Black Flag Down*, pp. 32, 163.

10 Dr Alison Davies, 'Beyond Tolerance: Young British Muslims Discuss Ways to Build Community Cohesion in Their City, and the Barriers They Experience', paper presented to the British Educational Research Association, 14 September 2016.

11 Bera, 'Press Release: Pupils Left Puzzled by the Term "British Values"', available at: https://www.bera.ac.uk/bera-in-the-news/press-release-pupils-left-puzzled-by-the-term-british-values.

12 Peter Oborne and James Jones, *Muslims Under Siege: Alienating Vulnerable Communities* (London and Essex: Democratic Audit, Human Rights Centre, University of Essex and Channel 4 *Dispatches*, 2008).

13 Religious hate crimes in England and Wales rose by 44 per cent between 2012/13 and 2013/14; 43 per cent between2013/14 and 2014/15; 34 per cent between 2014/15 and 2015/16; with a reported 41 per cent year-on-year increase following the Brexit vote: the number of racially or religiously aggravated offences recorded by the police in July 2016 was 41 per cent higher than in July 2015. In London alone, where Islamophobia statistics are available because the Metropolitan Police record data in this category, Islamophobia rose by 70 per cent between July 2014 and July 2015. ('Hate Crimes against Muslims Soar in London', *Guardian*, 7 September 2015, available at: https://www.theguardian.com/world/2015/sep/07/hate-crimes-against-muslims-soar-london-islamophobia.)

Race hate crime is the dominant type of hate crime, accounting for between 79 and 85 per cent, depending on the year, of all hate crime reported in England and Wales. (*Hate Crime England and Wales*, Home Office annual reports, 2013/14, 2014/15, 2015/16.)

The Crime Survey for England and Wales, a victim-based survey, posits the number of hate crimes at around 222,000 per year, showing a sharp shortfall in the volume of police-recorded hate crime compared with victim experiences. It also suggests that the rising volume of hate crime that is 'recorded' masks the true scale, given the huge level of under-reporting.

14 A Comres poll for the BBC Radio 4 *Today* programme, 25 February 2015, showed that 35 per cent of Muslims agreed with the statement 'I feel that most British people don't trust Muslims'; 46 per cent agreed with the statement 'Britain is becoming less tolerant of Muslims', compared with 49 per cent who disagreed; 46 per cent agreed with the statement 'Prejudice against Islam makes it very difficult being a Muslim in this country', compared with 51 per cent who disagreed. The 'Show Racism the Red Card' survey, 2012–14 collected responses from 6,000 schoolchildren from sixty schools around the country: 31 per cent of young people agreed with the statement 'Muslims are taking over England'; 35 per cent agreed Muslims 'contribute positively to society in England' compared to 19 per cent who disagreed; and a whopping 47 per cent said they 'don't know'. ('Racist and Anti-immigration Views Held by Children Revealed in Schools Study', *Guardian*, 19 May 2015,

available at: https://www.theguardian.com/education/2015/may/19/most-children-think-immigrants-are-stealing-jobs-schools-study-shows.)

15 Institute for Economics and Peace, *Global Terrorism Index 2015*, p. 2.

16 C. Kurzman, *Muslim-American Involvement with Violent Extremism, 2016* (North Carolina: Duke University, 2017). Statement by David Schanzer available at https://sites.duke.edu/tcths/2017/01/26/muslim-american-involvement-with-violent-extremism-2016.

17 Police Service of Northern Ireland, Security Situation Statistics 2015/16.

18 Brian Kilmeade on *The View*, Fox News, 15 October 2010; Brian Kilmeade, 'All Terrorists Are Muslims,' *Huffington Post*, 15 October 2010, available at: http://www.huffingtonpost.com/2010/10/15/brian-kilmeade-all-terror_n_764472.html.

19 'Boris Johnson Condemned for Blaming Munich Attack on "Global Sickness" of Islamist Terrorism', *Independent*, 25 July 2016, available at: https://www.independent.co.uk/news/uk/politics/boris-johnson-foreign-secretary-munich-shooting-attack-islamic-terrorism-isis-a7154371.html.

20 'Munich Shooting: Teenage Killer Ali Sonboly "Inspired by Far-right Terrorist Anders Breivik" and "Used Facebook Offer of Free McDonald's Food to Lure Victims"', *Daily Telegraph*, 24 July 2016, available at: http://www.telegraph.co.uk/news/2016/07/23/munich-shooting-german-iranian-gunman-targeted-children-outside/.

21 'How Islamic Inventors Changed the World', *Independent*, 11 March 2006, available at: http://www.independent.co.uk/news/science/how-islamic-inventors-changed-the-world-6106905.html.

22 M. Hafez, *Suicide Bombers in Iraq: The Strategy and Ideology of Martyrdom* (Washington, DC: United States Institute of Peace Press, 2007).

23 Majorities or near majorities of Muslims living in Great Britain, France, Germany and Spain view Westerners as generous, honest, tolerant and respectful of women. Similarly, minorities of Muslims in these countries associate Westerners with being violent, greedy, fanatical, and immoral. Report by the Pew Research Center, *The Great Divide: How Westerners and Muslims View Each Other*, 22 June 2006, available at http://www.pewglobal.org/2006/06/22/i-muslims-and-the-west-how-each-sees-the-other/.

24 Wind-Cowie, *A Place for Pride*.

25 The Gallup Coexist Index 2009: A Global Study of Interfaith Relations.

26 'UK Attitudes Towards Islam "Concerning" after Survey of 2,000 People', *BBC News*, 23 May 2016, available at: http://www.bbc.co.uk/newsbeat/article/36346886/uk-attitudes-towards-islam-concerning-after-survey-of-2000-people.

27 'Britain Divided by Islam, Survey Finds', *Daily Telegraph*, 11 January 2010, available at: http://www.telegraph.co.uk/news/religion/6965276/ Britain-divided-by-Islam-survey-finds.html; 'The Majority of Voters Doubt That Islam Is Compatible With British Values', *Daily Telegraph*, 30 March 2015, available at: http://www.telegraph.co.uk/news/ general-election-2015/politics-blog/11503493/The-majority-of-voters-doubt-that-Islam-is-compatible-with-British-values.html.

28 A recent refutation of the abuse of Islamic concepts to justify terrorism and violence can be found in the 'Open Letter to Al-Baghdadi', signed by hundreds of Muslim scholars from around the world and translated into seven European languages and Arabic, Persian and Turkish, available at: http://www.lettertobaghdadi.com/.

29 Speech by former Secretary of State Madeleine Albright at the 'Religion, Peace, and World Affairs: The Challenges Ahead' symposium at Georgetown University, 7 April 2016.

30 'Two Guys Tricked People Into Thinking Quotes From the Bible Were From the Qur'an', *Buzzfeed News*, 7 December 2015, available at: https://www.buzzfeed.com/alanwhite/these-guys-read-people-passages-from-the-bible-but-made-them?utm_term=.wkB59Omb3#.vcyxDX4q2.

31 For example, 'If a man lies with a male as with a woman, both of them shall be put to death for their abominable deed; they have forfeited their lives' (Leviticus 20:13); 'Think not that I am come to bring peace to the earth: I came not to send peace, but a sword. For I am come to set man at variance against his father, and the daughter against her mother, and the daughter in law against her mother in law. And a man's foes shall be they of his own household' (Matthew 10:34). See: ' "Violence More Common" in Bible than Quran, Text Analysis Reveals', *Independent*, 9 February 2016, available at: http://www.independent.co.uk/arts-entertainment/books/violence-more-common-in-bible-than-quran-text-analysis-reveals-a6863381.html.

32 A. Kundnani, 'Twenty-First-Century Crusaders', *Critical Muslim*, CM03: Fear and Loathing (London: C. Hurst, 2012), available at: http://critical-muslim.com/issues/03-fear-and-loathing/twenty-first-century-crusaders-arun-kundnani.

33 Quoted in Raymond Ibrahim. 'Are Judaism and Christianity as Violent as Islam?', *Middle East Quarterly*, Summer 2009, pp. 3–12, available at: http://www.meforum.org/2159/are-judaism-and-christianity-as-violent-as-islam.

34 'This Woman Was Told Muslims Don't Condemn Violence, So She Made a List to Show They Do', *Buzzfeed News*, 17 November 2016, available at: https://www.buzzfeed.com/krishrach/this-woman-was-told-

muslims-dont-condemn-violence-so-she-mad?utm_term=.fmbZKm39d#.jfQVBJ87k.

35 http://www.mohammedamin.com/Community_issues/Compendium-Muslim-condemnations-of-terrorism.html.

36 'CNN Anchor Blames French Muslims for Failure to Prevent Attacks', *Washington Post*, 16 November 2015, available at: https://www.washingtonpost.com/blogs/erik-wemple/wp/2015/11/16/cnn-anchor-blames-french-muslims-for-failure-to-prevent-attacks.

37 'We Prayed for Paris — But What About Istanbul?', *Huffington Post*, 29 June 2016, available at: http://www.huffingtonpost.com/entry/we-prayed-for-paris-but-what-about-istanbul_us_57741c57e4b042fba1ceeec2.

38 The Muslim Council of Britain placed an advert condemning the attacks in Paris on 13 November 2015. The advert appeared in the *Daily Telegraph*.

39 This, before his conviction, would be Anjem Chowdry of poppy-burning fame.

40 Robert Mackey, 'Clear Evidence Killing of British MP Jo Cox Was Politically Motivated', *The Intercept*, 18 June 2016, available at: https://theintercept.com/2016/06/17/far-right-britain-first-party-tries-avoid-blame-lawmakers-assassination/.

41 Speech by David Cameron to the Global Security Forum in Bratislava, 19 June 2015, available at: https://www.gov.uk/government/speeches/pm-at-2015-global-security-forum.

42 'UK Muslims Helping Jihadis, Says Cameron: Communities Must Stop "Quietly Condoning" Barbaric ISIS, PM Warns in Blunt Speech', *Daily Mail*, 19 June 2015, available at: http://www.dailymail.co.uk/news/article-3130540/David-Cameron-says-communities-stop-quietly-condoning-ISIS-blunt-speech.html.

43 'Remember, Prime Minister: British Muslims Hate Isis Too', *Guardian*, 19 June 2015, available at: https://www.theguardian.com/commentisfree/2015/jun/19/prime-minister-british-muslims-isis.

44 Speech by Theresa May to the Metropolitan Police Service Counter-Terrorism and Policing conference, London 18 June 2015.

45 'Remember, Prime Minister: British Muslims Hate Isis Too'.

46 '"New Jihadi John" Abu Rumaysah Warned 'Black Flag of Islam' Could Fly Over 10 Downing Street', *Daily Mirror*, 19 January 2016, available at: http://www.mirror.co.uk/news/uk-news/new-jihadi-john-abu-rumaysah-7202467.

47 'Swilling Beer, Smoking Dope and Leering at Porn, the Other Side of Hate Preacher "Andy" Choudary', *Daily Mail*, 5 January 2010, available at:http://www.dailymail.co.uk/news/article-1161909/Swilling-beer-smoking-dope-leering-porn-hate-preacher-Andy-Choudary.html.

48 D. Miller and T. Mills, 'Misinformed Expert or Misinformation Network?', *Open Democracy*, 15 January 2015, available at: https://www.opendemocracy.net/ourkingdom/david-miller-tom-mills/misinformed-expert-or-misinformation-network.

49 Office for National Statistics, *Religion in England and Wales 2011*.

50 Ipsos Mori, 'Perils of Perception' surveys, 9 July 2013, 29 October 2014, 14 December 2016, available at:https://www.ipsos-mori.com/researchpublications/researcharchive/3817/Perceptions-are-not-reality-what-the-world-gets-wrong.aspx. The latest poll in 2016 shows a somewhat less inaccurate perception of the number of Muslims, but at 15 per cent still represents a threefold overestimation of the actual figure.

51 ' "Have More Babies and Muslims Can Take Over The UK" Hate Fanatic Says, as Warning Comes That "Next 9/11 Will Be in UK" ', *Daily Mail*, 13 September 2008, available at: http://www.dailymail.co.uk/news/article-1054909/Have-babies-Muslims-UK-hate-fanatic-says-warning-comes-9-11-UK.html.

52 V. Cooper, 'The Islamic Future of Britain', *The Commentator*, 13 June 2013, available at: http://www.thecommentator.com/article/3770/the_islamic_future_of_britain.

53 *FactCheck: Will Britain Have a Muslim Majority by 2050?*, Channel 4, 17 June 2013, available at: http://blogs.channel4.com/factcheck/factcheck-will-britain-have-a-muslim-majority-by-2050/13690.

54 HMG Counter-Extremism Strategy, published October 2015, p. 19.

55 Byrne, *Black Flag Down*, p. 14.

56 This ratcheting-up of the issue and the sensationalist way in which the matter was dealt with was something I had come to expect from Michael. To me he rarely appeared interested in genuine solutions. I recall his terrible heel-dragging when both Theresa May, the then home secretary, and I tried to ensure the challenges of forced marriages were properly highlighted in schools, including that posters warning girls and providing helpline information were displayed.

57 P. Clarke, *Report into Allegations Concerning Birmingham Schools Arising From The 'Trojan Horse' Letter*. HC 576, 22 July 2014, para. 11.1, p. 95.

58 'Islamic "Radicals" at the Heart of Whitehall', *Sunday Telegraph*, 22 February 2015, available at: http://www.telegraph.co.uk/news/politics/11427370/Islamic-radicals-at-the-heart-of-Whitehall.html; see also Speech by Theresa May setting out the work of the Extremism Analysis Unit and its 'counter-entryist strategy', 'A Stronger Britain, Built on our Values: A New Partnership to Defeat Extremism', 23 March

2015, available at: http://press.conservatives.com/post/115395299770/theresa-may-speech-a-stronger-britain-built-on.

59 'Donald Trump Floats Conspiracy Theory That Huma Abedin Has Terrorist Ties', *Huffington Post*, 30 August 2016, available at: http://www.huffingtonpost.com/entry/donald-trump-huma-abedin_us_57c4aaafe4b09cd22d92273c.

60 'Islamic "Radicals" at the Heart of Whitehall'.

61 'Colossal Conspiracy in Whitehall as Sayeeda Warsi's Aftermath Assessed', blogpost, 23 February 2015, available at: http://islamexposedblog.blogspot.co.uk/2015/02/colossal-conspiracy-in-whitehall-as.html.

62 Examples of anti-Semitic legislation, 1933–9, taken from *Holocaust Encyclopedia* (Washington, DC: United States Holocaust Memorial Museum).

63 'Is the "Alt-Right" on the Rise in Europe?", https://m.youtube.com/watch?v=cNpt5KG5mis.

64 Nigel Farage, former UKIP leader, interviewed by Trevor Phillips for the programme *Things We Won't Say about Race That Are True*, Channel 4, 19 March 2015.

65 'Whatever They Do, Muslims Can't Win in Our Society', *Guardian*, 28 April 2016, available at: https://www.theguardian.com/commentisfree/2016/apr/28/muslims-society-london-mayoral-election-islam.

66 See 'Grooming and Race', *BBC News*, 9 May 2012, available at: http://www.bbc.co.uk/news/uk-18004153; see also: 'Are Asians Disproportionately Represented In Prosecutions For Sex Offences?', *Full Fact*, 10 May 2012.

67 'Cabinet at War Over Islamic Extremist Plot to Take Over Birmingham Schools', *The Times*, 4 June 2014, available at: http://www.thetimes.co.uk/tto/news/politics/article4108492.ece.

68 'Counter Extremism Bill Alarmed Me Most, says Independent Reviewer of Terrorism Legislation', National Secular Society, 3 November 2016, available at: http://www.secularism.org.uk/news/2016/11/counter-extremism-bill-alarmed-me-most-says-independent-reviewer-of-terrorism-legislation.

69 *Human Rights and Democracy: The 2012 Foreign and Commonwealth Office Report*, Cm 8593, April 2013 (London: HMSO), p. 72.

70 European Commission against Racism and Intolerance (ECRI), Report on the United Kingdom (fifth monitoring cycle), 4 October 2016.

71 'Aung San Suu Kyi Made Angry "Muslim" Comment After Tense Exchange With BBC Presenter Mishal Husain, It Is Claimed', *Independent*, 25 March 2016, available at: http://www.independent.co.uk/news/people/aung-san-suu-kyi-reportedly-said-no-one-told-me-i-was-going-to-be-interviewed-by-a-muslim-after-a6951941.html.

72 'BBC Presenter Signs Off "Inshallah" on Flagship Debate Programme', *Breitbart News*, 5 June 2016.

73 'Typecast as a Terrorist, Riz Ahmed', *Guardian*, 15 September 2016, available at: https://www.theguardian.com/world/2016/sep/15/riz-ahmed-typecast-as-a-terrorist.

74 'Nadiya Hussain: Racist Abuse Has Been Part of My Life "For Years" ', *Independent*, 14 August 2016, available at: http://www.independent.co.uk/news/people/nadiya-hussain-racist-abuse-great-british-bake-off-winner-interview-a7189816.html.

7. THE MUSLIMS

1 Regina Wagner, *The History of Coffee in Guatemala* (Bogota, Colombia: Villegas Editores, 2001), p. 19.

2 'Race and Religious Hate Crime Rose 41% after EU Vote, *BBC News*, available at: http://www.bbc.co.uk/news/uk-politics-37640982.

3 J. Burnett, *Racial Violence and the Brexit State* (London: Institute of Race Relations, 2016).

4 See a saying of the Prophet Muhammad: 'None of you truly believes until he loves for his brother what he loves for himself', Sahih Muslim, *Book of Faith* (*Kitab Al-Iman*), hadith 72, and Sahih al-Bukhari, vol. 1, book 2, hadith 13.

5 S. Akhtar Ehtisham, *A Medical Doctor Examines Life on Three Continents: A Pakistani View* (New York: Algora Publishing, 2008), p. 11.

6 Ultra-orthodox Islamic followers of an eighteenth-century preacher and scholar, Muhammad ibn Abd al-Wahhab, who started a revivalist movement in what is modern-day Saudi Arabia, advocating a purging of practices such as the popular 'cult of saints' and shrine and tomb visitation, widespread among Muslims, but which he considered to be *shirk*, idolatry. Al Wahhab eventually formed a pact with a local tribal leader, Muhammad bin Saud, when in exchange for propagation of his version of the faith he agreed political obedience. The pact was sealed with the marriage of Bin Saud's son to Al Wahhab's daughter, setting the foundations of the state of Saudi Arabia and the Saud royal family, which still rules today. N. C. Asthana and A. Nirmal, *Urban Terrorism: Myths and Realities* (Jaipur: Pointer Publishers, 2009), p. 61.

7 'On This Day: 5th May 1970 – Bashir Maan Becomes Councillor', *Glasgow Life* (undated), available at: http://www.glasgowlife.org.uk/

NOTES TO PP. 171–5

libraries/the-mitchell-library/archives/thisday/bashir-maan-councillor/
pages/default.aspx.

8 For example, Fatima al Firhi founded the first university in 859 in Fez,
Morocco; Razia al Din ruled the Delhi Sultanate in India in 1236;
Umm Darda, a scholar from Syria, taught imams.

9 F. Mernissi, *The Forgotten Queens of Islam*, translated by Mary Jo
Lakeland (London: Polity Press, 1993); 'The World's 100 Most Powerful Women', published by Forbes, June 2016.

10 'France's Sarkozy Says Would Change Constitution to Ban Burkinis',
Reuters, 29 August 2016, available at: http://uk.reuters.com/article/us-
religion-burqa-france-idUKKCN1130TW.

11 It was a British Muslim, crown prosecutor Nazir Afzal, who led the prosecutions in the Rochdale child abuse case, despite personal vilification. See:
'I Was Intimidated and Branded a Racist for Bringing Rochdale Abuse
Gang to Justice, Says Prosecutor', *Daily Mail*, 31 August 2014, available at:
http://www.dailymail.co.uk/news/article-2738804/I-intimidated-branded-
racist-bringing-Rochdale-abuse-gang-justice-says-prosecutor.html.

12 'Trump Recorded Having Extremely Lewd Conversation about Women
in 2005', *Washington Post*, 8 October 2016, available at: https://www.
washingtonpost.com/politics/trump-recorded-having-extremely-lewd-
conversation-about-women-in-2005/2016/10/07/3b9ce776-8cb4-11e6-
bf8a-3d26847eeed4_story.html?utm_term=.e16c73a93eda.

13 Home Office announcement 'Independent Review into Sharia Law
Launched', 26 May 2016, available at: https://www.gov.uk/government/
news/independent-review-into-sharia-law-launched.

14 There are in fact no statistics available on the number of polygamous
marriages in the UK, given that such marriages are unregistered; see
http://qna.files.parliament.uk/qna-attachments/92268/original/PQ%20
209506,%20209680%20ONS%20344,345.pdf.

15 'Law Seeks to Ease Jewish Divorces', *Guardian*, 27 July 2002, available at: https://www.theguardian.com/uk/2002/jul/27/religion.world1;
'Scandal of Women Trapped in Marriages by Jewish Courts', *Independent*, 31 July 2009, available at: http://www.independent.co.uk/news/uk/
home-news/scandal-of-women-trapped-in-marriages-by-jewish-courts-
1765888.html.

16 Shaista Gohir, *Information and Guidance on Muslim Marriage and
Divorce in Britain* (Birmingham: Muslim Women's Network UK, 2016).

17 Examples include Musawah, a global movement striving for equality
in the Muslim family, and Sisters in Islam, a Malaysia-based women's
organization for gender equality under Malaysia's Sharia rules.

18 'The Death Penalty for Homosexual Acts is a Violation of Shari'a', *AltMuslimah*, 14 June 2016, available at: http://www.altmuslimah. com/2016/06/death-penalty-homosexual-acts-violation-sharia/.

19 'Are Asians Disproportionately Represented in Prosecutions for Sex Offences?', *Full Fact*, 10 May 2012.

20 Ella Cockbain, 'Grooming and the "Asian Sex Gang Predator": The Construction of a Racial Crime Threat', *Race and Class*, vol. 54, no. 4, (London: Institute of Race Relations, 2013), pp. 22–32.

21 The Board of Deputies was at odds with much of the street-based activism of East End Jews in the 1930s; see 'How the Board of Deputies Infiltrated Britain's Fascists', *Jewish Chronicle*, 18 December 2014; D. Rosenberg, *Battle for the East End: Jewish Responses to Fascism in the 1930s* (Nottingham: Five Leaves Publications, 2011). In more recent times the Jewish Leadership Council and Campaign Against Antisemitism were set up in reaction to the Board of Deputies' perceived failures. And even today criticism of the Board of Deputies and the Jewish Leadership Council is not uncommon; see 'British Jews Break Away from "Pro-Israeli" Board of Deputies', *Independent*, 5 February 2007, available at: http://www.independent.co.uk/news/uk/ this-britain/british-jews-break-away-from-pro-israeli-board-of-deputies- 435146.html; 'A High Degree of Foolishness', *Jewish Chronicle*, 1 October 2015, available at: https://www.thejc.com/comment/columnists/a- high-degree-of-foolishness-1.59219.

22 I suggested as much in my inaugural lecture and Q&A session at St Mary's University, Twickenham, where I am a visiting professor. It generated quite a debate, with social network users from across the world posting me amazing pictures of mosques, many without minarets. But one religious scholar said my comments on minarets were akin to me suggesting pork was permissible.

23 Tariq Ramadan, *Western Muslims and the Future of Islam* (New York: Oxford University Press, 2005), p. 171.

24 Faith Minorities in Action project, Muslim Charities Forum, 10 January 2014, available at: https://www.muslimcharitiesforum.org.uk/media/ news/faith-minorities-action. The funding for the project was pulled by the then communities secretary in December 2014 amid claims some of the charities involved in the collaborative programme were 'linked to individuals who fuel hatred, division and violence'. One of the charities, Islamic Help, was accused of having invited 'an individual with extremist views' to speak at an event, although the government did not disclose who this alleged person was. The umbrella body, Mus-

lim Charities Forum, was accused of not having 'robust measures in place to investigate and challenge their members', though what these measures were and why they were deemed to fall short of them has yet to be disclosed. See 'Muslim Charities Lose Government Help over "Extremism"', *BBC News*, 18 December 2014.

25 One tradition of the Prophet Muhammad exhorts believers to 'Feed the hungry and visit a sick person, and free a captive if he be unjustly confined. Assist any person oppressed, whether Muslim or non Muslim.'

26 'Do Religious People Volunteer More?', Manchester Policy Blogs, 18 December 2014, available at: http://blog.policy.manchester.ac.uk/featured/2014/12/do-religious-people-volunteer-more-.

27 'Muslims "Are Britain's Top Charity Givers"', *The Times*, 20 July 2013, available at: http://www.thetimes.co.uk/tto/faith/article3820522.ece.

28 Different types of charity and Islamic rulings, Ummah Welfare Trust, see: http://www.uwt.org/site/article.asp?id=312#lillah-.

29 An open letter from Annie Ward-Pearson to the community of the Masjid Umar mosque in Evington Road, *Leicester Mercury*, 22 January 2013, available at: http://www.leicestermercury.co.uk/ndash-just-bus-firm/story-17928908-detail/story.html.

30 'British Universities Shouldn't Condone This Kind of Gender Segregation', *Guardian*, 26 November 2013, available at: https://www.theguardian.com/commentisfree/2013/nov/26/british-universities-gender-segregation-secular.

31 Maulana Muhammad Mohamedy, *Heavenly Ornaments (Bahishti Zewar) by Moulana Ashraf Ali Thanwi*, translated, 2nd edn (Karachi: Zam Zam Publishers, 2005).

32 'What Unites Englishness and Islam?', *British Future*, 15 September 2016, available at: http://www.britishfuture.org/articles/15300/.

33 Ramadan, *Western Muslims and the Future of Islam*, p. 80.

34 Mehdi Hasan, 'Why Islam Doesn't Need a Reformation', *Guardian*, Comment Is Free, 17 May 2015, available at: https://www.theguardian.com/commentisfree/2015/may/17/islam-reformation-extremism-muslim-martin-luther-europe.

35 Ramadan, *Western Muslims and the Future of Islam*, pp. 149–50.

8. THE POLITICIANS

1 'David Cameron Would Be in Favour of Leaving EU if He Weren't PM, Says Steve Hilton', *Guardian*, 26 May 2016, available at: https://www.the-

guardian.com/politics/2016/may/26/david-cameron-would-be-in-favour-of-leaving-eu-if-he-werent-pm-says-steve-hilton.

2 'I'm an Imam, and I'll Be Leading the Remembrance Sunday Services for the Muslims Who Died Fighting for Our Country', *Independent*, 11 November 2016, available at: http://www.independent.co.uk/voices/remembrance-sunday-muslim-soldiers-world-wars-cenotaph-a7410986.html.

3 'Murdered Soldier Lee Rigby's Mother Tells of Constant Pain', *BBC News*, 5 May 2016, available at: http://www.bbc.co.uk/news/uk-england-36205781.

4 'Sangin On Verge of Falling Back into Afghan Taliban Hands', *BBC News*, 7 February 2016, available at: http://www.bbc.co.uk/news/world-asia-35515517.

5 'Proud to be Muslim, a Soldier and British', *Daily Telegraph*, 4 July 2006, http://www.telegraph.co.uk/news/uknews/1523001/Proud-to-be-Muslim-a-soldier-and-British.html.

6 'David Cameron: More Muslim Women Should "Learn English" to Help Tackle Extremism', *Daily Telegraph*, 17 January 2016, available at: http://www.telegraph.co.uk/news/uknews/terrorism-in-the-uk/12104556/David-Cameron-More-Muslim-women-should-learn-English-to-help-tackle-extremism.html.

7 'National Archives: Britain Agreed Secret Deal to Back Mujahideen', *Daily Telegraph*, 30 December 2010, available at: http://www.telegraph.co.uk/news/worldnews/asia/afghanistan/8215187/National-Archives-Britain-agreed-secret-deal-to-back-Mujahideen.html.

8 M. Curtis, *Secret Affairs: Britain's Collusion with Radical Islam* (London: Serpent's Tail, 2012).

9 'The Secret History of Britain's Spanish Civil War Volunteers', *Guardian*, 28 June 2011, available at: https://www.theguardian.com/commentisfree/2011/jun/28/mi5-spanish-civil-war-britain.

10 It's an issue that came to the fore during the Gaza conflict in 2014, and one I discussed with the prime minister, when it transpired that children of a British parliamentarian were fighting for Israel during that conflict. (*What about the Britons Who Fight for Israel?*, Channel 4, 7 July 2014.) It's an issue I've raised in parliament and one we must resolve to ensure that there are no grey areas. The law in this country is still not clear. I am.

11 My speech to the Global Strategy Forum, 'British Policy Towards the Middle East: Getting It Right', 27 January 2015.

12 *National Security Strategy and Strategic Defence and Security Review 2015: A Secure and Prosperous United Kingdom*, November 2015.

13 *Speech by Robin Cook on the Government's Ethical Foreign Policy*, 12 May 1997, available at: https://www.theguardian.com/world/1997/may/12/indonesia.ethicalforeignpolicy.

14 Speech by Foreign Secretary William Hague at Lincoln's Inn, 15 September 2010. Available at: https://www.gov.uk/government/speeches/foreign-secretary-britains-values-in-a-networked-world.

15 Henry Farrell and Martha Finnemore, 'The End of Hypocrisy: American Foreign Policy in the Age of Leaks', *Foreign Affairs*, November/December 2013.

16 'Human Rights Are No Longer a "Top Priority" for the Government, Says Foreign Office Chief', *Independent*, 2 October 2015, available at: http://www.independent.co.uk/news/uk/politics/human-rights-are-no-longer-a-top-priority-for-the-government-says-foreign-office-chief-a6677661.html.

17 'Alok Sharma comments on UK-China Human Rights Dialogue', Foreign and Commonwealth Office, 28 October 2016.

18 'Don't Interfere on Human Rights, Says Chinese Envoy Before Xi's UK Visit', *Guardian*, 15 October 2015', available at: https://www.theguardian.com/politics/2015/oct/15/human-rights-chinese-ambassador-xi-jinping-uk-state-visit; 'Cameron to Welcome Modi to UK Despite Misgivings by Indian Muslims', *Financial Times*, 12 July 2015, available at: https://www.ft.com/content/db75592c-24b4-11e5-9c4e-a775d2b173ca.

19 The RSS, whose previous leaders have been inspired by the likes of Hitler, a member of whom assassinated Mahatma Ghandi, and who as an organization have been banned three times by the Indian government, is traditionally seen as the volunteer wing of the Bharatiya Janata Party, the BJP, the political party of Prime Minister Modi. Modi himself started his political life and student politics in the RSS and at the last cabinet reshuffle appointed ministers a third of whom had RSS links. And yet neither RSS hostility towards minorities nor the loss of British lives in the Gujerat riots at a time when Prime Minister Modi was the chief minister of Gujerat was actually raised by our government.

20 'UK Weapons Sales to Oppressive Regimes Top £3bn a Year', *Guardian*, 28 May 2016, available at: https://www.theguardian.com/world/2016/may/28/uk-weapons-sold-countries-poor-human-rights-saudi-arabia.

21 'UK Arms Sales to Countries with "Dubious Human Rights" Rise to £3bn', *Independent*, 29 May 2016, available at: http://www.independent.co.uk/news/uk/home-news/uk-arms-sales-to-countries-with-dubious-human-rights-rise-to-3bn-a7055206.html.

22 Ian Cobain, *Cruel Britannia: British Complicity in the Torture and Ill-treatment of Terror Suspects in Pakistan* (London: Portobello

Books, 2012); for 'hand grenade' comment, see https://www.opende
mocracy.net/ourkingdom/
nicholas-mercer/cruel-britannia-secret-history-of-torture.

23 *Cruel Britannia: A Secret History of Torture*, Open Democracy, 4
December 2012.

24 'Mau Mau Rebellion Victims Claim Parliament Was Misled Over Torture',
Guardian, 23 May 2016, available at: https://www.theguardian.com/
world/2016/may/23/mau-mau-rebellion-kenyan-victims-compensation-
claim.

25 'Ireland to Clash with UK at Human Rights Court over Hooded Men
Judgment', *Guardian*, 2 December 2014, available at: https://www.the
guardian.com/world/2014/dec/02/ireland-european-court-hooded-men.

26 'Public Need Answers in "Shocking" MI6 Rendition Scandal, Says
Senior Tory', *Guardian*, 1 June 2016, https://www.theguardian.
com/uk-news/2016/jun/01/mi5-chief-right-to-be-disgusted-over-mi6-role-
rendition-blair.

27 *National Security Strategy and Strategic Defence and Security Review
2015: A Secure and Prosperous United Kingdom*, November 2015.

28 'British Arms Sales to Israel Face High Court Challenge', *Guardian*, 16
August 2014, available at: https://www.the guardian.com/world/2014/
aug/16/british-arms-sales-israel-court-challenge.

29 *Review of Export Licensing Procedures for Israel*, Department for
Business, Innovation and Skills, 14 July 2015. Having been warned
about Israel's use of our supplied weapons during previous incursions
and conflicts, we simply reverted to business as usual after the bloodshed and carnage. Scrutiny of Arms Export Controls, *UK Strategic
Export Controls Annual Report 2007, Quarterly Reports for 2008,
Licensing Policy and Review of Export Control Legislation* (2009), a
report published after 2008/9 war in Gaza, said this about UK arms
sales to Israel at that time: 'We conclude that it is regrettable that com-
ponents supplied by the UK were almost certainly used in a variety of
ways by Israeli forces during the recent conflict in Gaza and that the
Government should continue to do everything possible to ensure that
this does not happen in future.'

30 *Draft Report on Young Muslims and Extremism*, UK Foreign and
Commonwealth Office/Home Office, April 2004; and HM Government, *Prevent Strategy*, June 2011, para 5.27.

31 'The World Has Broken Its Promises about Rebuilding Gaza – and the
Children Will Suffer', *Guardian*, 21 February 2015, available at: https://
www.theguardian.com/commentisfree/2015/feb/21/chris-gunness-gaza-
aid-broken-promises-children-suffer.

32 UN Office of the High Commissioner for Human Rights, *Human Rights Council Establishes Independent, International Commission of Inquiry for the Occupied Palestinian Territory*, 23 July 2014.

33 We had adopted this approach in 2012, when the Palestinians went to the United Nations General Assembly asking nations to vote to recognize Palestine as 'a non-member observer state'. The vote was passed with 138 votes to 9; 41 states abstained, of which one was the UK. At the time William Hague said: 'The only way to give the Palestinian people the state that they need and deserve, and the Israeli people the security and peace they are entitled to, is through a negotiated two-state solution, and time for this is now running out' (HC Deb, 20 November 2012, vol. 553, column 443, accessible at: http://www.publications.parliament.uk/pa/cm201213/cmhansrd/cm121120/debtext/121120-0001.htm#12112042001202). We thought an abstention would win us goodwill with the Israelis. It didn't. Within weeks of the vote Israel had announced more illegal settlement building and encroachment of Palestinian lands in breach of international law and United Nations resolutions. They did so again after the end of the Gaza conflict, when a major expansion of its illegal settlement building was announced, and once again no consequences followed. And I've failed to find a single occasion in government where Israel shifted its position because of our intervention, although there were many where we shifted our position at Israel's behest. See: 'Clinton and Hague Attack Israel Decision to Build New Settlements', *Guardian*, 1 December 2012, available at: https://www.theguardian.com/world/2012/dec/01/hillary-clinton-william-hague-israel-settlements.

34 House of Commons Foreign Affairs Committee, *'Political Islam', and the Muslim Brotherhood Review*, HC 118, published on 1 November 2016, para. 106, p. 39.

35 Ibid.

36 'Muslim Brotherhood Review: A Tale of UK–UAE Relations', *Middle East Eye*, 17 December 2015, available at: http://www.middleeasteye.net/news/muslim-brotherhood-review-tale-uk-uae-relations-378120043.

37 Interestingly the report found that the MB had 'not been linked to terrorist-related activity in and against the UK ... [and] the Muslim Brotherhood in the UK in the form of the Muslim Association of Britain has often condemned terrorist related activity in the UK associated with al Qai'da' and yet concluded that 'aspects of Muslim Brotherhood ideology and tactics, in this country and overseas, are contrary to our values and have been contrary to our national interests and our national security'. That word 'values' was back. The open-ended conclusion nei-

ther condemned nor exonerated groups and individuals in the UK, and once again policy-making was left hanging in mid-air. See: *Muslim Brotherhood Review: Main Findings*, 17 December 2015 (London: HMSO).

38 Lord Cromer, 'East and West', *Quarterly Review*, no. 226 (1916), pp. 21–39, quoted in Robert Tignor, 'Lord Cromer on Islam', *Muslim World*, vol. 52, no. 3 (1962), p. 227; *Lord Curzon's Anti-Suffrage Appeal*, Untold Lives blog, British Library, 4 June 2013.

39 Speech by the Rt Hon. Stephen O'Brien at the Roundtable on Transparency, Accountability and Good Governance: The Future of International Development, 'Transparency, Accountability and Good Governance', 16 May 2012.

40 Michael Gove, appearing on a Sky News Q&A session ahead of the referendum, declared, when asked to name any economist who supported Brexit, 'People in this country have had enough of experts.' ' "Britain Has Had Enough of Experts", Says Gove', *Financial Times*, 3 June 2016.

41 'David Cameron Is "Petrified" of Boris Johnson and Branded Michael Gove A "Maoist", New Memoirs Reveal', *Daily Telegraph*, 12 March 2016, available at: http://www.telegraph.co.uk/news/politics/david-cameron/12192322/David-Cameron-is-petrified-of-Boris-Johnson-and-branded-Michael-Gove-a-Maoist-new-memoirs-reveal.html.

42 House of Commons Home Affairs Committee, 'Radicalisation: The Counter-narrative and Identifying the Tipping Point', HC 135, 25 August 2016, p. 9.

43 'Only 4% of People Think David Cameron's Anti-extremist Policy Works', *Evening Standard*. 1 April 2016, available at: http://www.standard.co.uk/news/politics/only-4-of-people-think-david-camerons-antiextremist-policy-works-a3215961.html.

44 Home Affairs Select Committee, 'Radicalisation', p. 9.

45 'A Muslim Mayor of London Would "Send Message to the Haters", says Sadiq Khan', *Guardian*, 2 July 2015, available at: https://www.theguardian.com/politics/2015/jul/02/a-muslim-mayor-of-london-would-send-message-to-the-haters-says-sadiq-khan.

46 Letter by Khalid Mahmood MP and Shahid Malik, published in the *Guardian*, 15 July 2015, available at: https://www.theguardian.com/politics/2015/jul/15/sadiq-khans-version-of-77-meeting-is-at-odds-with-our-recollection.

47 'Preventing Extremism Together', working group's report to the Home Office, October 2005. The full list can be found at: http://wnc.equalities.gov.uk/publications/doc_download/240-preventing-extremism-2005-home-office-report.html.

48 *An Unquiet World*, paper by the National and International Security Policy Group presented to the shadow cabinet, July 2007.

49 'The Top Twelve Think Tanks in Britain', *Daily Telegraph*, 24 January 2008, available at: http://www.telegraph.co.uk/news/politics/1576447/The-top-twelve-think-tanks-in-Britain.html.

50 Ed Vaizey, 'The New Breed of Policy Wonk is a Doer and a Thinker', *Sunday Times*, 14 July 2002.

51 'Cameron Must Rein in These Toxic Neocon Attack Dogs', *Guardian*, 20 December 2007, https://www.theguardian.com/commentisfree/2007/dec/20/thinktanks.conservatives.

52 Munira Mirza, Abi Senthilkumaran, Zein Ja'far, *Living Apart Together: British Muslims and the Paradox of Multiculturalism* (London: Policy Exchange, 2007). Numerous criticisms are levelled at the report, from its weak methodological rigour to its suggestion that Islamophobia is a 'myth' which is 'given social credence by institutions, politicians, the media and lobby groups', p. 72.

53 On finances: 'Leading Think Tanks "Influencing Public Policy Without Disclosing Donors"', *i newspaper*, 29 June 2016, available at: https://inews.co.uk/essentials/news/uk/think-tanks-accused-influencing-public-policy-without-disclosing-donors/. On ideological links: T. Mills, T. Griffin and D. Miller, *The Cold War on British Muslims: An Examination of Policy Exchange and the Centre for Social Cohesion* (Public Interest Investigations, 2011). On Murray, see: https://policyexchange.org.uk/event/speech-wars/.

54 'Uniting the Country: Interim Report on National Cohesion': A response from the MCB, May 2007.

55 *Uniting the Country*, interim report of the Conservative Party Group on National and International Security, April 2007.

56 'Revealed: The Link Between Life Peerages and Party Donations', *Observer*, 21 March 2015, available at: https://www.theguardian.com/politics/2015/mar/21/revealed-link-life-peerages-party-donations; 'Tories to Make Donor Who Gave Party £6million a Lord Reigniting "Cash For Honours" Row', *Daily Mirror*, 3 August 2014, available at: http://www.mirror.co.uk/news/uk-news/tories-make-donor-who-gave-3974693; 'The Truth About Lobbying: 10 Ways Big Business Controls Government', *Guardian*, 12 March 2014, https://www.theguardian.com/politics/2014/mar/12/lobbying-10-ways-corporations-influence-government.

57 For example, 'Exclusive Ministers Using Middle Men and Mobile Phones to Circumvent Theresa May "Ban" on Making Contact with Nigel Farage', *Daily Telegraph*, 18 December 2016, available at: http://

www.telegraph.co.uk/news/2016/12/18/exclusive-ministers-using-middle-men-mobile-phones-circumvent/.

58 'Ros Altmann Claims "Short-Term Political Considerations" Thwarted Her Efforts to Improve Policy', *Daily Mail*, 18 July 2016, available at: http://www.dailymail.co.uk/news/article-3694899/Minister-quit-age-women-pension-Ros-Altmann-claims-short-term-political-considerations-thwarted-efforts-improve-policy.html; and G. Eaton, 'The Tories Woo The Grey Vote Again With Pledge To Protect Pensioner Benefits', *New Statesman*, 22 February 2015, available at http://www.newstatesman.com/politics/2015/02/tories-woo-grey-vote-again-pledge-protect-pensioner-benefit.

59 'PM's New Fixer in Racist Rant at Muslims: Foul-Mouthed Abuse by Campaign Chief Revealed as He Lands Top Tory Post', *Mail on Sunday*, 18 November 2012, available at: http://www.dailymail.co.uk/news/article-2234565/Lynton-Crosby-Foul-mouthed-abuse-campaign-chief-revealed-lands-Tory-post.html.

60 'Zac Goldsmith Must Take London's Indian Voters Seriously, Not Patronise Them', *Daily Telegraph*, 23 March 2016, available at: http://www.telegraph.co.uk/news/2016/03/23/zac-goldsmith-must-take-londons-indian-voters-seriously-not-patr/.

61 See: speech by the Rt Hon. David Cameron, Diwali 2014 reception at Downing Street, 21 October 2014, available at: https://www.gov.uk/government/speeches/diwali-2014-david-camerons-reception-speech; speech by the Rt Hon. David Cameron, Diwali celebration, 11 November 2015, available at: https://www.gov.uk/government/news/diwali-2015-david-camerons-message; David Cameron's speech to CST, *Jewish Chronicle*, 18 March 2015.

62 In a conversation with the current editor of Conservative Home, Paul Goodman, in 2016, this list was discussed. He too could recall it and said it was probably in their archieve material, and they would retrieve it and send it to me. To date I haven't received a copy.

63 Peter Oborne, 'What's the Conservative Party's Problem with Muslims?', *Middle East Eye*, 7 October 2016, available at: http://www.middleeasteye.net/columns/peter-oborne-whats-conservative-partys-problem-muslims-1757982215.

64 'Pious, Loyal and Unhappy', *The Economist*, 7 May 2009, available at: http://www.economist.com/node/13612116.

65 'Muslims Will Speak Up for British Values Only When They Know They Will Be Heard', *Guardian*, 24 January 2015, available at: https://www.theguardian.com/world/2015/jan/24/sayeeda-warsi-muslims-british-values.

66 Therese O'Toole et al., 'Governing through Prevent? Regulation and Contested Practice in State–Muslim Engagement', *Sociology*, vol. 50, no. 1 (2016), p. 164.

67 Supplementary written evidence submitted by David Anderson, QC (Independent Reviewer of Terrorism Legislation), to the Home Affairs Select Committee Inquiry, para. 13.

68 'Academics Criticise Anti-radicalisation Strategy in Open Letter', *Guardian*, 29 September 2016, available at: https://www.theguardian.com/uk-news/2016/sep/29/academics-criticise-prevent-anti-radicalisation-strategy-open-letter.

69 'CPS Twice Refused to Prosecute Abu Hamza', *Daily Telegraph*, 9 February 2006, available at: http://www.telegraph.co.uk/news/uknews/1510023/CPS-twice-refused-to-prosecute-Abu-Hamza.html. Details of the charges he was convicted on can be accessed here: http://www.cps.gov.uk/news/latest_news/105_06.

70 'BBC Apology to Queen over Abu Hamza Disclosure', *BBC News*, 25 September 2012, available at: http://www.bbc.co.uk/news/uk-19716941.

71 For example, Richard Reid, the 'Shoe Bomber'. See: 'Profile: Abu Qatada', *BBC News*, 26 June 2014.

72 'Swilling Beer, Smoking Dope and Leering at Porn'.

73 'MI5 "Blocked Scotland Yard from Arresting Radical ISIS Supporter Anjem Choudary for Years"', *Sunday Express*, 22 August 2016, available at: http://www.express.co.uk/news/uk/702521/MI5-Scotland-Yard-Anjem-Choudary-ISIS-Islamic-State-terror-police-MI5-Scotland-Yard.

74 'Muslim Protesters Pelt Tory Peer Baroness Warsi with Eggs during Walkabout in Luton', *Daily Mail*, 1 December 2009, available at: http://www.dailymail.co.uk/news/article-1232153/Baroness-Warsi-pelted-eggs-walkabout-Luton.html. My own experience of the police response to the Luton incident was surprising. The officers seemed neither worried by the presence of this gang on our streets nor forthright in their handling of the incident. As I was told by one of the officers, 'They have a right to protest.' I agree, they do, but politicians too have a right to appear in public without being physically attacked.

75 http://news.bbc.co.uk/1/hi/uk_politics/vote_2005/frontpage/4461695.stm.

76 'Cartoon Protest Slogans Condemned', *BBC News*, 5 February 2006, available at: http://news.bbc.co.uk/1/hi/uk/4682262.stm.

77 Initiatives included the Remembering Srebrenica project, something we'd developed in opposition in 2008 and which in government in 2012 took nearly a year to get ministerial agreement from my colleagues, to the Muslim Charities Forum project, to support mosques on governance, management and resilience against extremist

takeover, which was agreed and then shelved, to a Muslim Soldiers project focusing on the two World Wars, which was run once and never renewed, to a Muslim Jewish women's project which struggled to convince the government to fund it to the tune of less than £10,000.

78 Mrs Thatcher's government and gay rights is a case in point. Politicians talking up an issue magnifies the extent of the problem. The Thatcher government's anti-homosexuality position alongside a high-profile campaign on AIDS led to a higher percentage of the public being anti-gay. See Alison Park and Rebecca Rhead, *British Social Attitudes 30: Personal Relationships* (London: NatCen Social Research, 2013), p. 14.

79 'Harman's £70,000 Peace Pods', *The Sunday Times*, 27 June 2010.

9. THE REST OF US

1 'Can We Trust the People? After Trump, I'm No Longer Sure', *The Spectator*, 9 November 2016, available at: http://blogs.spectator.co.uk/2016/11/can-trust-people-trump-im-no-longer-sure/.

2 George Orwell, 'Freedom of the Park', available at: http://www.george-orwell.org/Freedom_of_the_Park/0.html.

3 'Nigel Farage Defends Trump: Ukip Leader Urges Americans to Focus on the "Real Issues"', *Daily Express*, 8 October 2016, available at: http://www.express.co.uk/news/politics/719118/Nigel-Farage-Ukip-Donald-Trump-Hillary-Clinton.

4 'Hate Crime Inquiry Head Warns Against "Whipping up Prejudice" in Campaigns', *Guardian*, 14 November 2016, available at: https://www.theguardian.com/society/2016/nov/14/uk-hate-crime-inquiry-yvette-cooper-prejudice-brexit-trump-campaigns.

5 A letter to all political parties in Westminster by David Isaacs and Rebecca Hilsenrath, Equality and Human Rights Commission, 25 November 2016, available at: https://www.equalityhumanrights.com/en/our-work/news/letter-all-political-parties-westminster.

6 'Hate Crime: Avoid Polarising Language, Politicians Urged', *BBC News*, 27 November 2016, available at: http://www.bbc.co.uk/news/uk-38120596.

7 'Alarmism Saved My Family from Hitler: Why I Won't Tell Anyone to Calm Down about Trump', *The Times of Israel*, 10 November 2016, available at: http://blogs.timesofisrael.com/alarmism-saved-my-family-from-hitler-why-i-wont-tell-anyone-to-calm-down-about-trump/.

8 In the UK the BNP won many a council seat on persuading those that didn't normally vote to turn out and vote. In 2014 a House of Commons Select Committee inquiry found an electorate who feel politics in its current form doesn't work for them, questions the motivations of politicians and the party whip system, are concerned at the behaviour politicians display in parliament, especially at PMQs, and believe that politicians aren't people like them. See: Political and Constitutional Reform Committee report, Voter Engagement in the UK, HC 232, 14 November 2014 (London: HMSO).

9 Policy Paper on Democratic Engagement, 8 May 2015 (HM Government: Cabinet Office), available at: https://www.gov.uk/government/publica tions/democratic-engagement/democratic-engagement-programme.

10 The British Social Attitudes survey 30 (2013) shows a British public increasingly disengaged with politics, with fewer people turning out to vote, fewer identifying with a political party, trust in politicians falling, and these trends being more acute amongst those with few or no education. See: L. Lee and P. Young, 'A Disengaged Britain? Political Interest and Participation Over 30 Years', in A. Park, C. Bryson, E. Clery, J. Curtice and M. Phillips (eds.), British Social Attitudes: The 30th Report (London: NatCen Social Research, 2013), available at: www.bsa-30.natcen.ac.uk, pp. 62–86.

11 'Donald Trump's Victory Represents a Racist "Whitelash"', New Statesman, 9 November 2016, available at: http://www.newstatesman.com/politics/staggers/2016/11/make-no-mistake-donald-trumps-victory-represents-racist-whitelash; Torsten Bell, 'Four Decades of Discontent Trumps a Strong 2015 for US Jobs and Pay in the Race to the White House', Resolution Foundation, 9 November 2016, available at: http://www.resolutionfoundation.org/media/blog/four-decades-of-discontent-trumps-a-strong-2015-for-us-jobs-and-pay-in-the-race-to-the-white-house/; 'Why Did Trump Win? In Part Because Voter Turnout Plunged', Washington Post, 10 November 2016, available at: https://www.washingtonpost.com/blogs/plum-line/wp/2016/11/10/why-did-trump-win-in-part-because-voter-turnout-plunged/?utm_term=.c0af863933ca.

12 'George Osborne Warns Theresa May She Must Work Closely with Donald Trump to Curb His Disastrous Ideas', Sun, 10 November 2016, available at: https://www.thesun.co.uk/news/2159155/george-osborne-warns-theresa-may-must-work-closely-with-donald-trump-to-curb-his-disastrous-ideas/.

13 'This Is How Steve Bannon Sees the Entire World', Buzzfeed News, 15 November 2016, available at: https://www.buzzfeed.com/lesterfeder/

this-is-how-steve-bannon-sees-the-entire-world?utm_term=.ra9pGaba1#.
ic5xV6Y60.

14 'Stephen Bannon and Breitbart News, in Their Words', *New York Times*,
14 November 2016, available at: http://www.nytimes.com/2016/11/15/us/
politics/stephen-bannon-breitbart-words.html?smprod=nytcore-iphone
&smid=nytcore-iphone-share; 'Why ISIS Supports Donald Trump', *Time*
magazine, 7 September 2016, available at: http://time.com/4480945/isis-
donald-trump/.

15 The poem 'First They Came' by Pastor Martin Niemöller appears in several versions – this version is from the United States Holocaust Museum.

16 'White Supremacists Chant "Hail Trump" While Performing Hitler Salutes
at Alt-Right Conference', *Independent*, 22 November 2016, available
at: http://www.independent.co.uk/news/world/americas/donald-trump-
president-elect-alt-right-white-supremacists-nazi-hitler-salutes-richard-b-
spencer-a7431216.html; 'Alt-right Founder Urges Donald Trump to Freeze
Immigration For 50 Years', *Independent*, 21 November 2016, available
at: http://www.independent.co.uk/news/world/americas/donald-trump-
immigration-freeze-richard-spencer-alt-right-50-years-demands-a7429
666.html.

17 A recording of my speech is available at: https://www.youtube.com/
watch?v=DyoHbcLGG9Q.

18 'What Makes the EDL's Former Leader, Who Says He Is a Friend of
the Jews, Tick?, *Jewish Chronicle*, 5 March 2015, available at: https://
www.thejc.com/print/131131.

19 My speech at Georgetown University, Washington DC, 'An International Response to a Global Crisis'. 16 November 2013.

20 'Rowan Williams Raps Government for Treating Religion as a "Problem"',
Guardian, 12 December 2009, available at: https://www.theguardian.
com/uk/2009/dec/12/rowan-williams-government-religion-problem.

21 Anglicans are still the majority among Christian denominations in the
UK, though their fall in numbers has been steepest; see http://www.
stmarys.ac.uk/benedict-xvi/docs/2016-may-contemporary-catholicism-
report.pdf, although, in terms of praxis, more Catholics are churchgoing
than Anglicans: see 'Britain Has Become a Catholic Country', *Daily
Telegraph*, 23 December 2007, available at: http://www.telegraph.co.uk/
news/uknews/1573452/Britain-has-become-a-Catholic-country.html.

22 WIN/Gallup International End of Year Survey 2014, published 13
April 2015.

23 'Church Attendance Has Been Boosted by Immigrants, Says Study',
Daily Telegraph, 3 June 2014, available at: http://www.telegraph.co.

uk/news/religion/10873405/Church-attendance-has-been-boosted-by-immigrants-says-study.html.

24 *Living with Difference: Community, Diversity and the Common Good*, report of the Commission on Religion and Belief in Public Life (Cambridge, Woolf Institute, 2015).

25 Scott Thomas of the University of Bath argues: 'Traditionally seen as a Western or European religion steeped in that continent's culture, Christianity evolved from its Jewish origins in Palestine, conquered the pagan world, and spread east to Iraq, India, and China before the Mongol invasions reduced it to its European setting. It is now returning to its roots by becoming a post-Western religion dominated by the peoples, cultures, and countries of the global South. For U.S. policymakers – many of whom currently consider Islamism to be the most urgent religious challenge to Washington's foreign policy – the politics of global Christianity may soon prove just as pivotal.' See: Scott M Thomas, 'Globalized God: Religion's Growing Influence in International Politics', *Foreign Affairs*, vol. 89, no. 6 (November/December 2010). See also: http://www.wingia.com/en/news/losing_our_religion_two_thirds_of_people_still_claim_to_be_religious/290/.

26 In the 2001 Census about 85 per cent of Brits identified themselves as belonging to a faith. Of them just over 70 per cent said they were Christian. By the time of the 2011 Census 75 per cent of Brits identified themselves as belonging to a faith, and of them just under 60 per cent said they were Christians. (*Religion in England and Wales 2011*, Office for National Statistics 11 December 2012.)

A poll conducted by YouGov in March 2011 on behalf of the British Humanist Association asked the census question 'What is your religion?' 61 per cent of people in England and Wales ticked a religious box (53.48 per cent Christian and 7.22 per cent other), while 39 per cent ticked 'No religion'. When the same sample was asked the follow-up question, 'Are you religious?', only 29 per cent of the same people said 'Yes' while 65 per cent said 'No', meaning over half of those whom the census would count as having a religion said they were not religious. Less than half (48 per cent) of those who ticked 'Christian' said they believed that Jesus Christ was a real person who died and came back to life and was the son of God. Asked when they had last attended a place of worship for religious reasons, most people in England and Wales (63 per cent) had not attended in the previous year, 43 per cent of people last attended over a year earlier, and 20 per cent of people had never attended. Only 9 per cent of people reported having

attended a place of worship within the previous week. (https://human
ism.org.uk/campaigns/religion-and-belief-some-surveys-and-statistics/.)

The 2012 British Social Attitudes survey found that the biggest
group remains people who say they have no religion, which accounts
for around half (49 per cent) of all people in Britain, up from 43 per
cent a decade ago and 31 per cent in 1983. (*British Social Attitudes 28*,
National Centre for Social Research, 2012, p. 173.) It also showed a
marked decline in Christian affiliation. However, a closer look at the
figures shows that most Christian denominations have remained fairly
stable over the last thirty years: Roman Catholics and 'others', which
includes Methodists, Presbyterians and Christians without a denomi-
nation, make up 8 per cent and 17 per cent of the population respectively
and remain at a similar level as in 1983. The sharp decline has occurred
in the numbers identifying as Anglican, where the proportion fell from
40 per cent in 1983 to 17 per cent in 2014, with the most dramatic
decline over the last decade. In real terms the number of Anglicans in
Britain has fallen by as many as 4.5 million over the last ten years from
around 13 million people to about 8.5 million. (*British Social Attitudes: Church of England Decline Has Accelerated in Past Decade*, 31
May 2015.)

A WIN/Gallup international poll from 2015 also found that of those
polled in the UK only 30 per cent described themselves as religious, as
opposed to 63 per cent worldwide. ('Losing Our Religion? Two Thirds
of People Still Claim to Be Religious', press release, WIN/Gallup International. 13 April 2015.)

The British Humanist Association, however, makes an important
point that religions and beliefs are notoriously difficult to measure.
Just because an individual says he is Christian doesn't mean he believes
in the tenets of the faith, nor does it indicate active worship or attendance at church. The form of Christianity within the UK that is on
the rise is one which simply reflects a global shift from German Luther-
anism and Anglicanism to eastern churches, a dramatic spread of
Pentecostalism and evangelical Protestantism, reflecting the demographic shift toward the global South. This version of Christianity is
more literal, morally prescriptive and socially conservative, in other
words, more in line with our Christian heritage but less in tune with
our current British values and out of step with many of the UK's
present-day societal norms.

The British Social Attitudes Survey also mapped the relevance of
being a Christian to British identity and recorded a drop from 32

per cent in 1995 to 24 per cent in 2013. (Zsolt Kiss and Alison Park, *British Social Attitudes 31: National Identity* (London: NatCen Social Research, 2014), p. 5.) The British Social Attitudes survey from 2013 draws correlations between religious belief and attitudes to issues of moral conflict such as premarital sex, children out of wedlock, homosexuality and others. The survey maps out the decline in religious observance and the rise in liberal attitudes and an ever more secular public space, and measures the impact on attitudes towards these issues. It was an acute awareness of these changing trends that convinced a new generation of politicians that moralizing on family issues and gay-bashing were no longer politically profitable.

27 'Warsi's Speech on "Militant Secularism" in Full', 14 February 2012, available at: http://www.politics.co.uk/comment-analysis/2012/02/14/warsi-s-speech-on-militant-secularism-in-full.

28 See chapter 4 above.

29 In a country where it's becoming increasingly fashionable to not believe, politicians and the civil service are no exception. I found the disdain and eye-rolling that many a civil servant and politician shows for faith and all things religion quite startling. The most awful example of it for me was during the preparations for the Pope's visit in 2010. Two Foreign Office civil servants circulated a memo which suggested that Britain should mark the visit by asking the Pope to open an abortion clinic, bless a gay marriage and launch a range of Benedict-branded condoms. The memo also suggested that the Pope could apologize for the Spanish Armada or sing a song with the Queen for charity. It was a paper mocking the Catholic Church, not one challenging a friend on policy – which would be welcomed. It was described by the Foreign Office as 'a foolish document . . . the ideas in the document are clearly ill-judged, naive and disrespectful'. Jim Murphy, MP for East Renfrewshire and the then secretary of state for Scotland, who led the preparations for the visit, described the memo as 'absolutely despicable' and 'vile'. ('Leaked FCO Memo 'Will Not Affect Pope's Visit', *BBC News*, 26 April 2010, available at: http://news.bbc.co.uk/1/hi/uk/8643370.stm.) And although this was a uniquely ignorant and public display of officialdom's lack of understanding of faith, it was systematic of what I came across regularly in government.

30 Christianity and its extensive UK-wide networks can invariably be the glue in a fractious country that locally holds communities together. The Church, and specifically the Church of England, can be the faith

hub around which other faiths can coalesce, the convener, the enabler and, on issues like equal marriage, which most faith communities were vexed over, the leader in both raising objections and finding solutions. The 'quadruple lock' negotiated by the Church of England, which amongst other things ensured that the Marriage (Same Sex) Couples Act, 2013, didn't compel religious organizations and their representatives to conduct or permit same-sex marriages, was a solution that many other faiths were grateful for. (Factsheet about Equal Marriage, Department for Culture, Media and Sport, 15 July 2013.) This unique role of the Church is what formed the basis of my political thinking on a programme in opposition we called 'Active Faith', which eventually came to life as the 'Near Neighbours' programme, which successive governments have over the last six years supported to the tune of £9.5 million. ('New £1.5 Million Funding to Bring Communities Together', press release, Department for Communities and Local Government, 4 April 2016.)

In government the argument that faith and religion had a role to play in public life wasn't an easy one to win. A lack of understanding of what faith communities did and why, a mistrust of all things faith, with faith-based social action interpreted as proselytizing and conservative faith being confused with extremism and thus the basis of terrorism, created the backdrop for the space in which politicians operated.

Support from colleagues such as Eric Pickles, Caroline Spelman and eventually David Cameron helped to get the Christian view on the table. 'Near Neighbours', which seeks to encourage communities to work together using the Church of England's network, and the Cinnamon Network, self-described as faith-based, motivated by Jesus to serve and founded by Matt Bird, a practising Christian, were two early successes in 'doing God' and recognizing the value of social action, volunteering and charitable giving inspired by faith. (The Cinnamon Network, *Our Story*, available at: http://www.cinnamonnetwork.co.uk/our-story/.) A partnership between the Department for International Development and the Disaster Emergency Committee (DEC), charities which included CAFOD, Christian Aid and Islamic Relief, was another. DFID's partnership with Islamic Relief in Ramadan 2012 led to £5 million of match funding by government, resulting in informed and effective fundraising. ('DFID to Match Public Donations to Islamic Relief's Ramadan Appeal', *UK Fundraising*, 18 July 2012, available at: http://fundraising.co.uk/2012/07/18/dfid-match-public-donations-islamic-relief039s-ramadan-appeal/#.WFAp9PmLRnJ.)

31 In 2014/15 race accounted for 82 per cent of all hate crime, in 2015/16 the figure is 79 per cent.

32 *British Muslims in Numbers: A Demographic, Socio-economic and Health Profile of Muslims in Britain Drawing on the 2011 Census* (Muslim Council of Britain, 2015), p. 16.

33 H. Corcoran and K. Smith, *Hate Crime, England and Wales, 2015/16*, Home Office, Statistical Bulletin 11/16, 13 October 2016; '9/11-Era Ignorance of Islam Is Infecting the Age of Isis. We Should Know Better', *Guardian*, 9 September 2014, available at: https://www.theguardian. com/commentisfree/2014/sep/09/ignorance-islam-isis-hate-crimes; 'Tesco Knife Attack: Man Who "Shouted White Power Slogans" Arrested on Suspicion of Attempted Murder in Mold Supermarket', *Independent*, 15 January 2015, available at: http://www.independent.co.uk/news/uk/ crime/tesco-knife-attack-man-who-shouted-white-power-slogans-arrested- on-suspicion-of-attempted-murder-in-9980488.html.

34 Channel, part of the Prevent strategy, is a programme which focuses on providing support at an early stage to people who are identified as being vulnerable to being drawn into terrorism. See: https://www.gov. uk/government/publications/channel-guidance.

35 Figures released by the NPCC for the period 2015–16 shows 22 per cent of referrals accepted into Channel were for far-right extremism; see: National Police Chiefs Council, FOI disclosure 043 16.

36 'Far Right Extremism: A Growing Problem?', *Full Fact*, 24 November 2016.

37 'Jo Cox Murder: Judge's Sentencing Remarks to Thomas Mair', *BBC News*, 23 November 2016, available at: http://www.bbc.co.uk/news/ uk-38076755.

38 John Denham, the last Labour secretary of state for the Department of Communities and Local Government, started a programme and commissioned research looking at white far-right extremism and white alienation called 'Connecting Communities'. This was closed down by the Coalition government. See: 'Labour Battles the BNP on Class and Race', *BBC News*, 14 January 2010, available at: http://news.bbc. co.uk/1/hi/uk_politics/8454590.stm.

39 'Far-Right Group National Action to be Banned Under Terror Laws', *BBC News*, 12 December 2016, available at: http://www.bbc.co.uk/ news/uk-38286708.

40 ICM poll, April 2016, for Channel 4, 'What British Muslims Really Think'. 'Half of All British Muslims Think Homosexuality Should Be Illegal, Poll Finds', *Guardian*, 11 April 2016, available at: https://www.

theguardian.com/uk-news/2016/apr/11/british-muslims-strong-sense-of-belonging-poll-homosexuality-sharia-law.

41 'Cameron Announces "Funding" for English Classes Six Months after £45 Million Cuts', *Independent*, 18 January 2016, available at: http://www.independent.co.uk/news/uk/politics/cameron-announces-funding-for-english-classes-six-months-after-45-million-cuts-a6819656.html.

42 'The Rise and Fall of FGM in Victorian London', *The Conversation*, 12 March 2015.

43 Leyla Hussein, 'FGM: A Muslim Issue?', *Huffington Post*, 23 February 2013, available at: http://www.huffingtonpost.co.uk/leyla-hussein/fgm-female-genital-mutilation_b_4490603.html.

44 *Report of the Inquiry into the Culture, Practices and Ethics of the Press*, vol. 2, para. 8.51, p. 673; see: 'Leveson Report Finds Sensational or Unbalanced Reporting in Relation to Immigrants and Asylum Seekers Is Concerning', Electronic Immigration Network, 29 November 2012, available at: https://www.ein.org.uk/news/leveson-report-finds-sensational-or-unbalanced-reporting-relation-immigrants-and-asylum-seekers; 'Daily Star reporter Quits in Protest at Tabloid's "Anti-Muslim" Coverage', *Guardian*, 4 March 2011, available at: https://www.theguardian.com/media/2011/mar/04/daily-star-reporter-quits-protest.

45 Key recommendations of the Leveson Report are an independent regulator recognized by the Press Recognition Panel and mandated, under Section 40 of the Crime and Courts Act, 2013, to impose stern financial penalties on newspapers found to be wanting in their adherence to the voluntary Code of Practice under which they self-regulate standards in the press.

46 'There Are Far-Right Wannabe Terrorists in the UK – But We're Only Focusing on Islamic Extremists', *Independent*, 24 November 2016, available at: http://www.independent.co.uk/voices/jo-cox-trial-thomas-mair-terrorist-nazi-isis-jihadis-far-right-police-only-focus-a7436426.html.

47 For example, Andrew Marr's interview of Marine le Pen; see: Peter Oborne, 'The BBC and Andrew Marr Let Marine Le Pen Off Easy on Islamophobia'. *Middle East Eye*, 15 November 2016, available at: http://www.middleeasteye.net/columns/andrew-marr-marine-le-pen-islamophobia-france-elections-1912026295.

48 'BBC Receives Almost 1200 Complaints Over Ukip Election Coverage', *Guardian*, 30 May 2014, available at: https://www.theguardian.com/media/2014/may/30/bbc-complaints-ukip-election-coverage-bias.

49 Press Watchdog Independence Questioned After *Sun* Columnist Attacks Fatima Manji', *Huffington Post*, 26 October 2016, available at: http://www.huffingtonpost.co.uk/entry/press-watchdog-independence-

fatima-manji-trevor-kavanagh-kelvin-mackenzie_uk_5810f3f8e4b067
2ea687a487.

50 'Sun Forced to Admit "1 in 5 British Muslims" Story Was "Significantly
    Misleading"', *Independent*, 26 March 2016, available at: http://www.
    independent.co.uk/news/media/ipso-sun-british-muslims-story-headline-
    significantly-misleading-a6953771.html.

51 'Sun Front Page Nazi Shame', Zelo Street blog, 25 June 2016, available at:
    http://zelo-street.blogspot.co.uk/2016/06/sun-front-page-nazi-shame.html.

52 *The Scale of Economic Inequality in the UK*, The Equality Trust
    (undated), available at: https://www.equalitytrust.org.uk/scale-economic-
    inequality-uk.

53 'The UK's Growing Divide between North and South', *Financial
    Times*, 14 December 2014.

54 'From the North East and on Free School Meals? What's the Chances
    of You Going to Oxbridge?', *Chronicle*, 30 April 2016.

55 'IFS Chief: "Worst Decade for Living Standards"', *BBC News*, 24
    November 2016, available at: http://www.bbc.co.uk/news/business-
    38089044.

56 'The Last Liberals', *Economist*, 29 October 2016, available at: http://
    www.economist.com/news/briefing/21709291-why-canada-still-ease-
    openness-last-liberals?fsrc=scn/tw/te/pe/ed/thelastliberals.

57 *Poverty and Income Inequality in Scotland: 2014/15* (Scottish Gov-
    ernment, June 2016).

58 *Scottish Social Attitudes 2015: Attitudes to Discrimination and Posi-
    tive Action* (Scottish Government, September 2016).

59 'Scotland Becoming a More Tolerant Place According to Study', *Scots-
    man*, 30 September 2016, available at: http://www.scotsman.com/news/
    scotland-becoming-a-more-tolerant-place-according-to-study-1-4245520.

60 D. Peukert, *Inside Nazi Germany: Conformity, Opposition and Racism
    in Everyday Life* (New Haven: Yale University Press, 1989), pp. 144–5.

61 *The Chronicles of Nadiya*, Part 2, BBC1, broadcast on 20 September
    2016.

62 *Migrant Entrepreneurs: Building Our Businesses, Creating Our Jobs*,
    Centre for Entrepreneurs and DueDil, March 2014.

63 S. Janmohamed, *Generation M: Young Muslims Changing the World*
    (London: IB Tauris, 2016), p. 7.

64 'David Cameron: The Conservatives Have Become the Party of Equal-
    ity', *Guardian*, 26 October 2015, available at: https://www.theguardian.
    com/commentisfree/2015/oct/26/david-cameron-conservatives-party-of-
    equality; Lester Holloway, 'PM's Blind-spot on 20/20 Vision', Runny-

mede Trust, 14 April 2016, available at: http://www.runnymedetrust.
org/blog/pms-blind-spot-on-2020-vision.

65 See 'The Holy Quran Experiment', http://www.inquisitr.com/2616980/
the-holy-quran-experiment-prank-turns-into-social-experiment-in-sur
prising-way-video/.

66 J. Burnett, *Racial Violence and the Brexit State* (London: Institute of
Race Relations, 2016).

67 'White Nationalists, Anti-Fascists Come to Blows at Refugee Port in
Dover, UK', Reverb Press, 30 January 2016.

68 The statement is a definition of fascism by historian Robert Paxton;
see: R. O. Paxton, *The Anatomy of Fascism* (New York: Alfred A.
Knopf, 2004), p. 218.

APPENDIX I:
WHO SPEAKS FOR 'THE MUSLIMS'?

1 The UMO's objectives, according to its website, are: to promote unity
amongst Muslims in the UK and Ireland; to safeguard Islamic values and
heritage; to facilitate the upbringing of Muslim children in accordance
with the holy Qur'an and Sunnah; to operate as a spokesman on behalf
of all Muslims in the UK and Ireland on all matters relating to their religious, cultural, social, educational and economic issues; to strengthen the
bonds of brotherhood between Muslims throughout the world; to promote Dawah Islamiya. See: http://www.umouk.org/index.html.

2 UMO press release, 26 June 1989.

3 Aspects of the bill are considered here: http://www.wynnechambers.
co.uk/pdf/UMO060304.pdf.

4 T. an-Nabhani, *The Islamic State* (London: Al Khilafah Publications,
1953), available at: http://www.hizb-ut-tahrir.org/PDF.EN/en_books_
pdf/IslamicState.pdf.

5 It was during this golden era that the MCB's first secretary general, Sir
Iqbal Sacranie, rose to prominence and was decorated with honours
including a knighthood in 2005. Interestingly Sir Iqbal and others had
felt the need to pull away from the UMO because of the authoritarian
leadership; the founder, Dr Pasha, was still at the helm some twenty-five
years on, and yet Sir Iqbal went on to serve as secretary general for
nearly a decade and continues to wield power today. There is rarely a
high-level meeting of the MCB where Sir Iqbal is not present, if anyone
who matters is present. Despite changes in secretary generals, Sir Iqbal

continued to be the face of the MCB long after his tenure, appearing to take more of a back seat when the MCB was relegated by the government, through its process of disengagement, to the second and then third division and eventually not even considered to be professional players.

6   Speech by former communities and local government secretary Ruth Kelly, 'Britain: Our Values, Our Responsibilities', at Local Government House, London, on 11 October 2006. The speech was widely seen as heralding a break with the MCB and offering conditional funding to Muslim organizations the government felt were more effective in tackling extremism. Kelly said: 'In future, I am clear that our strategy of funding and engagement must shift significantly towards those organisations that are taking a proactive leadership role in tackling extremism and defending our shared values.' The MCB refused to be cowed and issued a statement saying: 'The MCB will not be deflected from its duty or commitment to speak out on issues where we believe the government's actions domestically and overseas have contributed to undermining our national security.' ('MCB Responds to Ruth Kelly's Speech', 15 October 2006, available at: http://www.mcb.org.uk/mcb-responds-to-ruth-kellys-speech/.)

7   P. Goodman 'After the Bomb Plots', *Conservative Home*, 9 July 2007, available at: http://www.conservativehome.com/platform/2007/07/paul-goodman-mp-5.html.

8   The BMF focused on Islam and the community: 'Islam strictly, strongly and severely condemns the use of violence and the destruction of innocent lives. There is neither place nor justification in Islam for extremism, fanaticism or terrorism. Suicide bombings, which killed and injured innocent people in London, are haram – vehemently prohibited in Islam – and those who committed these barbaric acts in London are criminals not martyrs. We pray for the defeat of extremism and terrorism in the world. We pray for peace, security and harmony to triumph in multicultural Great Britain'. ('Full Text: Fatwa Issued after London Bombs', *BBC News*, 19 July 2005, available at: http://news.bbc.co.uk/1/hi/uk/4697365.stm). A statement drafted and signed by over forty scholars and imams from around the country presented by the MCB focused on the root causes of terrorism: 'The tragedy of 7th July 2005 demands that all of us, both in public life and in civil and religious society, confront together the problems of Islamophobia, racism, unemployment, economic deprivation and social exclusion – factors that may be alienating some of our children and driving them towards the path of anger and desperation . . . youth need under-

standing, not bashing . . . we urge the media to refrain from character assassinations of our reputable scholars and denigration of the community . . . We also call on the international community to work towards just and lasting peace settlements in the world's areas of conflict and help eliminate the grievances that seem to nurture a spiral of violence.' ('Full Text: Muslim Leaders' Declaration on Bombs', *BBC News*, 19 July 2005, available at: http://news.bbc.co.uk/1/hi/uk_poli tics/4696969.stm.)

9   'UK's Top Muslim Backs 42 days', *Islamophobia Watch*, 10 June 2008, available at: http://www.islamophobiawatch.co.uk/uks-top-muslim-backs-42-days/.

10 Haris Rafiq, a wannabe Conservative politician, and Azhar Ali, a wannabe Labour politician, were the men behind the group. I first came across Rafiq during a 2005 post-7/7 appearance on *The Politics Show*, where he struck me as both articulate and ambitious. This was a man who could both speak well and was prepared to say whatever it took to further his political career. Ali, on the other hand, was less eloquent. Meeting the two together left me with visions of George and Lennie from *Of Mice and Men*. Rafiq tried and failed in later years to become the Conservative candidate for police and crime commissioner in Lancashire, and Ali stood and failed as a Labour parliamentary candidate in Pendle, Lancashire. The SMC's links with the neo-conservatives Hudson Institute in the US and the lack of any substance to Ali and Rafiq's new found Sufism resulted in the group lacking credibility and simply being seen as a tool to further personal careers and earn a crust. See: http://sufimuslimcouncil.blogspot.co.uk/2006/08/neoconservative-sufi-muslim-council.html. The SMC has its advocates, Paul Goodman, who also championed the British Muslim Forum, was one of them. Support from across the Atlantic came from the Hudson Institute's Zeyno Baran, who approvingly cites the SMC as a 'non-Islamist' organisation and an example of instrumentalizing Sufism to serve policy objectives. Baran herself contributed to the SMC's website and its magazine, *Spirit*. Baran's connections to neo-conservative bodies in the US, such as the Hudson Institute, present important contextual detail on the intersection of Cold War strategies, neo-con bodies and Sufi Muslim organizations decrying 'Islamist' influence in politics. It is deeply ironic that, while they presented an 'apolitical' stance, the SMC published the work of Baran, whose 'Understanding Sufism and Its Potential Role in US Policy' would suggest anything but an apolitical orientation.

11 Mark Sedgwick, 'The Support of Sufism as a Counterweight to Radicalization: An Assessment', in Marco Lombardi et al., *Countering Radicalisation and Violent Extremism Among Youth to Prevent Terrorism* (IOS Press, 2015), pp. 113–19.

12 In my first official meeting with Husain and Nawaz was in 2008, I saw two very different individuals. Husain struck me as thoughtful, measured and in some ways still on a journey. He seems to have stopped being starkly black and white and accepted that most positions are nuanced and most areas are grey. His early statement to me that not all Wahhabis were terrorists but all terrorists were Wahhabi now sounds childlike, but his more recent statements around the development of democracies in Muslim countries are more thoughtful. Nawaz is in many ways the same today as he was when in HT. He is charming, dapper and attentive until he disagrees, when he can quickly switch to being confrontational, antagonistic and argumentative.

13 Nafeez Ahmed, *How Violent Extremists Hijacked London-based 'Counter-Extremism' Think Tank*, AlterNet, 28 April 2015, available at: http://www.alternet.org/world/how-violent-extremists-hijacked-london-based-counter-extremism-think-tank.

14 Nafeez Ahmed and Max Blumenthal, *The Self-Invention of Maajid Nawaz: Fact and Fiction in the Life of the Counter-Terror Celebrity*, AlterNet, 5 February 2016, available at: http://www.alternet.org/grayzone-project/self-invention-maajid-nawaz-fact-and-fiction-life-counter-terror-celebrity.

15 https://www.splcenter.org/20161025/journalists-manual-field-guide-anti-muslim-extremists.

16 See also Appendix 3 below and http://www.conservativehome.com/thetorydiary/2011/02/robert-halfon-raises-engage-case-in-commons.html.

17 'Muslim Hate Monitor to Lose Backing', Daily Telegraph, 9 June 2013, available at: http://www.telegraph.co.uk/journalists/andrew-gilligan/10108098/Muslim-hate-monitor-to-lose-backing.html.

18 'Islamic "Radicals" at the Heart of Whitehall', *Daily Telegraph*, 22 February 2015, available at: http://www.telegraph.co.uk/news/politics/11427370/Islamic-radicals-at-the-heart-of-Whitehall.html.

19 Metropolitan Police Service Crime Figures, Rolling 12 month, December 2016.

20 It claims 2009, though in the evidence and counter-evidence to the Home Affairs Select Committee there is some confusion about whether it was 2008 (when they appeared to have done some work that was publicly funded) or 2009 (which is the date it claims it was set up).

21 Home Affairs Committee Oral Evidence: Countering Extremism, HC 428, 17 November 2015, available at: http://data.parliament.uk/writtenevidence/committeeevidence.svc/evidencedocument/home-affairs-committee/countering-extremism/oral/24795.pdf.

APPENDIX 2:
PARTY POLITICKING AND 'THE MUSLIMS'

1 Michael Ashcroft '45 Years On, Do Ethnic Minorities Remember "Rivers of Blood"?', Lord Ashcroft Polls 19 April 2013, available at: http://lordashcroftpolls.com/2013/04/45-years-on-do-ethnic-minorities-remember-rivers-of-blood/.

2 Paul Foot, *Immigration and Race in British Politics* (London: Penguin Books, 1965).

3 *Statement of Changes in Immigration Rules*, 20 February 1980 (London: HMSO). It required anyone wishing to follow his or her spouse into Britain to prove that 'the marriage was not entered into primarily to obtain admission to the UK'. Proving a negative, as the rule obliged the candidate to do, was extremely difficult, and large numbers of spouses were refused entry into Britain. I was aware of many horrific stories of couples and families being separated for years as immigration officers approached each application with the premise of 'keep them out', and delays in the appeals system meant the cases languished in the bowels of bureaucracy.

4 Migration Watch, *How Did Immigration Get Out of Control?*, Immigration System and Policy: MW 116, 10 February 2016.

5 *Family Migration: A Consultation* (London: Home Office, UKBA), July 2011.

6 K. Young (1983), 'Ethnic Pluralism and the Policy Agenda', in N. Glazer and K. Young, *Ethnic Pluralism and Public Policy: Achieving Equality in the United States and Britain* (London: Dartmouth, 1983), p. 297.

7 The Act passed with the support of the majority of Conservative MPs. Dudley Smith, the Conservative MP for Warwick and Leamington (1968–97), called for a 'crusade to overcome racial discrimination and give fellow Brits who are in the minority a new confidence which they have significantly lacked in recent years'.

8 Even the famous Smethwick general election of 1965, known for its racist Tory election slogan, hid a nasty racism on the left of politics: it

turned out that Smethwick's Labour club, like a number of Labour clubs at the time, operated a colour bar.

9 Robert Ford and Matthew Goodwin, 'Angry White Men: Individual and Contextual Predictors of Support for the British National Party', *Political Studies*, vol. 58, pp. 1–25.

10 'MCB Welcomes William Hague's Commitment to Family Values and Greater Muslim Representation in the Conservative Party', MCB Press Release 22 March 2001.

11 Speech by David Cameron, 'Bringing Down the Barriers to Integration', 29 January, 2007, accessible at: http://conservativehome.blogs.com/torydiary/files/bringing_down_the_barriers_to_cohesion.pdf.

12 Speech by David Cameron to the British American Project, 11 September 2006.

13 Labour Party, *Fairer Britain, Your Choice* (April 2010); Liberal Democrat Party, *Policies for Racial Equality* (April 2010).

14 Jamil Sherif, Anas Altikriti and Ismail Patel, 'Muslim Electoral Participation in British General Elections: An Historical Perspective and Case Study', in Timothy Peace (ed.), *Muslims and Political Participation in Britain* (London: Routledge, 2015), pp. 32–52.

15 *Ethnic Minority Voters And Non-Voters at the 2005 British General Election*, Ipsos Mori, 9 September 2006; B. Clements, *The Ethnic Minority British Election Study (EMBES): British Religion in Numbers*, 7 March 2011, available at: http://www.brin.ac.uk/2011/the-ethnic-minority-british-election-study-embes.

16 Anthony Heath and Omar Khan, *Ethnic Minority British Election Study: Key Findings* (London: Runnymede Trust, 2012).

17 'Ministers May Be Told to Focus on Minorities in Key Seats', *Independent*, 5 April 2012, available at: http://www.independent.co.uk/news/uk/politics/ministers-may-be-told-to-focus-on-minorities-in-key-seats-7622358.html; 'The Number-One Driver of Not Voting Conservative Is Not Being White', Conservative Home, 6 April 2012, available at: http://www.conservativehome.com/majority_conservatism/2012/04/the-number-one-driver-of-not-voting-conservative-is-not-being-white.html; UK Conservatives Face Defeat Unless They Woo Ethnic Voters', *Financial Times*, 16 February 2014, available at: http://www.ft.com/cms/s/0/ff842b74-94c6-11e3-9146-00144feab7de.html#axzz4J1iHiWk.

18 Michael Ashcroft, *Degrees of Separation: Ethnic Minority Voters and the Conservative Party* (2012), pp. 8–13, available at: http://lordashcroftpolls.com/wp-content/uploads/2012/04/DEGREES-OF-SEPARATION.pdf.

19 Speech by David Cameron to Conservative Party conference, 2007, available at: http://news.bbc.co.uk/1/hi/7026435.stm.

20 'Are the Conservatives Really Breaking Through with Ethnic Minority Voters?', extended discussion by Robert Ford, Laurence Janta-Lipinski and Maria Sobolewska, 12 June 2015, available at: https://yougov.co.uk/news/2015/06/12/are-conservatives-really-breaking-through-extend/.

APPENDIX 3:
WE DON'T LIKE 'THE MUSLIMS'

1 *A Very Light Sleeper: The Persistence and Dangers of Antisemitism: Review by the Runnymede Commission on Antisemitism*, January 1994 (London: Runnymede Trust). See: http://www.runnymedetrust.org/uploads/publications/pdfs/AVeryLightSleeper-1994.PDF.

2 *Islamophobia: A Challenge for Us All* (London: Runnymede Trust, 1997).

3 Robin Richardson, 'Islamophobia or anti-Muslim Racism – or What? – Concepts and Terms Revisited' (Insted Consultancy, 2013).

4 'Islamophobia pervades UK - Report', *BBC News*, 2 June 2004, available at: http://news.bbc.co.uk/1/hi/uk/3768327.stm.

5 The Holocaust Educational Trust was set up in 1998, and the Inquiry into Anti-Semitism, which preceded the All Party Parliamentary Group on Anti-Semitism, took place in 2005, and shows greater political will to address anti-Semitism via initiatives targeting public policy and public institutions. On the other hand, the Metropolitan Police did begin to record specifically Islamophobic hate crime from 2002 to meet the fears of Muslim communities after 9/11 of religiously motivated hate crime.

6 Report of the All-Party Parliamentary Inquiry into Antisemitism, September 2006.

7 Report of the All-Party Parliamentary Inquiry into Antisemitism: Government Response, 29 March 2007.

8 'ENGAGE Statement on Comments Made by Robert Halfon MP', 3 February 2011, available at: http://mend.org.uk/engage-statement-on-comments-made-by-robert-halfon-mp/.

Index

In Arabic names the definite article (Al, al- or El), used as a prefix, is ignored in the ordering of entries.

Clegg, Nick 96, 125, 258
Clinton, Hillary 60
Coalition government (UK) 101,
    118–19, 195, 263
  Strategic Defence Review 195
Cobain, Ian: *Cruel Britannia* 199
COBRA 65
Cold War 59, 192
colonialism 33
  anti-colonial sentiment 58
  French 69
Commonwealth Immigrants Act
    (1962) 18
Communications Act (2003)
    292n16
Community Engagement Forum 215
Community Security Trust (CST)
    260
Conservative Christian
    Fellowship 269
Conservative Friends of India 269
Conservative Friends of Israel 269
Conservative Home 149, 213
Conservative Muslim Forum
    (CMF) 268
Conservative Party
  2015 Election campaign 270
  and the AK Party, Turkey 93
  and blacks 261, 268
  conferences 126, 213, 274
  counter-terrorism approach *see*
    counter-terrorism
  Counter Extremism Strategy
    149–50
  'Educate against Hate' website 132
  and the EU referendum 188–9
  far-right appeal 264
  and the Hindu vote 213
  and homosexuality 35, 36, 44,
    51, 88

and immigration 8, 18, 43, 262,
    268, 288n31
  and the Jewish vote 213
  London mayor 2016 campaign
    128, 213
  and multiculturalism 40, 43,
    106–7, 211, 293n37
  and the Muslim vote/Muslim
    relations 168–9, 211, 212–16,
    262, 265–70
  National Security Review 195
  paranoid state under Cameron
    124, 132
  racism 261, 263–4
  and single-sex wards 183
  Smethwick election slogan 262,
    350–51n8
  Strategic Defence and Security
    Review (2015) 199
  and the term 'Islamism' 154
  Thatcher government 88, 336n78
CONTEST 86–9
  Prepare strategy 87
  Prevent strategy *see* Prevent
    strategy
  Protect strategy 87
  Pursue strategy 87
  referrals and support 110
Conway, Gordon 271
Cook, Robin 195
Cooper, Vincent 148
Corbyn, Jeremy 115
counter-terrorism
  alienation through 86, 87, 103,
    109–10, 131
  child referrals 109
  CONTEST strategy *see*
    CONTEST
  and conveyor-belt theory of
    radicalization 103